Systems of Health Care

Also in This Series

Assuring Quality Ambulatory Health Care: A Case Study, Donald Angehr Smith and Gitanjali Mukerjee

Westview Special Studies in Health Care

Systems of Health Care
Douglas R. Mackintosh

This comprehensive introductory text describes health systems in the United States and in other countries, with emphasis on their ability to deliver goods and services, their cost, and their operation within a legal framework. Included is a discussion of such major developments as pre-paid group practice, automated multiphasic health testing, national health insurance, professional standards review organizations, comprehensive health planning, and malpractice arbitration. The author underlines the salient features of the various systems by presenting and discussing advertisements for health products and services. Flow diagrams, charts, tables, and discussion questions help the reader understand the complexities and interrelationships of health care systems. Extensive references and suggestions for further reading are also included.

Douglas R. Mackintosh works in the health systems division of Analytic Services, a Washington-based consulting firm. He previously taught in the Department of Management and Marketing at the University of New Orleans. While in New Orleans, he worked at a multiphasic health-testing facility, participated in a pediatric arteriosclerosis research project, and helped establish an outpatient abortion clinic. Dr. Mackintosh holds degrees in chemistry, business administration, hygiene, and public health. His publications include *The Economics of Airborne Emissions*.

Systems of Health Care

Douglas R. Mackintosh

Westview Press/Boulder, Colorado

Epigraph Credits

p. 45: reprinted by permission from Leonard Tushnet, *The Medicine Men*, published by St. Martin's Press, Inc., New York. Copyright © 1971 by St. Martin's Press.

p. 77: reprinted by permission of the publisher from Ken Kesey, *One Flew over the Cuckoo's Nest*, published by the Viking Press, Inc., New York. Copyright © 1962 by Ken Kesey.

Westview Special Studies in Health Care

Published in 1978 in the United States of America by
  Westview Press, Inc.
  5500 Central Avenue
  Boulder, Colorado 80301
  Frederick A. Praeger, Publisher

Library of Congress Cataloging in Publication Data
Mackintosh, Douglas R.
  Systems of health care.
  (Westview special studies in health care)
  Bibliography: p.
  1. Medical care—United States. 2. Medical care. I. Title. II. Series. [DNLM: 1. Delivery of health care—Standards—United States. 2. Quality of health care—United States. 3. Evaluation studies. W84 AA1 M156s]
Ra395.A3M28   362.1'0973   78-3134
ISBN 0-89158-330-0
ISBN 0-89158-818-3 pbk.

Printed and bound in the United States of America

To Dr. Cicely Williams,
a beautiful, genuine person

In this life we must consider ourselves lucky indeed if we have the good fortune to be befriended by one or two great individuals. Dr. Williams was the first to identify *kwashiorkor*, the "weaning disease," which she came in contact with while serving as a pediatrician in the British Colonial Service in Ghana in 1931. Her rich and remarkable life is reflected in the warmth and enthusiasm she shares with her students and friends even as she approaches her eighty-third year. I consider myself extremely lucky to have been exposed to her wisdom and her values.

For a closer look at Dr. Williams' life and work, see Ann Dally's *Cicely: The Story of a Doctor* (London: Victor Gollancz Ltd., 1968—now out of print); and *Mother and Child Health: Delivering the Services* (New York: Oxford University Press, 1972), by Cicely D. Williams and Derrick B. Jelliffe.

Contents

List of Figures xv
List of Tables xix
Foreword, by Andrew B. Dott xxiii
Introduction xxvii

1. Systems and Health Care 1

   A System 1
   A Health Care System 2
   Another Description of a Health Care System 5
   Summary 7
   Questions 8
   Notes 8
   Further Reading 8

2. Understanding the Semantics of Health Care 11

   Abstracting a Few Concepts and Terms 13
   Macro Health Indicators 15
   Access to Health: Right or Privilege? 17
   Social Responsibility: A Divergence 20
   The Meaning of Socialized Medicine 22
   Psychosemantics of Care 24
   Summary 26
   Questions 27
   Notes 27
   Further Reading 29

3. The U.S. Health Care Delivery System: Background 31

   The Consumer as Patient 31
   Affluence and Expectations 34

The Physician as Provider 35
Other Medical Clinicians 40
Summary 42
Questions 44
Notes 44
Further Reading 47

4. Organized Care 49

Primary Care and the Community Physician 49
Group Practice 50
Hospitals 55
Summary 71
Questions 71
Notes 71
Further Reading 74
Further Viewing 75

5. Mental Health 77

Psychiatric Hospitals 78
Community Mental Health Centers and Clinics 84
Zone Mental Health and Integrating Long-Term and
    Short-Term Care 86
Summary 89
Questions 89
Notes 89
Further Reading 93
Further Viewing 94

6. Health Services for the Aged 95

Problems of the Aged 95
Nursing Homes 97
Home Health Services 101
Summary 103
Questions 104
Notes 104
Further Reading 106

7. Disjointed Community Efforts To Organize the Delivery
    of Health Care 109

Voluntary Agencies and Problems in Organizing Services ... 109
Emergency Transportation 111
Red Cross 115
Blood Banks 120

Summary 123
Questions.. 123
Notes.. 124
Further Reading 125

8. Medical Business in the Private Sector...................... 127

Consulting Firms and Contractual Arrangements 127
Medical Supplies and Equipment 127
Clinical Laboratories 130
Drug Manufacturing and Wholesale Distribution 131
Pharmacy 139
Summary 144
Questions.. 144
Notes.. 145
Further Reading 147

9. Government Health Care Activities 149

State and Local Government.............................. 150
Federal Government Efforts at the State and Local Level 151
Family Planning 154
Inside the Federal Government 157
Summary 168
Questions.. 168
Notes.. 169
Further Reading 170

10. Independent Practitioners.................................. 173

Faith Healers and Marginal Practitioners.................... 173
Chiropractic 184
Podiatry 186
Dentistry.. 187
Optometry... 190
Veterinary Medicine 191
Intermediate-Level Health Practitioners 193
Summary 194
Questions.. 194
Notes.. 194
Further Reading 200

11. Economics and Finance of Health Care 203

Gross National Indicators 203
Macro Model of the Health System 207
Supply and Demand for Services......................... 210

Deviance from the Competitive Model 211
Price and Income Effects 214
Insurance 215
Alternative Methods of Financing Health Care 226
Summary 227
Questions. 228
Notes. 228
Further Reading 229

12. Negligence and Medical Malpractice. 231
Frequency and Distribution of Claims 231
Principles of Negligence 235
Effects of Malpractice Suits 237
Summary 237
Questions. 237
Notes. 239
Further Reading 239

13. Sociopolitical Aspects of Health Care. 241
Poverty and Minority Participation in the Health System 241
Community and Consumer Control 244
State and Areawide Control 246
Provider Control 249
Summary 254
Questions. 255
Notes. 255
Further Reading 261

14. Future Delivery of Health Care: Emerging Concepts 263
Automated Multiphasic Health Testing (AMHT). 263
Computer Diagnosis 265
New Facility Arrangements 266
New Financial Arrangements 267
Summary 275
Questions. 275
Notes. 276
Further Reading 278

15. National Systems of Health Care 279
Health Care in the United Kingdom. 279
Health Care in Sweden 282
Health Care in the Soviet Union 283
Health Care in the People's Republic of China 286

Health Care in Emerging and Developing Countries 292
Summary 294
Questions. 294
Notes. 295
Further Reading 297

16. Two Directions for a Health System 299

Toward Less Government Involvement 299
Toward More Government Involvement. .302
Note 304

17. Spaceship Earth, Evolution, and Health Care 305

Begin at the Beginning. 305
Ecologic Systems 306
The Economic System 307
Spaceship Earth 307
Survival and Growth 308
Summary 309
Question 310
Notes. 310
Further Reading 311

Appendix: Gourmand and Food—A Fable. 313
Selected Secondary Sources. 317
Index. 319

Figures

1.1   A Cybernetic Model of Human Systems 2
1.2   Conceptual Model of a Health Care System 4
1.3   Disease Causation: A Hypothetical Historical Interpretation 6
2.1   Health-Illness Thermometer 14
2.2   A Balance of Conflicting Rights: Equality versus Freedom 18
2.3   Lorenz Curve of U.S. Income Inequality 23
3.1   Distribution of Demand for Medical Care by a Typical
      Population in One Year (1970) 41
3.2   The Expanding Pyramid of Roles and Occupations in
      the U.S. Health Care Delivery System 43
4.1   Organization of Health Care by Practitioner Groups 55
4.2   Per Diem Costs at a Large Urban Teaching Hospital 64
5.1   Number of Resident Patients at Year End in State and
      County Mental Hospitals, 1950-1972 79
5.2   Psychiatric Patient-Care Episodes per 100,000
      Population, Selected Years 1955-1973 80
5.3   A Model of a Zone Mental Health Delivery System 87
6.1   Deaths at Home versus Deaths in Institutions,
      New York City, Selected Years 1955-1967 96
6.2   Percentage of Deaths in U.S. General Hospitals, Mental
      Hospitals, and Nursing Homes, 1949 and 1958 97
7.1   Organizational Chart of the International Red Cross
      and the American National Red Cross 116
7.2   Local Government Authority Disaster Coordinator 118
8.1   The Process of New Drug Development 133
8.2   Number of New Drugs Introduced, 1958-1972 134
8.3   Manufacturers' Sales of Prescription Drugs, 1962-1971 136
8.4   Consumer Expenditures for Nonprescription Drugs,
      1960-1971 138

8.5   Major Pharmacy Organizations and Their Constituents 142
9.1   Family Health Foundation Program Thrust 156
9.2   Federal Health Outlays by Activity, 1969 and 1974 158
9.3   Total Federal Health Outlays by Agency, 1969 and 1974 158
9.4   Federal Outlays for the Prevention and Control of
      Health Problems and Distribution by Agency, 1969
      and 1974...159
9.5   Number of People Eligible for Services Provided or
      Financed by the Department of Defense, 1969-1974 160
9.6   Outlays by the Department of Defense per Eligible
      Beneficiary, 1969-1974...................................160
9.7   Outlays by the Veterans Administration per U.S.
      Veteran, 1969-1974.......................................162
9.8   Department of Health, Education and Welfare, 1974 163
9.9   Indian Health Service 167
11.1 Distribution of Aggregate National Health Expenditures,
      Selected Fiscal Years, 1929-1975 204
11.2 Sources of Funds for Personal Health Care Expenditures,
      Selected Years, 1929-1975.................................204
11.3 Estimated Per Capita Personal Health Care Expenditures,
      Fiscal Years 1967-1972 205
11.4 Medical Care Price Index and Consumer Price Index,
      Selected Years, 1950-1977.................................206
11.5 National Health Expenditures as a Percent of GNP,
      Selected Fiscal Years, 1950-1975 206
11.6 Circular Flow of Economic Activity in the Health
      Care Delivery System 207
11.7 Supply and Demand Curves 210
11.8 Shifts in Supply and Demand 212
11.9 Supply Curve for Independent Health Care Practitioners.....214
11.10 Effect of Price and Income on the Demand for Three
      Types of Health Services 216
11.11 Hospital Cost per Patient Day, 1950-1972 220
12.1 State to State Differences in Number of Claims Closed
      in 1970 per 100 Physicians Providing Patient Care.............232
12.2 Duration of Closing Files for Auto Claims versus
      Medical Malpractice Claims, 1970 235
13.1 Visits to Dentists and Physicians in the U.S.
      per Person per Year by Color and Income, 1973.............242
13.2 Spectrum of Consumer-Provider Control of Various
      Health Resources...245
13.3 Health Planning Structure in the United States, 1977.........248
13.4 Percentage Distribution of Annual Earnings of Providers
      of Health Services versus Workers in a Composite of
      Nineteen Nonhealth Industries 251

14.1 Computer Printout of AMHT Questionnaire 264
14.2 Computer Printout of Comparative Results for Several
     Examinations and Standardized Ranges 265
14.3 The Garfield Delivery System 267
14.4 Typical Cost of National Health Insurance as a
     Percentage of Family Income under the Administration
     and Kennedy-Mills Plans, 1975 273
15.1 Administrative Structure of the National Health Service 280
15.2 Specified Health Services as a Proportion of the Total
     Cost of the National Health Service, 1971 281
15.3 Administration of Swedish Hospital, Health, and Social
     Services 283
15.4 Governmental Structure of Health Care in the USSR 284
15.5 Flow of Urban and Rural Families through the Health
     System of the USSR 285
15.6 Urban Health Care in the People's Republic of China 288
15.7 Rural Health Care in the People's Republic of China 289
17.1 Spaceship Earth 308

Tables

2.1 A Matrix of Health and Illness 14
2.2 Infant Mortality for Selected Countries, 1965-1967 15
2.3 Ten Leading Causes of Death, United States, 1900 and 1967 16
2.4 The Probability of an Individual Dying in the Next
      Ten Years 17
3.1 Average Remaining Years of Life at Specified Ages,
      Selected Years, 1900-1971 32
3.2 Maternal Mortality Rates by Race, Selected Years,
      1940-1971 32
3.3 Infant Mortality Rates by Age and Color, Selected Years,
      1940-1971 33
3.4 Net Migration for Metropolitan Areas of the United
      States, 1960-1965 33
3.5 Federal and Nonfederal Physicians by Specialty and
      Activity, 31 December 1973 36
3.6 Percentage of Physicians in Each Type of Practice and
      Primary Specialty of Active Physicians, 31 December 1972 37
3.7 Number of Employed Nursing Personnel by Category,
      January 1973 42
4.1 Number and Percentage of Groups and Full- or Part-Time
      Group Physicians, by Type of Group 51
4.2 Distribution of Physician Groups by Form of
      Organization and Type of Group 52
4.3 Comparison of Average Net Income per Physician and
      Percent of Business Receipts, 1968 53
4.4 Hospitals and Hospital Beds, 1972 and 1967 57
4.5 Ownership of Hospitals and Hospital Beds, 1972 59
4.6 An Example of an Organization Chart for a Large
      Community General Hospital 60

4.7   Selected Measures of U.S. Community Hospital Inpatient
      Utilization, Selected Years, 1950-1973 62
4.8   Community Hospital Outpatient Statistics, 1963-1973 66
5.1   Utilization Rates for Psychiatric Specialty Hospitals, Long
      and Short Term, Selected Years, 1950-1973 81
5.2   Extent of Insurance Coverage of 1,000 Psychiatric Patients
      at Ten Hospitals, 1968 87
5.3   Federal Staffing Funds for Mental Health Centers 88
6.1   Comparison of Nursing and Related Homes, 1971 98
6.2   Nursing and Related Homes by Type of Ownership, 1971 99
6.3   Home Health Agencies Participating in the Medicare
      Program, by Type of Agency, 1973 102
7.1   Types of Ambulance Services, California, 1972 112
7.2   Statement of Income and Expenditures of the American
      National Red Cross, for the Year Ending June 30, 1973 119
7.3   Number of Blood Banks and Transfusion Services and
      Units of Blood Drawn, 1961 and 1971.......................120
7.4   Estimates of Source of Blood by Donors and Blood Units,
      United States, 1965-1967 121
8.1   Net Profit for Drug Companies and Manufacturing
      Corporations 134
8.2   1972 Dollar Volume of Prescription Drugs and Percentage
      Share of Prescription Market, Sixteen Largest Companies 135
8.3   Pricing Methods of Pharmacists 143
9.1   Health Formula and Matching Grants Received by State
      Agencies, Louisiana FY 1974 152
9.2   Ratio of Indian and Alaska Native Age-Adjusted Death
      Rates to U.S. Rates, All Races, 1967........................166
10.1 Number of Dental Specialists by Specialty, 1972 189
10.2 Number of Dental Auxiliaries by Type, 1972 189
10.3 Comparison of Opticianry, Optometry, and
      Ophthalmology 191
10.4 Type of Activity of Members of the American Veterinary
      Association, 31 December 1972 192
11.1 Types of Health Insurance 217
11.2 Ratio of Claims Incurred to Net Premiums Written for
      Twenty-two Large Insurance Companies, 1970-1972...........219
11.3 Alternative Financial Arrangements for Health Care 227
12.1 The Ratio of the Base Rate for Classes Two through Five
      Physicians and Surgeons to the Base Rate for Class One
      Physicians, 1966-1972......................................232
12.2 Location within Hospital Where Incidents Which Give
      Rise to Malpractice Claims Occur 233
12.3 Percentage of Medical Malpractice Claims Files Closed
      at Each Stage in the Process, with and without Payment.......234

12.4 Distribution of Amounts Paid on Medical Malpractice
       Claims Closed in 1970 234
14.1 Coverage, Financing, and Type of Provider Reimbursement
       under Alternative National Health Insurance Plans,
       Based on Prices and Population Projected for 1975 272
14.2 A Comparison of Two National Health Insurance Plans 273
15.1 Birthrates of Countries, by Continent and Level, 1974 or
       Most Recent Date 290

Foreword

Man ain't really evil, he jest ain't got any sense.
—William Faulkner

It is difficult to review and evaluate the U.S. health care delivery system because it is not a comprehensive, formal, rational structure, such as exists in Great Britain or the Soviet Union, with the exception of a few subcomponents such as the military medical system or the Indian Health Service. The U.S. health care system has been criticized by consumers, planners, politicians, lawyers, and, of course, by the health providers themselves. No one is satisfied, it would seem, and as a result, the same evolutionary forces of change, in a fragmented and disorganized fashion, are occurring as they have since health services first developed in the Americas. The major issue today, as it has been for several decades, is whether a revolutionary change should occur in this "nonsystem," a change leading to a comprehensive, rational, centrally controlled, planned national health service, or whether change should be a gradual process representing a dynamic balance among the various political, technological, social, and economic processes in the United States.

The criticisms of the U.S. health care delivery system are many. They include: (1) maldistribution of resources, (2) the exclusion of large components of our society from adequate health services, (3) excessive cost, (4) excessive concentration of resources on technologically advanced curative services rather than on preventive services, (5) unfavorable national health statistics, (6) excessive allocation of resources to irrelevant basic science research, (7) the existence of powerful interest groups that block innovation and change, (8) excessive profits by suppliers and providers, and (9) unreasonable expectations by consumers. The reader should consider these problems and others as he or she attempts to understand the factors behind these criticisms, explores their validity, formulates solutions, and finally assesses whether the changes that would be proposed would really improve the situation.

A major aspect of these problems is that good health and the factors that contribute toward it bear little relationship to medical care. The World Health Organization defines health as "a state of complete physical, mental, and social well-being and not merely the absence of disease or infirmity." The U.S. health care delivery system—referred to here occasionally as medical care—really provides medical, dental, pharmacological, social, nursing, and custodian services, among others. Of course, medical care contributes to the good health of individuals in a few circumscribed areas such as preventive health care services to mothers and children and in the care of certain acute major medical and surgical problems such as appendicitis and infectious diseases. For the most part, however, medical services merely supervise the inevitable and, at best, make people feel comfortable because they have been exposed to shiny modern technology in amenable surroundings. Many a wise physician has observed that 85 percent of patients get well and 10 percent die regardless of what one does, so that the primary service provided is supportive. The old dictum *primum non nocere* ("first of all do no harm") is quite relevant here. Only in about 5 percent of encounters will medical skills really make any difference. For this reason, many unorthodox providers, such as chiropractors, faith healers, and the like are quite successful.

From the most cynical perspective, one might perceive the medical system and all its glittering technology as a twentieth-century response to the same motives that compelled Ponce de Leon to seek the fountain of eternal youth. For example, the average life expectancy of individuals age forty and above has not materially improved in this century. Virtually all improvement in life expectancy has resulted from control of childhood diseases as well as from an improved standard of living associated with improved nutrition, occupational conditions, housing, sanitation, and education. Most health problems affecting Americans today are self-inflicted and reflect the stress, poor habits, and self-indulgence that characterize our society. The biological effects of obesity, inappropriate diet, alcoholism, and smoking on pulmonary, dental, vascular, endocrine, orthopedic, and gastrointestinal disease, to mention a few, are well known. For a certain subset of our society, poverty contributes to poor health. For most, ignorance is also a problem. For a few, mainly older women, health problems reflect longevity and the final failure of a finite biological system to sustain itself. Any effort to improve the overall health of the American people through modification of the health care delivery system must consider the question of whether a changed medical care service will indeed improve overall health.

The current irrationality of health care reflects a free-market response toward consumer demands for services. Granted, many of these demands are generated by the provider's subtle, or not so subtle, manipulation of consumer behavior through various communication modalities, but the consumer, who is least informed, still makes and pays for most final decisions. For these same reasons, some of the best medical care in the

United States today is provided in publicly funded facilities where free-market forces are not operative and rationality prevails. Unfortunately, this same care is most criticized by the consumer precisely because it does not meet his perceived needs. Thus he is not motivated to use these services properly, and disasters occur. The government then intervenes, and the political process reimposes the irrationality with which the system is comfortable. Without exception, every provider of services has been forced to modify his rational, disciplined training to cope with the irrational pressures of the marketplace. Certain individuals are successful in partially modifying consumer behavior through education. Others simply follow the line of least resistance. Attempts to rationalize the health care delivery system inevitably meet with considerable resistance because of irrational components of the system.

If overall health is the optimal goal, where should efforts of change be directed? Obviously, human behavior must be modified by education, not merely in school but rather in homes and society itself, so that individuals enter into a constructive pursuit of health. Individuals also need the means to fulfill their behavioral expectations. Finally, services should be provided. Many grand educational experiments affecting health—such as prohibition or control of tobacco, marijuana, heroin, and the like—have failed. Others have succeeded. An alternative to manipulation of human behavior is overt political coercion, which is generally not compatible with the U.S. life-style. Optimism and change are essential national characteristics. Therefore, the reader should view with caution the pessimism expressed above and continue to work toward achieving good health and a reasonably sane and balanced state of existence for his fellow individuals.

Andrew B. Dott
M.D., M.P.H.

Introduction

Systems of Health Care is a comprehensive, introductory text that describes health systems in the United States and other countries. It stresses fundamental principles and relationships. It emphasizes law, economics, and systems of delivering goods and services. Each chapter segments a series of interrelated subsystems; by focusing on these subsystems, the reader can better comprehend the complexities of a health care system. As each chapter is covered, a more holistic perception and understanding occurs.

The systems concept is a powerful tool for organizing and analyzing extensive, complex material. Each descriptive segment of information becomes more meaningful if you remember its relationship to other components of the health system. Therefore, if you are looking for continuity as the text flows along—if you are looking for a "theme"— consider a *systems* approach. The systems approach to descriptive material is what separates this book from all others that attempt to analyze health care delivery. The book is designed to meet the following objectives:

1. to prepare individuals to help raise levels of wellness for individuals, families, and the community
2. to prepare individuals capable of assuming supervisory responsibility
3. to develop change agents and leadership characteristics
4. to provide materials that individuals can use to develop teaching abilities in working with other individuals and groups
5. to help an individual learn to interpret and implement research findings
6. to prepare an individual capable of functioning effectively as a member of a multidisciplinary health team

7. to enhance an individual's creativity and competency in coping with health care delivery problems

In order to accomplish these goals, the text covers most of the significant changes in health care over the past twenty years. "Dated" materials (graphs, etc.) are used, in a few instances, to point out an important trend. Toward the end of the book, major developments in the delivery of health care—including prepaid group practice, automated multiphasic health testing, national health insurance, professional standards review organizations, comprehensive health planning, and malpractice arbitration—are covered. Extensive references are listed for further reading on each subject. Throughout the text, advertisements for health products and services illustrate the characteristics of a particular health service. Flow diagrams, charts, and tables are also used to reinforce concepts and trends. Questions are included at the end of each chapter to stimulate further reading and discussion.

I have attempted to remain emotionally detached from the significant controversies that surround the delivery of health care. Chapter 16 is a futuristic trip in two directions the reader might wish to take health care. It is important that you make up your mind, based on a thorough understanding of the important issues involved in delivering health care, about the future direction of the health care delivery system. There are no right and wrong answers—only more sophisticated and less sophisticated answers.

Parts of this text have been read by my friends. They are not responsible for my mistakes, but they are responsible for keeping my mind on a somewhat even track. My thanks go to them, to Beth McKnight who labored over the manuscript many a long day, and to my wife, Dr. Stephanie Heidelberg, who drew the figures and illustrations.

I hope you enjoy the material and remain awake during the duller sequences. Mastery of the concepts contained herein will make you a more competent practitioner, administrator, and person. Be patient and, at the same time, actively critical.

D.R.M.

Systems of Health Care

1. Systems and Health Care

The spread of specialized deafness means that someone who ought to know something that someone else knows isn't able to find it out for lack of generalized ears.
—Kenneth E. Boulding

Attempting to describe and analyze a health care system is like trying to describe and analyze the human body. The task is complex and endless, but necessary if we want to change and fine-tune the mechanism. The simplest way to start is by examining the anatomy of the system and then studying the functions of these parts. Next, we want to know the relationship between and among these parts. Finally, we want to find out how changing a small part of the system will change the functioning of other components of the system. To complicate matters, in some instances a relationship holds, and in other instances, a relationship becomes confused and can completely break down. For example, measles vaccination appears to be a simple answer to preventing measles in children and thus its serious complications. However, because of failures on the part of drug manufacturers, medical researchers, and public health officials, the measles vaccination program, in contrast to the simple polio vaccination model, is undergoing revision; preventing measles turns out to be a complicated process. Or, for example, spending more money on family planning programs sometimes leads to lower birthrates—but not always.

The best thing we can do is explain what are the most likely causes of an event or outcome. In this chapter we will begin to explore the most likely relationships and the organization of components of the health care system.

A System

A *system* is defined as a set of objects together with relationships between the objects and between their attributes, or as a set of elements standing in interaction. Objects or elements are simply the parts or components of a system; attributes are the properties of objects or

1

Figure 1.1   A Cybernetic Model of Human Systems

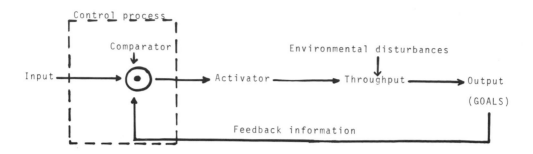

elements; relationships tie the system together. All systems have a *teleology,* or purpose in functioning. A system is a part of reality, and a model is an abstract attempt to represent reality and in some cases, to represent a system. No one is quite sure whether health care is or is not delivered in a systematic fashion. Models can be developed that can begin to explain both the way health care is delivered now (descriptive) and the way health care ought to be delivered in the future (normative).

An extremely simple model of a system might be:

Input ———→ Throughput ———→ Output

If this model were applied to education, books, students, desks, tuition, and teachers would be input; classes and the writing of term papers would be throughput; and learning and the awarding of a diploma would be output. Missing from this model are the *endogenous variables* (factors inside the system), such as teacher evaluating student (grading) and student evaluating teacher (dozing off, complaining to the dean, etc.), and *exogenous variables* (factors outside the system), such as bus strikes, family problems that affect performance, and how much homework is assigned in other classes. Therefore, a more complex model (Figure 1.1) can be devised. The heating of a house with a thermostat is a simple cybernetic system; the eye-foot coordination system of a human (i.e., walking) is a more complicated process.

A Health Care System

Let us group the ingredients of health care under the headings of the cybernetic model:

Heading	Elements of health care
Input	Patients, illnesses, providers, person-

	nel, equipment, institutions, finances, research, knowledge
Comparator	Administrators, public, professional associations, government, courts, peer review
Activator	Patient, provider, courts, screeners, patient's family
Environmental disturbances	Wars, overpopulation, epidemics, natural disasters, pollution, changes in preferences, technological advances, and economic upturns and downturns
Output	Wellness, data, jobs, wealth, education, long life, happier outlook
Feedback	Information, complaints, records, legal suits, praise, analysis of waiting times and occupancy rates, number and amount of gifts.

Although this list is by no means exhaustive, it allows us to begin making some discoveries about a health system. Perhaps the most important environmental disturbances relative to health care are:

1. the development of refrigerated transportation
2. the development of indoor plumbing
3. the discovery of antibiotics
4. the increased affluence of the developed countries
5. the payment for medical care by third parties, i.e., by the government and insurance companies

The first three disturbances have significantly influenced nutrition, sanitation, and infections. Affluence has affected the expectations and preferences of both those who are well off and those who are less well off. Private and public insurance has had a major impact on the demand for health care. Within any system, feedback is a useful guide in controlling expenses, increasing efficiency, and achieving satisfactory quality.

We are ready to cluster some of our components further into a larger conceptual model of a health care system. Figure 1.2 shows how these components of the system are grouped together in particular categories that can be applied to any provision of a service: population, demand, supply, utilization, revenue and expenses, and monitoring and evaluation of performance. For example, the same headings apply to educational and banking systems. In any system, the difference between demand and

Figure 1.2 Conceptual Model of a Health Care System

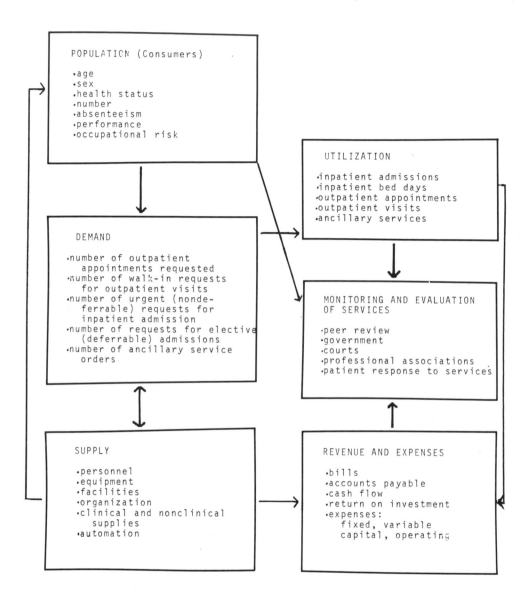

POPULATION (Consumers)

•age
•sex
•health status
•number
•absenteeism
•performance
•occupational risk

DEMAND

•number of outpatient
  appointments requested
•number of walk-in requests
  for outpatient visits
•number of urgent (nonde-
  ferrable) requests for
  inpatient admission
•number of requests for elective
  (deferrable) admissions
•number of ancillary service
  orders

SUPPLY

•personnel
•equipment
•facilities
•organization
•clinical and nonclinical
  supplies
•automation

UTILIZATION

•inpatient admissions
•inpatient bed days
•outpatient appointments
•outpatient visits
•ancillary services

MONITORING AND EVALUATION
OF SERVICES

•peer review
•government
•courts
•professional associations
•patient response to services

REVENUE AND EXPENSES

•bills
•accounts payable
•cash flow
•return on investment
•expenses:
   fixed, variable
   capital, operating

utilization is unmet demand, e.g., those consumers who requested services but did not receive them. As discussed in the sections on family planning and the sociopolitical aspects of health care (Chapter 13), much recent activity in the delivery of health care has been directed toward reducing unmet demand. As discussed in the section on the economics of health care (Chapter 11), a special relationship exists between supply and demand. Increasingly, monitoring and evaluation have become an important part of the health care system (see Chapter 12 on malpractice).

Our discussion of the health care system begins with the simplest components: consumers and providers (Chapter 3). However, before we can understand these components, we need to "speak their language" by understanding the special terms and symbols that apply to their world (Chapter 2). After we begin to master their system of semantics, we can analyze their relationships and other parts of the supply side of health care services:

- primary care, hospitals, clinics, and group practices
- mental health care
- care for the aged
- voluntary care agencies
- drug, equipment, and supply companies
- government-financed and government-supplied health care
- independent practitioners

Any description of the way in which these elements are organized seems to depend on three factors: the country being described, the point in time (1920 vs. 1980, for example), and the perceptual background of the analyst. Later chapters in this book discuss the health systems of other countries and the future possibilities for the delivery of health care. As for the analysts' philosophy, there are numerous ways to describe the important features of a health care system.

Another Description of a Health Care System

For example, Mark Field, a medical sociologist and physician, has developed a sociological description of the inputs and outputs of a health care system.[1] He suggests that four analytically distinct inputs from a society comprise a system: mandate and trust, knowledge, personnel, and instrumentalities. Health professionals receive a mandate from society in the form of monopolistic license that grants them certain privileges. This symbolic contract results in a fiduciary commitment; medicine will police its own house. In return, health professionals are granted a relatively free hand by the government to set their own standards and "lay on hands." Knowledge is the state of the art that is handed down from one generation of health providers to the next. Personnel, obviously, are those individuals whose central occupational concern is health care. Because of the surprising diversity in their background, they must be "motivated, recruited, taught, trained, socialized, and placed"; and once on the job, they must be continuously motivated through varying rewards (money, success, status, and security). Instrumentalities support health providers with the necessary supplies, instruments, and powers to perform their mandate. These instrumentalities can be derived from either the political or the economic system.

Field identifies four analytically distinct responses to the needs associated with illness, incapacity, and the ever-present possibility of

Figure 1.3   Disease Causation: A Hypothetical Historical
             Interpretation

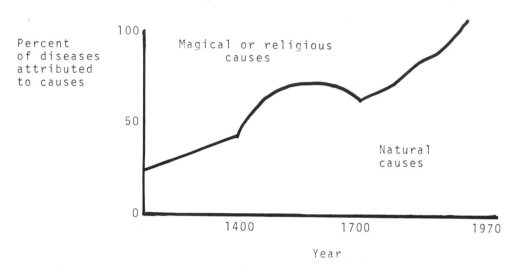

death. These responses or elements—magical, religious, compassionate, and technological—can be considered an amplification of the concept of wellness, a definite output that patients seek.

The magical response is closely aligned with ritual and the mystique of medicine. The "laying on of hands" (the administration of an injection, or the writing of a prescription) often satisfies the patient's need to undergo active treatment.

Historically, medicine and religion have been bound together. Until the introduction of germ theory into medical care, most diseases were attributed to magical or religious causes (Figure 1.3). Patients have believed and will continue to believe that disease is the work of some higher purpose and providence. They therefore look for higher meaning in their illness; this often requires the additional interpretation or reinforcement of a friend, provider, or minister. Because disease is unpredictable and death is both unpredictable in youth and predictable in old age, mankind has developed a large number of religious rationalizations to compensate for the inadequacy of scientific explanations. Much of our discussion of independent practitioners deals with our continuing reliance on faith healers and religious cures.

The compassionate response "stems from the need for comfort, reassurance, love, support, consolation, and 'tender loving care' that the suffering, anxiety-ridden, frightened, and often disturbed or regressed patient, and sometimes those near him, needs in the course of the illness, suffering, or disability."[2] The roots of this response probably lie in the mother-child relationship.

Last, and most obvious in this scientific age, is the technological response. Patients anticipate the rational application of clinical science— sometimes known as the "medical model." This output involves an active, interventionist approach by the provider. A curious by-product of the need for a technological response is role playing: shiny instruments, white coats, a visual display of diplomas and certificates, and a semidetached mannerism that symbolically represents the scientific approach to solving empirical problems.

Now that we have gained a clearer notion of the input and output of a health care system, we can discuss some implications and trends. As the number of personnel who handle a patient increases and as the hospital becomes a medical factory where a patient feels he or she is going through an assembly line, the compassionate response suffers.[3] Patients become alienated: they have to wait long periods of time before a physician sees them, only to be treated as if they were an interesting diagnostic problem or "good teaching material." With technology has come the specialization of personnel (economists call this "division of labor") and the industrialization or institutionalization of medicine. The result is a bewildering maze of fragmented units through which patients wander. This fragmentation has made it difficult to find an activator, a primary care physician in some instances, or a point of entry into the system.

Complex institutions require administration, sometimes known as a bureaucratic structure. Bureaucracies alienate consumers and providers. Comparators threaten the traditional physician-patient relationship with the potential problem of the invasion of privacy and loss of privileged communication. As the system becomes more differentiated and depersonalized, there are more and more attempts to "manage" the system or make it more efficient through the use of automation, computers, and sophisticated machinery.

When an independent system appears to be malfunctioning, the government may take steps to make assessments and regulate its activities. This trend, the greater role played by public agencies in the health care system, is expected to continue. On a regional and national level, this phenomenon is called "health planning." The objective of the planning process is to eliminate unnecessary, duplicated services and to introduce a comprehensive system of health care in which patients will have coordinated access and continuity of care.

Summary

In order to begin the complex task of describing a health care system, we have broken it down into its simplest elements and their relationships. There is no generally accepted method for grouping or clustering these components. The relationships among components can be complicated, hidden, and tenuous. The growth technology and the demands for efficiency in the delivery of health care appear to be at odds with the need for compassionate responses unencumbered by bureaucratic alienation.

Questions

1. Refer back to Figure 1.1. Draw your own diagram of a health care system and include the elements you consider important. What elements and relationships in your system do you feel are most likely to change?

2. Write a paragraph describing the stereotypical bureaucracy. Can a bureaucracy occur in any system? What about a well-managed system?

3. Both the quality and quantity of a health care system could be increased. Using a graph of input and output, show the relationship between input and quantity and input and quality.

4. What is the teleology of the U.S. health care delivery system?

5. Using Mark Field's concepts in describing the inputs and outputs of a health care system, diagram a health system. Compare your results with Dr. Field's own diagram ("The Concept of the 'Health System' at the Macrosociological Level," *Social Science and Medicine* 7 (1973):763-85).

Notes

1. Mark G. Field, "The Medical System and Industrial Society: Structural Changes and Internal Differentiation in American Medicine," in *Systems and Medical Care*, ed. Alan Sheldon, Frank Baker, and Curtis P. McLaughlin (Cambridge, Mass.: MIT Press, 1970), pp. 143-81.

2. Ibid., p. 148.

3. Ibid. Field describes this process, "the patient is manipulated, percussed, exhibited, trundled, cut into, connected to tubes, swabbed, and wrapped, all the while moving from one person to another."

Further Reading

Blum, Henrik L. *Expanding Health Care Horizons: From a General Systems Concept of Health to a National Health Policy.* Oakland, Calif.: Third Party Association, 1976.

Buckley, Walter, ed. *Modern Systems Research for the Behavioral Scientist.* Chicago: Aldine, 1968. (Selected readings, pp. 490-513.)

Cardus, David, and Thrall, Robert M. "Overview: Health and the Planning of Health Care Systems." *Preventive Medicine* 6:134-42, March 1977.

LaPatra, J. W. *Health Care Delivery Systems: Evaluation Criteria.* Springfield, Ill.: Charles C. Thomas, 1976.

Levey, Samuel, and Loomba, N. Paul, eds. *Health Care Administration: A Managerial Perspective.* Philadelphia: J. B. Lippincott, 1973. (Selected readings, pp. 58-104.)

Robertson, Leon S., and Heagarty, Margaret C. *Medical Sociology: A General*

Systems Approach. Chicago: Nelson-Hall, 1975.

Trussell, Patricia. "Theories of Health." *Proceedings of the Southeast Chapter of the Society for General Systems Research,* 28 April 1973, pp. 5-9.

White, K. L. "Medical Care Research and Health Service Systems." *The Journal of Medical Education* 42 (August 1967):729-41.

2. Understanding the Semantics of Health Care

People in general attach too much importance to words. They are under the illusion that talking affects great results. As a matter of fact, words are, as a rule, the shallowest portion of all the argument. They but dimly represent the great surging feelings and desires which lie behind. When the distraction of the tongue is removed, the heart listens.
—Theodore Dreiser

Individuals from different disciplines or from diverse backgrounds but who make a contribution to health care often get together to discuss the future of the system. Heated arguments follow. If they have an audience, the audience gets excited. Passions rise, and perhaps a few strong words are used. Several people graphically describe the failures of medicine. Several others jump up to defend the system as "the greatest in the world." As the discussion comes to an end, most of the participants realize that little genuine understanding has taken place.

Our perception of reality as well as our behavior and thought processes are greatly influenced by our language, our symbolic maps. Our world of symbols—that is, words, labels, and inferences—deals with life on an abstract level, one that is removed from the silent, objective world. With our language, our symbol system, we have not only a way of talking, but also a way of seeing, a way of organizing experience, a way of discriminating among events.[1] Why is it that two experts can travel to Great Britain to observe the National Health Service and "see" and subsequently describe the NHS in dramatically different terms? There are many semantic difficulties in attempting to describe a health care delivery system.[2]

Recognizing that words have no meaning in and of themselves, we are ready to discuss some of the key terms and concepts of health care. We will plunge into, but make no attempt to resolve, the emotional controversy of whether access to health care is a right or a privilege and subsequently cover the fundamentals of socialized medicine. Finally, the psychosemantics of both the provider-provider and the provider-consumer relationships will be discussed. We must remember that no two perceptions of what we are describing will be precisely the same.

11

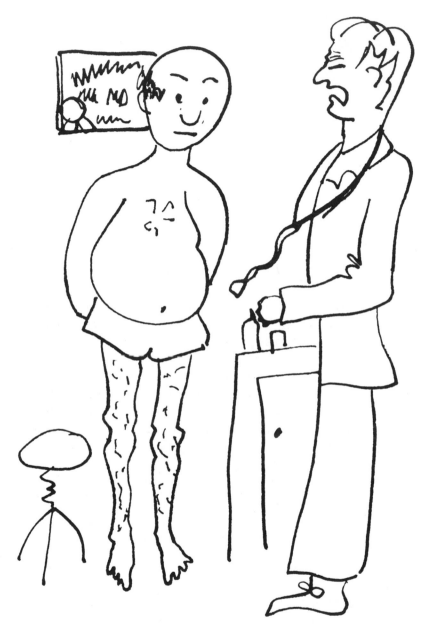

"If you want it simple, get a Reader's Digest!"

Abstracting a Few Concepts and Terms

The first distinction that requires some scrutiny is *health care* versus *medical care. Medical care* is a narrower term and traditionally refers to the type of care delivered by physicians.[3] Nurses practice nursing care. Optometrists practice optometric care. All three deliver health care.

The term *organized medicine* refers to the various groups and associations that physicians join, such as the American Medical Association, state and local medical societies, state licensing boards, and other professional organizations

The prevailing definition of *optimal health,* as provided by the World Health Organization, is "a state of physical, mental and social well being." Optimal health is sometimes known as *optimal wellness.* Health, when examined in this sense, is a broad concept. If a boss grants an employee's request for a sizable raise in pay, has not he or she elevated the employee's health (the employee feels better)? Does not a beautiful poem contribute to the reader's sense of well-being? Does not a shot of vitamin B-l2 or a glass of beer on a hot day contribute to our sense of physical health? When a shot is administered by a physician, is it medical care, and when administered by a nurse, nursing care? What if the shot is self-administered? We must recognize how arbitrary many definitions are.

Disease can be broken down into two parts: *dis* and *ease* which symbolize a malfunction or anxiety or both. *Illness* is difficult to define. Besson asks whether an individual is ill or well in the following examples:[4]

1. the "well" patient with subclinical disease discovered accidentally on a routine examination
2. the "well" patient with no subclinical disease, but who is a heavy smoker and is incubating emphysema
3. the "well" patient with no subclinical disease, who is not exposed to a chronic hostile environment as the smoker is, but now happens to be temporarily overwhelmed by the vexations and complexity of contemporary urban life
4. the "well" patient who, assuming an attitude of dependency may prefer the sick role
5. the "ill" patient who, because of social, ethnic, cultural, and family background, may refuse to accept the sick role or may feel uncomfortable in the traditional health institution and prefer not to risk rejection implied by being out of familiar surroundings

Perhaps these five cases can best be viewed by setting up a 2 x 2 matrix as in Table 2.1. The problem with asking, "Is the patient healthy or sick?" is that the question sets up a false dichotomy, a semantic trap: One can be both healthy and sick at the same time, but a health-illness spectrum or

Table 2.1 A Matrix of Health and Illness

Perceived Need (suffering)

	Yes	No
Yes Existing Need (malfunctioning) **No**	Illness	Other defined problems
	Hypochondria and malingering	Health

continuum turns a false contradictory into a thermometer of contraries (see Figure 2.1).[5] If health or lack of health is viewed as a matter of degree, we see the idea of preventive medicine more clearly. *Preventive medicine* is the practice of detecting and altering the natural progression of disease before it reaches the clinical manifestation. Ideally, all disease can be halted before pain sets in and costly treatment becomes necessary. For asymptomatic individuals, an annual physical checkup represents a form of preventive medicine. For many people, however, physicians and hospitals are providers one visits only when one is sick. Sometimes, unfortunately, physicians and hospitals themselves cause disease, known as *iatrogenic disease.*[6] Iatrogenic diseases can result from negligence, from the effects of long-term institutionalization, which can cause acute dependency, or from other side-effects of treatment. Another curious phenomenon is *transference,* which occurs when a patient imputes to a health provider a significance that is not appropriate to the situation, but that derives from the psychological needs of the patient. A particularly important form of transference is the attribution of parental roles (a male physician becomes a father figure; a female nurse becomes a mother).

Besides preventive medicine, many health educators are teaching the importance of treating people rather than diseases. Instead of concentrating all their efforts on one part of the body, providers are supposed to treat the whole patient, or take a holistic approach toward the delivery of care. Thus, by implication, they are supposed to deal with the problems a patient might have that would make him feel less than optimal.

Figure 2.1 Health-Illness Thermometer

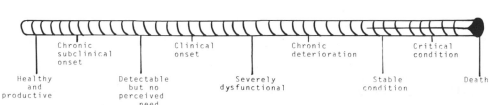

Macro Health Indicators

A common mistake is to equate health as measured by health status indicators with the quality of care delivered by a health system. The quality and availability of medical care do not have a simple cause-and-effect relationship with mortality levels (death rates). The same can be said for morbidity rates (the incidence and prevalence of different diseases). The reason is that between the independent and dependent variables there are all kinds of other variables: control, uncontrolled, confounding, distorter, suppressor, explanatory, intervening, moderator, and component variables.[7] Therefore, it may be inaccurate to say that poor maternal care by physicians and hospitals is responsible for the high infant mortality rate in the United States. Similarly, low birth weight in the ghettos of U.S. cities is regularly associated with failure of the mother to obtain prenatal care. However, the association, in part, is explained by the fact that premature delivery gives rise to low birth weight and by the inability of women to attend prenatal care clinics during the last months of pregnancy.[8] Premature labor may be caused by a number of factors, such as nutrition, heredity, or even cigarette smoking. Because in France and West Germany there is a high rate of deaths due to cirrhosis of the liver, should we therefore conclude that the health systems in those countries are deficient in treating problems related to alcohol?

Because of geographical variations in reporting (death certificates vary from country to country) and even different fashions in diagnosis, it is impossible to prove a direct cause-and-effect relation between the delivery of health care and the level of national health.[9] With these caveats in mind, we can examine a few health status indicators, such as infant mortality rates for selected countries (Table 2.2[10]). Despite appearances, it would be erroneous to conclude from Table 2.2 that the Scandinavian health systems are superior to those of other countries.

Life expectancy is another national health indicator. In the United States in 1967, life expectancy at birth was 71.3 years for whites and 64.6 years for nonwhites. Women have a longer life expectancy—7.2 years more—than men, a differential that is approximately the same for whites

Table 2.2   Infant Mortality for Selected Countries, 1965-1967

Country	Deaths per 1000 Infants Born Alive
Sweden	12.9
Norway	11.4
Denmark	17.1
USA	22.1
Italy	34.4
Israel	26.2
Ireland	24.8
Belgium	24.4
West Germany	23.4

Table 2.3 Ten Leading Causes of Death, United States, 1900 and 1967

	Rank of Cause		Deaths Per 100,000 Population	
	1900	1967	1900	1967
Influenza and pneumonia, other than in newborns	1	5	202.2	28.8
Tuberculosis, all forms	2		194.4	3.5
Gastroenteritis	3		142.7	3.8
Diseases of the heart	4	1	137.4	364.5
Vascular lesions affecting central nervous system (stroke)	5	3	106.9	102.2
Chronic nephritis	6	*	81.0	*
All accidents	7	4	72.3	57.2
Malignant neoplasms(cancer)	8	2	64.0	157.2
Certain diseases of early infancy	9	6	62.6	24.4
Diphtheria	10		40.3	0.0
General arteriosclerosis		7		19.0
Diabetes mellitus	*	8	*	17.7
Other diseases of the circulatory system		9	12.0	15.1
Other bronchopulmonic diseases		10	12.5	14.8
All causes			1,719.1	935.7

*Not comparable because of change in classification.

and nonwhites.[11] One statistic has puzzled experts for yers: why has the U.S. life expectancy at age 65 remained at about 13.0 years since 1955?[12] Has the health care system failed to help individuals over the age of 65?

Table 2.3 shows the dramatic shift in the causes of death in the United States between 1900 and 1967.[13] As is evident, the contagious diseases—tuberculosis and influenza—have declined in frequency, and cancer and diseases of the heart and central nervous system have increased. Accordingly, health resources have been shifted into the chronic diseases. The increase in diabetes may be the result of technological advances in health care: because insulin and changes in diet allow diabetics to live longer and because diabetes may be hereditary, diabetics can now have more children, which in turn leads to an increase in the incidence of diabetics per 100,000 population.

Another interesting health indicator is the cause of death in young people. Table 2.4 shows that motor vehicle accidents and other violent activities are the leading causes of death for white males in this age group.[14] By age twenty-five, arteriosclerotic heart disease begins to take its toll. As we can see from Table 2.3, however, accidents remain an important factor in mortality for the entire population. Accidents—their frequency, type, and severity—are a direct input into the emergency health care system.

Despite the shortcomings of health indicators, we would still like to have some measurement of the end product or output of whatever health systems we can manage to isolate and study. The following indexes are the best currently available:[15]

1. mortality—death certificates
2. morbidity—how sick, type of complaints

Table 2.4 The Probability of an Individual Dying
in the Next Ten Years

WHITE MALE, AGE 10	%	WHITE MALE, AGE 20	%
1. Motor vehicle accidents	.30	1. Motor vehicle accidents	.58
2. Drowning	.07	2. Suidide	.13
3. Accidents due to firearms	.04	3. Homicide	.06
4. Suicide	.03	4. Drowning	.04
5. Leukemia		5. Aircraft accidents	.04
Total probability of dying within 10 years	.88	Total probability of dying within 10 years	1.58

WHITE MALE, AGE 15		WHITE MALE, AGE 25	
1. Motor vehicle accidents	.60	1. Motor vehicle accidents	.38
2. Suicide	.09	2. Suicide	.15
3. Drowning	.07	3. Arteriosclerotic heart disease	.10
4. Homocide	.05	4. Homicide	.06
5. Accidents due to firearms	.04	5. Chronic rheumatic heart disease	.04
Total probability of dying within 10 years	1.44	Total probability of dying within 10 years	1.62

  a. days lost from work
  b. days in hospital (length of stay)
  c. extent of activity limitations
3. activity counts
  a. M.D./population ratio
  b. R.N./population ratio
  c. hospital beds/population ratio
4. the average fraction of the year in which the individual is healthy
5. risk profile for each patient under care
6. probability models of movement along the health-illness continuum
7. proxy measures
  a. self-administered questionnaire
  b. socio-economic index (income, employment/residence)
8. Q index, example:

$$\frac{\text{T.B. Mortality—American Indian}}{\text{T.B. Mortality—U.S. Population}}$$

A careful examination of these indexes will reveal their inadequacies. Even combining a few of them does not produce a better result. If physical health is difficult to measure, the mental health of an area or country is next to impossible to measure. The best we can say is that health is an elusive concept and that elusive concepts are hard to measure.

Access to Health: Right or Privilege?

We are now ready to take on a far more controversial aspect of health care.[16] Is access to high-quality health care a right or a privilege? Almost any discussion of health care eventually will boil down to this basic

Figure 2.2   A Balance of Conflicting Rights: Equality Versus Freedom

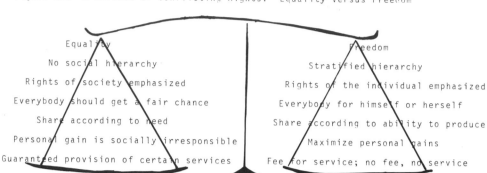

question. If health care is a right, then it ought to be accessible and delivered to everyone, even to the extent of making it free at the point of delivery in the system. This also suggests that someone, perhaps the government, has a positive duty to provide health services to the holder of the right. On the other hand, the libertarian view is that no one has the right to medical care nor the duty to provide it on any terms except those satisfactory to the provider. Illness is seen as one of life's normal risks.

This controversy represents a continuing tension between the polar concepts of freedom and equality, between the rights of the individual and the collective rights of society. Figure 2.2 shows the conflicting goals of the two ideals. White contends that an equilibrium between freedom and equality must be maintained if the sytem is to estabish order, preserve its essential characteristics, and survive.[17] However, it is by no means clear why one side of the balance must be chosen over the other.

The United States has slowly been moving away from viewing health care as a privilege, recognizing it instead as a right. The first step in this direction was public education. Public schools were founded on the premise that individuals can and will benefit according to their abilities. This principle, known as equity, could be interpreted to mean equal opportunity—but not equality. One look at the public education system in the United States is enough to see that students come out with grossly unequal amounts and qualities of education.

Subsequent steps have moved the country toward equal access to health care. By 1948, all states had passed legislation recognizing rights given by workmen's compensation. The employee's duty was to work and the employer's duty was to pay the premiums necessary to cover health accidents occurring on the job. The employer also had to provide a safe place of work. Workmen's compensation was the culmination of a long, tough drive on the part of unions to establish sick benefits for workers.

The armed forces has had its own health care system, as have merchant seamen and other groups. The U.S. Public Health Service and the Indian Health Service have had their own socialized system of hospitals and salaried providers. The right to health care has also been recognized— through the Veterans Administration system for service-related conditions and some non-service-related conditions—as an extension of armed-forces-related work.

A series of court decisions have recognized the right to emergency care. The Delaware Supreme Court, in *Wilmington General Hospital* v. *Manlove*, held that if a private hospital has emergency facilities, it can be held liable if its refusal to render emergency service to a person in an unmistakable emergency results in further injury—it must render timely and appropriate care.[18]

Similarly, one who is involuntarily committed to a mental health institution has a right to treatment. If he or she receives inadequate care, such detention may amount to punishment that exceeds that allowed for the crime or alleged crime committed (cruel and unusual punishment). It may thus raise a question of due process and may violate one's other constitutional rights. *Rouse* v. *Cameron* and *Wyatt* v. *Stickney*, a 1972 decision by the U.S. District Court for the Middle District of Alabama, have set this precedent.[19]

Cook County Hospital in Chicago, Charity Hospital in New Orleans, Bellevue Hospital in New York City, and Washington General Hospital in Washington, D.C., were among the first to provide health services for persons unable to care for themselves. In 1965, medicare and medicaid legislation was passed to help the aged and the poor even more. This legislation does not guarantee health care; instead, it guarantees payment for health care. State and city health departments have also established health care as a right in such cases as epidemics and communicable disease, through techniques such as inoculation, vaccination, and quarantines. Recently, these agencies have actively provided treatment for alcohol-related and narcotics-related ailments. For these "diseases," state intervention comes in direct conflict with individual freedom.

National health insurance may be the next step in turning health care into a right. Some providers are disturbed by these trends, which seem to make the provider subservient to a third party, namely, to the government.[20] Saxon, for example, objects to intervention in the fee-for-service negotiations between provider and patient:

> When physicians or their associations individually or collectively allow third parties to interfere with this basic doctor-patient relationship they have made it possible for them to trespass in areas where they should not be permitted to participate. Such third party participation, eventually by its mere presence on the scene nullifies medical ethics and opens the doors to a new ethic that would make a public utility of professional medical services to be controlled by a political force, trade unions, or consumer pressure groups, etc.
>
> Political agencies of the government, insuring agents or companies,

accrediting institutions and isolated pressure groups who would provoke and enforce a "social conscience" on a community hospital and seduce its board of trustees by a token subsidy of government gain a management influence over the hospital and, in part, relieve the board of trustees of their prime obligation—the total management of hospital affairs.[21]

Saxon's arguments open up a discussion over the rights and obligations of providers. Is the provision of health care ethically and perceptually different from the provision of goods and services by other business enterprises, such as grocery stores and banks? Is medicine a special case?

Social Responsibility: A Divergence

Social responsibility is a fuzzy concept. It is often invoked to incite action. It sometimes takes the form of asking the affluent to relinquish some of their wealth in order to allow others to receive a good or service. The following case study dramatizes how difficult it can be to resolve an individual's or institution's social responsibility.

Case Analysis: The Social Responsibility of Health Providers

To the public, Joe Maywood was "the big man" at Maywood Hospital, but, people within the hospital knew very well that his sister Carol was at least as important, though very much a quieter person. Together, the two had taken over, in the early days of the Depression, a small proprietary hospital started by their physician uncle Ben Maywood. From the beginning Joe was the public figure and aggressive leader. Carol, however, was the administrative genius who not only developed a considerable number of new financial innovations, but who had a nose for future technology and future developments, and who had brought new procedures to the hospital which later on turned into highly productive areas.

The two siblings complemented one another, got along very well, and enjoyed each other and their work. Within twenty years they had turned a small hospital into a substantial complex with an annual budget amounting to almost twelve million dollars. After World War II, Maywood Hospital expanded its role and services. The hospital increased its acute bed complement, built a new physicians' office building, added long-term care beds, and instituted a home health service.

From the beginning, even before the Maywoods took over, the hospital had been particularly active in employee welfare and employee benefits —old Dr. Maywood having been an ardent churchman who felt deeply responsible for the condition of his work people. Wages were always at least five percent, if not ten percent, above prevailing industry rates—it was the boast of Joe Maywood that his workers were paid the highest wages in the community. The hospital was among the first to install a pension plan, health and medical insurance for its employees, and a credit union. In 1974, in response to the Report of the Secretary's Advisory Committee on Hospital Effectiveness, Joe Maywood announced that it was the intention of the hospital to give the employees the full benefit of any increase in productivity and output per man hour as well as savings resulting from employee suggestions.

The community within which Maywood Hospital was located was in the Midwest. In the fall of 1974, the midwestern economy went into a recession. Joe Maywood carefully studied the outlook for his hospital complex and came to the conclusion that his revenue would in all likelihood at least remain unchanged and would probably continue to go up. To reassure his employees, he therefore came out, in November 1974, with a statement (mailed over his signature) to every Maywood employee, in which he guaranteed to each employee that he would, during 1975, be fully employed at least at his present wage rate for fifty-two weeks—minus vacation—and for forty hours in each week.

No sooner had this pledge been made than employee productivity and output began to fall. The first drop was in January—complaints from patients, supervisors, and the medical staff increased considerably. Although by June the number of patients had increased and the cost of supplies had risen a normal amount, quality control and work performance were at the point of collapse. For the first time in seventy years, rumblings were heard throughout the community about the quality of medical care and even research at Maywood Hospital. Operating income began to drop to the break-even point.

Joe Maywood called an emergency meeting of the trustees, at which he presented a program of drastic action to reverse the trend   conferences, meetings, training sessions, and so on.

When he was through, his sister Carol suddenly spoke up—something that happened very rarely in these meetings. What Carol said surprised everybody even more than the fact of her speaking at all. For Carol lashed out against the entire social philosophy of the hospital. Carol said,

> What has happened could have been predicted. Just because you were worried about business, you assumed that the workers would be worried too. You, therefore, tried to reassure them—but since they were not worried to begin with, the fact that you felt the need to reassure them, only panicked them. What you did is like a doctor saying to a man who is afraid that he has cancer, "well, you should have six more months." This is all that's needed to confirm the man's fear that he is incurable.
>
> I think this is the time to realize that we have been wrong all along with our approach to our responsibilities to the employees. We have been gratifying our egos and feeding vanity at the expense of our real social responsibility. That our employees have no real confidence in us—and I think the events of the last five months show this clearly—is only too

understandable. We must look like complete phonies to them. We do indeed have a social responsibility: to deliver the best medical care we know how and to sell it at the best price. Our first social responsibility to the employee is to make sure that he will have a job tomorrow and a better one than he has today. We discharge this by maximizing operating income. Everything else is frosting on the cake. Actually we have no right to hand over the fruits of increased productivity to the worker, who, as a rule, has done little to produce them. Our social responsibility is to hand them over to the patient in the form of better quality and lower prices, and to strengthen the economy thereby. This we have refused to do.

Altogether our social responsibility as medical care administrators is realized through medical performance and medical success rather than through philanthropy and the attempt to make people happy. Our paying ten percent or so above the prevailing rate is antisocial. Just because we can afford to do so does not give us the right to impose wage rates on our competitors or on the small hospitals in the community in which we operate—and yet, those people have to meet our wage rate. And the worst default of social responsibility is to guarantee jobs when we ought to have made clear all along that there are jobs only because there are patients for what we produce. If we, in management, exist only to produce jobs rather than hospital care services, then is there no difference between a free-enterprise and a socialist economy?

The board of trustees, and two of its ministers in particular, were outraged. The discussion continued over whether to guarantee jobs and whether to pay ten percent over the average prevailing wage rate. Suddenly the conversation switched to whether the hospital ought to continue to render free care.

The Meaning of Socialized Medicine

The question of whether health care is a right or a privilege is another semantic trap, a two-sided contradictory question. Health care is in some respects a right; in other respects, it is a privilege. How far to go toward one side or the other is a political question. As for social responsibility, we must ask whether the maldistribution of health care in the United States and elsewhere is not just a reflection of the maldistribution of wealth. Figure 2.3 shows how wealth is actually distributed (Lorenz curve, line *AYB*) and how wealth might be ideally distributed (line *AXB*). The closer the Lorenz curve approaches the imaginary line AP, the more maldistributed wealth is. Those who want access to health care to be an absolute right may actually be proposing that the health care system be used to redistribute income and wealth. In any case, most proposals to make health care a right mean a movement into socialized medicine.

Depending on who you are and your frame of reference, socialized medicine may be attractive or terrifying. There are two kinds of socialized

Figure 2.3   Lorenz Curve of U.S. Income Inequality

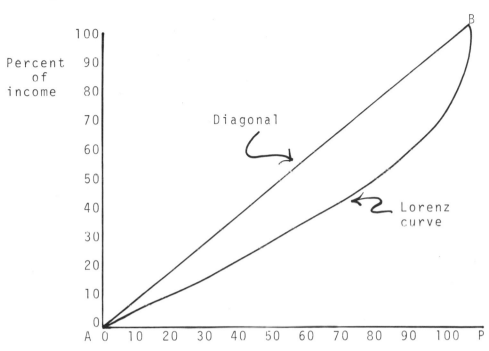

Percent of population

medicine: (1) national health insurance or third-party reimbursement for health care by the government, and (2) direct provision of services by government employees in government hospitals (Charity, Los Angeles, and Cook County hospitals).

Rather than explore the details of socialized medicine in all the countries where it exists, let us instead make a few generalizations about socialized medicine and try to stay away from emotionally charged issues. There are several reasons why a system might move toward socialized medicine:

1. short supply of medical facilities and providers
2. not enough money to pay for high-priced services
3. an excessive amount of hospitalization
4. fear by the government of loss of control over the providers
5. gaps in private insurance plans[22]
6. government has already nationalized other industries

When the providers realize that socialized medicine is imminent, they vigorously protest through their professional organization and insist on provider control of the new system. In many instances, they are successful in achieving three goals:

1. physicians who would like to continue in private practice can do so
2. physicians are reimbursed at a fixed dollar amount per patient (capitation fee) or at a fixed fee per patient visit or procedure
3. physicians administer the socialized system and retain control over peer review

According to Glazer, the quality of medical care is not affected by the transition to socialized medicine. Instead, more patients have access to and utilize the system; for a certain period of time, moreover, providers' salaries, through their combined incomes from private and public practices, exceed what they would have been with solely private practices. After several years of experience with socialized medicine, however, a government may attempt to (1) reduce or eliminate private practice, (2) put a lid on the income health providers can earn, and (3) eliminate "freedom of choice" in choosing a provider.

Psychosemantics of Care

Just as heated, but perhaps better hidden from public view, are transactional conflicts between providers and between providers and consumers. The health care delivery system is plagued by the same interpersonal problems that exist in any labor-intensive system (a high concentration or proportion of the system's resources are employees). These problems are sometimes humorous, sometimes troublesome, and sometimes painful. Why, indeed, do people respond so irrationally to our directions, or why cannot others seem to say what they mean or at least relate to us in a meaningful way?

Stein's articulation of "the doctor-nurse game" is a splendid example of the psychosemantics of provider-provider transactional conflicts.[23] The objective of the "game" is for the nurse to be bold, have initiative, make significant recommendations and at the same time appear passive. The nurse's recommendations must appear to be initiated by the physician. The nurse must communicate recommendations without appearing to be making a diagnosis or prescribing treatment, which is the physician's "territorial imperative." Likewise, the physician, in requesting a recommendation from the nurse, must do so without appearing to do so. Open disagreement in front of a patient is definitely to be avoided.

Stein provides us with an example of how a successful doctor-nurse game is played. The medical resident on hospital call is awakened by telephone at 1:00 a.m. because a patient on a ward not his own has not been able to fall asleep. Dr. Jones answers the telephone, and the conversation goes like this:

"This is Dr. Jones." (An open and direct communication.)

"Dr. Jones, this is Miss Smith on 2 W—Mrs. Brown, who learned today of her father's death, is unable to fall asleep." (This message has two levels. Openly, it describes the circumstances: a woman who is unable to sleep and who that morning received word of her father's death. Less openly, but just as directly, it is a diagnosis and recommendation: Mrs. Brown is unable to sleep because of her grief, and she should be given a sedative.)

Dr. Jones, accepting the diagnosis and replying to the recommendation, answers "What sleeping medication has been helpful to Mrs. Brown in the past?" (Dr. Jones, not knowing the patient, is asking for a recommendation from the nurse, who does know the patient, about what sleeping medication should be prescribed. Note, however, that he does not appear to be asking for her recommendation.)

Miss Smith replies, "Pentobarbital mg 100 was quite effective night before last." (A disguised recommendation.)

Dr. Jones replies with a note of authority in his voice. "Pentobarbital mg 100 before bedtime as needed for sleep, got it?" (Miss Smith ends the conversation with the tone of a grateful supplicant.)

When the game is played successfully, the physicians and nurses function efficiently, and everyone is happy. However, unskilled players are barely tolerated. Physicians who fail to recognize the nurses' subtle recommendations are "dolts." If they interpret these recommendations as insolence, nurses can make life miserable for physicians by being less than cooperative. On the other hand, if nurses fail to make suggestions, then they are perceived as "dolts" and are ignored. Outspoken nurses may not be tolerated by physicians.

This game evolves from the attitudes that physicians and nurses learn during their training. As medical students, physicians quickly learn that lives depend on their judgment and that they had best not make mistakes. Carefully nurtured, this attitude turns into a phobia: the pervasive fear of making a mistake. In order to cope with it, physicians develop a phobic defense or defensive manner. They assume a facade of superiority. They are omnipotent, omniscient, and therefore incapable of admitting a mistake to anyone other than fellow physicians. This sets up an approach-avoidance conflict: physicians want to do their best for a patient and therefore get the best possible advice, but accepting advice from non-physicians is highly threatening to their mask of omnipotence. The only way out is to play the game.

Similarly, nursing students are often taught that physicians must be shown the utmost respect and deference. Nursing schools used to instruct nurses to stand when physicians enter the room, to offer their chair, and even open the door and allow the physician to enter first. Student training took on a military flavor, and this subservience inevitably led to a fear of independent action. The fear of being humiliated for a blunder while assisting a procedure became a general fear of humiliation for taking an action independent of a physician. At the same time, nursing students receive a contradictory message during their training. They are told that they are an invaluable aid to the physician in the treatment of the patient; often nurses are the closest provider to the patient, the persons most likely to hear the details of a patient's troubles. In short, they are an important contributor to total patient care. Thus the nurse is also placed in an approach-avoidance conflict and must play the game.

Social reinforcement during medical and nursing school reinforces the game. Female nursing students accuse male medical students of thinking they can "walk on water." Male medical student accuse female nursing students of having weak self-concepts and limited intellectual horizons. Sexual roles of male dominance and female passivity perpetuate the game. The rewards for playing well and the punishments for playing poorly are sufficient to keep the game flourishing.

Stein believes the doctor-nurse game inhibits open dialogue, is stifling and anti-intellectual, and hinders the team approach to patient care. Role playing is likewise deeply ingrained in the health care system. These patterns of semantic interchange may be difficult to change—given legal liability and current trends in malpractice claims.

Let us turn to the provider-consumer transaction. Why do patients fail to respond to medical advice? Why do they fail to take their medicine? Does increased social distance between patient and provider lead to greater compliance by the patient? How important is warmth—often a nonverbal form of communication—in the increasingly complicated, fragmented health care system?

Although there is no consensus on these questions, Francis et al. have found three key factors in noncompliance: the extent to which a patient's expectations from the medical visit were left unmet, lack of warmth in the physician-patient relation, and failure to receive an explanation of diagnosis and cause of the patient's illness.[24] Thus, there seems to be a significant association between compliance and a patient's satisfaction with the patient-provider transactions. Although a patient's satisfaction is of course subjective, a matter of his or her individual personality, Francis et al. found that the provider—the physician—and his or her ability to communicate during the exchange can greatly affect the outcome, or output, of the system.

Summary

Health is a broad term and is difficult even to define, much less guarantee. What makes health care different from other goods and services is also unclear. Social responsibility is likewise a fuzzy concept. Income inequality is often confused with unequal access to health care. The U.S. health care delivery system is moving toward a socialized or nationalized system that would recognize access to health care as a right. Genuine understanding between providers and between providers and consumers, as well as recognition of each group's rights, is an important part of an efficient and effective system.

Questions

1. What should health providers do when they encounter hypochondria and malingering? When is transference appropriate?

2. List as many factors as you can why the U.S. infant mortality rates are higher than Scandinavian rates.

3. What imagery is conjured up by the words *socialized medicine*?

4. Medical school classes now are one-quarter female. How will increased female admissions affect the doctor-nurse game?

5. You are a trustee of Maywood Hospital (case study, p. 20). The hospital buys a $500,000 radiology unit. Should the entire cost of the equipment be passed along to patients through higher radiology fees, or should some of the increase be defrayed through higher daily room rates? How about lowering employee wage increases as well?

Notes

1. Alfred Korzybski, *Science and Sanity. An Introduction to Non-Aristotelian Systems and General Semantics* (Lakeville, Conn.: Institute of General Semantics, 1933); and Alfred Korzybski, "The Role of Language in the Perceptual Processes," *General Semantics Bulletin* 36:15-50 (1969). In his article on perceptual processes, Korzybski, the father of general semantics, tells the following story:

> We have all seen a box of Aunt Jemima pancake flour, with the picture of "Aunt Jemima" on the front. Dr. William Bridges of the New York Zoological Society has told this story about it: A United States planter in the Belgian Congo had some 250 natives working for him. One day the local chieftain called him and said he understood that the planter was eating natives, and that if he did not stop, the chief would order his men to stop work. The planter protested that he did not eat natives and called his cook as a witness. But the cook insisted that he did indeed eat natives, though he refused to say whether they were fried, boiled, stewed, or what not. Some weeks later the mystery was cleared up when the planter was visited by a friend from the Sudan who had had a similar experience. Between them they figured out the answer. Both had received shipments of canned goods from the United States. The cans usually bore labels with pictures of the contents, such as cherries, tomatoes, peaches, etc. So when the cooks saw labels with the picture of "Aunt Jemima," they believed that an Aunt Jemima must be inside!

2. Korzybski also is credited with the profound statement, "Whatever you say something is, it is not." For example, the label on a bottle of Valium or Seagram's Seven provides only a crude description of what is inside.

3. There are many different "doctors" working in the health care system (Ph.D, Dr. P.H., D.Eng., D.D.S., M.D., D.O., O.D., D.C., D.S.W., etc.) Fortunately or

unfortunately, the public has trouble distinguishing these individuals from an M.D. or what we will refer to in this book as a physician. An osteopathic physician (Doctor of Osteopathy, D.O.) also is considered a physician in this book. For an interesting though biased article on osteopathy, see Carl J. Denbow, "Osteopathy: Packing More Professional Punch," *Medical Dimensions* 6:19-24 (May 1977).

4. Gerald Besson, "The Health-Illness Spectrum," *AJPH* 57:1901-5 (November 1967).

5. G. B. Hutchinson, "Evaluation of Preventive Services." *Journal of Chronic Diseases* 11:479-508 (1960).

6. R. M. Markus, "We Report: President's Commission on Medical Malpractice." *Trial* 9:32 (March-April 1973). A limited study conducted for the commission concluded that some "medical injury" was sustained by as many as 7.5 percent of patients in two (supposedly representative) hospitals studied.

7. Mervyn Susser, *Causal Thinking in the Health Sciences* (New York: Oxford University Press, 1973), pp. 64-135.

8. Susser explains why it may be spurious to infer a causal association: "Low birthweight in the ghettos of American cities . . . is regularly associated with failure of the mother to obtain prenatal care. This association is explained in part by the fact that premature delivery gives rise to low birthweight and the inability of women to attend prenatal care clinics late in gestation. Premature delivery prevents the late attender from signing up and entering the statistics of prenatal clinics late in pregnancy." Therefore, it appears that

less prenatal care ⎯⎯⎯⎯⎯▶ lower birth weight

when actually the relationship is

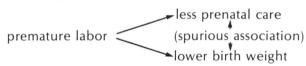

9. For an excellent discussion of this proposition, see Rita R. Campbell, *Economics of Health and Public Policy* (Washington D.C.: American Enterprise Institute, 1971), pp. 41-52.

10. *Statistical Bulletin* (Metropolitan Life Insurance Company, February 1970), p. 2.

11. *Statistical Bulletin* (Metropolitan Life Insurance Company, April 1970), p. 8.

12. *Statistical Bulletin* (Metropolitan Life Insurance Company, July 1970), pp. 4 and 6.

13. Petersen, *Population*, p. 223; U.S. Dept. of Commerce, *Statistical Abstract of the United States*, 1969 (Washington, D.C.: U.S. Government Printing Office, 1969), pp. 58-59.

14. *Commentary*, June 1970, p. 64.

15. Seth B. Goldsmith, "The Status of Health Status Indicators," *Health Services Report* 87:212-20 (March 1972).

16. Robert L. White, *Right to Health: The Evolution of an Idea* (Iowa City, Iowa: University of Iowa, 1971).

17. Ibid., p. 47.

18. *Problems in Hospital Law* (Pittsburgh, Pa.: Aspen System Corp., 1968), pp. 9-13.

19. Donald S. Burris, ed., *The Right to Treatment* (New York: Springer-Verlag New York, 1969).

20. Robert N. Sade, "Health as a Right: A Refutation." *New England Journal of Medicine* 285:1288-92 (2 December 1971); also John S. Millis, "Is Private Practice Dead?" *California Medicine* 109:499-503 (1968).

21. M. R. Saxon, *The Social Conscience of Medical Associations—A Mythical Impossibility* (Aurora, Ill.: Saxon Foundation, 1970), pp. 3 and 5.

22. W. Glazer, "Socialized Medicine in Practice." *The Public Interest* 1:90-106 (1966).

23. Leonard I. Stein, "The Doctor-Nurse Game." *Archives of General Psychiatry* 16:699-703 (1967).

24. Vida Francis et al., "Gaps in Doctor-Patient Communication." *New England Journal of Medicine* 280:535-40 (6 March 1969).

Further Reading

Arrow, Kenneth J. "Government Decision Making and the Preciousness of Life." In *Ethics of Health Care*, edited by Laurence R. Tancredi. Washington, D.C.: National Academy of Sciences, 1973, pp. 33-47.

Boorse, C. "On the Distinction between Disease and Illness." *Philosophy and Public Affairs* 5:49-68 (Fall 1975).

Duff, R., and Hollingshead, A. *Sickness and Society*. New York: Harper & Row, 1968.

Health is a Community Affair: Report of National Commission on Community Health Services. Cambridge, Mass.: Harvard University Press, 1968.

Illich, Ivan. *Medical Nemesis: The Expropriation of Health*. London: Calder & Boyars, 1975.

Kasl, S. V., and Cobb, S. "Health Behavior, Illness Behavior and Sick Role Behavior." *Archives of Environmental Health* 12:246-66 (February 1966).

Lee, Philip R. "Health and Well Being." *Annals of the American Academy of Political and Social Science* 373:193-207 (September 1967).

Parsons, Talcott. "Definitions of Health and Illness in Light of American Values and Social Structure." In *Patients, Physicians, and Illness*, edited by E. Jaco. New York: Free Press, 1958.

Rashkis, Harold A., and Yanovski, Alexander. "Towards a Systems Definition of Psychiatric Practice." *Diseases of the Nervous System* 37:177-81 (April 1976).

U.S. Congress, Subcommittee on Health and Environment. *A Discussive Dictionary of Health Care*. Washington, D.C.: U.S. Government Printing Office, February 1976.

Wessen, A.F. "Hospital Ideology and Comunication Between Ward Personnel." In *Medical Care*, edited by W. R. Scott and E. H. Volkhart. New York: John Wiley & Sons, 1966, pp. 458-75.

Wylie, G.M. "The Definition and Measurement of Health and Disease," *Public Health Reports* 85:100-04 (February 1970).

3. The U.S. Health Care Delivery System: Background

Our mortality figures reflect convincingly the fact that most Americans die of excess rather than neglect or poverty.
—Michael Halberstam

The system of delivering health care in the United States is made up of many components and smaller subsystems that interact with one another. The principal players in this system are the consumer and the physician, although many other participants provide care. Our objective here is to describe some of the characteristics and trends of the major participants so that we can then examine the organization of these components.

The Consumer as Patient

As of 1 July 1972, the total population of the United States (including armed forces overseas) was 208,837,000. About 51 percent of this total was female, 11 percent was black, 4.5 percent of Hispanic origin, and 10 percent was sixty-five years and over.[1] An important characteristic of the U.S. population is its rate of growth, especially the net reproduction rate—the number of females born. The net reproduction rate is approaching one; that is, females are replacing themselves with but one daughter. Since the number of reproducing females will not increase, zero population growth is a real possibility. The preferences for smaller families already has affected the demand for obstetrical care and baby products, and it may well affect the gap between supply and demand for other health care services. This decrease in the birthrate is not as marked in minority groups.

Because the percentage of young people in the population is decreasing, the percentage of the over-sixty-five population is increasing. More older Americans means more demand for nursing homes and geriatric care. Eventually, as the population stabilizes, this demand should level off. Older individuals, babies and young children, and women in their child-bearing years all have above-average health needs. Tables 3.1,[2] 3.2,[3] and 3.3[4] show the insignificant change in life expectancy (1900-1971)

31

Table 3.1   Average Remaining Years of Life at Specified Ages,
             Selected Years 1900-1971

| Age | Average Years of Remaining Lifetime | | | | Average Increase in Remaining Lifetime |
	1900-02	1969	1970	1971	1900-02 to 1971
At birth	49.2	70.4	70.8	71.1	21.9
1	55.2	71.0	71.2	71.5	16.3
5	55.0	67.2	67.4	67.7	12.7
25	39.1	48.1	48.3	48.6	9.5
45	24.8	29.9	30.1	30.3	5.5
65	11.9	14.8	15.0	15.2	3.3
85 and over	4.0	5.0	5.3	5.4	1.4

Table 3.2   Maternal Mortality Rates by Race, Selected Years 1940-1971
             (rates per 100,000 live births[a])

Year	Total	White	All Other
1940	376.0	319.8	773.5
1950	83.3	61.1	221.6
1955	47.0	32.8	130.3
1960	37.1	26.0	97.9
1965	31.6	21.0	83.7
1966	29.1	20.2	72.4
1967	28.0	19.5	69.5
1968	24.5	16.6	63.6
1969	27.4[b]	N.A.[c]	N.A.
1970	24.7[b]	N.A.	N.A.
1971	20.5[b]	N.A.	N.A.

a In 1971 the deaths of an estimated 730 women were
assigned to complications of pregnancy, childbirth,
and puerperium. The 1971 provisional maternal mortality
rate was 20.5 per 100,000 live births.
b Preliminary data.
c N.A.: Not Available.

for those aged sixty-five and over and, in contrast the marked changes in infant and maternal mortality, particularly since 1940. Despite this general improvement in maternal and child health, nonwhites still have much higher mortality rates for certain selected health problems.

Purchasers of health care continue to shift their place of residence, primarily from rural to urban and suburban areas. The moves made during the 1960-1965 period in the United States (Table 3.4) were primarily attempts to optimize their own chances in life.[5] California, Texas, and Florida have grown and continue to grow based on "images of locale" and certain specialized activities.

Table 3.3 Infant Mortality Rates by Age and Color, Selected Years, 1940-1971[a]

	Total			White			All Other		
Year	Under 1 Year	Under 28 Days	28 Days to 11 Months	Under 1 Year	Under 28 Days	28 Days to 11 Months	Under 1 Year	Under 28 Days	28 Days to 11 Months
1971(est.)	19.2	14.3	4.9	16.8	12.9	3.9	30.2	20.8	9.4
1970(est.)	19.8	14.9	4.9	17.4	13.5	3.9	31.4	21.6	9.8
1969(est.)	20.7	15.4	5.4	1814	14.1	4.4	31.6	21.6	10.0
1968	21.8	16.1	5.7	19.2	14.7	4.5	34.5	23.0	11.6
1967	22.4	16.5	5.9	19.7	15.0	4.7	35.9	23.8	12.1
1966	23.7	17.2	6.5	20.6	15.6	5.0	38.8	24.8	13.9
1965	24.7	17.7	7.0	21.5	16.1	5.4	40.3	25.4	14.9
1964	24.8	17.9	6.9	21.6	16.2	5.4	41.1	26.5	14.6
1963	25.2	18.2	7.0	22.2	16.7	5.5	41.5	26.1	15.4
1962	25.3	18.3	7.0	22.3	16.9	5.5	41.4	26.1	15.3
1961	25.3	18.4	6.9	22.4	16.9	5.5	40.7	26.2	14.5
1960	26.0	18.7	7.3	22.9	17.2	5.7	43.2	26.9	16.4
1950	29.2	20.5	8.7	26.8	19.4	7.4	44.5	27.5	16.9
1940	47.0	N.A.[b]	N.A.	43.2	N.A.	N.A.	73.8	N.A.	N.A.

a For 1969 through 1971 based on a 10 percent sample of deaths; for all other years, based on final figures. Rates per 1,000 live births.
b N.A.: Not Available.

Table 3.4 Net Migration for Metropolitan Areas of the United States, 1960-65

	Net Gain (in thousands)
Greater Los Angeles (Riverside to Ventura to Orange County)	865
New York (Bridgeport to Princeton)	332
San Francisco-San Jose	271
Washington (with adjoining Maryland and Virginia)	222
Miami-Palm Beach	204
Houston	139
Atlanta	106
Dallas	104
Phoenix	90
Las Vegas	85
Tampa-St. Petersburg	77
Denver	61
Philadelphia	60
Sacramento	56
Huntsville	50

	Net Loss (in thousands)
Pittsburgh	143
Boston-Lawrence-Haverhill-Lowell	82
Buffalo	65
Detroit	55
Milwaukee	53

As one would expect, growth in medical services has followed shifts in migration. The suburban population of our metropolitan areas has increased dramatically and is 96.6 percent white; the inner cities, on the other hand, have become high-density nonwhite areas. The migration of health providers out of the cities and into the urban fringe has left the central city with understaffed facilities and unmet health needs. Many factors preserve this pattern, including suburban realty–development cliques, bureaucratic city governments, and racial prejudices.[6]

Since the end of World War II, there has been unparalleled prosperity in the United States. Per family real income (income divided by a price index) after taxes rose by 50 percent from 1950 to 1970. Although cyclical, employment remained high (under 5 percent unemployed). In 1974, however, inflation and recession broke both these trends. Furthermore, although unemployment may have been low, underemployment—being employed in a job that requires far less skill or time than an individual has—was and is a problem. Amid the United States' affluence lies a hard core of individuals on welfare, more than 14.4 million in 1973. Half of these welfare recipients are children in the Aid to Families of Dependent Children program (AFDC). In 1975, an estimated 30 million people lived below the poverty levels established by the 1970 census, and another 4.5 million were classified as near-poor—those with incomes of less than 25 percent above the poverty line. The near-poor have enough income to be ineligible for public assistance, but too little income to afford needed medical care.

Education levels continue to rise. In 1967, the proportion of young people completing college was as great as the proportion who completed high school in the early 1920s.

Affluence and Expectations

Affluence is not without its problems. Many Americans overeat, eat the wrong foods, consume too much alcohol, puff away at cigarettes, and get little exercise. The obese who smoke die early. Those whose lives are rushed and who do not take time to relax between business deals also die early. Affluence and urbanization have produced an extraordinary situation: more people live alone than live with somebody else, whether family or an unrelated individual. "Anomie," depression, social isolation, and excessive consumption of stimulants and depressants are the result, especially for those who are ill prepared to cope with loneliness. The implications of affluence register with the cardiologist and psychiatrist.

Rising incomes and rising education levels have brought rising expectations vis-à-vis health services. One might expect that with more money and education, people would be healthier and therefore use services less. Instead, we find a greater per capita demand for health services, especially for the treatment of minor ailments that might have been neglected during hard times. Both the "haves" and "have-nots" have rising expectations. The discrepancy between the "haves" and "have-nots" is disturbing to the "have nots" and, when care is unavailable, has contributed to alienation. One has only to view "Marcus Welby" from a cold-water inner-city flat to appreciate the great gaps between promise and performance. "Marcus Welby" misleads even the middle-class suburbanite: where can one find unhurried, readily accessible, comprehensive, compassionate care where bills never are discussed, difficult cases are resolved, and the physician is an unending source of strength? Rural America sometimes has to travel long distances to get to health care. Everywhere, waiting time hangs heavy for countless patients.

Industrialization and urbanization have brought another change: random violence. Weekend nights in the emergency rooms of the large, urban public hospitals look like a scene after a battle. Victims of, and participants in, crimes against persons straggle in. Violence due to accidents, stabbings, and handguns is evident. Rape victims, half of them children, are brought in by the police. The result is fear, paranoia, a pervasive distrust of strangers, a boom in the security-protection industry, and flight to the relative calm of the suburbs. The owners of small pharmacies located in urban areas are well aware of this.

We end up with what Somers describes as "a longer-lived, less disease-ridden, better educated, richer patient than ever before, but at the same time, needing and demanding more health care than ever before (this applies both to the affluent majority and the poor minority), increasingly critical of existing health care institutions, and determined to change these institutions, by whatever means he can command, in order to get what he thinks he needs."[7] The consumer increasingly feels he is powerless to effect any changes in a health care system dominated and controlled by the providers. Subsequently, he turns toward the third parties—the government and even the courts—to intervene in his behalf, to negotiate for him, and to force providers to be more responsive to his needs. (He wants readily available, high-quality care at low cost.)

The Physician as Provider

The average practicing physician is in great demand. Primary care physicians, general practitioners, obstetrician-gynecologists, and pediatricians, as well as the newest specialty—family practitioners—are in scarce supply. High demand and low supply mean high incomes. The average income for physicians is now about $55,000 per year, a sum unsurpassed by any other occupational group. Yet with all the financial and status rewards accorded to physicians, a number of trends make physicians unhappy. In order to understand these trends, we must first examine the number and distribution of physicians.

At the end of 1973, according to the AMA Masterfile of Physicians, there

Table 3.5 Federal and Non-Federal Physicians by Specialty and
          Activity, 31 December 1973

Specialty	Total Physicians	Patient Care	Medical Teaching	Adminis- tration	Research	Other
General practice	53,946	52,918	133	574	113	208
Medical specialties	86,924	77,598	2,318	2,751	3,807	450
Surgical specialties	91,549	88,050	1,168	1,183	896	252
Other specialties	91,984	76,691	2,564	7,451	3,516	1,726
Total physicians	366,379[a]	295,257	6,183	11,959	8,332	2,636

a Includes 42,012 physicians (22,624 inactive; 13,744 not classified;
and 5,644 address unknown) not distributed throughout the table.

were 366,379 physicians in the United States, but, as seen in Table 3.5, not all these physicians were active or involved in patient care.[8] Only about 80 percent (295,257) of these physicians were involved in direct patient care, that is, about 137 direct patient care physicians per 100,000 population and 171 physicians per 100,000. However, the AMA's survey omits doctors of osteopathy, and since we have included them in our definition of physicians, this brings the total physicians to approximately 381,579, or 179 physicians per 100,000 population, or one physician for every 562 people. The number of physicians is growing relatively faster than the population, and the physician/population ratio therefore continues to increase in a direction favorable to consumers.

Despite the growth in the number of physicians and medical schools (115 M.D. and D.O. schools in 1971-1972 with several more about to open), the United States relies heavily on graduates of foreign medical schools. In December 1972, there were 68,009 such graduates in the United States, or 18 percent of all physicians in 1972. It is estimated that 8,000 to 10,000 enter the United States each year, that is, almost as many physicians as U.S. medical schools graduate each year (10,000).[9] This "brain drain" from the developing countries, where many of these foreign physicians come from, raises serious questions about U.S. foreign policy. Countries such as Haiti, which graduates about 100 physicians annually, find that over 90 percent of the graduating class ends up in the United States and Canada.[10] In effect, foreign governments that subsidize foreign medical educations end up subsidizing U.S. health care. In addition, many U.S. students head for foreign medical schools, particularly just across the border in Mexico where admission is easier. Migration into the United States seems to be motivated primarily by the promise of a higher income.

The geographic distribution of physicians is uneven. In 1973, 86 percent of all physicians and about 90 percent of all specialists practiced in metropolitan areas. But an unexpectedly high proportion of general practitioners (32 percent) were located in nonmetropolitan areas.[11] In 1967, there were 318 physicians/100,000 in the District of Columbia, 199

Table 3.6   Percentage of Physicians in each Type of Practice and
             Primary Specialty of Active Physicians, 31 December 1972

Type of Practice	Percentages	Type of Practice	Percentages
General practice	22.0	Psychiatry and Neurology (8.8)	
		Child psychiatry	0.7
Medical Specialties (26.5)		Neurology	1.1
Allergy	0.5	Psychiatry	7.0
Cardiovascular	1.8		
Dermatology	1.3		
Gastroenterology	0.6	Other specialties (10.9)	
Internal medicine	15.0	Aerospace medicine	0.3
Pediatrics	6.4	General preventive	
Pulmonary diseases	0.6	medicine	0.3
		Occupational medicine	0.8
Surgical Specialties (32.2)		Pathology	3.5
Anesthesiology	3.7	Physical medicine and	
Colon and rectal	0.2	rehabilitation	0.5
General surgery	9.7	Public health	0.9
Neurological	0.9	Radiology	4.6
Obstetrics and			
gynecology	6.3		
Ophthalmology	3.3		
Orthopedic	3.2		
Otolaryngology	1.8		
Plastic	0.6		
Thoracic	0.6		

physicians/100,000 in New York, and 69 physicians/100,000 in Mississippi. Does this mean that residents of the District of Columbia receive better care than residents of Mississippi? In order to answer this question, we would have to know more about the relative productivity of the two groups of physicians, their specialties, their patients, and the other providers and facilities available in the two areas.

More and more physicians are specializing, primarily because they can earn more money and prestige as a specialist, and because medical schools seem to encourage it. Table 3.6 shows the distribution of physicians in the various specialties as of 1972.[12] The number of physicians in administrative positions has increased, and the number of general practitioners has decreased.[13] Specialties and their specialty boards are recognized and approved by the American Board of Medical Specialties in conjunction with the AMA Council on Medical Education. Although a physician need not be certified by a specialty board in order to practice a specialty, many physicians, after internship, take further training in a residency program of two to five years' duration. After this training, a physician becomes *board eligible* and may apply to the appropriate specialty board. After passing written and oral examinations and, in some cases, after practicing this specialty a few more years, the physician becomes *board certified* or a *diplomate* of that board. In 1969, the new specialty of "family medicine" was established, in part to induce more physicians into primary care functions.

In 1968, the average physician saw 132 patients per week and the general practitioner saw 173 patients per week (in 1938, the average physician saw 50 patients per week).[14] Despite this increase, Fein has argued that the so-called physician shortage could be alleviated if, instead of a drastic increase in the number of physicians, the physicians now in practice increase their work load.[15] He estimates that a 4 percent increase in the productivity of current physicians would add more medical supply than the medical schools' current graduating class would. Both physicians and consumers are apprehensive about this possibility. If patient visits or procedures per day or per week were increased, there would be less time for establishing rapport, ministering to the patient's need for compassion, and injecting genuine concern into the relationship. Instead, there would be assembly line diagnosis and treatment: the use of multiple examining rooms, allied health personnel tramping around helter-skelter, crowded waiting rooms, long waits before the physician and patient actually see each other, confused orders, problems of privacy, and ultimate frustration. Gone are the days of quiet house calls (they are inefficient—while a physician is driving around, he or she could be seeing far more patients at the office), solo practices, and "out-of-pocket" fees for service.

A physician used to be reimbursed directly out of a patient's pocket on a fee-for-service basis. He or she simply decided on a fee,[16] and the patient paid by cash or check. This transaction was considered an important part of the physician-patient relationship. Along came private health insurance and then government reimbursement programs:

These third parties began to impose all sorts of rules and regulations on physicians, rules and regulations that physicians regard as an unnecessary and harmful intrusion into the traditional physician-patient relationship. Medical care review, PSRO (Professional Standards Review Organization), the federal government's attempt to determine the need for medical care and set and enforce standards for its quality—all have alienated physicians.[17]

The spread of malpractice suits, (approximately 10,000 annually) and the subsequent rise in premium rates for malpractice insurance have also frustrated physicians. Physicians engaged in anesthesiology and complicated surgery can pay annual premiums as high as $20,000 to $40,000. But even higher rates are needed, the insurance companies contend, to offset losses caused by higher court settlements awarded to patients. Generous juries have awarded plaintiffs (injured patients) amounts that stagger the imagination, sometimes millions of dollars (but similar amounts are awarded for occupational accidents, so we should not be completely taken aback by malpractice awards).

Physicians have traditionally been reluctant to refuse their services en masse, but 1975 marked a significant departure from the "no-strike" ethic.

A Doctors' Strike?

Unthinkable? Maybe, but the unthinkable is about to happen.

More than 3,000 interns and residents in eleven major New York City voluntary hospitals plan to strike at 7:00 a.m. March 17. From that moment these skilled, highly trained and dedicated doctors will be on the picketline rather than at patients bedsides.

Why?

The League of Voluntary Hospitals represents:

Bronx-Lebanon (all divisions)
Brookdale
Jewish Hospital of Brooklyn/Greenpoint
Catholic Medical Center (all hospitals)
Hospital for Joint Diseases
Long Island Jewish/Hillside/South Shore Division/Queens General
Mt. Sinai/Elmhurst
Maimonides/Coney Island
Flower Fifth Avenue/Metropolitan/Coler
Montefiore/Morrisania
University Hospital

Since January 24, the League has adamantly refused even to discuss the lengthy hours doctors work or the practice of recurrent out-of-title work assignments. Our union, the Committee of Interns and Residents has asked that hours be limited to 80 per week and 15 per day. We don't think such a limitation is an unreasonable request.

We now work as many as 110 hours per week and often 56 hours at one stretch.

We know that after 50 hours of work we cannot possibly be as alert and as responsive to patient needs as we should be. We want to be good doctors. How alert would you be after 50 hours on duty?

In January the Federal mediator urged that the issue of excessive hours "be worked out." Rejecting the mediator's recommendation, The League has chosen instead to turn its back on us and the general public. But as the mediator warned this is an issue which "will not go away."

As to recurrent out-of-title work, so long as doctors do the work of nurses and orderlies, the more nurses and orderlies will be out of jobs and the more doctors will be kept from providing the medical services for which they have been trained.

If you plan to enter one of these hospitals for an elective procedure it may be wise to defer your admission until the strike is settled. If you plan to enter one of these hospitals for a non-elective procedure it may be wise to ask your doctor about using another hospital with house-staff which will be able to better care for you.

It is the legal responsibility of the League of Voluntary Hospitals to provide for patient coverage during the strike. The law provides for a 10-day strike notice so the hospital can discharge or transfer patients whenever possible and so that elective admissions will be reduced.

We deeply regret the necessity for this strike which will greatly inconvenience the public. Only the continued refusal of the hospitals to make any concessions on these key issues will prevent us from being at the bedsides of patients. We hope that you will urge the League to reconsider their position and re-open negotiations. The Interns and Residents stand ready to bargain in good faith.

COMMITTEE OF INTERNS AND RESIDENTS

Richard A. Knutson, M.D., President
666 Third Avenue, N.Y.
Affiliate of Physicians' National Housestaff Association

As a result of rising malpractice insurance, anesthesiologists initiated a work stoppage, which spread quickly on the West Coast.[18] Physicians also are willing to strike (see p. 39) over excessive working hours and performance of tasks that should be delegated to other providers.[19] Work stoppage probably alienates patients and physicians even more.

As a result of such fictional fantasies as Sinclair Lewis's novel, *Arrowsmith,* and "Marcus Welby," "Medical Center," and other medical TV shows, patient expectations do not always accord with physician performance. Although physicians can occasionally perform miracles, are highly trained, and are often adored by their patients, they can also make mistakes.[20] Furthermore, there are gaps in their training: for example a physician's training may differ markedly from the type of practice he or she eventually establishes. As Figure 3.1 suggests, the few people who are admitted to a university hospital may be quite different from those who visit physicians in their offices.[21]

As Somers characterizes the ambiguity of the physicians' situation: "More and better trained doctors than ever before, performing many near-miracles, seeing more patients, earning more money . . . but a continuously increasing imbalance between supply and demand that is producing tremendous emotional and financial pressures, resentment on the part of doctors and patients, and public depreciation of the medical profession."[22] Clearly, both physicians and patients are frustrated over exactly the same trends and forces—over which they individually have little control.

Other Medical Clinicians

In the U.S. system of health care, numerous occupations contribute to a patient's well-being. These medical clinicians range from highly skilled to practically unskilled.

Technologist, Therapist	Requires education at or above the baccalaureate level
Technician Assistant	Requires education at, or beyond, the two-year college level
Aide	Requires less than two years beyond high school or on-the-job training

In 1973, 4.4 million persons were employed in the health system; a total of 600 primary and alternate job titles were used for these individuals. For every physician, there are twelve other health personnel. It is not surprising that health care is the nation's second-largest occupational grouping (after construction and before agriculture; education and tourism are rising fast).

Figure 3.1   Distribution of Demand for Medical Care by a Typical
             Population in One Year (1970)

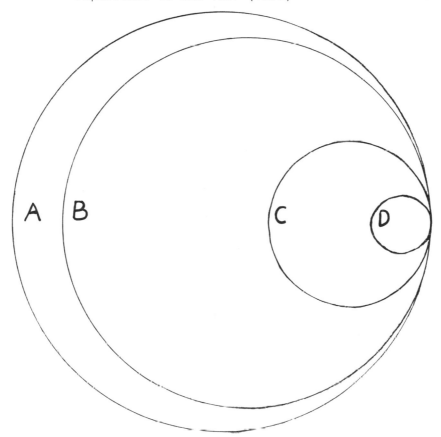

Circle A: Total population at risk = 1,000.
Circle B: People who visited a physician in an ambulatory
            setting at least once = 720.
Circle C: People who were admitted to a hospital
            at least once - 100.
Circle D: People who were admitted to a university hospital
            at least once = 10.

The largest single occupation group within the health system is nurses. Table 3.7 shows the numerical size of nursing and related services.[23] If are about 2,200,000 employed nursing personnel, then roughly half of all health personnel are involved in nursing care. Moreover, a 1972 inventory conducted by the American Nurses' Association found that of 1,125,657 registered nurses in the United States, 316,611, or 28 percent, were not employed in nursing.[24] In addition, of those registered nurses employed in nursing, approximately 29 percent work part-time. Therefore, a large number of registered nurses do not practice their skills at full capacity.

Because nursing is such a large segment of the health care system and

Table 3.7   Number of Employed Nursing Personnel by Category,
             January 1973

Nursing Personnel	Number Employed
Licensed registered nurses (R.N.)	815,000
Licensed practical nurses (L.P.N. or L.Y.N.)	459,000
Nursing aides, orderlies, attendants	910,000
Home health aides (homemakers)	25,500

because physicians are less and less able to spend much time with patients, nurses are an important source of medical care and compassion. The nurse is the active listener and more and more frequently the single most significant intervener in a patient's health-illness spectrum.

In the health professions, thus, responsibility devolves to lower and lower levels (physician to registered nurse, registered nurse to licensed practical nurse, licensed practical nurse to nurse's aide, etc.); jobs are "deskilled" to permit those with less formal training to do what more skilled individuals previously did. Figure 3.2, an expanding pyramid of health roles and occupations, shows both these processes.[25]

Providers are reluctant to give up their responsibilities and power, even though they do so voluntarily and sometimes involuntarily. Legal liability for patient care often makes delegation of tasks an extremely complex situation. Pride is also at stake, and interpersonal frictions can develop. Patients can become alarmed if a task normally performed by a physician is suddenly being performed by a nurse or even a medical student. Administrators find it difficult to distinguish among the skills of a medical technician, an operating room technician, a laboratory technician, and a licensed practical nurse. On the one hand, the proliferation of roles and occupations has provided a large number of jobs to those who in the past might not have been skilled enough to participate in the delivery of health care. On the other hand, it has created a complicated, confusing, difficult-to-coordinate system deeply in need of sophisticated managerial expertise and direction.

Summary

Because of their increased affluence and potential for well-being, patients and physicians ought to be satisfied with each other. Yet both are dissatisfied: the remaining gaps between supply and demand produce excessive waiting time, frustrations over minimal patient-contact time, and intervention by third parties. Even the expansion of roles within the health care system, which has brought added assistance to the physician, has not as yet brought the expected relief to the strained physician-patient relationship. Indeed, it may have intensified existing tensions.

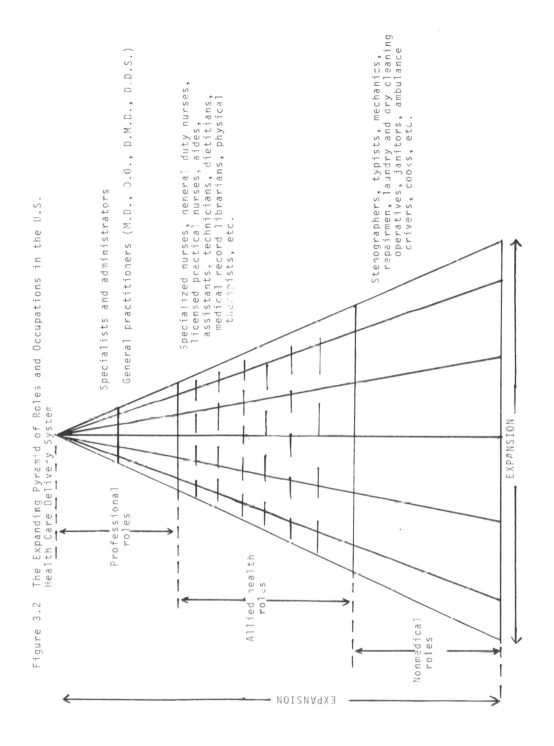

43

Figure 3.2   The Expanding Pyramid of Roles and Occupations in the U.S. Health Care Delivery System

Specialists and administrators

General practitioners (M.D., D.O., D.M.D., D.D.S.)

Specialized nurses, general duty nurses, licensed practical nurses, aides, assistants, technicians, dietitians, medical record librarians, physical therapists, etc.

Stenographers, typists, mechanics, repairmen, laundry and dry cleaning operatives, janitors, ambulance drivers, cooks, etc.

Professional roles

Allied health roles

Nonmedical roles

EXPANSION

EXPANSION

Questions

1. A few economists argue that in the early 1980s, the United States will have an excess or surplus of physicians. This prediction is based on an ideal physician/population ratio. What do you feel is an ideal physician/population ratio; what factors should you take into account in determining such a ratio?

2. Why are so many registered nurses not practicing at full capacity?

3. What is the difference in skills among an M.T., an O.R.T., an L.T., and an L.P.N.?

4. Obviously, the two cases from Leonard Tushnet's *The Medicine Men: The Myth of Quality Medical Care in America Today* (see p. 45) are extreme examples of poor medicine. Write up an example of a successful medical procedure that you personally know about. Why are Tushnet's and your examples misleading? What is a better method of analyzing the quality of U.S. health care?

Notes

1. American Medical Association, *Socioeconomic Issues of Health* (Chicago: AMA Center for Health Services Research and Development, 1973), pp. 1 and 2.

2. Ibid., p. 15.

3. Ibid., p. 27.

4. Ibid., p. 35.

5. Richard Meier, "The Metropolis as a Transaction-Maximizing System," *Daedalus* 97:1292-1313 (fall 1968).

6. Anthony Downs, "Alternative Futures for the American Ghetto," *Daedalus* 97:1331-78.

7. Anne R. Somers, *Health Care in Transition: Directions for the Future* (Chicago: Hospital Research and Educational Trust, 1971), p. 25.

8. "AMA's Annual Study Describes Distribution of M.D.'s in U.S.,"*Research Notes* (Center for Health Services Research and Development, AMA), vol. 1, August 1974.

9. The magnitude of migration of foreign physicians to the United States since 1965 may have been overstated. See Rosemary Stevens et al., "Physician Migration Reexamined," *Science* 190:439-42 (31 October 1975).

10. Discussion by the author with various Haitian officials.

11. "AMA's Annual Study Describes Distribution of M.D.'s in the U.S."

12. *Health Resource Statistics* (National Center for Health Statistics, PHS. HEW, 1974), pp. 167-79.

13. "AMA's Annual Study Describes Distribution of M.D.'s in the U.S."

14. *Medical Economics* 30:88 (September 1968). A 1967 survey of Kentucky G.P.'s found that the average length of time spent by the physician with each patient was 6.1 minutes, with the median 4.7 minutes. "What Is General Practice Really Like Today," *Medical World News*, 19 May 1967, p. 38). Doing some quick mathematics we find the following:

Assuming a work week of	63 hr	173 patients/week
	x 60 min	x 6.1 min/patient
	3,680	1055.3 patient min

1055.3/3,680 = 28.7% of working time spent seeing patients

What activities account for the remaining time? If the typical physician is rushed, Marcus Welby is not typical. For example, Dr. Welby makes house calls, has plenty of time to convince patients of the error of their ways, is adored by his patients, treats the "whole" patient (and sometimes his family), and despite difficult ethical dilemmas, seems to be attuned to the precise resolution that will please Middle America. We know little of his medical record system, the business side of his practice, and his methods of bill collecting. Miracles are not impossible. Dr. Welby has time, compassion, and understanding for even the most illiterate, recalcitrant individuals. His mere presence is enough to cure distress, hardship, and illogical thinking. He also happens to almost always be in the right place at the right time (like emergencies).

15. Rashi Fein, *The Doctor Shortage: An Economic Diagnosis* (Washington, D.C.: Brookings Institution, 1967), p. 138.

16. This is known as *price discrimination* and is discussed in a subsequent chapter.

17. "Medical Care Review Stirs a Fiery Debate Among U.S. Physicians," *Wall Street Journal,* 24 June 1974. PSRO are discussed in a subsequent chapter.

18. "Doctors' Protest Spreads in California: Bay Area Hospitals Feel Financial Pinch." *Wall Street Journal,* 21 May 1975. Malpractice and malpractice insurance also are discussed in a subsequent chapter.

19. *New York Times* and *New York Daily News,* 13 March 1975.

20. Two examples follow that are from Leonard Tushnet's *The Medicine Men: The Myth of Quality Medical Care in America Today* (New York: St. Martin's Press, 1971), pp. 167-68 and pp. 209-10.

Case 1

A forty-year-old woman trying to recapture her youth began to wear very short skirts. She noticed that her right thigh was quite a bit smaller than her left. She went to an orthopedist, who measured both thighs and found she was correct. The circumference of the left thigh was three inches more than that of the right.

The orthopedist put her through a series of exercises. He found that there was no muscle or joint weakness. The woman could stand and walk without trouble. He was puzzled by what he considered an atrophy of the right thigh. He sent the woman into the hospital for a thorough checkup.

The intern took a complete history and did a physical examination of the woman lying in bed. Because atrophy of the thigh may have resulted from a neurologic disorder and because he was going to be an ophthalmologist, the intern paid particular attention to the eye grounds, a valuable indicator in multiple sclerosis, brain tumors, and related disorders. The eye grounds were normal.

The resident went over the intern's history and physical. Because he planned to be a gynecologist, the resident did a careful vaginal examination and found nothing of moment. He made a note on the chart to that effect and ordered a laboratory workup.

After $450 worth of laboratory tests (that cost the hospital less than $50 to do) came back negative, a neurologist examined the patient in consultation. He found no nerve disorder that would account for the right thigh being smaller than the left.

After the tests were finished with and while the doctors were making up their minds what the diagnosis was, they ordered physiotherapy to be given to the thigh (heat, massage, muscle stimulation). The physiotherapist by error started massaging the left thigh while the patient lay on her abdomen. "What's this?" she asked. "What's what?" asked the patient. "You're on the wrong side." The physiotherapist made a note on the chart: "Lump at back of left thigh."

The attending doctor read the note and went over the left thigh. He found a flat fatty tumor, apparently under the posterior muscle of the left thigh. It was ordinary lipoma, a benign growth that needed no treatment except for cosmetic reasons.

The doctors all realized that the right thigh had nothing wrong with it. The difference in circumference from the left was due to the presence of the tumor on the left.

Case 2

A young man had an acutely inflamed throat. He went to his doctor, who gave him an injection of penicillin. The sore throat quickly got better.

Three days later, the young man began to itch. The itching got worse and he developed hives all over his body. The doctor made the correct diagnosis of an allergic reaction to penicillin. He prescribed anithistamines. The hives disappeared.

The young man, a machine operator, got drowsy from the antihistamines and cut his hand at work. The nurse in the dispensary gave him first aid and put on an antibacterial ointment containing penicillin. The hives returned and now the young man had swelling of the eyes and lips. The doctor recognized that a potentially dangerous allergic reaction was present; he ordered a course of corticosteroid treatment. Result—the itchiness, the hives, and the swellings disappeared, and the patient was well again.

Except that now he had pain in his belly plus heartburn, and he began to show signs of blood in his stools. The correct diagnosis of a peptic ulcer (induced by the corticosteroid) was made. The young man did not do well on medical treatment; he continue to bleed from his ulcer. His doctor, therefore, had a surgeon in consultation. The two doctors agreed that partial gastrectomy was necessary, an operation to remove the ulcer-bearing portion of the stomach. The operation was successful.

But because of the previous bleeding and the unavoidable blood loss at the operation, a transfusion of 1,000 milliliters (two pints) of blood was given. Hepatitis (inflammation of the liver) followed. The young man became intensely jaundiced; he vomited his food and had to be fed intravenously for a few days. His youth did him in good stead. He recovered from his hepatitis.

At the right ankle, where the intravenous needle and the plastic tube had been inserted into a vein exposed by cutting through the skin, a tender nodule appeared. It became red and inflamed, evidence of infection. Because of the bad experience the patient had had with penicillin, the doctor prescribed tetracycline. The inflammation promptly subsided.

Because of the antibiotic, diarrhea came on and the patient had severe colicky cramps. The doctor ordered a special diet and gave a new synthetic antispasmodic drug to control the cramps. Diarrhea stopped.

The new drug was in the belladonna class. It relaxed smooth muscle all over the body, and by its action on the iris, it caused dilation of the pupil.

The young man's vision was impaired. He drove his car into a tree. Exitus young man.

21. Kerr L. White, "Life and Death and Medicine," *Scientific American* 229:23-33, (September 1973).

22. Somers, *Health Care in Transition,* p. 13.

23. *Health Resources Statistics,* p. 199.

24. Ibid. There are several reasons why nurses are not in practice. See the chapter on economics for one explanation.

25. Mark G. Field, "The Medical System and Industrial Society. Structural Changes and Internal Differentiation in American Medicine," in *Systems and Medical Care,* edited by Alan Sheldon, Frank Baker, and Curtis P. McLaughlin (Cambridge, Mass.: MIT Press, 1970), pp. 162-63.

Further Reading

Anderson, Odin. *The Uneasy Equilibrium.* New Haven: College and University Press, 1968.

Arasteh, Josephine D. *Factors Influencing Practice Location of Professional Health Manpower.* Washington, D.C.: H.E.W., 1975.

Magraw, Richard. *Ferment in Medicine.* Philadelphia: Saunders, 1966.

Pratt, Lois. *Family Structure and Effective Health Behavior: The Energized Family.* Boston: Houghton Mifflin Co., 1976.

Rutstein, D. D. *The Coming Revolution in Medicine.* Cambridge, Mass.: MIT Press, 1967.

Strickland, Stephan P. *U.S. Health Care: What's Wrong and What's Right.* New York: Universe Books, 1972. Results of Gallup opinion survey of consumers and providers.

U.S. Public Health Service. *Health in America 1776-1976.* Washington, D.C.: U.S. Government Printing Office, 1976.

4. Organized Care

The American hospital is large, impersonal, and dominated by elaborate technology. The American hospital is small, inefficient, underequipped, and understaffed. The American hospital exists primarily to further the professional and economic interests of physicians. The American hospital exists to serve the community. The American hospital is crowded to the point of inefficiency and even danger, and serious delays are encountered in obtaining admission. The American hospital is often half-empty, and many of its patients should be at home or in extended-care facilities. The American hospital is the noblest expression of the philanthropic impulse. The American hospital is a business run to show a profit for its owners. Will the "real" American hospital please stand up?
—Victor Fuchs

The U.S. health care delivery system has been described as a "cottage industry," that is, its providers tend to resist organizing themselves into larger organizational units. In most other industries, smaller units have been combined into more efficient units, which allow for greater economies of scale (greater purchasing power leads to lower cost per unit of volume). To some extent, medicine has reluctantly followed this trend: there is increasing use of group practice, more ambulatory care centered within the hospital, and, in general, more centralization of primary care. Yet, at the same time, medicine still fosters the idea that it is practiced or ought to be practiced out of a "cottage"—that the independent solo practioner is, in effect, what medicine all boils down to—the lowest single, most important denominator.

Primary Care and the Community Physician

Primary care is a term used to denote general, including first-contact, health care. *Secondary* or *tertiary* care takes place on referral to specialists or subspecialists. A provider renders *"usual-place"primary care* if the patient turns to that provider for general health services, including prevention, health monitoring, counseling, diagnosis and treatment of disease, and rehabilitation. A *community physician* is a physician in a solo or group practice that is not hospital-related; this physician, although he or she spends some time in the hospital, maintains an office outside the hospital and spends most of his or her working time delivering ambulatory care.

The community physician has four roles in delivering ambulatory care:[1]

Function

1. providing care for an acute condition
2. serving as family physician
3. covering or substituting for patient's family physician
4. providing specialist care for an acute or chronic condition

Terminology for Function

1. "single-visit primary care"
2. "usual-place primary care"
3. "providing primary care coverage and backup"
4. "single or multiple visit secondary care"

Single-visit primary care is usually for an acute condition, but consumers often lack a defined provider of usual-place primary care, and must therefore turn to strangers for nonacute conditions (physical checkups and minor ailments). Because of the difficulties of establishing usual-place primary care and of approaching strangers with problems appropriate for a family physician, consumers may forgo treatment or bypass community physicians in favor of other sources of care. A critical problem facing the consumer is finding and identifying a reliable source of usual-place primary care. Physicians face the same problem: how to tell the consumer where this care is available.

The simplest defined form of organized ambulatory care in the community is group practice.

Group Practice

There is no standard definition of group practice. Although a *group practice* is a formal association of providers, we also must consider *group care*, which is distinguished more by function than by form and which concerns the actual sharing of responsibility for joint management of patients.[2] We could define group practice as including all physicians or all providers not in solo practice. The Council on Medical Service of the AMA uses the following definition:

> Group medical practice is the application of medical services by three or more physicians formally organized to provide medical care, consultation, diagnosis or treatment through the joint use of equipment and personnel, and with income from medical practice distributed in accordance with methods previously determined by members of the group.[3]

In 1969, the average size of a group medical practice was 6.3 physicians. In recent years, there has been a tendency toward smaller groups of 3 to 6 physicians. As for geographic distribution, in 1969 New England had the lowest percentage of group physicians (3.8 percent), and the Pacific census division had the highest percentage of group physicians.

The most common method of classifying groups is by type of practice:

1. *single-specialty groups:* medical group providing services in only one specialty, except groups composed exclusively of general practitioners
2. *general practice groups:* groups composed exclusively of general practitioners
3. *multispecialty groups:* groups providing services in at least two specialties

Table 4.1 shows the distribution of groups and group physicians in 1969.[4] Single-specialty groups make up almost 50 percent of the total number of groups and tend to be composed of such specialists as anesthesiologists and radiologists. The number of general practice groups, much like the number of general practitioners, is decreasing. In most group practices, physicians are in multispecialty practice (61 percent) and include general practitioners as well as general surgeons and internists. Of the 303,800 active practicing physicians (M.D.'s only) in 1969, 13 percent were engaged in formal group practice. But this percentage is misleading: it excludes physicians engaged in full-time hospital-based practice and physicians working in partnerships, professional corporations, or in buildings where expenses, but not income, are shared. Adjusting for these factors and projecting the data to 1974, it appears that nearly 60 percent of actual patient care in the United States is rendered by physicians in some form of grouping.[5]

Group practices can also be classified by their organization. As seen in Table 4.2, partnership (three or more physicians) is the predominant form

Table 4.1   Number and Percentage of Groups and Full- or Part-time Group Physicians by Type of Group

Type of Group	Groups	Group Physicians		
		Total	Full-time	Part-time
		Number		
Single specialty	3.169	13,053	12,751	302
General practice	784	2,691	2,641	50
Multispecialty	2,418	24,349	21,098	3,251
All types	6,371	40,093	36,490	3,603
		Percentages		
Single specialty	49.7	32.6	34.9	8.4
General practice	12.3	6.7	7.2	1.4
Multispecialty	38.0	60.7	57.8	90.2
All types	100.0	100.0	100.0	100.0

Table 4.2   Distribution of Physician Groups by Form of
            Organization and Type of Group (in percentages)[a]

Form of Organization	Total	Type of Group		
		General Practice	Single Specialty	Multi-Specialty
Single owner	2.8	2.3	1.3	4.9
Partnership	68.7	78.2	69.7	64.2
Corporation	15.6	9.6	17.8	14.7
Association	9.2	7.0	8.5	10.9
Foundation	0.3	0.0	0.2	4.7
Total percent	100.0	100.0	100.0	100.0
Total number	6,263 [a]	772	3,114	2,377

a   This figure excludes nonrespondents to the question.

of organization, but the corporate form of grouping is the fastest growing form of organization.[6] Each form of organization has its own advantages and disadvantages—which are primarily financial. Substantial savings can be achieved by limiting liability, by investing in pension, retirement, and profit-sharing plans, and by utilizing other tax provisions not available to solo practitioners.[7] In 1969, 10,000 physicians were incorporated; by 1972 about 60,000 were incorporated, and 72 percent of them were in some form of group. In 1974 the laws governing self-employment retirement plans were changed, and physicians have found incorporation less financially advantageous. Single-ownership arrangements are the least popular form, because physicians traditionally have refused to work for anyone else unless they share in the financial benefits of ownership. Foundations for medical care, based on the format established by the Medical Foundation of San Joaquin, California, join physicians with individual practices into an organization that reviews utilization, monitors insurance claims, and sets criteria for benefits and fees.[8] Associations perform the same activities, but are more likely to be prepaid group practices.

Physicians can earn more net income (gross income minus office expenses) in group practice than in solo practice or in informal associations, as can be seen in Table 4.3.[9] There are exceptions, of course: well-known, successful specialists (neurosurgeons, for example) can earn more in solo practice. Weighing such factors as specialty, seniority, productivity, and prestige, a group can divide its earnings in a number of ways, ranging from not rewarding the energetic nor penalizing the lazy, to dividing earnings entirely according to each physician's productivity.[10]

Table 4.3 Comparison of Average Net Income per Physician,
and Percent of Business Receipts, 1968

Type of Practice	Internal Revenue Service	American Medical Association	Medical Economics
	Average Net Income (dollars)		
Solo	30,337	35,049	35,100
Partnership (2-member)	37,377a	39,853	42,820a
Group practice		39,065	
Informal association	--	29,537	--
Average all physicians	32,045	36,646	37,620
	Net Income as a Percent of Business Receipts		
Solo	61.7	64.0	64.8
Partnership (2-member)	59.0a	63.5	66.8a
Group practice		65.1	
Informal association	--	64.9	--
Average all physicians	60.9	64.2	64.8

a Includes partnerships and group practices.

Group practice has many other advantages:

1. personnel, equipment, and facilities are shared and therefore less costly;
2. more vacation and sick-leave time plus a system for providing night, weekend, vacation, and sick-leave coverage;
3. more opportunity for cross-fertilization of ideas and consultation with colleagues;
4. more opportunity for continuity of care;
5. less worry over administrative details, i.e., more opportunity to hire skilled administrators;
6. a simple method for new practitioners to establish a large practice in a short period of time.

Group practice also has some unexpected disadvantages:

1. an incorrect diagnosis or large malpractice suit can reflect disparagingly upon each member of the group;
2. irreparable conflicts among members of the group can develop—individual members may not like or be compatible with the group's policies;
3. physicians outside the group may be reluctant to refer to physicians in the group.

Since the advantages seem to outweigh the disadvantages by far, one might expect formal group practice to be the predominant form of practice among physicians. The Mayo Clinic introduced private group practice in 1883, and other famous groups—the Ross-Loos Medical Group in Los Angeles, the Palo Alto Clinic, Glisinger, Marshfield, and Ochsner— have developed it. In short, as a means of stimulating more efficient and meaningful use of all types of providers, group practice would seem to be the wave of the future. Yet uncertainties over national health insurance and peer review, plus the traditional fee-for-service structure, have slowed the growth in group practice and in experimentation with new forms of staffing, facilities, and organization.

Group practice is not limited to physicians. For example, dentists, optometrists, veterinarians, and chiropractors form group practices— sometimes together with physicians. Registered nurses, usually with master's degrees, are beginning to form groups, although this is not exceptionally profitable as yet.[11] When independent practitioners form a group, it is easier to negotiate and contract out services to consumers or other providers.

Perhaps the most radical departure from traditional community-based medical practice is the prepaid group practice. For a fixed annual per capita fee, a group of physicians agrees to treat a group of consumers for varying ranges of illnesses. Because group profit is based on utilization (the more services and physician time used, the less money is left over to be divided up among the physicians), physicians practicing in a prepaid group practice have a strong incentive to keep utilization down and their consumers healthy. The largest of these groups is Kaiser-Permanente, which has a membership of 2,531,000 (1972), twenty-three hospitals and fifty-six outpatient facilities, a health plan, a business and administrative service organization, a school of nursing, and a research foundation.[12] The Health Insurance Plan of Greater New York (HIP), the second largest, has about 800,000 members. Group Health Cooperative of Puget Sound, a consumer cooperative with approximately 173,000 enrollees, is another well-known prepaid group practice. Independent health insurance plans show a 1972 enrollment of 5,865,000 in prepaid group practice plans for office, clinic, or health center visits.[13]

Prepaid group practice plans have been fought by organized medicine, but they have managed to survive and have produced some of the most significant, yet controversial, results in the delivery of health care. They have demonstrated a method for reducing costly inpatient care, improving manpower utilization, and increasing efficiency with the use of electronic data processing equipment (EDP). Some innovative plans have devised ways of serving both affluent and needy consumers simul- taneously. In 1974, as a result of these successes, the government began to subsidize the initial stages of health maintenance organizations (HMO).[14] There is little question that prepaid group practice has had a sizable impact on plans to alter the methods for delivering ambulatory and primary care.

Whether a group practice is prepaid or not, it provides a method for organizing health care in a more rational fashion. Figure 4.1 shows how a

Figure 4.1   Organization of Health Care by Practitioner Groups

```
┌─────────────────────────┐  ┌─────────────────────────┐  ┌─────────────────────────┐
│                         │  │                         │  │ INPATIENT               │
│ PRIMARY CARE            │  │ SECONDARY CARE          │  │ LONG-TERM CARE          │
│                         │  │                         │  │                         │
│ G.P. (Family            │  │ Psychiatrist            │  │ Hospital                │
│   practitioner)         │  │ Dermatologist           │  │ Nursing home            │
│ OB/GYN                  │  │ Radiologist             │  │                         │
│ Pediatrician            │  │ Cardiologist            │  │                         │
│ Internist[a]            │  │ Opthalmologist          │  │                         │
│ General surgeon[a]      │  │ Internist[a]            │  │                         │
│                         │  │ General surgeon[a]      │  │                         │
└─────────────────────────┘  └─────────────────────────┘  └─────────────────────────┘
```

Multispecialty groups may be housed
in the same facility, or in adjacent
buildings (such as a medical arts
building near a hospital).

[a] These practitioners may belong in either category, depending on the location of their practice.

family flows through such a system. As we have seen, some large groups own or have special arrangements with hospitals and other institutions: theoretically, at least, care can be carefully coordinated, patient records are more accessible, and a patient can (without extensive trips back and forth across town) find comprehensive care. But organized medicine has discouraged these arrangements, arguing that they limit the patient's free choice of physician and that they are a form of fee splitting.[15] Indeed, radiologists and other specialists sometimes make exclusive agreements with the leasers of medical arts buildings so as to ensure that they are the only such specialists in the building, thereby preventing any competition. Group practice and the way it organizes health care do not necessarily mean more compassionate, less expensive treatment of illnesses.

Hospitals

Hospital comes from the Latin *hospes,* meaning "host or guest." *Hospital, hotel,* and *hostel* were at one time used interchangeably. Until the twentieth century, hospitals cared for the poor and for transients, and their services were limited to bed and board and rudimentary nursing. It was not unusual for more than one patient to occupy a bed. Until late in the nineteenth century, when Florence Nightingale improved nursing services, hospitals often did patients more harm than good (itinerant apothecaries and blood-letting surgeons got to the patients first; "hospitalism," or cross infection, occurred among patients). The U.S. hospital did not assume its present form until the twentieth century, when it was transformed "from a passive receptacle for the sick poor to an active caring institution for all social and economic classes."[16]

In the early 1900s, x-ray machines were installed and x-ray departments established. In the 1910s and 1920s, single rooms for the affluent were built. In the 1920s and 1930s two-to-four bed (semiprivate) rooms were installed. Hospital architecture changed dramatically. With the introduction of sulfanilamide in the 1930s and penicillin in the 1940s, surgery no longer involved a prohibitive risk of infection. As consumer affluence increased and the number of physicians increased, so did the number of hospital beds, hospital admissions, and patient days.

In 1946, Congress approved a proposal by Senators Lister Hill (D., Ala.) and Harold Burton (R., Ohio) for a program to deal with the shortage of hospitals that had developed during the depression and World War II, a shortage that was especially acute in the South and other economically depressed, rural areas. The Hill-Burton grants (these grants pay about 25 percent of the total cost for health facilities receiving assistance; churches, charities, and state and local governments put up the rest of the money) were aimed at precisely these areas. By 1973, they had distributed $3.8 billion to nearly 11,000 hospitals and other health facilities. Critics of the program feel that hospitals have been overbuilt in rural areas, that central city hospitals have been allowed to decay, and that inpatient bed care has been overbuilt relative to ambulatory outpatient care.[17]

The Division of Health Manpower and Facilities Statistics of the National Center for Health Statistics collects data on all inpatient health facilities in the United States. This national data system, known as the Master Facility Inventory (MFI), uses the following definition of *hospital*:

> A hospital is a facility with at least 6 beds that is licensed by the State as a hospital, or that is operated as a hospital by a Federal or State Agency and is therefore not subject to State or local licensing laws.

The states—in establishing rules, regulations, minimum standards, and licensing laws—define *hospital* variously, that is as to the number of beds necessary to qualify for their jurisdictional control.[18]

Table 4.4 shows the number of hospitals in the United States reported in the Master Facility Inventory.[19] General medical and surgical hospitals provide diagnostic and treatment services for patients with a variety of medical conditions. In 1972, the MFI classified 87 percent of these hospitals as *short-term-care* hospitals. The large general hospital of this type appears to be growing faster than all other types of hospitals; the average general hospital had 143 beds in 1967 and 156 in 1972. Specialty hospitals usually limit their admissions to patients with specified illnesses or conditions. In 1972, the MFI classified most specialty hospitals as

Table 4.4 Hospitals and Hospital Beds, 1972 and 1967

Classification	Number of Facilities		Beds		Beds per 1,000 Population	
	1972	1967	1972	1969	1972	1967
General medical and surgical	6,491	6,685	1,014,064	958,729	4.9	4.9
Specialty						
Psychiatric	497	573	372,603	545,913	1.8	2.3
Chronic disease	78	333	23,962	61,211	0.1	0.3
Tuberculosis	75	169	12,351	33,335	0.1	0.2
Other[a]	340	387	44,060	31,913	0.2	0.2
Total	990	1,462	452,976	672,372	2.2	3.4
Total hospitals	7,481	8,147	1,467,040	1,631,101	7.0	8.3

a Includes eye, ear, nose, and throat hospitals; epileptic hospitals; alcoholism hospitals; narcotic hospitals; maternity hospitals; orthopedic hospitals; and physical rehabilitation hospitals.

long-term-care hospitals. As we can see from Table 4.5, the number of specialty hospitals is declining, which has contributed to the decline in the total number of all hospitals. The average specialty hospital had 460 beds in 1967 and 458 in 1972.

Table 4.5 shows the ownership of hospitals and hospital beds in 1972.[20] As indicated, there are slightly more government hospital beds than private proprietary (for-profit, or as those in the industry like to say, "investor-owned") and nonprofit (voluntary) hospital beds. In recent years, state and local governments have done most hospital construction. State and local governments own far more hospitals than the federal government does. Likewise, they own more specialty hospitals. For general and surgical hospitals, on the other hand, voluntary ownership predominates. For-profit ownership accounts for 13 percent of all hospitals and about 5 percent of all hospital beds, but these percentages are expected to increase. The percentage of church-owned hospitals by contrast is expected to decrease.

The distinction between profit and nonprofit is one of incorporation. In a state where a hospital is incorporated to do business, the hospital must specify its form of organization on the articles of incorporation. If it is nonprofit, it must (1) not distribute any "profits" to the owners and (2) plow all "profits" back into the facility. However, nothing, including the Internal Revenue Service (which checks to see that rules are followed), prevents the hospital's owners or fiduciaries from paying themselves excessively high salaries ("operating expenses," not "profits") and from instructing the hospital to contract with companies they own to provide goods and services to the hospital.[21] Voluntary hospitals are exempt from real estate taxes as well as some other local taxes.

In theory, voluntary hospitals put patient needs first, and proprietary hospitals put profits first. More and more proprietary hospitals are run by large corporations: in 1970, twenty-nine chains ran hospitals in the United States. Voluntary hospitals accuse proprietary hospitals of "cream skimming," that is, of taking away their paying patients and thereby leaving them with more indigent patients, and of only performing profitable services, thus leaving the voluntary hospitals to take up the slack. Proprietary hospitals contend that they eliminate waste, cut back on unnecessary services, and provide high-quality services at less cost because they have a strong incentive to minimize costs.

Before we look specifically at inpatient and outpatient use, it might be helpful to examine how a hospital is run. Table 4.6 is an organization chart for a large general hospital.[22] The governing board is legally responsible for policy decisions and fiscal solvency. The administrator is responsible for carrying out the policy of the board and thus for making operating (day-to-day) decisions. The hospital organization sometimes is referred to as a duopoly with essentially autonomous administrative and medical staff

Table 4.5 Ownership of Hospitals and Hospital Beds, 1972

| Classification | Government | | | | Proprietary | | Non-Profit | | | |
| | Federal | | State-Local | | | | Church | | Other | |
	Number	Beds	Number	Beds	Number	Beds	Number	Beds	Number	Beds
General medical and surgical	369	108,409	1,879	214,070	811	60,916	797	185,763	2,635	444,906
Specialty										
Psychiatric	29	32,093	239	325,823	88	6,959	14	1,742	67	5,986
Chronic diseases			49	19,900	8	573	5	792	16	2,697
Tuberculosis			70	12,011			1	65	4	275
Other	7	2,171	68	20,197	79	3,001	37	1,991	149	16,700
Total	36	34,264	486	377,931	175	10,533	57	4,590	236	25,653
Total hospitals	405	142,673	2,365	592,001	986	71,149	854	190,353	2,371	470,564

60

Table 4.6 An Example of an Organization Chart for a Large Community General Hospital[a]

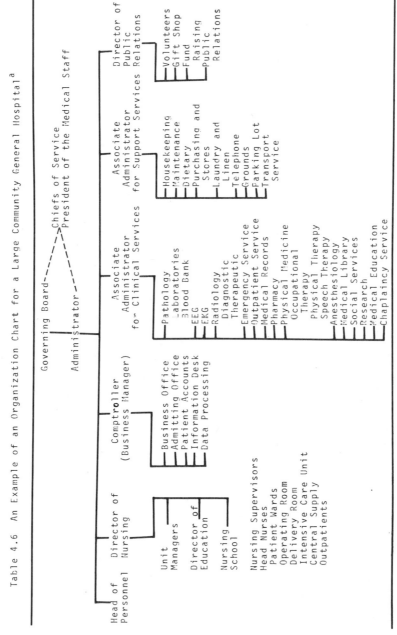

a The internal organization of the medical staff is not shown.

organizations: The medical staff may emphasize provision of service, but the administrative staff may emphasize maintenance of the organization's operation. Thus administrative-medical staff conflict can arise. Nurses can become caught between multiple lines of authority (the nursing department is the largest component of the hospital). Although fewer hospitals now operate nursing schools, the dichotomy between teaching and patient care continues to be a source of conflict. Resolution and prevention of power struggles is a constant activity in hospitals, large and small.[23]

Patients and, increasingly, outside agencies expect the hospital to maintain high standards and quality. In 1965, the Supreme Court of Illinois, in *Darling* v. *Charleston Memorial Hospital*, affirmed that a hospital can be held legally and financially responsible for the quality of care rendered by all employed or affiliated health providers, including physicians and nurses.[24] The hospital can be sued, therefore, for unqualified or inappropriate medical practice. Of course, if a suit against a hospital for negligence on the part of an individual provider is successful, the hospital may bring suit against the provider.

Most, but not all, hospitals (61 percent of all hospitals; 79 percent of all beds) are inspected and accredited by the Joint Commission on Accreditation of Hospitals (JCAH).[25] To qualify for accreditation, a hospital must have twenty-five beds or over and be accepted for registration by the American Hospital Association. If it qualifies, it is surveyed by an on-site visit, which includes conferences with professional staff, service chiefs, and governors of the facility. JCAH, after reviewing the survey report, may leave the hospital unaccredited or accredited for one or two years. Major factors in the accreditation decision include evidence of overall compliance with standards, progressive advancement toward more complete compliance, and absence of any serious impediment to patient safety or the quality of care. If accredited, a hospital is resurveyed periodically and placed in one of three categories:

> Certified A: in substantial compliance with no significant deficiencies
> Certified B: in substantial compliance with deficiencies
> Certified C: special or "access" certification

If it does not correct its deficiencies, a hospital can lose its accreditation. If it does not receive JCAH accreditation, it may still accept medicare patients if it passes government inspection.[26] All states and the District of Columbia license specialty hospitals; all states except Ohio license general hospitals.

Inpatient Care

In general, the nation's inpatient hospital facilities are being used less than optimally (see Table 4.7 for recent trends[27]). Consider, for example, the occupancy rate (the average daily census divided by the total number of beds): 85 percent is an ideal occupancy rate for an acute-care community hospital, a rate at which hospitals are operating at peak efficiency and utilization. The current average occupancy rate in the United States has dipped below 75 percent, which implies that we are overbedded and are underutilizing high-cost facilities. However, this conclusion does not apply to all general hospitals: e.g., hospitals that are the only ones within a large geographic area must be prepared for emergencies, and hospitals with a large pediatric patient distribution have seasonal fluctuations (respiratory diseases increase during the winter). Occupancy rates seem to vary directly with the size of a hospital (more beds—higher occupancy). Admissions have increased, and length of stay has fluctuated.

Two companion pieces of legislation have been enacted to reduce length of stay and overbedding. The Professional Standards Review Organization (PL 92-603) will examine the care provided to patients under Titles 5, 18, and 19 of the Social Security Act, namely, it will carry out a detailed review for:

1. the necessity of the services rendered
2. the appropriateness of the facility
3. the quality of care

The National Health Planning and Resource Development Act (PL 63641) established health agencies that will control the supply of hospital beds through their power to deny a certificate-of-need for most planned capital expansion projects. These agencies will use data gathered by the PSROs. If a region has too many hospital days because it has too few extended-case beds, plans for additional nursing home beds will most likely be approved, and plans for expansion of acute short-term beds will not.[28] There is considerable disagreement over whether Hill-Burton

Table 4.7   Selected Measures of U.S. Community Hospital Inpatient
            Utilization, Selected Years 1950-1973

Measure	1950	1960	1970	1974
Inpatient admissions (number per 1000 population)	108.0	125.3	143.9	152.6
Average length of stay (in days)	3.1	7.6	8.2	7.8
Patient days per year (number per 1000 population)	877.0	952.0	1180.0	1190.0
Occupancy rate (in percentages)	73.7	74.7	78.0	75.4

monies have lowered the occupancy rate and should, therefore, be terminated.[29]

The cost of inpatient care has risen dramatically over the past fifteen years. Figure 4.2 shows this increase in cost for a large urban teaching hospital.[30] Hospital inpatient costs include "routine" costs and ancillary expenses. In 1971-1972, certain routine costs, that is, hotel costs (costs necessary to maintain and manage the physical plant) were about $23 per day, which is what you might pay for a reasonable hotel room. Other routine costs are meals and the salaries of nurses, physicians, and other providers (social workers and so on). Total routine costs amount to $92 per day. Ancillary costs bring the total to $170.45 per day. This figure does not include charges for the intensive care unit, surgeons' and anesthesiologists' fees, and any bills a patient might have to pay for aftercare.

Some states, notably Maryland and Connecticut, have created new state agencies, called health services cost review commissions, which are attempting to clamp down on hospitals' operating costs. Armed with sweeping legal mandates and strong statehouse support, they are scrutinizing expensive nursing education; wasteful use of computers; costly arrangements with pathologists, anesthesiologists, and radiologists; and unapproved rate increases.[31] Similarly, the President's Cost-of-Living Council may attempt to put a 9 percent "lid" on hospital costs in 1978. Finally, Blue Cross is attempting to hold down hospital costs through a method known as "prospective" reimbursement. In this method, if a hospital exceeds what Blue Cross budgets for its fiscal year, it, not Blue Cross, must absorb the difference.

Until 1974, private, nonprofit hospitals enjoyed some protection from ordinary labor costs. That is, they were exempt from the National Labor Relations Act and minimum wage laws. With removal of these exemptions, union organizing and labor costs are expected to increase. Three-fifths of all health care workers work in hospitals, and few workers (approximately 10 to 15 percent) belong to unions. In 1974, the average hourly earning of hospital employees was $3.33 an hour, 73¢ an hour less than the average for manufacturing employees.[32] Hospitals are labor-intensive.[33] A large portion of a budget is spent on labor costs (60 per cent). Furthermore, hospitals do not install laborsaving devices to the extent that other industries do. Indeed, advances in technology have created a need for more and better-trained health personnel, not less—for example, in intensive care units.

As if hospitals were not burdened already with enough outside interference (utilization review, licensing and accreditation agencies, medicare review, and other cost-of-living review committees), they must now comply with a 1974 federal directive stating that if a hospital has received any Hill-Burton financing for construction in the past, it must devote the equivalent of 5 percent of its gross revenues for free patient

64

Figure 4.2   Per Diem Costs at a Large Urban Teaching Hospital

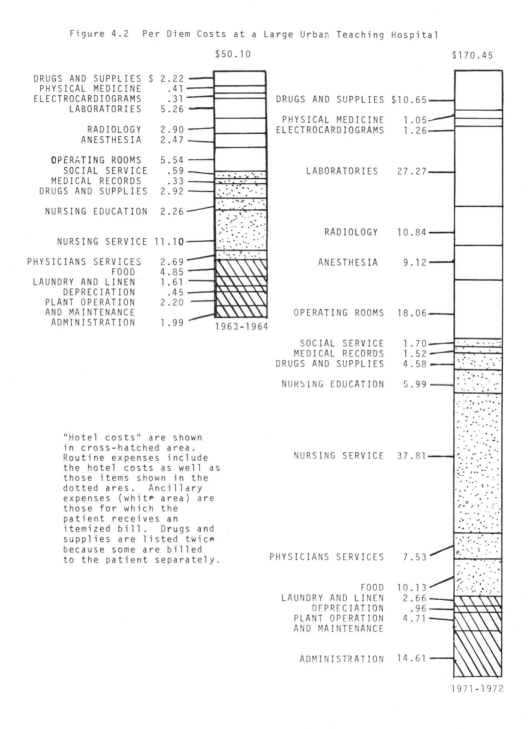

$50.10

DRUGS AND SUPPLIES $ 2.22
PHYSICAL MEDICINE   .41
ELECTROCARDIOGRAMS   .31
LABORATORIES   5.26

RADIOLOGY   2.90
ANESTHESIA   2.47

OPERATING ROOMS   5.54
SOCIAL SERVICE   .59
MEDICAL RECORDS   .33
DRUGS AND SUPPLIES   2.92

NURSING EDUCATION   2.26

NURSING SERVICE   11.10

PHYSICIANS SERVICES   2.69
FOOD   4.85
LAUNDRY AND LINEN   1.61
DEPRECIATION   .45
PLANT OPERATION   2.20
AND MAINTENANCE
ADMINISTRATION   1.99

1963-1964

$170.45

DRUGS AND SUPPLIES $10.65

PHYSICAL MEDICINE   1.05
ELECTROCARDIOGRAMS   1.26

LABORATORIES   27.27

RADIOLOGY   10.84

ANESTHESIA   9.12

OPERATING ROOMS   18.06

SOCIAL SERVICE   1.70
MEDICAL RECORDS   1.52
DRUGS AND SUPPLIES   4.58

NURSING EDUCATION   5.99

NURSING SERVICE   37.81

PHYSICIANS SERVICES 7.53

FOOD   10.13
LAUNDRY AND LINEN   2.66
DEPRECIATION   .96
PLANT OPERATION   4.71
AND MAINTENANCE

ADMINISTRATION   14.61

1971-1972

"Hotel costs" are shown
in cross-hatched area.
Routine expenses include
the hotel costs as well as
those items shown in the
dotted ares. Ancillary
expenses (white area) are
those for which the
patient receives an
itemized bill. Drugs and
supplies are listed twice
because some are billed
to the patient separately.

WHY CONNECTICUT IS A GOOD STATE TO GET SICK IN.

A couple of years ago, the rise in Connecticut's hospital costs was running along at the national average.

Today, it's significantly below the national average.

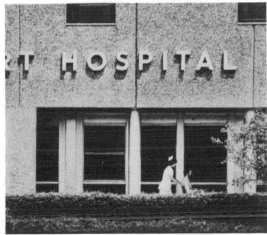

No, people in Connecticut didn't stop getting sick. Nor did hospitals start giving away services or reducing the quality of care.

The big difference is that Connecticut instituted a commission to contain hospital costs.

The facts show that it is working.

Over $50,000,000 have been saved since 1973.

At the same time the rate of increase was slowing, Connecticut patients saw no loss of services or their own freedom in choosing a particular hospital or clinic.

Maryland and Massachusetts have seen encouraging results doing what Connecticut did.

Perhaps you'd like some more detailed information on Connecticut's experience. Just write our Office of Consumer Information, One Tower Square, Hartford, Conn. 06115. Or dial, toll-free, 800-243-0191. In Connecticut, call collect, 277-6565.

By keeping hospital costs a little more in line, you know, the people in Connecticut have made their state a pretty nice place to get well in, too.

THE TRAVELERS
Raising our voice, not just our rates.

The Travelers Insurance Company, The Travelers Indemnity Company, and Affiliated Companies, Hartford, Conn. 06115 care for the poor. Some hospitals have sidestepped this directive by assigning unpaid patient bills to the required Hill-Burton percentage.[34]

Outpatient Care

Although the quantity of inpatient care has increased at a slow pace, the quantity of outpatient care has risen rapidly. Table 4.8 shows this increase from 1963 to 1973.[35] In this period, the number of visits per 1,000 population nearly doubled. The ratio of outpatient visits to inpatient admissions increased from 3:1 to 5:1. The cost of an outpatient visit more than doubled. In addition, outpatient services have become an increasingly important source of hospital revenue: outpatient revenue has expanded from 7.9 percent of total revenue in 1963 to 10.3 percent in 1973.

Hospital outpatient services may be divided into three categories:

1. outpatient department—an organized unit of a hospital, with facilities and medical services exclusively or primarily for those patients who are generally ambulatory and who do not currently require or are not currently receiving services as an inpatient of the hospital (an OPD may range from a treatment room next to the emergency department to a fully staffed satellite clinic several miles from the hospital);
2. emergency department—a hospital outpatient care unit for the provision of medical services that are urgently needed to sustain life or prevent critical consequences and that should be performed immediately (ES);
3. ancillary department—an organized unit of a hospital, other than an operating room, delivery room, or patient care unit, with facilities and personnel to aid physicians in the diagnosis and treatment of patients through the performance of diagnostic or therapeutic procedures.[36]

Table 4.8 Community Hospital Outpatient Statistics, 1963-1973

Year	Outpatient Visits (per 1,000 population)	Admissions (per 1,000 population)	Outpatient Visits per Admission	Outpatient Revenue per Outpatient Visit (in dollars)
1963	416.63	139.43	3.0	8.06
1964	452.25	140.41	3.2	8.36
1965	476.13	138.35	3.4	8.41
1966	503.86	139.40	3.6	8.76
1967	533.80	139.31	3.8	9.84
1968	564.07	140.88	4.0	11.77
1969	594.34	142.38	4.2	13.09
1970	676.99	149.35	4.5	13.68
1971	713.95	148.15	4.8	14.79
1972	767.55	150.33	5.1	15.82
1973	807.21	154.36	5.2	17.54
Changes 1963-1973 (in percentages)	93.7	10.7	73.3	117.6

In 1974, the Columbia University Center for Community Health System surveyed the country's 5,509 community hospitals (72.4 percent response) to find out about the availability of outpatient services. Its findings were as follows:

1. Availability of services:
   a. community hospitals with both ES and OPD   23 percent
   b. community hospitals with only ES or with ES plus specialized clinics   70 percent
   c. community hospitals with no ambulatory care or with arrangements other than those categorized above   7 percent
2. The distinction between having or not having an outpatient department seems to be of considerable importance in the context of primary care
3. The volume of primary care that is being provided in the emergency services of community hospitals is enormous
4. Hospital emergency services covering or substituting for private physicians occurs very widely in hospitals with or without an outpatient department
5. The emergency room frequently backs up the outpatient department in two-thirds of the hospitals having an outpatient department
6. Many emergency service patients apparently have no other source of care
7. Many emergency service patients without another source of care seem to use the emergency service mainly on an acute-care basis
8. The emergency service is often the entry point to continuing primary care outside the hospital
9. Continuing primary care may be provided most often in the outpatient department or its offshoots[37]

Obviously, the number of emergency department visits has increased at a faster rate than either hospital inpatient admissions or other outpatient visits. This increase, however, may only reflect availability: a 1968 study indicated, for example, that of 60,000 emergency cases treated in the 312 hospitals responding to the survey, only two-thirds were bona fide emergencies.[30] In recent years, many emergency rooms have been staffed by groups of physicians with contracts with the hospital, contracts that frequently allow for coverage of emergency room patients but that do not allow for follow-up or the taking over of care for patients these physicians have treated in the emergency room. The emergency room is a poor source of continuing primary care, but an increasingly important source of first-contact acute care as well as nonacute care.

Since most inpatient care in community hospitals involves surgery, the recent changes in the delivery of low-risk surgical care are not unexpected: e.g., outpatient surgery (particularly for elective abortion and tonsillectomy) performed in outpatient departments or "free standing" clinics (no formal hospital affiliation). As a result, the patient's cost and waiting time have decreased.

Other specialty clinics include:

1. emergency access clinics: instead of building a small community hospital, the central hospital is enlarged, and a satellite emergency clinic is built twenty to forty minutes' drive from the central hospital;
2. weight reduction and obesity clinics: may or may not be staffed by physicians; a new specialty is developing called *bariatric medicine;*
3. sex and marital therapy clinics: sometimes patterned after the Masters and Johnson clinic in St. Louis, Missouri;
4. longevity clinics: through dietary and life-style changes, these clinics help reduce the risk factors associated with diabetes and heart disease;
5. acupuncture clinics: acupuncturists, on an outpatient basis, attempt to relieve the pain associated with arthritis and other musculo-skeletal disorders;
6. birthing clinics: these clinics create a "homelike" atmosphere for labor and delivery; family and backup equipment are usually present; if there are no complications, women and children return home six hours after delivery.

Long-Term Care

Long-term care embraces a wide variety of health care facilities, from special long-term hospitals providing intensive care to the boarding home providing only the simplest of supportive services. Long-term care facilities are primarily for the following groups of patients:

1. mental disability
2. chronic, degenerative disability
3. geriatric
4. slow-acting contagious diseases

When such patients are hospitalized, we sometimes say they have been "institutionalized" and that they are being either "maintained" or "rehabilitated." But, in general, long-term patients have been neglected—they have been institutionalized and forgotten. Neglect has led to abuses and eventually to attempts at reform. Public and legislative outcries have called for the end of dehumanized long-term care.

A *long-term care facility* is a facility where the average length of stay for

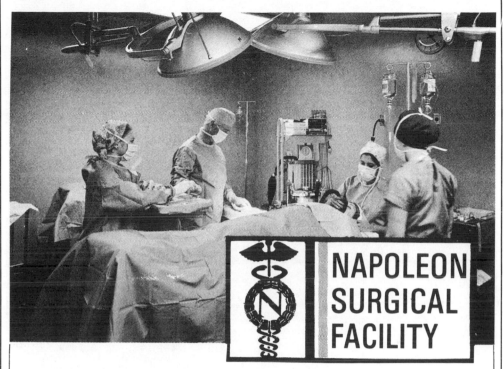

How a hospital can make a profit without taking something away from patient care.

"Humana, a private enterprise hospital company, has proved that a profitable hospital can provide <u>improved</u> services for the patient and the physician.

There is nothing mystical about Humana's achievements. By applying private enterprise incentives, and the skills of the Humana professional, our hospitals are able to operate efficiently and profitably."

David A. Jones. Chairman. Humana Inc.

Profitability is what assures Humana's ability to attract the financial resources needed to set standards for higher quality hospital care, at a time when many hospitals must struggle to maintain the status quo.

The Humana approach to hospital services has already resulted in a successful, growing company, owning and operating hospitals in seventeen states. But we are actually just at the threshold of our growth potential. Looking ahead, the need to renew America's hospitals cannot be met by traditional means. Humana will play an important role in fulfilling this need through private enterprise.

If you would like to know more about a leadership company in the rapidly growing 47 billion dollar hospital services industry, we would be pleased to send you a copy of our annual report. Please write. Humana Inc., 1800 First National Tower, Dept. 4 A. Louisville. Kentucky 40201.

Humana
The Hospital Company

Where private enterprise is making possible a better kind of hospital.

all patients is thirty days or more, or where over 50 percent of all patients are admitted to units in which the average length of stay is thirty days or more.

Summary

Group practice and outpatient departments are two methods of organizing the delivery of primary care. With increasing frequency, consumers are seeking primary care from the emergency rooms of urban community hospitals. Specialty hospitals have been declining as less costly and more efficient ways are sought to deliver long-term care.

Questions

1. A 1972 Gallup survey found that most Americans have considerable confidence that they can obtain good medical care when they or their families need it, but that they recognize serious problems in the health care system that require basic changes. U.S. physicians, in the same poll, do *not* agree that there is a health crisis in the United States, but most recognize serious problems. Discuss these problems, their causes, and the effect of "organized" care on these problems.

2. How would you find a primary-care physician for your family?

3. List the managerial advantages of being a solo practitioner with *no* employees.

4. What evidence is there that hospital inpatient bed space has been overbuilt relative to hospital space allocated to ambulatory care?

5. Which costs of a hospital are fixed (will not change with increases or decreases in the average daily census), and which costs are variable (will change with changes in the volume or output)?

6. Assume you are a rural general practitioner in an area where no telephone answering services are available. You have a listed phone number. What types of patient education and procedure policies can you suggest to minimize unnecessary home phone calls?

Notes

1. Adapted from Margaret C. Olendzki's "The Present Role of the Community Hospital in Primary Ambulatory Care" in *Community Hospitals and the Challenge of Primary Care*, a report by the Center for Community Health Systems (Columbia University, New York: The Center, 1975), pp. 55-68.

2. Jerome Pollack, "The Grouping of Medical Practice" in *Community Hospitals and the Challenge of Primary Care* (Columbia University, New York: The Center, 1975), pp. 36-37.

3. American Association of Medical Clinics; American Medical Association; Medical Group Management Association (publishers), *Group Practice: Guidelines to Joining or Forming a Medical Group* (Chicago: The American Medical Association, 1970), p.1.

The American Association of Medical Clinics defines a medical group as:

> Any group of seven or more full-time physicians maintaining a private organization for the purposes of providing general medical care of high quality. Such groups or clinics shall have on their full-time staff at least five physicians in different major specialties, two of which specialties shall be internal medicine and general surgery."

The Medical Group Management Association definition is:

> An organized medical group of three or more doctors of medicine which shall employ a person or persons in the active supervision of its business affairs.

4. Mary E. McNamara and Clifford Todd, "A Survey of Group Practice in the United States," *AJPH* 60:1304 (July 1970).

5. This conclusion is based on three sources: Jerome Pollack, "The Grouping of Medical Practice," pp. 39-40; Anne Sommers, *Health Care in Transition: Directions for the Future* (Chicago: Health and Hospital Trust, 1971), p. 9; and *Medical Economics*, 15 October and 26 November 1973.

6. Mary E. McNamara and Clifford Todd, "A Survey of Group Practice in the United States," pp. 1303-13.

7. A partnership is not a legal entity. Each individual partner, unless the partnership agreement is to the contrary, has the power to purchase and sell partnership property, either real or personal, with or without the other partners' agreement. Each partner shares in the operating and capital profits and losses. Each partner can put in and take out money from the business's bank account. With the exception of dissolving and winding up the business, the courts are reluctant to entertain suits by partners against each other. A partner is liable for the torts (personal injury) of a fellow partner if they are committed while the latter partner is acting within the scope of the normal business. Because of the nature of a partnership, partners must get along with each other.

A corporation is a legal entity and does not require close personal relationships. A business corporation is carried on primarily for the profit of its shareholders. A corporation has the power to buy, sell, and hold both real and personal property in its own name, but only as long as the particular situation contributes to the purposes of the business. The personal property of participants in a corporation cannot be attached through a legal suit; instead, only corporate property can be attached. Corporations require bylaws and other specified documents, and thus the relationships among participants is more carefully defined. Willful or negligent mismanagement and other failures on the part of participants in the corporation have distinct legal remedies.

See Don Votaw, *Legal Aspects of Business Administration* (Englewood Cliffs, N.J.: Prentice-Hall, 1963), pp. 376-437.

8. R. H. Egdahl, "Foundations for Medical Care," *New England Journal of Medicine* 288:491-98 (8 March 1973).

9. *Income of Physicians, Osteopaths, and Dentists from Professional Practice, 1965-69*, Social Security Administration, Office of Research and Statistics, DHEW publication no. (SSA) 73-11852.

10. These methods include the 100-point plan, the incentive factor plan, the

points-plus-percentage plan, and the progressive sharing plan. See Robert I. Pfeffer, "Bad, Good, Better Ways to Divide Group Income," *Medical Economics*:139-45 (8 January 1973).

11. Betty C. Agree, "Beginning an Independent Nursing Practice," *American Journal of Nursing* 74:637-42 (April 1974), and Rhea Felkner, "An All-R.N. Fee-For-Service Group Practice," *Registered Nurse* 37:41 (May 1974).

12. *Kaiser Foundation Medical Care Program, '72* (Oakland, Calif.: The Foundation, 1973).

13. *Independent Health Insurance Plans in 1972, Preliminary Estimates* (Washington, D.C.: Social Security Administration, 1974).

14. The controversial aspects of prepaid group practices are discussed in the section of this book on provider control; utilization and HMO aspects are discussed in the sections on alternative methods of financing health care and new financial arrangements.

15. Fee splitting occurs when one provider, B, "kickbacks" or returns part of his or her fee to another provider, A, who made the referral. In turn, provider A has a strong incentive to make a referral to provider B. Suppose provider A and B form a group practice. Does not provider A have a strong incentive to refer a patient to provider B if they share income and expenses? Does not provider A have a strong incentive to refer a patient to a hospital or nursing home he or she owns or jointly owns with provider B and a group of physicians? Conflict of interest can be one trade-off with better organized delivery of health care.

16. John Knowles, "The Hospital," *Scientific American* 229:128-37 (September 1973).

17. "Finding the Best Way to Upgrade Old Hospitals in Cities Is at the Heart of the Hill-Burton Dispute," *Wall Street Journal*, 5 March 1973, p. 26.

18. For example, Louisiana's definition varies with the MFI definition. Louisiana defines a hospital as follows:

> "Hospital" means any institution, place, building or agency, public or private, whether for profit or not, devoted primarily to the maintenance and operation of facilities for *ten or more* individuals for the diagnosis, treatment or care of persons admitted for overnight stay or longer who are suffering from illness, injury, infirmity or deformity or other physical condition for which obstetrical, medical or surgical services could be available and appropriate.

Rules, Regulations, and Minimum Standards Governing Hospitals and the Hospital Licensing Law (Baton Rouge, La.: Louisiana State Department of Hospitals, 1962), p. 7. There is a curious difference between the definition of a hospital and that of a nursing home. See Chapter 6.

19. *Health Resources Statistics*, 1974, p. 350.

20. Ibid., pp. 365-66

21. Hospital trustees are often lawyers and bankers who subtly influence the hospital to contract for their services and to deposit idle cash at low interest rates in their banks.

22. Florence Wilson and Duncan Neuhauser, *Health Services in the United States* (Cambridge, Mass.: Ballinger Publishing Co., 1974), p. 18.

23. Rockwell Schulz and Alton C. Johnson, "Conflict in Hospitals," _Hospital Administration_ 16:36-50 (Summer 1971). See also David B. Smith and Arnold D. Kaluzny, _The White Labyrinth_ (Berkeley: McCutchan, 1975), and Alan Sheldon, _Organizational Issues in Health Care Management_ (New York: Spectrum, 1975).

24. _Darling v. Charleston Memorial Hospital,_ 33 111. 2nd 326, 211 N.E. 2d 253 (1965); _certiorari_ denied 383 US 946 (1966).

25. The hospital accrediting program of JCAH was started in 1952. The governing board currently consists of representatives of the American Medical Association (seven seats), the American Hospital Association (seven seats), the American College of Surgeons (three seats), and the American College of Physicians (three seats). JCAH's standards primarily stress maintenance of medical records, facility safety and sanitation, and medical staff organization. See JCAH Accreditation Manual for Hospitals, 1976.

26. Problems with accreditation and licensing are covered in Chapter 12.

27. _Hospital Statistics,_ American Hospital Association, 1974. This survey did not include osteopathic hospitals, federal hospitals, and hospitals not registered with the American Hospital Association.

28. Comprehensive health planning and utilization review legislation are discussed in detail in Chapter 13.

29. Judith R. Lave and Lester B. Lave, _The Hospital Construction Act: An Evaluation of the Hill-Burton Program, 1948-73_ (Washington, D.C.: American Enterprise Institute, May 1974).

30. Knowles, "The Hospital," p. 137.

31. "Some States Try Surgery on Hospital Costs, with Maryland and Connecticut Leading the Way," _Wall Street Journal,_ 10 December 1974, p. 36.

32. "Organizing Workers in Non-profit Hospitals Begins: Move Is Likely to Boost Wage Costs," _Wall Street Journal,_ 29 July 1974, p. 22.

33. Hospitals could be contrasted with electrical utilities, which are capital-intense: a large proportion of an electrical utility's budget must be spent on equipment.

34. Marilyn G. Rose, "Federal Regulations of Services to the Poor Under the Hill-Burton Act: Realities and Pitfalls," _Northwestern University Law Review_ 70:168-201 (March-April 1975).

35. National Hospital Panel Survey in _Hospitals_ 48:31-33 (16 June 1974). This survey did not include osteopathic hospitals and hospitals not registered with the American Hospital Association.

36. _Health Resources Statistics,_ 1974, p. 471.

37. Margaret C. Olendzki, "The Present Role of the Community Hospital in Primary Ambulatory Care," pp. 64-66.

38. Western Hospital Association, _Hospital Forum_ 12 (March 1970).

Further Reading

Andrepoulos, Spyros. _Where Medicine Fails: A Look at Primary Care in the United States._ New York: John Wiley & Sons, 1974.

Annas, George J. _The Rights of Hospital Patients._ New York: Avon Books, 1975.

Friedson, Eliot. _The Hospital in Modern Society._ New York: Free Press, 1963.

Garrett, Raymond D. *Hospitals—A System Approach.* Philadelphia: Anerbach Inc., 1973.
Hamilton, James A. *Patterns of Hospital Ownership and Control.* Minneapolis: University of Minnesota Press, 1961.
Knowles, J., ed. *Hospitals, Doctors and the Public Interest.* Cambridge, Mass.: Harvard University Press, 1965.
MacColl, William A. *Group Practice and the Prepayment of Care.* Washington: Public Affairs Press, 1966.
Riedel, Donald C. and Fitzpatrick, Thomas B. *Patterns of Patient Care.* Ann Arbor: University of Michigan Press, 1964.
Shindell, Sidney; Salloway, Jeffrey C.; and Oberembt, Colette. *A Coursebook in Health Care Delivery.* New York: Appleton-Century-Crofts, 1977.
Wasyluka, Ray G. "New Blood for Tired Hospitals." *Harvard Business Review* 70:65-74 (September-October 1970).

Further Viewing

"Medicine in America: Life, Death, and Dollars," National Broadcasting Company, fall 1977. This three-hour TV special is a balanced consideration of the U.S. health care delivery system. Even controversial subjects such as unnecessary surgery, malpractice, and empty hospital beds are handled with an unbiased perspective.

5. Mental Health

When they first used that fog machine on the ward, one they bought from Army Surplus and hid in the vents in the new place before we moved in, I kept looking at anything that appeared out of the fog as long and as hard as I could, to keep track of it, just like I used to do when they fogged the airfields in Europe. Nobody'd be blowing a horn to show the way, there was no rope to hold to, so fixing my eyes on something was the only way I kept from getting lost. Sometimes I got lost in it anyway, got in too deep, trying to hide, and every time I did, it seemed like I always turned up at the same place, at the same metal door with the row of rivets like eyes and no number, just like the room behind that door drew me to it, no matter how hard I tried to stay away, just like the current generated by the fiends in that room was conducted in a beam along the fog and pulled me back along it like a robot. I'd wander for days in the fog, scared I'd never see another thing, then there'd be that door, opening to show me the mattress padding on the other side to stop out the sounds, the men standing in a line like zombies among shiny copper wires and tubes pulsing light, and the bright scrape of arcing electricity. I'd take my place in the line and wait my turn at the table. The table shaped like a cross, with shadows of a thousand murdered men printed on it, silhouette wrists and ankles running under leather straps sweated green with use, a silhouette neck and head running up to a silver band goes across the forehead. And a technician at the controls beside the table looking up from his dials and down the line and pointing at me with a rubber glove. "Wait, I know that big bastard there—better rabbit-punch him or call for some more help or something. He's an awful case for thrashing around."

So I used to try not to get in too deep, for fear I'd get lost and turn up at the Shock Shop door. I looked hard at anything that came into sight and hung on like a man in a blizzard hangs on a fence rail. But they kept making the fog thicker and it seemed to me that, no matter how hard I tried, two or three times a month I found myself with that door opening in front of me to the acid smell of sparks and ozone. In spite of all I could do, it was getting tough to keep from getting lost.

Then I discovered something: I don't have to end up at that door if I stay still when the fog comes over me and just keep quiet. The trouble was I'd been finding that door my own self because I got scared of being lost so long and went to hollering so they could track me. In a way, I was hollering for them to track me; I had figured that anything was better'n being lost for good, even the Shock Shop. Now, I don't know. Being lost isn't so bad.

I'm further off than I've ever been. This is what it's like to be dead. I guess this what it's like to be a Vegetable; you lose yourself in the fog. You don't move. They feed your body till it finally stops eating; then they burn it. It's not so bad. There's no pain. I don't feel much of anything other than touch of chill I figure will pass in time.
        —Chief Broom, also known as Big Chief Bromden, institutionalized with
    the Chronics and Acutes in Ken Kesey's *One Flew Over the Cuckoo's Nest.*

There are no (nor have there ever been) fog machines in mental institutions, but there are "shock shops." Psychiatric therapies have grown and diversified tremendously since World War II. Our purpose here is not to evaluate these therapeutic modes; instead, we describe the more important changes in the treatment of mental patients. In the United States, one out of every ten receives some form of psychiatric therapy during his or her lifetime. We will examine the progress being made toward more efficient use of mental health resources and more humane treatment of the large numbers of people in need of psychiatric assistance.

Psychiatric Hospitals

The history of mental health services is quite different from that of other kinds of health services: until the last few decades, progress in patient care for mental disorders has been social, administrative, and legal rather than clinical. During the seventeenth century, mental illness was not recognized as a major medical problem. The mentally ill were "treated" through confinement and punishment. Vincenzo Chiarugi of Italy, Philippe Pinel of France (best known for removing chains binding lunatics in 1793), and William Tuke of England, responding to the humanistic ideas of the eighteenth century, pioneered in the recognition that the way mental patients are treated affects the way they behave. Waves of reform, neglect, reform, and neglect followed.

Most of the mentally ill remained in workhouses or prisons as "simple lunatics" under the care of a guardian. Before the industrial changes of the first half of the nineteenth century, many problems of mental disorder could be treated casually but effectively in small, mainly rural community settings. But industrial growth and urbanization accentuated problems. The hospital movement began in urban areas as a result of private philanthropy. During the second quarter of the nineteenth century, responsibility for mental patients shifted toward public hospitals under state authority. Funding came from state and local government sources in the United States. The old physical methods of treatment and restraint— bleeding and purging, leg-locks and strait jackets—gradually disappeared. The asylum physician began to acquire professional standing. However, unmanageably large, poorly staffed, and grossly underfunded state mental hospitals rapidly became isolated, self-contained worlds still unable to provide significant treatment.

Not much happened in the mental health services until after World War II, when the large number of soldiers who returned from the war in a state of shock rekindled the public's interest in mental health. Sociologists and hospital superintendents began to propose more patient self-government, less institutional dependency, and more bonds with families and the surrounding community. They emphasized that the mentally ill should live in the community and that mental hospitals should become places of treatment rather than places of custody. Far fewer first admissions became chronic, and the continuous growth of the inpatient population came to an end.

In the early 1950's effective chemotherapeutic means of managing acute psychotic disorders became available. Chlorpomazine and other members of the phenothiazine class of drugs were found to help episodic, overactive cases of schizophrenia. Then, two classes of antidepressants— the monamine oxidase inhibitors and the tricyclics—were found to be effective in the management of from 70 to 80 percent of depressive episodes; reliance on electroconvulsive therapy, then the only known effective treatment for depression, was reduced. Lithium was discovered to be—with proper attention to dosage and careful monitoring of levels in the blood—a safe, effective prophylactic agent against the recurrence of psychotic episodes in manic-depressives. These drugs have reduced durations of stay and allowed some long-term patients to return to the community.

Two other developments have affected the inpatient population. In the early 1960s, new legislation was passed to create more outpatient facilities at the local level. In addition, newer methods of short-term treatment, including behavior modification and transactional analysis, began to replace the older forms of long-term psychotherapy, which included psychoanalysis.[1]

As seen in Figure 5.1, the resident mental-patient population peaked in 1955 in state and county mental hospitals.[2] As seen in Figure 5.2, the rate of outpatient care, measured in psychiatric patient-care episodes per 100,000 population, doubled from 1965 to 1971 and accounted for nearly all the increase in the total patient-care rate.[3] The inpatient care rate has held steady (800 to 900 per 100,000) for almost two decades.

As we saw in Table 4.5, the number of beds in specialty psychiatric hospitals and the number of beds per 1,000 population have sharply

Figure 5.1   Number of Resident Patients at Year End in
State and County Mental Hospitals

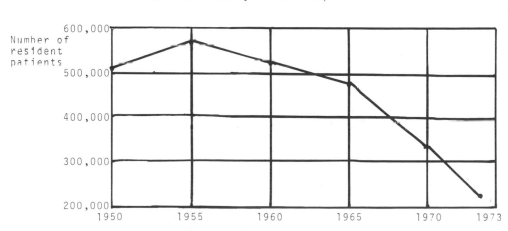

Year

Figure 5.2   Psychiatric Patient-Care Episodes per 100,000
             Population, Selected Years 1955-1973

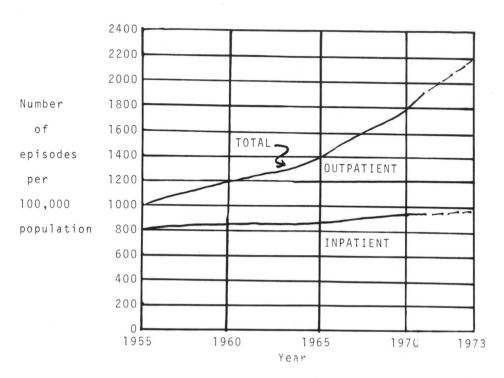

declined. Table 5.1 shows additional changes in utilization rates for specialty psychiatric hospitals, both long-term and short-term.[4] In psychiatric hospitals, few beds are allocated to short-term stays (fewer than thirty days). Occupancy rates have been decreasing slowly but steadily, as has the average daily census and, more recently, admissions. Interestingly, alcoholism is currently a major cause of first admissions.

These figures do not include public and private facilities specifically designed for the mentally retarded. During the nineteenth century, a number of "asylums" were established for the teaching of "idiots." The term *school* gradually replaced the term *asylum* at the turn of the century, and today many of the state institutions that were formerly large, isolated facilities are smaller units distributed geographically over each state. In 1971, the MFI reported 1,236 public and private facilities for the mentally retarded with 213,821 beds, 195,316 residents (91 percent occupancy rate), and 123,247 staff members employed full-time (1.6 patient/staff ratio). About 61 percent of these facilities had fewer than 25 beds, and about 60 percent of all facilities for the mentally retarded are proprietary.[5] Patient eligibility for these facilities is based on intelligence quotients (IQ) and other measures of learning ability and educational aptitude.

Private mental hospitals tend to be smaller (87 beds on the average) than

Table 5.1 Utilization Rates for Psychiatric Specialty Hospitals,
Long and Short Term, Selected Years 1950-1973

	Long Term Hospitals				Short Term Hospitals			
	1950[a]	1960	1970	1973	1950[a]	1960	1970	1973
Number of beds	607,327	719,317	551,847	442,861	--	3,176	16,542	9,633
Number of admissions	292,874	317,972	549,599	538,264	--	44,431	118,812	112,340
Occupancy rate (in percentages)	98.0	93.2	84.9	81.8	--	69.9	79.2	67.6
Average daily census	N.A.[b]	670,060	468,267	362,247	--	2,220	13,101	6,512

a In 1950, psychiatric hospitals were not broken down into long and short term.
b N.A.: Not Available.

government mental hospitals (1,091 beds on the average) and dramatically different from government mental hospitals. One reason is funds. For example, at the Menninger Clinic, a high-quality private mental hospital in Topeka, Kansas, the cost of hospitalization is $100 a day. For the average stay of about eight months, the total is $25,000 to $30,000. By comparison, Topeka State Hospital, a publicly supported psychiatric hospital a few blocks away, charges $37 a day for the first sixty days and $9 a day after that. An eight-month stay costs around $4,000. At such rates, it is not surprising that private institutions generally treat affluent patients and that public institutions treat less affluent patients. But even the $4,000 charge in public institutions is a barrier for the voluntary commitment of poor patients.

There is good reason for private psychiatric patients to seek treatment at Menninger. Here, and in similar institutions, patients have a voice in governing the hospital—this allows staff members to observe patient behavior and teaches patients how to deal with responsibility. Furthermore, favorable patient/staff ratios allow private hospitals such as Menninger to bring about basic changes in a patient's personality. Most public hospitals and even community outpatient clinics, on the other hand, help a patient only to deal with an emotional crisis and get back to ordinary life.[6] Patients at private mental hospitals are usually referred by their private physician; at the state hospital, in contrast, the courts, social agencies, and the public are the main sources of referral.

What obligations does the state mental hospital have toward its patients? What are the rights of mental patients? First, we must distinguish between *mental illness* and *mental incompetence* (definitions vary from state to state). *Mental incompetence* means that an individual is unable to take care of his business or legal affairs (his taxes, property, bank account, etc.). *Mental illness* means that an individual is unable to take care of his personal affairs (health, safety, and so on). The terms are mutually exclusive. In most states, a person can legally be declared "mentally incompetent" even though he or she has not been committed to a mental hospital. If so, he or she legally cannot make contracts, buy and sell property, decide what to do with his or her money or estate, marry or get a divorce. In several states, hospitalization for "mental illness" automatically results in adjudication of "mental incompetence." In other states, the hospital superintendent or the department of mental hygiene can petition the court for the adjudication of incompetence of a specific patient.

Due process of law,[7] a constitutional right, requires that before life, liberty, or property may be taken from anyone, he has a right to a court hearing on all relevant issues. A superintendent's certification that the patient is incompetent is often considered prima facie evidence (sufficient evidence to declare mental incompetence unless rebutted), and a decision may be rendered without the patient's ever appearing in court, either because he is ignorant of what is going on or is powerless to prevent it. The state can then take the patient's money to pay for his maintenance and therapy. This is the "Catch 22" of the rights of mental patients. The state assumes that if a person exhibits antisocial behavior and the symptoms of mental illness, he or she is no longer able to act in his or her best interest and that therefore the state should and will act in his or her best interest. But if the individual protests that the state is not acting in his or her best interest, the state disregards the protest—it is coming from someone it considers mentally ill.

There are hundreds of procedures for putting people in mental hospitals against their will; this is known as *involuntary hospitalization* or *involuntary commitment.* Most hospitalized psychiatric patients are committed involuntarily in one of two ways: (1) emergency and (2) nonemergency hospitalization. The emergency procedure is supposed to be used only in exceptional cases. But in almost every state, almost all involuntarily committed individuals are initially hospitalized under the emergency procedure, whether there is a true emergency or not. In most states, the standard for emergency hospitalization requires some proof, or at least an allegation, that the prospective patient is (1) mentally ill and (2) dangerous—dangerous either to himself, or to others, or to property (all in the future). In some states, a layman (a spouse, parent, neighbor, or policeman, for example) can so allege; in other states one or more physicians can do so; and in still others, a judge can do so through court order. An emergency commitment is similar to arrest or detainment and, though it authorizes treatment, is ostensibly for the purpose of observation and diagnosis. In most states, the maximum period of emergency hospitalization is five to fifteen days.

Nonemergency hospitalization is for the purpose of treatment, usually for an indefinite period or for long periods (two months, six months, or a year), which can be renewed again and again. Most states require a court order after a judicial hearing before one can be hospitalized involuntarily for a nonemergency, but a few states require only the certification of two physicians (they need not be psychiatrists) that an individual is mentally ill and needs treatment. In most states, proof "beyond a reasonable doubt" is not necessary during the judicial hearing; if the "preponderance" of the evidence is against the prospective patient, hospitalization is permitted.

Voluntary patients, more accurately described as nonprotesting patients, are free to enter the hospital but are not always free to leave it. Most states require only the prospective patient's application. Almost every state provides that the voluntary patient can leave within five or ten (or in some cases thirty) days after he notifies the hospital that he wants to leave, unless during that time the hospital begins involuntary commitment proceedings. If a patient, either voluntary or involuntary, feels he is being unjustly held against his will, he may file with the courts a petition for a writ of *habeas corpus*,[8] and in many cases, the mere filing of a writ induces the hospital to discharge the patient. However, many patients are unaware of their rights, and in many cases, old, confused patients have remained in the hospital year after year as voluntary patients, even though they might be better off at home or in some other facility. So that patients are not forgotten, many states have statutory provisions for periodic review. Depending upon the state, the review may be conducted by the hospital staff or by the courts with limited and sometimes full-scale hearings. In some states, a procedure known as *informal admission* allows a patient to enter and leave the hospital freely. The informal patient cannot be held once he demands release.

Because a mental patient in a state mental hospital is a ward of the state, the state sometimes denies him or her rights other than those previously discussed, including such civil rights as voting and religious freedom as well as rights of communication and visitation, confidentiality of records, payment for work, control of personal property, notice of rights (only nine states specifically require that a voluntary patient be advised of his right to request release),[9] the right to a free lawyer, and most important, the right to treatment and the right to deny treatment. In many states, the mental patient's consent is not required either for emergency or other surgery. Many states authorize the "eugenic sterilization" of the "probable potential parent of socially inadequate offspring." Mental patients do not have the right to refuse insulin coma therapy (ICT) or electroshock therapy (ECT); consent may be given by a close relative, or if none can be found, by the hospital superintendent.

Several court cases have established that adequate and effective treatment in a mental hospital is a right. In *Ragsdale* v. *Overholser,* the court held that without treatment the hospital is transformed "into a penitentiary where one could be held indefinitely for no convicted offense."[10] In *Rouse* v. *Cameron,* the case concerned Charles Rouse, who had been found not guilty by reason of insanity of carrying a deadly weapon, and who had been summarily committed to Saint Elizabeth's Hospital for treatment. Rouse's therapeutic commitment was noncriminal in nature and continued for three years before he filed a *habeas corpus* petition. He challenged his continued detention on the ground that he was receiving no treatment. Chief Judge Bazelon, speaking for the majority, declared, "The purpose of involuntary hospitalization is treatment, not punishment."[11] The court concluded that an individual committed to a mental hospital has a right to treatment and that the courts will enforce that right. In 1972, in a historic decision, a federal judge ruled that Alabama's state mental hospitals did not provide adequate treatment: Judge Johnson, in *Wyatt v. Stickney,* ordered that the hospital be completely reorganized and that specific minimum standards of adequate staffing and treatment be met—in short, that involuntary mental patients have a *constitutional* right to treatment.[12] The opinion spells out the rights of hospitalized patients, and a companion opinion spells out the rights of the mentally retarded.

One of the benefits of outpatient therapy is that patients and providers need not be as concerned over questions of law. All outpatient treatment is voluntary, except care rendered under the threat of involuntary hospitalization.

Community Mental Health Centers and Clinics

In 1946, Congress passed the National Mental Health Act, which established a training program for mental health manpower and grants-in-aid for mental health clinics; authorized financing of research on the cause, diagnosis and treatment of mental disorders; and established the National Institute of Mental Health. In 1955, Congress passed the Mental Health Study Act which authorized a comprehensive study of the mental health field. In its final report on this study, the Joint Commission on Mental Illness and Health sent its recommendations to Congress in December 1961.[13] The report stimulated further action on community mental health services. In 1963, President Kennedy, in a special message to Congress, called for a new national program for mental health and to combat mental retardation. Later that year, Congress passed the Mental Retardation Facilities and Community Mental Health Centers Construction Act, which authorized federal grants for the construction of community-based facilities. In addition, under the Aid to Totally and Permanently Disabled programs, the financial necessity of remaining in a mental hospital as a means of subsistence was removed for the totally disabled mentally ill.

Under terms of the 1963 act, a *community mental health center* may be either a discrete physical entity or a network of services joined by administrative arrangement to form a comprehensive program that provides continuity of care. In order to be considered a comprehensive mental health center and thus be eligible for funding, a center had to provide the following five services:

1. inpatient service
2. outpatient services
3. day care services
4. twenty-four-hour emergency service
5. consultation and educational services for community agencies and professional personnel

As of 1976, centers must also provide:

6. special services for children and the elderly
7. follow-up care for discharged patients
8. transitional services
9. screening for referral to a state mental health facility
10. alcohol and drug abuse services unless provided by other agencies

Inpatient services may provide acute intensive psychotherapy for the patient who requires temporary hospitalization. Emphasis is placed on quickly switching the patient to an outpatient status. Therapies range from group to individual psychotherapy sessions to electroshock therapy in the case of deep psychotic depressions. If the patient shows no improvement, he is referred to a facility providing long-term care. Some patients require only partial hospitalization, that is, they leave the facility at night and return in the day for therapy and drug treatment. Emergency services usually include a central phone number and psychiatric services on twenty-four-hour call.

By September 1973, there were 541 funded comprehensive community mental health centers, of which 392 were operating.[14] Their total number of employees was 42,769. The average community mental health center has an annual budget of nearly $1 million, employs 100 persons, may receive funds from as many as ten or more different sources, and may be composed of as many as eighteen decentralized, different organizations.[15] Approximately one-third of the U.S. population resides in areas with funded centers.

The development of community mental health centers has placed increased emphasis on community psychiatry. Patient problems are more effectively treated if diagnosis and treatment can be administered during the initial visit. Programs may include the early detection of incipient difficulties in populations, and assistance to inhabitants to enable them to cope with societal stresses. Health education and consultation may be provided to such institutions and agencies as school systems, welfare agencies, police departments, courts, and correctional institutions. Community mental health clinics, despite the traditional reluctance of organized medicine and the turmoil political activism can engender, have begun to deal with the relationship between mental illness and social problems such as overcrowding, mobility, and cultural and racial conflict.

Zone Mental Health and Integrating Long-Term and Short-Term Care

In order to apportion the responsibility for care, catchment areas have been established for each community mental health center. These centers generally serve catchment areas of 70,000 to 200,000 persons. In order for them to function properly, however, they must have the appropriate linkage and networks to serve populations of the projected size, particularly in the inner city.[16] The mental health center often has to field requests for help in the school sytem, other parts of the health system, the legal system, and in other human services of the community. So before the zone system becomes operative, it also must plan linkages with these other systems.

As seen in Figure 5.3, a state may have four echelons of mental health services.[17] The first echelon is a neighborhood outpost, which does screening and works with other agencies in a neighborhood. The second echelon is the community mental health center, which is usually linked to three to six outposts. The third echelon is the zone center, and is usually linked to six to eight mental health centers which is the administrative hub of the echelon network. The fourth echelon—primarily the state mental hospital system—is made up of long-term, extended-care facilities or categorical programs that require a lengthy period of residence.

One of the interesting features of a continuous closed-circuit network is a "no-decline" option for providing services. Patients who apply for services must be treated within their own catchment area; if they choose not to and seek treatment outside of the catchment area, they must pay a higher fee for service. In many community mental health clinics, patients pay on a sliding scale based on income and number of dependents. However, scales may vary; residents of one catchment area justifiably may complain that the same treatment in a different area costs less.

The Social Security Amendments of 1965 (medicare and medicaid) provided national programs of health insurance for the aged and medical assistance payments for the less affluent. Both programs include mental health care benefits but limit benefits that do not apply to care for physiological diseases. Although private health insurance policies also have discriminatory provisions against mental illness (as opposed to other conditions), group coverage appears to be tending toward comparable benefits for mental illness for hospital care and in-hospital physicians' services. The principal difference continues to be in outpatient psychiatric care, where several exclusions and limitations are still common.[18] Table 5.2 shows the extent of coverage by type of hospital for 1,000 psychiatric patients admitted to ten hospitals.[19] A smaller percentage

Figure 5.3   A Model of a Zone Mental Health Delivery System

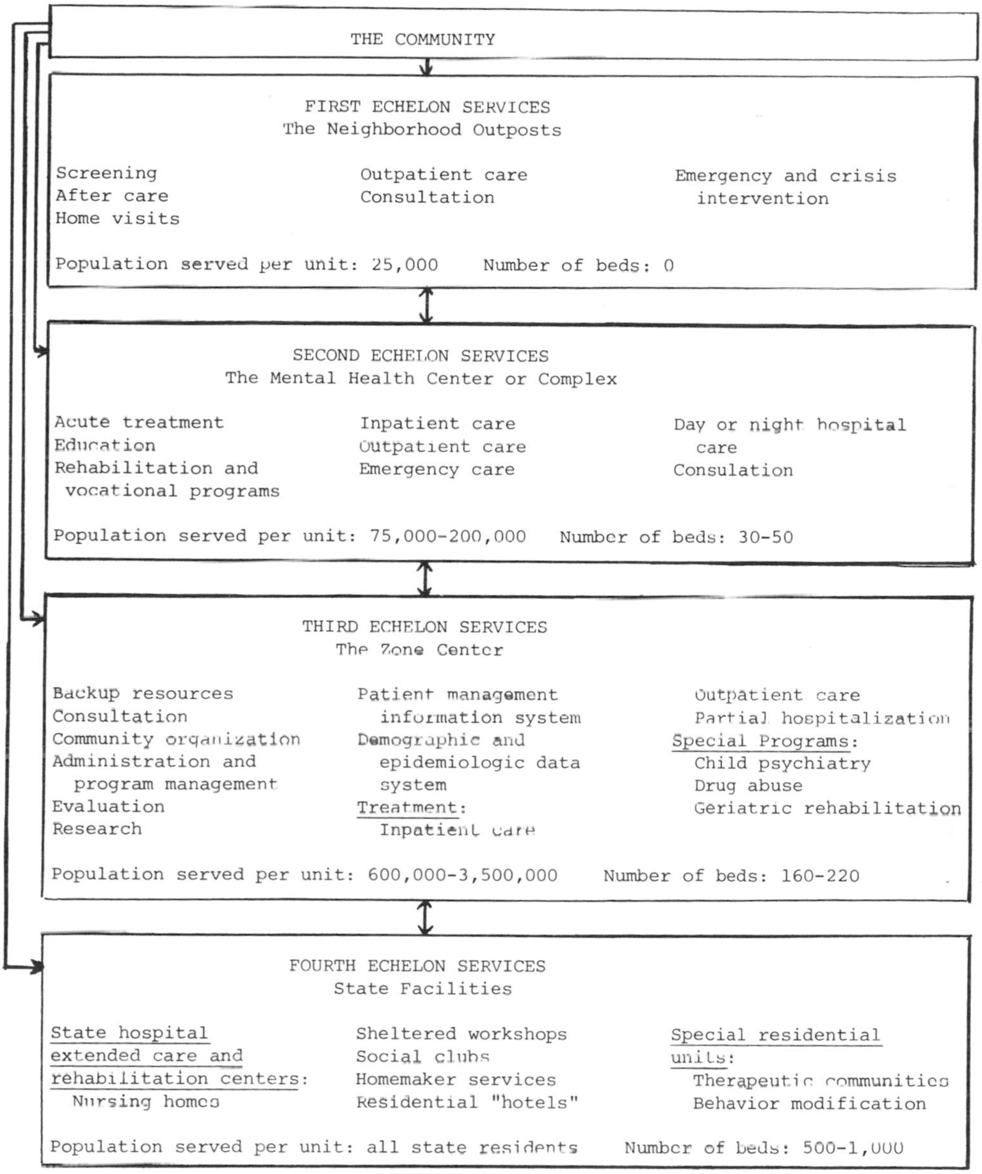

```
┌─────────────────────────────────────────────────────────────┐
│                       THE COMMUNITY                           │
└─────────────────────────────────────────────────────────────┘

┌─────────────────────────────────────────────────────────────┐
│                   FIRST ECHELON SERVICES                      │
│                  The Neighborhood Outposts                    │
│                                                               │
│ Screening          Outpatient care       Emergency and crisis│
│ After care         Consultation              intervention     │
│ Home visits                                                   │
│                                                               │
│ Population served per unit: 25,000    Number of beds: 0       │
└─────────────────────────────────────────────────────────────┘

┌─────────────────────────────────────────────────────────────┐
│                  SECOND ECHELON SERVICES                      │
│             The Mental Health Center or Complex               │
│                                                               │
│ Acute treatment       Inpatient care      Day or night hospital│
│ Education             Outpatient care        care             │
│ Rehabilitation and    Emergency care       Consulation        │
│   vocational programs                                         │
│                                                               │
│ Population served per unit: 75,000-200,000  Number of beds: 30-50│
└─────────────────────────────────────────────────────────────┘

┌─────────────────────────────────────────────────────────────┐
│                   THIRD ECHELON SERVICES                      │
│                      The Zone Center                          │
│                                                               │
│ Backup resources      Patient management    Outpatient care   │
│ Consultation            information system   Partial hospitalization│
│ Community organization Demographic and       Special Programs: │
│ Administration and      epidemiologic data    Child psychiatry │
│   program management    system                Drug abuse       │
│ Evaluation            Treatment:              Geriatric rehabilitation│
│ Research                Inpatient care                        │
│                                                               │
│ Population served per unit: 600,000-3,500,000  Number of beds: 160-220│
└─────────────────────────────────────────────────────────────┘

┌─────────────────────────────────────────────────────────────┐
│                  FOURTH ECHELON SERVICES                      │
│                     State Facilities                          │
│                                                               │
│ State hospital        Sheltered workshops   Special residential│
│ extended care and     Social clubs          units:           │
│ rehabilitation centers: Homemaker services    Therapeutic communities│
│   Nursing homes       Residential "hotels"    Behavior modification│
│                                                               │
│ Population served per unit: all state residents  Number of beds: 500-1,000│
└─────────────────────────────────────────────────────────────┘
```

Table 5.2   Extent of Insurance Coverage of 1,000 Psychiatric
Patients at Ten Hospitals, 1968

Type of Hospital	Percentage of Patients Covered	Average Percentage of Bill Paid by Insurance
Public, general	35	70
Voluntary, general	74	71
Private psychiatric	69	58

of the private psychiatric hospital's bill was paid by insurance. Insurance programs, especially for outpatient services, have been slow to include mental health benefits for several reasons:

1. existing public responsibility for the care of the mentally ill
2. continuing stigma attached to mental illness
3. the belief of many that they will never need mental health care
4. fear of many that the use of psychiatric services will affect their employment status adversely

Funds for mental health will still probably come primarily from state government—with assistance from the federal government. Federal staffing funds are provided on a declining percentage basis for the first eight years of a mental health center's operations (shown in Table 5.3).[20] In 1970, schizophrenia and affective disorders were the most common diagnoses for persons admitted to mental health centers. Alcoholism and drug abuse were other common diagnoses.

New short-term treatment modalities have been developed for outpatient care. *Group therapy,* which draws on learning theory and group dynamics, involves those who cannot cope unaided with their psychiatric or social problems, a staff trained to treat such problems, and the use of the psychiatric patient or social casualty as a resource in the treatment process itself. In effect, the patient becomes a therapist. Group therapy may take the form of sensitivity sessions, psychodrama, family therapy, encounter groups, and so on.

Behavior therapy emphasizes altering undesirable symptoms and behavior rather than personality review and modification. Reciprocal inhibition and psychological desensitization, and forms of behavior therapy, are relearning processes: in the presence of an anxiety-evoking stimulus, a non-anxiety-producing response is continually repeated until it extinguishes the old, undesirable response. In aversive conditioning, undesirable behavior can be eliminated by systematically "punishing" the patient in situations that might ordinarily elicit unwanted behavior.

Nonverbal therapies such as *art and dance therapy* are enjoying a revival among providers who work with the mentally retarded. *Direct*

Table 5.3   Federal Staffing Funds for Mental Health Centers
            (in percentages)

Year of Operation	Funds for Designated Poverty Areas	Funds for Other Areas
First and second	90	75
Third	80	60
Fourth	75	45
Fifth	75	30
Sixth through eighth	70	30

psychoanalysis, based upon the discoveries of Freud, is a psychiatric recreation and revision of the patient's relationship with his or her early parental environment and attempts to focus on unconscious dynamic factors. In contrast, *existential therapy, reality therapy,* and *Gestalt therapy* place considerable emphasis upon a patient's life in the present; *Rogerian therapy* focuses heavily on the client-therapist relationship. All these modalities emphasize an active therapist (as opposed to a passive, nonresponding therapist). Patients who enter a community health center are likely to encounter some of these newer treatment techniques; in theory, less hospitalization is the result.

Summary

The psychiatric hospital has come a long way, but it still has a long way to go. Patients used to be confined, punished, and neglected, but now they aimlessly wander around the ward, fogged in by thorazine, many unaware of or unable to exercise their rights. Recent court cases have confirmed that confined mental patients have a right to treatment. Fortunately, as a result of changing attitudes, treatment, and advances in psychobiology, inpatients are outpatients, and outpatients do not become inpatients. Community mental health centers have begun systematically to deliver short-term inpatient and neighborhood outpatient care. Emphasis is placed on helping the patient cope with his or her immediate problems. Demand for these outpatient services has been brisk.

Questions

1. In *O'Connor v. Donaldson* (docket no. 74-8, U.S. Supreme Court, 26 June 1975) the Supreme Court ruled in favor of Kenneth Donaldson that an involuntarily hospitalized mental patient has a right to be released if not dangerous to himself or others. What should the mental health delivery system do with people who are so psychotic that their family and the community are unable to care for them, but who are not dangerous to themselves or others?

2. Assume you are writing a writ of *habeas corpus* for an involuntarily committed patient. What points would you stress?

3. Discuss the differences between custodial care in a mental institution and the services rendered by a large hotel.

4. Assume you are the administrator of a community mental health center. You are making your annual presentation before the state budgeting and appropriations committee. You would like to see your funding level increased for the upcoming fiscal year. What kinds of statements would you make to justify this increase?

Notes

1. This history of mental health treatment has been condensed from three sources: Gerald N. Grob, *Mental Institutions in America: Social Policy to 1875*

(New York: Free Press, 1973); *The Cost of Mental Care* (London: Office of Health Economics, 1965), pp. 4-7. Leon Eisenberg, "Psychiatric Intervention," *Scientific American* 229:117-27, September 1973).

2. Eisenberg, "Psychiatric Intervention," p. 120.

3. Ibid., p. 121.

4. *Hospital Statistics, American Hospital Association,* 1974; *Hospitals* 45:464-66 (1 August 1971) (Guide Issue) part 2; *Hospitals* 35:396 (1 August 1961) (Guide Issue) part 2; *Hospitals* 25:9 (June 1951) (Guide Issue) part 2.

5. *Health Resources Statistics* (National Center for Health Statistics, 1974), p. 401.

6. "The Menninger Clinic is Changing Its Ways: Patients Help Run It." *Wall Street Journal,* 13 March 1974, pp. 1 and 19.

7. *Due Process* requires (1) that an individual be notified in *advance* that someone has begun a proceeding which, if successful, will result in the loss of his liberty, and (2) that an individual be given a meaningful opportunity *in court* to oppose that proceeding *before* he loses that liberty. Most of this section on patient rights is drawn from Bruce Ennis and Loren Siegel, *The Rights of Mental Patients* (New York: Avon Books, 1973).

8. A writ of *habeas corpus* may be filed in a state or federal court by anyone who believes he or she has been unjustly confined, whether in a mental institution, a prison, or the armed forces.

9. The following is a list of patient rights handed to patients before they are admitted to Southeast Louisiana Hospital:

Patient's Rights According to Act 154 of the 1972 Louisiana Legislature Amending Title 28 of the Louisiana Revised Statutes of 1950

Every patient shall have the right:

1. To wear his own clothes; to keep and use his personal possessions, including toilet articles; to keep and be allowed to spend a reasonable sum of his own money for canteen expenses and small purchases, and to have access to individual storage spaces for his private use.

2. To correspond by sealed letter with people outside of the hospital and to have access to reasonable amounts of letter writing materials and postage.

3. To be visited at all reasonable times.

4. To be employed at a useful occupation depending upon the patient's condition and available facilities.

5. To sell the products of his personal skill and labor at the discretion of the superintendent and to keep or spend the proceeds thereof or to send them to his family.

6. To be discharged as soon as he has been restored to reason and has become competent to manage his own affairs. The medical director or superintendent of the treatment facility shall have the authority to discharge the patient without the approval of the court which committed him to the treatment facility.

7. To be visited in private by his attorney at all times.

8. To request an informal court hearing to be held within five days of receipt of the request. If the patient does not have an attorney of his own, the court shall appoint an attorney who shall represent the patient at the hearing. The purpose of the hearing shall be to determine whether or not the patient should be discharged from treatment.

9. To apply for a writ of habeas corpus.

10. To be visited and examined at his own expense by a physician designated by him or a member of his family or a near friend. The physician may consult and confer with the medical staff of the treating facility and have the benefit of all information contained in the patient's medical record.

The medical director or superintendent of this treating facility may for good cause only, deny a patient's rights under this section, except that the rights enumerated in (6), (7), (8), (9), and (10) shall not be denied under any circumstances.

10. *Ragsdale* v. *Overholser,* 281 F. 2d 943 (D.C. Cir 1960).
11. *Rouse* v. *Cameron,* 373 F. 2d 451 (D.C. Cir 1966).
12. *Ricky Wyatt et al.* v. *Dr. Stonewall B. Stickney et al.* Civil action No. 3195-N, U.S. District Court for the Middle District of Alabama, Northern Division. The court set seventy-four constitutional and medical standards. The order was—by far—the broadest and most specific ever handed down in this area of law. For a definitive summary of this decision, see "The First Landmark: Mental Patients' Rights," *Civil Liberties,* September 1972. For a discussion of the effect of this decision on the lives of the mentally ill, see "Federal Court Order Brings Big Changes in Lives of Mentally Ill and Retarded Patients in Alabama," *Wall Street Journal,* 18 December 1973, p. 32. One must always keep in mind, however, that there is an enormous difference between the rights mental patients have in theory and the rights they have in practice.

In sum, for the mentally ill the Court ordered:

1. Use of the least restrictive conditions necessary to achieve the purposes of commitment.
2. Freedom from "unnecessary or excessive" medication. Medication may be given only upon a physician's written order and may not exceed U.S. Food and Drug Administration standards.
3. Weekly review by a physician of each patient's drug regimen, with prescriptions to terminate within 30 days.
4. No use of medication as punishment or "substitute for program."
5. Freedom from physical restraint and isolation except for emergencies—that is, the danger of physical harm to the patient or others, upon a professional's written order after that professional has seen the patient.
6. Freedom from experimental research without consent of the patient or next-of-kin *after* review by a human rights committee.
7. No use of hazardous treatment without the patient's express and informed consent.
8. Provision of medical treatment for physical ailments.
9. An end to peonage, with the minimum wage to be paid to patients who voluntarily engage in hospital maintenance and other labor.
10. No patient labor that interferes with the patient's treatment.
11. The housing of a maximum of six patients to a room with adequate space for each. Screens or curtains must be provided to insure privacy.
12. Provision of one toilet for each eight patients, one lavatory for each six, one shower or tub for each 15. Toilet and bathing facilities must be private.
13. Appropriate recreational and dining facilities.
14. Bed linen changes at least once a week.
15. Regulation of temperature between 68 degrees and 83 degrees, with adequate ventilation.

16. Refuse disposal.

17. Observance of fire and safety standards set by the state, the locality, and the National Fire Protection Association.

18. Adequate diet, following menus developed according to the moderate cost food plan of the U.S. Department of Agriculture.

19. No denials of food as punishment.

20. The use of only state licensed professionals in professional capacities.

21. The employment, for each 250 patients, of two psychiatrists, four M.D.'s, 12 registered nurses, six licensed practical nurses, one Ph.D. level psychologist, one M.A. psychologist, two B.S. psychologists, seven social workers, 102 aides and orderlies and a variety of other personnel, including half a chaplain.

Within 48 hours of admission, the Court said, each patient shall have a comprehensive physical and mental examination. An individualized treatment plan shall be developed for each patient. It shall specify the least restrictive treatment conditions necessary to achieve the purposes of commitment and it shall specify criteria for discharge of the patient. There shall also be an individualized post-hospitalization plan for each patient.

Each patient shall have a mental examination at least every 90 days. Complete, accurate records shall be kept and shall be accessible to personnel who treat the patient. Every week a professional shall make a progress report on each patient. Children shall be given education, recreation and play opportunities.

Within 15 days after commitment, each patient must be examined to determine whether he or she still requires hospitalization and is being treated according to standards. Otherwise that patient must be released or kept only voluntarily. Finally, the Court specified that the mental health board has the duty to provide adequate transitional treatment for the patients it releases—including psychiatric day care, treatment at home, the use of nursing homes, out-patient treatment, and treatment in the psychiatric wards of general hospitals.

For the mentally retarded the Court ordered physical living conditions similar to those for the mentally ill. Also:

1. "Normalization," that is, conditions of living and treatment which are, insofar as possible, like those of normal life.

2. No use of isolation or seclusion.

3. Use of physical restraints only to prevent physical injury, on the order of professionals and for no more than 12 hours at a time. A patient under restraint must be checked every 30 minutes.

4. The employment, for each 60 patients, of one psychologist, one social worker, an educator, a therapist and a large number of attendants and aides.

5. Reevaluation of each patient within 90 days of the commitment order. At that point he or she must be discharged, if possible, with "transitional habilitation assistance."

6. A halt to new admissions at the school for retardates until all of the guidelines are met.

13. Joint Commission on Mental Illness and Health, *Action for Mental Health* (New York: Basic Books, 1961).

14. *Health Resources Statistics*, 1974, pp. 437-41. A note of caution: inpatient/outpatient, partial or emergency services located in the psychiatric ward of a general hospital may be counted in these statistics.

15. Saul Feldman, "Problems and Prospects: Administration in Mental Health," *Administration in Mental Health* 1:4-11 (winter 1972).

16. There apparently is a high negative correlation between income and incidence of psychological disorder.

17. Harold M. Visotsky, "Modern Approaches to Community Mental Health," in *Handbook of Psychiatric Therapies*, ed. Jules H. Masserman (New York: Grune and Stratton, 1966) pp. 476-97.

18. *Financing Mental Health Care in the United States* (Rockville, Md.: National Institute of Mental Health, 1973) pp. 97-112.

19. P. L. Scheidemandel et al., *Health Insurance for Mental Illness* (Washington, D.C.: The Joint Information Service of the American Psychiatric Association and the National Association for Mental Health, 1968).

20. *Financing Mental Health Care in the United States*, p. 99. See also Marjorie S. Miller, "Private Health Insurance in 1970: Population Coverage, Enrollment, and Financial Experience," *Social Science Bulletin* 35: 3-19 (Feburary 1972).

Further Reading

American Journal of Psychiatry 129: entire issue (September 1972).

Beigel, A., and Levinson, A. F., eds. *Community Mental Health Center: Strategies and Programs*. New York: Basic Books, 1972.

Brakel, Samuel J., and Rock, R. S. *The Mentally Disabled and the Law*. Chicago: University of Chicago Press, 1971.

"The Changing Role of the State Mental Hospital." *Hospital and Community Psychiatry* 25: entire issue (June 1974).

Foley, Henry A. *Community Mental Health Legislation*. Lexington, Mass.: D.C. Heath & Co., 1975.

Ginsberg, Leon. "The Mentally Committed." *Nation* 25 (May 1974), p. 656.

Giordano, Joseph. "Mental Health and Middle America." *Mental Hygiene* 59:28-31 (fall 1975).

Glasscott, Raymond, et al. *The Community Mental Health Center: An Interim Appraisal*. Baltimore, Md.: Garamond, 1969.

Goffman, Erving. *Asylums—Essays on the Social Situation of Mental Patients and Other Climates*. New York: Doubleday & Co., 1961.

Goldblatt, Phillip B. "Catchmenting and the Delivery of Mental Health Services." *Archives of General Psychiatry* 28:478-82 (April 1973).

Greenblatt, P. "The Phasing Out of Mental Hospitals in the United States." *American Journal of Psychiatry* 132:135-40 (November 1975).

Kittrie, Nicholas. *The Right to be Different—Deviance and Enforced Therapy*. Baltimore, Md.: Penguin Books, 1973.

Kramer, Kenneth. "The Subtle Subversion of Patients' Rights by Hospital Staff Members." *Hospital and Community Psychiatry* 25:475-76 (July 1974).

Mirelowitz, Seymour. "Alienation and Bureaucratization of Mental Health Organizations." *Mental Hygiene* 56:6-12 (fall 1972).

Schulberg, H. C., and Baker, F. *The Mental Hospital and Human Services*. New York: Behavioral Publications, 1973.

Silverstein, Harry, ed. *The Social Control of Mental Health*. New York: Thomas Y. Crowell Co., 1968.

Steward, David W. "Future of State Mental Hospitals." *Perspectives in Psychiatric Care* 13:120-22 (July-September 1975).

Szasz, Thomas S. *The Myth of Mental Illness.* New York: Dell Publishing Co., 1961.

Talbott, John. "Stopping the Revolving Door—A Study of Readmission to a State Hospital." *Psychiatric Quarterly* 48:159-68 (1974).

Tancredi, L. R.; Lieb, J.; and Slaby, A. E. *Legal Issues in Psychiatric Care.* New York: Harper & Row, 1975.

Thompson, M. G. "New Perspectives for Mental Health Care Delivery Systems." *Canadian Psychiatric Association Journal* 18:501-4 (December 1973).

Further Viewing

"Titticut Follies." A film documentary by Frederick Wiseman on the callous treatment at Bridgewater State Hospital in Massachusetts. All Wiseman's films, including those on juvenile courts, high school, hospitals, basic training, and primate research, are highly recommended as studies of American institutions and their effects. For a review of Wiseman's films, see Hecht, Chandra. "Total Institutions on Celluloid." *Society* 9:45-48 (April 1972).

6. Health Services for the Aged

Mere length of life . . . may be a poor concern on which to focus. Most would agree that the quality of life, rather than its duration, should be the prime issue.
—Alexander Leaf

In the developed countries, nearly two-thirds of all deaths are associated with the infirmities of old age. Our concern here is precisely with the aged—where we institutionalize them, the treatment and long-term care they receive, and the alternatives available to them.

Problems of the Aged

Those over sixty-five are the fastest growing "minority group" in the United States—by 1990, they will increase by another 25 percent. They are also the largest single group of the chronically ill. Biologically, the body gradually loses its ability to renew itself. During advanced adulthood (which begins in middle age when an individual first notices that he or she is growing old), changes occur in sensory processes, perception, motor skills, intelligence, problem-solving, understanding, learning drives, emotions, attitudes, expectancies, motives, self-image, social roles, and total personality. Activity limitation, incontinence, and sometimes family rejection and loneliness occur. Old age has become a stigma based on stereotypes. Many companies have policies that arbitrarily require retirement. Despite the mounting evidence that health practitioners can rehabilitate the elderly, the elderly are often still seen as unresponsive and unrehabilitable.[1]

The denial of dignity at the end of life perhaps is one of the aged's worst problems. Legally and socially, the autonomy of the aged is difficult to protect. Increasingly, the aged are out of view and deprived of the protection of their families. In New York City, for example, there have

Figure 6.1   Deaths at Home versus Deaths in Institutions in
             New York City, Selected Years 1955-1967

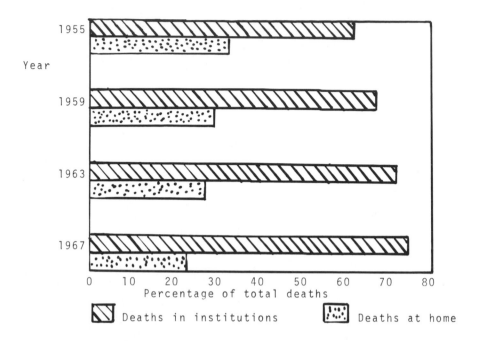

been fewer and fewer deaths at home than in institutions since 1955
(Figure 6.1[2]). In 1955 more than 31 percent of all deaths occurred at home
(the national average was about 40 percent), but by 1967 home deaths had
fallen below 25 percent. Figure 6.2 shows the types of institutions in which
deaths away from home occur.[3]

The large majority of deaths occurred in general hospitals, a smaller
number in mental hospitals and nursing homes. A rise in the percentage
of deaths occurring in nursing homes mirrors the growth of these
institutions and their use as depots for the irreversibly ill, older American.
As the period of dependency and weakening has lengthened for the
aged, the nature of the care given has shifted dramatically toward long-
term institutionalization. Bok sums up the increased vulnerability to
paternalism and the "intensive care syndrome":

> The family units have shrunk, and many elderly live alone; when they
> need help, institutional help is overwhelmingly more frequent. Patients
> who are severely ill often suffer a further distancing and loss of control
> over their most basic functions. Electrical wiring, machines, intravenous
> administration of liquids creates new dependency, and at the same time
> new distance between the patient and all who come near.[4]

Despite increases in Social Security payments, the aged must also live on a
fixed income during inflationary periods. Nothing produces insecurity

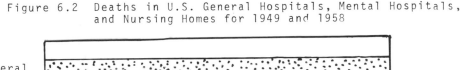

Figure 6.2   Deaths in U.S. General Hospitals, Mental Hospitals, and Nursing Homes for 1949 and 1958

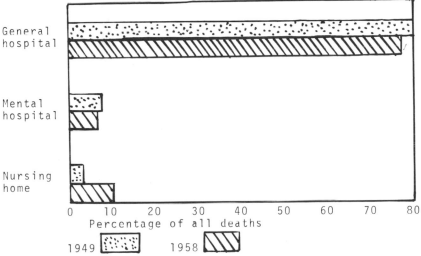

faster than watching inflation push the necessities of life out of financial reach. Inability to participate in the economic system—first as a producer and then as a consumer—is likely to be interpreted as personal failure. Rejected by family, out of money, many older individuals turn to, almost surrender to, the health care delivery system as a last resort.

Nursing Homes

In 1935, as part of the New Deal, the Social Security Act was passed. It provided Old Age Assistance (OAA) in the form of monthly payments to the employed and their dependents upon retirement. A proviso in the act also withheld OAA payments from residents of state and local public institutions. As one might expect, the aged, the sick, the crippled, and the blind left the public institutions in large numbers in order to qualify for the Social Security payments. Private boarding homes—typically run by widows, unemployed couples, and aging nurses—became nursing homes. In 1950, amendments to the Social Security laws extended OAA payments to residents of public medical institutions and required each state to establish minimum standards for nursing-home care and to enforce them through licensing laws. In 1965, the Social Security Act was again amended to create medicare and medicaid. These programs authorized payments to two classes of nursing homes: skilled nursing homes and extended-care facilities. In 1967, Congress recognized a third type of nursing home: the intermediate-care facility.

Table 6.1 shows the different types of nursing homes, their type of care, method of reimbursement, percent of total homes and beds, and the

98

Table 6.1 Comparison of Nursing and Related Homes, 1971

Home	Type of Service	Type of Care	Paid for by	Total Number of Beds	Percentage[a] Number of Beds	Average Bed Size
I. Skilled nursing home[b] II. Extended care facility[b]	I and II provide skilled nursing	Long term skilled nursing, continuous nursing, r.t., p.t., o.t., diet care; post-hospital skilled nursing	I. Medicaid II. Medicare	58	76	I. NA II. 72
III. Intermediate care facility	Provides personal care with or without nursing	Long term supportive care	Medicaid (optional)	41	23	33
IV. Residential facility, rest home, or boarding house	Provides domiciliary room and board	Custodial room and board	--	1	1	NA

a Based on 22,004 nursing and related homes with a total of 1,201,593 beds.
b Licensed in all 50 states, primarily by health departments.

average bed size.[5] Both skilled nursing homes and extended-care facilities are considered skilled nursing facilities and offer continuous nursing care plus auxiliary services, including different forms of therapy. In 1972, medicaid payments (for care in skilled nursing homes) financed almost half of all nursing-home care in the country. Intermediate-care facilities, known also as personal-care homes, offer less care than that in a skilled nursing home, but more than just room and board. Some intermediate homes offer regular nursing care, and others offer only the most rudimentary nursing care. Although states must participate in the reimbursement of skilled nursing-home care under medicaid, they may choose not to participate in the reimbursement of intermediate-care facilities.[6] Intermediate-care facilities tend to be about half as large as skilled nursing facilities and offer a less expensive alternative to the skilled nursing home. To make matters more confusing, some facilities may be certified as both intermediate-care facilities and skilled nursing homes (or as skilled nursing homes and extended-care facilities). Rest homes and boarding houses represent a small proportion of nursing homes and an even smaller proportion of the total number of beds; not much is known about their average bed size or how they are paid for. The average size nursing home is now around 54 beds, but new facilities under construction have at least 100 beds—staffing requirements make facilities under that size unprofitable.

Nationally, for every 1,000 persons aged sixty-five and over in the civilian population, 52 were residents in nursing and related homes (approximately 1 in 20). Ninety percent of nursing-home patients fall into this age group. Residents of urban nursing homes tend to be between 75 and 84, female, and widowed; only about 5 percent are nonwhite; and they have lived in a facility from two to three years.[7] From 10 to 15 percent of the residents die each year. The number of beds in 1971 was approximately double that in 1963. One reason for the growth in nursing homes and beds (other than the advent of the reimbursement programs) is the high occupancy rate (90 percent) and high profitability. Table 6.2 shows the type of ownership of nursing homes.[8]

Most nursing homes are owned and run for profit. Proprietary homes serve more men and more persons with disturbed marital histories; they

Table 6.2 Nursing and Related Homes by Type of Ownership, 1971

Type of Ownership	Percentage of Total Homes
Proprietary (for profit)	78
Voluntary (non-profit)	16
Public	6

are more likely to be available to former mental patients and black persons; and their residents have fewer and more distantly related community contacts and fewer visitors.[9] On the other hand, nonprofit church-related homes (one-third of all nonprofit homes) serve a more socially advantaged population who actively have community persons interested in them.

There is pervasive evidence that nursing homes are excessively utilized. It is estimated that 27 to 79 percent of nursing-home patients do not need nursing-home care.[10] There is also evidence of underutilization. Because medicare only reimburses up to 100 days of care, a patient ineligible for medicaid may be discharged after 100 days, regardless of whether continued care is needed.[11]

Investigations continue to reveal serious, nationwide deficiencies.[12] Professional care (physicians, nurses, therapists, and so on) is theoretically available as a condition for reimbursement; yet personnel actually may spend little time with patients.[13] *Transplantation shock*—a severe depression resulting from giving up lifelong belongings and familiar surroundings—can occur when patients enter a place where they very likely will die. Adequate medical supervision is a major problem. Recreation programs turn out to be little more than a few checkerboards. Medication is administered haphazardly. Records are kept poorly. Preventive measures against fires,[14] patient falls, and contaminated food are not taken. Absentee ownership contributes to neglect. As in mental institutions, patient rights are violated. Some homes are human warehouses, dumping grounds for the dying, halfway houses between society and the cemetery. A few notorious operators have been arrested for flagrant abuses of funding programs,[15] but many studies have found that the government still provides financial support for care in homes with numerous, prolonged deficiencies.[16] Federal standards have not been enforced. Boarding homes, which most states do not regulate, have been found to have serious structural violations, overcrowding, inadequate dietary preparation, and lack of personal and medical care.[17]

Control of nursing-home quality has largely been illusory. The Hill-Burton legislation attempted to use construction financing to integrate nursing homes into areawide systems of health care and link them closely to hospitals; but nursing-home owners, to guard themselves against controls mandated by Hill-Burton, have turned instead to FHA (Federal Housing Assistance) loans.[18] State licensing laws are not uniform; life safety codes vary. The Joint Commission on Accreditation of Hospitals has attempted to accredit nursing homes that meet relatively high standards.[19] By the end of 1973, 2,056 facilities—or less than one-tenth of all facilities— were accredited.[20] In deciding whether to build a skilled nursing home, an intermediate-care facility, or an extended-care facility, owners often choose one of the first two options so as to avoid coming under the higher standards of medicare certification.

Depending on whom one talks to, nursing homes are unprofitable, marginally profitable, or highly profitable. In recent years, many homes that were owned as a single facility after having been converted from a normal residential household have been driven out of business by stricter enforcement of standards (certification, licensing, fire and safety, zoning ordinances, and so on) and by mismanagement. The trend now is toward multiple-facility organizations that are parent or holding corporations.[21] The holding company may issue stock to raise funds to acquire facilities, or the stock may be swapped to acquire the property.

Although many parent corporations operate and construct their own institutions, several of the larger companies are also franchisers. The franchiser sells its name and services for a set fee. If the investor is to be owner, he or she puts up the initial capital costs of the facility (this money may be borrowed from a lending institution). The franchiser's major return is on the construction and furnishing of the facility. The investor may contract with the franchiser or another company to manage the facility, usually agreeing to pay a percentage of gross revenue (7 to 10 percent) to the franchiser, who in turn will provide certain services and assistance. Although the stock market performance of these corporations has been spectacular and their share of the nursing home market is expected to increase, they, too, are not exempt from mismanagement, corruption, and collapse.[22]

In 1967, the first of an estimated thirty geriatric day care centers opened.[23] These centers provide an alternative for patients who are physically ill but who wish to live in their own homes and do not need round-the-clock nursing services. Instead, these patients may receive a full range of services five days a week, including transportation, meals, daily baths, group counseling, a sheltered workshop, arts, crafts, and physical therapy. There is now a definite trend toward alternatives that permit chronically ill senior citizens to live longer in their own homes.

Another related movement is the growth of the *hospice* concept—a method of (1) caring (psychological and emotional support, treatment of symptoms) for those cancer patients who do not respond to treatment and (2) providing an environment for the patient to die with dignity. Instead of trying to cure a terminally ill patient, health providers working in a hospice attempt to minimize pain while maintaining a psycho-dynamically rewarding environment.

Home Health Services

Historically, before the emergence of hospital-based care, health care was provided in the home. In 1796, the Boston Dispensary developed the first home care program. In 1946, Montefiore Hospital in New York City began the first hospital-centered program. The term *home health services* describes an array of services—both therapeutic and preventive—that patients in their homes or foster homes receive for acute illness and exacerbations of chronic illness or disability. A coordinated home care program is centrally administered and, through coordinated planning, evaluation, and follow-up procedures, provides for physician-directed medical, nursing, social, and related services to selected patients at home.

There are three "levels" of care: (1) concentrated or intensive services, (2) intermediate services, and (3) basic services. Table 6.3 shows the number of home health agencies participating under the medicare program in 1973.[24] As is evident, official health agencies predominate. The total number of agencies, 2,215, is down from a high of 2,333 in 1971. To be approved for participation under medicare as a home health agency, an agency must provide both skilled nursing care and at least one other therapeutic service, such as physical therapy, speech therapy, occupational therapy, medical social services, or home health aide services. It must also comply with state and local licensure requirements (seven states license home health agencies) and maintain clinical records. Most agencies (74 percent) offered physical therapy services in 1973. Under medicare legislation, proprietary home health agencies must be licensed to participate. As of April 1973, there were 76 home health agencies accredited by a joint voluntary accreditation program of the National League of Nursing and the American Public Health Association.

In a 1963 survey of thirty-three coordinated home care programs, the average daily census was 110.[25] Hospital-based programs, notably those of larger institutions, carried a larger patient census than did other types of programs. A 1970 survey of hospital-based programs found that 84 percent charge per visit and 22 percent charge per hour (some programs use both methods). Per diem, per service, and per month methods were also used for reimbursement.[26] A 1966-1968 Health Interview Survey indicated that in the United States as a whole, 4.9 percent of the civilian, noninstitutional population fifty-five years or over receive intermittent to full-time care at home.[27] It also showed that with the exception of the age group seventy-five and over, proportionally more low-income and non-

Table 6.3   Home Health Agencies Participating in the
            Medicare Program, by Type of Agency, 1973

Type of Agency	Number
Official health agency	1,255
Visiting nurse association	531
Combined government and voluntary agency	55
Hospital based program	231
Other[a]	140
All agencies	2,215

a Includes extended care facility-based programs, rehabilitation facility-based programs, proprietary or other home care programs.

white persons receive care at home rather than in a nursing home or other residential institutions for the aged and chronically ill. Proportionally more persons living outside standard metropolitan statistical areas (SMSA) received health-related home care than those living in SMSAs.

A study of matched groups of patients—one group placed in home care and the other retained in a general hospital—revealed that the results of care did not differ significantly.[28] It thus indicated that home care is an acceptable alternative to hospitalization. Organized home health care can reduce patient cost, the effects of institutionalization (particularly "transplantation shock" for the elderly), and the effects of isolated, neglected care. Hospital home care programs can free hospital beds and reduce average length of stay. Yet home care has many problems. Many agencies have no social service component, many physicians never use the home care program, hospital-based home care programs pay little attention to the possibility of shortening the acute care period in the hospital through preadmission services, and agencies often cannot provide or arrange for essential household supporting services.[29]

The nutritional component of home care is an important alternative to institutionalized care. The aged, chronically ill, handicapped, disabled, convalescing, malnourished, undernourished, and the poor sometimes lack the strength, ability, or motivation to prepare nutritious meals or to obtain adequate food services. In response, many communities are developing meals-on-wheels programs funded by local, state, and federal monies.[30] Food that is relatively inexpensive and retains temperature well is prepared in a central kitchen, often in a church or school, and is transported, usually by volunteers, to recipients' homes. Meals are designed to meet at least one-third of the recommended daily allowance established by the Food and Nutrition Board of the National Research Council; the appearance and temperature of the food is also an important factor in recipient participation. Some communities have found that a congregate meal site is a more efficient alternative to meals-on-wheels.

For many families, a chronically ill older person who lives with them is an emotional and financial burden. As an alternative to nursing homes, home health care could be reimbursed under a program for "aid to families with dependent parents."[31] Perhaps in the future, medicare funds could be made available for a broad spectrum of home health and social services.

"Gray Power" may be the next emerging political force.

Summary

The aged are a neglected, growing minority group. Increasingly, they die in institutions, particularly in general hospitals. Three types of nursing homes—the skilled nursing home, the extended-care facility, and the intermediate-care facility—are reimbursed by medicaid, medicare, and medicaid, respectively. Each type of home provides a different level of nursing care and rehabilitative services. Despite reforms and governmental monitoring, nursing homes can perpetuate the same conditions that other long-term facilities have in the past—depression and human defeat. An alternative to nursing homes is health care reimbursed by medicare. Home health care can reduce patient costs as well as the effects of institutionalization.

Questions

1. What can be done about the "intensive care syndrome" and its effect on older people?

2. In cities with an acute shortage of nursing-home beds, should the government be more lenient in cutting off financial reimbursement for care in homes with numerous, prolonged deficiencies?

3. Assume you are a provider of health care to the aged—many of your patients live on fixed incomes. The local utility company, Harper Valley Power and Light (HPVL), wants to raise its rates 20 percent for the coming year. If the rate increase is granted by the regional utility commission, your patients will be less able to afford health care if they consume the same amount of electricity and gas next year as they did this year. In your role as a patient advocate, is it appropriate for you to come before the commission and argue against the HVPL rate increases? What other measures could you take besides fighting the rate increase? Assume that the local hospitals receive a discount on their electricity and gas rates (pay less per unit of power than other consumers); would you argue for or against the continuation of this discount?

4. What electrical appliance, if any, would you, as a nursing home administrator, allow patients to keep in their rooms?

Notes

1. Jerome Kaplan, "In Search of Policies for Care of the Aged," in *Ethics of Health Care,* edited by Laurence R. Tancredi (Washington, D.C.: National Academy of Sciences, 1974), pp. 281-303.

2. Robert S. Morison, "Dying," *Scientific American* 229: 55-62 (September 1973).

3. Ibid., p. 62.

4. Sissela Bok, "Commentary" on Jerome Kaplan's "In Search of Policies for Care of the Aged" (1974), p. 306.

5. Combined from two sources. Kenneth D. Frank, "Government Support of Nursing Home Care" *New England Journal of Medicine* 287:538-45 (14 September 1972); *Health Resources Statistics* (National Center for Health Statistics, 1974), p. 383.

6. In 1972, thirty-two states included intermediate-care facilities in their medicaid programs.

7. Leonard E. Gottesman, "Nursing Home Performance as Related to Resident Traits, Ownership, Size and Source of Payment," *AJPH*, pp. 269-76 (March 1974).

8. *Health Resources Statistics* (1974), p. 394.

9. Gottesman, "Nursing Home Performance," p. 274.

10. Kenneth D. Frank, "Government Support for Nursing-Home Care," *New England Journal of Medicine* 287:540 (14 September 1974).

11. President's Task Force on Aging, "Toward a Brighter Future for the Elderly" (Washington, D.C.: U.S. Government Printing Office, April 1970), pp. 31-32.

12. Frank, "Government Support," provides an extensive bibliography of these investigations.

13. J. L. Barney, "Community Presence as a Key to Quality of Life in Nursing Homes," *AJPH* 64:265-68 (March 1974).

14. Carroll Cihlar, "Ohio Nursing Home Fire: An Analysis," *Hospitals* 44:28a-28d (1 March 1970).

15. "Two Grand Juries Indict Hollander," *New York Times*, 3 July 1975, p. 1. Eugene Hollander, a major nursing home operator in New York State, was indicted by state and federal grand juries on charges of stealing more than $1.2 million in medicaid and medicare funds by using fraudulent billings. In addition moves were under way to remove the licenses of all of Hollander's homes because of inadequate food and care.

16. C. Townsend, *Old Age: The Last Segregation* (Ralph Nader's Study Group Report on Nursing Homes) (New York: Grossman, 1971). M. A. Mendelson, *Tender Loving Greed* (New York: Vintage, 1975). Charles H. Percy, *Growing Old In the Country of the Young* (New York: McGraw-Hill, 1974). Richard M. Gavin, *Where They Go to Die—The Tragedy of America's Aged* (New York: Delacorte Press, 1968). J. Braverman, *Nursing Home Standards: A Tragic Dilemma in American Health* (Washington: American Pharmaceutical Association, 1970).

17. Pearl R. Roberts, "Human Warehouses: A Boarding Home Study," *AJPH* 64:277-82 (March 1974). Quoting from this article:

> Since most boarding homes are staffed by owner/managers with little outside help, individual care is totally lacking. No special provisions were found for the dietary needs of diabetics. Amputees were sometimes housed on second and third floors, as were the blind. Many occupants relied on other boarders for their personal needs. Medication was haphazard and not administered by trained personnel. One home was found where all the medication of all boarders was kept in one cupboard and distributed without fixed schedules and apparently at random.

Some nursing homes are not much better at providing custodial care than these boarding homes.

18. W. C. Thomas, *Nursing Homes and Public Policy: Draft and Decision in New York State* (Ithica, N.Y.: Cornell University Press, 1969), pp. 49-56.

19. Standards for Accreditation of Extended Care Facilities, Nursing Care Facilities and Resident Care Facilities (Chicago: Joint Commission on Accreditation of Hospitals, January 1968).

20. *Health Resources Statistics*, p. 383.

21. Paul W. Earle, "The Nursing Home Industry—Part 1" and "The Nursing

Home Industry—Part 2," *Hospitals* 44:45-50 and 60-64 (16 February and 1 March 1970).

22. In 1970, Four Seasons Nursing Centers, Inc., was the largest publicly owned nursing and extended care corporation. The corporation experienced a tumultuous crash; the U.S. government has called this case one of the biggest stock conspiracies on record. See *New York Times,* 5 June 1973; 31 August 1973, p. 33; and 19 September 1973, p. 65.

23. "Alternatives to Nursing Homes," *Wall Street Journal,* 4 April 1975, p. 10.

24. *Health Resources Statistics,* p. 465. A note of caution: perhaps only half of all agencies participate in medicare.

25. Survey of Coordinated Home Care Programs (PHS publication no. 1062) (Washington, D.C.: U.S. Government Printing Office, 1963).

26. Lorraine Richter and Alice Gonnerman, "Hospital-Administered Home Care Programs," *Hospitals* 46:41-44 (1 May 1972).

27. "Persons 55 Years and Over, Receiving Care at Home, July 1966—June 1968," *Monthly Vital Statistics Report* 19:1-4 (January 1971).

28. J. R. Stone, E. Patterson, and L. Felson, "The Effectiveness of Home Care for General Hospital Patients," *JAMA* 205:145-48 (15 July 1968).

29. Frank Van Dyke and Virginia Brown, "Organized Home Care: An Alternative to Institutions," *Inquiry* 9:3-16 (June 1972).

30. *A Home Delivered Meals Program for the Elderly,* DHEW (SRS) 73-20234 (Washington, D.C.: Administration on Aging, September 1971).

31. "Alternatives to Nursing Homes," p. 10.

Further Reading

Chiswick, Barry. "The Demand for Nursing Home Care." *Journal of Human Resources* 11:295-316 (summer 1976).
Eckman, Judith, and Furman, Walter, eds. *Handbook and Directory of Nursing Homes.* New York: Basic Books, 1975.
Eckman, Judith, and Furman, Walter, eds. "Health of the Elderly: A Special Section." *Public Health Reports* 92: entire issue (January-February 1977).
Korcher, Charles, Jr. "Family Rejection of the Aged and Nursing Home Utilization." *International Journal of Age and Human Development* 5:231-44 (Summer 1974).
Mendelson, M. A., and Hapgood, D. "The Political Economy of Nursing Homes." *Annals of the American Academy* 415: 95-105 (October 1974).
Miller, Duley B. *The Extended Care Facility: A Guide to Organization and Operation.* New York: McGraw-Hill Book Co., 1969.
National Council on Aging. *Older Americans: Special Handling Required.* Washington, D.C.: The Council, 1975.
Nursing Home Care in the United States: Failure in Public Policy (report no. 93-1420). Senate Subcommittee on Long-Term Care, November 1974.
Trager, Brahna. "Home Care: Providing the Rights to Stay Home." *Hospitals* 49: 93-98 (16 October 1975).
U.S. Congress. "Special Congress on Aging: Home Health Services." Working paper, 1973.

Warner, George M. "Nursing Home Investigations and Reform: Their Effects on Quality of Care in New York State." One Hundred and Fourth Annual Meeting of the American Public Health Association, Miami Beach, Fla. October 17-21, 1976.

Weiner, Leonard; Becker, Alvin; and Friedman, Tobias. *Home Treatment: Spearhead of Community Psychiatry.* Pittsburgh, Pa.: University of Pittsburgh Press, 1967.

7. Disjointed Community Efforts To Organize the Delivery of Health Care

He that passeth by and meddleth in a war not his own is like unto a man
that lifteth a dog by the ears.
—Proverbs 26:17

Many of us are well-meaning, friendly, and sympathetic toward others. We wish to improve local, national, and worldwide human conditions. We have a penchant for reforms and tend to form and join organizations to accomplish these goals. Many of us unselfishly devote time and money to voluntary health agencies and causes that espouse high ideals and hope to relieve the misery of others. We are told we have a moral responsibility to give our fair share, to do our part, to exercise our social responsibility, to help others who are needier than we. Our concern here is with efforts, usually voluntary, fragmented, and decentralized on a community basis, to arrange emergency transportation, to provide disaster relief, and to collect and distribute blood. The purpose of these activities is noble, but their organization is often inefficient, rigid, secretive, and bewildering.

Voluntary Agencies and Problems in Organizing Services

Voluntary health organizations are supported by private or nontaxable funds and have few legal powers. There may be as many as 100,000 separate voluntary agencies in the United States.[1] These agencies fall into several categories. A large group of agencies is supported by individual donations:

1. agencies concerned with specific diseases, such as the American Cancer Society
2. agencies concerned with certain organs or structures of the body, such as the American Heart Association
3. agencies concerned with the health and welfare of special groups, such as the American Geriatric Association
4. agencies concerned with particular phases of health and welfare, such as the National Safety Council

109

Another large group consists of foundations established and financed by private philanthropy, such as the W. K. Kellogg Foundation, the Commonwealth Fund, and the Johnson Foundation. A third group of health agencies is composed of professional associations, such as the National League for Nursing, which attempt to influence health policy at the national level. All three types of agencies are nonprofit and tax exempt. Some foundations are tax shelters for wealthy individuals or families. All contributions to any of these agencies are tax deductible; even the dues members pay to professional associations are tax deductible. By allowing for these deductions, the government encourages (or subsidizes, depending on one's viewpoint) participation and contributions.

The fund-raising activities of these voluntary agencies are important and sometimes costly—10 to 36¢ per dollar raised (but many organizations fail to use uniform accounting procedures in determining expenses).[2] There is an increasing trend toward joint fund-raising efforts. The United Fund, a once-a-year community effort, raises funds for member organizations, whose local, state, and national offices receive specified amounts. There are about 1,500 United Fund agencies and about the same number of community chests, which collect money primarily for local agencies.[3]

Toward the end of the 1950s, a number of national agencies, notably those concerned with cancer, poliomyelitis, tuberculosis, and crippled children, forbade their local chapters to participate in the United Fund or community chest campaigns. Separate appeals can add confusion and siphon money off which might have been expended locally. During the "big sell" or "torch drive" or "give once for all" campaign, many United Funds draft officials of the agencies they give money to. This means that the executives' salary is being spent for fund raising, but this amount is not recorded as a fund-raising expense on the agency books or on the United Fund books.[4] Each year the agencies that desire continued funding or initiation of funding make a pitch to the United Fund and community chest. In order to be successful, those who present the requests must paint a compelling picture, complete with dramatic stories of children snatched from the perils of disease and pictures of volunteers in action.[5] Pet agencies of board members, usually individuals drawn from the elite of the community, are not likely to have their funds cut, nor are newer, smaller, more innovative agencies likely to be funded.[6] Perhaps the most interesting problem with United Funds is the overt and covert pressures applied to encourage employees to do their fair share. Goals are set for corporations, divisions, and departments; supervisors are anxious to please their superiors through a good showing; the pressure falls hardest on lower-income employees with greatest job vulnerability.

Another curious problem of fund raising is that independent organizations concerned with diseases of low incidence sometimes raise more money than organizations concerned with diseases of high incidence. There may be an imbalance between campaign goals or amounts raised and the relative importance of a disease. Again, this may be the result of pet donors, fund-raising activities based on the social life of community elites, and apathy on the part of knowledgeable individuals who fail to take an advocacy role.

Reform has been slow in coming. In 1961, Hamlin published a study of the voluntary health and welfare agencies in the United States and recommended the development of a uniform accounting and financial reporting system for voluntary agencies.[7] In 1964, uniform standards were devised.[8] Although eventual compliance seemed possible in 1966, many local and national agencies, as we shall see with the Red Cross, do not adhere to generally accepted principles of accounting.

We know little about the impact of voluntary agencies and voluntary efforts. Obviously, volunteers play a role in organized care within the hospital (see the hospital organizational chart, Figure 4.7). We do know that philanthropy comprises an extremely small percentage (5 percent) of total research expenditures, just as it does in the overall health expenditures. We will examine how voluntary efforts get mixed in with private and public efforts to provide goods and services that have been inadequate, disjointed, and sometimes in conflict and turmoil.

Emergency Transportation

The three primary objectives of the emergency medical care system are (1) resuscitation and maintenance of life, (2) transportation of the patient, and (3) rapid diagnosis and treatment of the basic medical problem.[9] A key factor is not the speed of the ambulance, but the time it takes to stabilize the patient's condition. Much time is saved if the patient's condition can be stabilized at the site of the accident or heart attack. From 10 to 20 percent (a conservative estimate) of the prehospital deaths due to illnesses and accidents can be prevented if proper care is administered at the scene and en route to a medical facility.[10] As comparisons between survival rates for military injuries in early wars with those in more recent wars suggest, mortality decreases when time to treatment decreases.

Before the turn of the century, ambulances were drawn mainly by mules or horses; around 1900, gradual motorization of ambulance vehicles began. Funeral homes were active in providing ambulance services because they had vehicles that could accommodate injured people on stretchers. Through the years, requirements for staffing and equipping ambulances have been upgraded as well as the attendants' qualifications; many of the funeral homes found providing the service was much less profitable than accommodating the dead and bereaved, so the trend in providing ambulance services by morticians has decreased. As of March 1973 there were 14,072 ambulance services, 25,891 vehicles, and 206,824 personnel. That is 1.8 vehicles per service and 8.0 personnel per vehicle. Obviously, many ambulance services are small. In order to provide twenty-four hour service with one attendant per vehicle, an average of five attendants per vehicle is required. One attendant per vehicle is inadequate if (1) that attendant is untrained, or (2) the patient is hard to move, or (3) the patient requires treatment en route (one attendant must drive).

Ambulance services can be divided into two categories: (1) those serving the public and (2) those serving special groups. Table 7.1 shows the distribution of ambulance services in California.[11] Approximately 62 percent of the ambulances serve the public, and 38 percent serve special groups. The fire department plays a significant part in serving the public. Hospitals rarely enter the ambulance system, because (1) they are open to charges of conflict of interest in deciding on what hospital to take the patient to and (2) ambulance services are expensive to run.

As a hypothetical case, let us take a male, age fifty, who has just had a heart attack in his suburban home. What problems does he face in getting an ambulance quickly enough to save his life? First, whom should he call? There may be no centralized phone number (911), and it may be difficult (to put it mildly) to find a service in the phone book. If he gets through to a dispatcher, he will, on the average, have to wait forty-four minutes for the arrival of an ambulance. The dispatcher may or may not have triage experience.[12] If he calls more than one ambulance service, two ambulances may arrive on the scene. If there is no central number, dispatchers of different services may not coordinate dispatches. Finally, just because he has called a service does not mean the service has any legal obligation to dispatch an ambulance; indeed, their ambulances may already be out on runs.

Table 7.1   Types of Ambulance Services, California, 1972

	Percentage of total ambulances in state
Serving the Public	
Commercial	33
Funeral	7
Hospital-based	3
Fire department	12
Police	1
Volunteer	3
Other governmental	3
Serving Special Groups	
Military	17
Industrial	12
State government	5
Federal government (non-military)	2
Other	2

When an ambulance arrives, the attendants—who are likely to have had the standard and advanced Red Cross first aid course (65 percent of all attendants) but are unlikely to be registered emergency medical technicians (EMT) (which requires passing an eighty-one-hour course sponsored by the Committee on Trauma of the American College of Surgeons) will in most instances, instead of administering care to the heart attack victim, pick him up and transport him to a hospital at five mph over the posted speed limit. An attendant's background should include cardiopulmonary resuscitation, emergency childbirth, light extrication, and the ability to start I.V.'s, restore breathing, control hemorrhaging, splint fractures, and administer injections and oxygen.

However, most ambulances are far from temporary field hospitals. A fully equipped ambulance costs $25,000 and has, besides minimal first aid equipment, oxygen tanks and a defibrillator. In many cases ambulances are nothing more than "horizontal taxis." Although our coronary patient may protest, only 46 percent of all ambulance trips are for emergencies; most ambulance trips are for escort transportation. Ambulances are just beginning to get sophisticated and expensive telemetry equipment that will allow physicians in emergency rooms to monitor a patient's vital signs in the ambulance. Our heart attack patient may need a shot of lidocaine to prevent erratic heartbeat, but the paramedic may not be able to administer the shot: (1) the drug may not be on board, or (2) the paramedic may first need to get an M.D. order, which is impossible either because he has no communication system with which to contact an M.D. or because there is no M.D. available at the other end of his communication system. Only 10 percent of all ambulances have room for two litters, adequate space between them, and head room for the attendent to work over the patients. Some states set standards for ambulances (equipment, headroom, design, and so on), but there is no practical enforcement of these standards. Rural areas need more equipment because there is often a delay in discovery, less adequate emergency treatment (more volunteers and less training), more hazardous occupations, and a longer distance to the nearest hospital.[13]

Ambulance operators and their employees, as well as physicians, often express concern about legal liability or suits involving patient care. There is a good deal of mythology in this area. There has yet to be an officially reported decision of any court of record within the United States in which an injured party has sued a physician for rendering emergency medical care.[14] In states that have Good Samaritan laws, there apparently is no greater effort to aid the emergency-injured patient than in the several states that do no have such legislation. Suits against ambulance companies and personnel are not based on medical care per se, but instead on traffic accidents, delays in reaching or delivering patients to the hospital, and patients falling off cots or gurneys.

Individual companies do have some restrictions. Private operators are not allowed to pick up a patient unless they are called for that purpose. If a private ambulance is called to a scene and after arriving finds that a patient cannot pay for the service, he can refuse to transport the patient. Many companies, however, feel bound morally to carry all patients, only to find that they provide a significant amount of "free" transportation. The average charge is $75 per trip; some companies have a charge per mile or a fixed fee within a certain radius plus a per mile charge for trips outside the radius; some companies charge for extra services such as the administration of oxygen. Some towns and cities assess a fixed fee per resident and provide ambulance services to all residents.

Back to our heart attack patient—which hospital should he be taken to? Does he have a family physician who would prefer he were in one particular hospital? Not all hospitals have emergency rooms, and those that do, do not necessarily have a physician or nurse there twenty-four hours per day—these providers may be "on call." If the ambulance has no way of warning the emergency room of its impending arrival, the staff "on call" will be notified only upon arrival of our patient instead of being on hand when he arrives. From start to finish, only an organized system of emergency medical care will save our heart attack patient.

In 1966, Congress passed the Highway Safety Act, which required states to undertake a systematic evaluation of existing ambulance services. This led to state laws on standards of care, criteria of competence, licensure regulations, duty to render aid and Good Samaritan laws, consent to treatment, and traffic regulations. One intention of the act was to upgrade emergency medical services nationwide while leaving the particulars of local operation up to the states. In 1973, the Emergency Medical Services Systems Act was passed. Its purpose was to authorize the secretary of HEW to provide grant and contract money to states, city governments, and public or private nonprofit agencies to plan, improve, and expand comprehensive and integrated systems for providing emergency medical services. Despite these grants, many cities still have a long way to go before their services can be considered both adequate and coordinated.

Weekends (particularly Saturday) generate the most demand for ambulance services, 3:00 P.M. to 6:00 P.M. are the busiest hours, and summer is the busiest season. Demands are highest in urban census tracts with high concentrations of (1) people of low socioeconomic status, (2) families of high mobility, (3) commercial land and high employment (people on the job generate more calls for heart attacks), and (4) freeways. Demand also increases with housing density, nonwhite population, male unemployment, females in the labor force, and increased numbers of aged and children.[15] Because of these ingredients, commercial ambulance services find it difficult to make a profit. Many commercial agencies prefer to contract with clinics and businesses to provide ambulance services in case of emergency. Volunteer services are decreasing as their questionable quality leads government officials toward paid "professional" attendants. Communities thus find themselves with a "crazy-quilt" pattern of emergency medical systems consisting of services working in a vacuum.

Red Cross

The American Red Cross can be classified as a "voluntary social welfare agency," since it provides primary medical care only in the military and in civilian nursing. A congressional charter authorizes the American Red Cross to act as the medium of voluntary relief and communication between the American people and their armed forces and to carry on a system of national and international relief to prevent and mitigate suffering caused by disasters. But the American Red Cross has been plagued by misunderstanding and a "bad image." Our purpose here is to examine how this massive volunteer structure functions, and how it affects the delivery of health care at the community level.

War provided the original inspiration for the Red Cross. Henri Durant (1829-1910), a Swiss citizen, helped provide relief and supplies to the thousands of wounded on the battlefield at Solferino, Italy, and was so moved by the experience that he wrote A Memory of Solferino (1862), which proposed the training of volunteers and international cooperation for wartime relief efforts. In 1864, the Geneva Convention formalized the following principles: (1) in every country a national volunteer committee should be set up to aid the wounded, and (2) international agreements should proclaim neutrality for all ambulances, hospital personnel, and wounded. Eleven countries signed the Geneva Convention. Because of strong isolationist views, however, the United States did not sign until 1882; ratification was due to the single-minded efforts of Clara Barton, who had cared for the wounded on the battlefields of the Civil War. As the symbol of neutrality and as its logo, the Red Cross adopted a red cross on a white field, the reverse of the Swiss flag. Periodic Geneva conventions formulated principles covering shipwrecks, prisoners of war, and the treatment of civilians.

In 1905, the American National Red Cross became the contracting party of the Geneva Treaties. The 1905 charter, still in force, gives the American Red Cross two unique responsibilities. First, it renders health and welfare services to the armed forces in time of war. A 1953 congressional amendment allows the Red Cross to render peacetime services to the military; in turn, the military absorbs some of the Red Cross's expenses. (Inteference with Red Cross activities still is punishable under the Espionage Act.) Second, the American Red Cross provides national and international relief for victims of disasters such as pestilence, famine, fire, and floods. Until 1964, it was the only agency in the United States allowed to provide aid *in cash* and welfare to victims of major disasters. From 1964, when the Alaskan earthquake occurred, until April 1973, the federal government provided loans at 1 percent interest with a $5,000 forgiveness feature. The 1905 charter also exempted the American National Red Cross from all taxes and established it as an independent governmental agency, much like the postal service. Although the U.S. Supreme Court has never passed on the legal authority of the Red Cross, congressional committees, federal tax authorities, and the lower courts agreed that it is an integral part of the U.S. government.

Figure 7.1 shows the relationship between the International Red Cross and the American National Red Cross as well as the organization of the American National Red Cross. Eight members of the board of governors are appointed by the president of the United States, who is honorary chairman; thirty governors are elected by the chapters at a national convention; the governors themselves elect another twelve as "members-at-large." All properties, funds, rights, and interests acquired for or held by the local chapters are owned by the national corporation. Basic membership costs $1.00, and there are approximately 36 million members. Although the Red Cross is primarily a voluntary organization, it maintains a career staff that is responsible for the coordination and continuity of programs as well as for certain specific services to local chapters. Half the local chapters only have volunteer workers; the rest employ staff members in management, program direction, and fund raising.

Figure 7.1   Organizational Chart of the International Red Cross
and the American National Red Cross

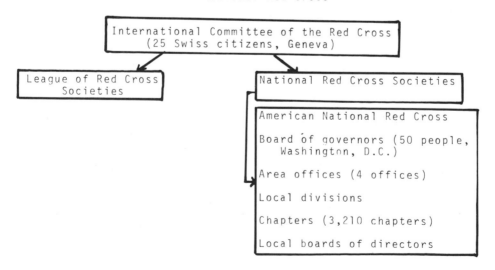

The American Red Cross has five areas of responsibility:

1. armed forces and veterans
2. disasters
3. international relations
4. voluntary services
5. health, education, and youth
    a. nursing program
    b. first aid, small craft, water safety activities
    c. blood programs
    d. youth programs

The Red Cross provides more funding for its armed forces–related activities than for any of its other activities. It provides all sorts of auxiliary services, including financial assistance to military personnel, military patients, and military dependents. Figure 7.2 shows the relationship between the responsibilities of the Red Cross and the government in natural disasters. The Red Cross cannot legally assume its responsibilities unless a responsible local government official requests it to do so. It gets involved in international relations by interceding on behalf of U.S. servicemen captured by hostile forces. It carries on an effort to recruit and train volunteers in every community. Volunteers provide personal services in nursing homes, hospitals, and prisons; they transport patients and provide laboratory and pharmacy assistance.

In 1971 54,600 registered nurses participated in the Red Cross nursing program, whose objectives are to maintain a volunteer staff for disaster relief, aid in community health projects, assist in the blood program, conduct health education courses, and provide information on general health, nutrition, and nursing skills. The Red Cross is the nation's largest collector of blood from voluntary donors. In 1971, 1700 chapters operating through fifty-nine regional programs collected 3.5 million units of blood. The Red Cross operates a computerized Rare Donor Registry and conducts research on human organ and platelet freezing and the use of immunoglobins. Youth programs are the Red Cross's greatest source of volunteers (6.5 million in 1971).[16]

The Red Cross claims that it is financed entirely by individual contributions. This claim, which may once have been true, is incorrect. In fact, income (as seen in Table 7.2[17]) is generated in a number of ways: 1,700 chapters conduct their own "March campaigns"; 750 chapters, because only part of their territory is included in the United Fund, must participate in both types of campaigns; 25 percent of the Red Cross's income comes from blood-related activities, either from federal research money or from the fees it charges for collecting, processing, and storing blood. In addition, the federal government pays all salaries and expenses of Red Cross personnel participating in military activity outside the United States.

FIGURE 7.2
Local Government Authority Disaster Coordinator

RESPONSIBILITIES OF GOVERNMENT	RESPONSIBILITIES OF RED CROSS
Protection of life, property, public health and welfare and the maintenance and repair of public property.	The relief of persons in need as a result of a disaster.
Financed by public agencies from tax funds.	Financed by Red Cross from voluntary contributions.

WHEN DISASTER THREATENS

GOVERNMENT:	RED CROSS:
-Issues official warnings and designates hazardous zones -Enforces evacuation from threatened areas -Provides means of rescue and evacuation and directs those operations -Organizes and coordinates all government departments and agencies involved	-Assists government agencies in disseminating official warnings -Coordinates Red Cross resources for voluntary evacuation -Mobilizes trained volunteers to assist in rescue -Transports and temporarily stores household goods.

WHEN DISASTER STRIKES

GOVERNMENT PROVIDES:	RED CROSS PROVIDES:
Emergency Community Services: Special police and fire protection Temporary housing, if disaster is declared major by the president Safeguards to public health and sanitation: repairs sewage and water systems Identification of the dead and care of the bodies, including temporary mortuaries Warning signs for hazardous buildings and dangerous areas	Emergency Mass Care Assistance: Food for disaster sufferers and volunteer workers Temporary shelter for those in need Medical and nursing aid Clothing
Community Welfare Services: Financial and medical assistance to eligible persons Social services for families, including rehabilitation; foster family placement; day care for children; services and care for the aged, the mentally retarded, and others with special needs; and basic casework	Emergency Services on an Individual Family Basis: Welfare inquiry and other information services Emergency orders for food, clothing, rent money, bedding, and similar essentials
Assistance in Community Restoration: Repairs highways and local roads Removal of debris from public property Restoration of public transportation and communication facilities Repair of public buildings like schools and hospitals Inspection of private property for health and safety concerns Salvage of unclaimed property	Aid for Recovery to Families: Casework services Food, clothing, and other maintenance until normal sources of support are restored Building and repair of owner-occupied homes Household furnishings Medical and nursing care Occupational supplies and equipment
Aid for Recovery to Families: Disaster loan programs, provided by such groups as the Small Business Administration or the Farmers Home Administration Specialized counseling and advice to families provided through public health, agriculture and other government agencies	

Table 7.2   Statement of Income and Expenditures of the American
National Red Cross, For the Year Ending June 30, 1973

Income:

Contributions:
Fund campaign contributions	$117,493,484
For disaster relief operations	18,297,511
For youth service programs	769,323
Legacies and bequests	3,982,115
Other contributions	6,058,891
Total contributions	146,601,324
Interest and dividends from investments	7,824,181
Blood program products, civilian and federal hospital participation fees, U.S. Government research grants and contracts and miscellaneous	48,186,889
Other	8,276,867
Total income	210,889,261

Expenditures:

Service to the members of the armed forces, veterans, and their families	50,012,784
Disaster preparedness and relief	37,692,842
Blood program	59,873,522
Community health and safety programs:	
Home nursing, mother and baby care, mother's aide, and other health training	4,137,445
First aid, small craft, water safety, and accident prevention training	9,640,799
Youth service programs:	
For general programs	4,339,703
For local and international projects	755,414
Community volunteer programs	9,871,313
International relations	854,701
Membership and fund raising	3,845,379
Management and general	16,331,427
Acquisition of and capital improvements to land and buildings	5,152,952
Total expenditures	202,503,341
Excess of Income over expenditures	8,380,920

Overhead—expenditures for membership and fund raising, management, and general expenses—is approximately 9 percent of expenditures. But Red Cross accounting is deceptive: Red Cross staff actively participates in United Fund drives (many local United Funds give up to 20 percent of the money they collect to the Red Cross); for some mysterious reason, their salaries are not classified as overhead. In 1972, it should be noted, income exceeded expenditures by some $8 million. Where this money goes is unclear; it may well go into a reserve fund for disasters. The Department of Defense audits the Red Cross's books. In June 1973, the director of the Red Cross claimed that several years of severe catastrophes had reduced the disaster reserves to absolute zero.[18]

Much of the criticism directed at the Red Cross is petty.[19] However, some of it is serious and deserves further examination. Some of the most frequent charges are:[20]

1. lethargic bureaucratic bungling during recent disasters
2. boards chosen on the basis of status rather than performance
3. stodgy conservatism toward the initiation of new programs
4. no effort made to devise a national policy on blood supplies
5. duplication of services, often in a less proficient manner
6. internal friction between local and national staffs

The Red Cross even denies its denial that it has performed inefficiently. It has made attempts to initiate new health-related programs, but often these efforts amount to tokenism. It still maintains enough strength in its collection and delivery of blood products, but its participation in armed forces–related activities can be expected to decline, at least temporarily.

Blood Banks

Two battles—one philosophical, the other territorial—have shaped up over a small, but important, component of the health care delivery system. Should blood be considered a gift or a commercial product, a drug or a medical service? We shall look at the implications in the answers to this question.

In 1937, the first civilian blood bank was established in Chicago's Cook County Hospital. In 1943, an anticoagulant was developed that preserved blood for twenty-one days and allowed for the widespread use of blood banks. In 1948, the American National Red Cross established the first of its fifty-nine regional blood centers to supply blood for both civilian and military medical procedures. Table 7.3 shows the growth in blood banks from 1961 to 1971.[21] Most blood banks are hospital-based; only a few are free-standing. The American Association of Blood Banks (AABB) defines a *blood bank* as a medical facility that recruits at least 100 donors per year, draws, processes, stores, and distributes human whole blood and its derivatives. An institution that does not meet these criteria but receives sources is sometimes classified as a transfusion service. In addition, pharmaceutical firms directly operate an unknown number of commercial blood banks, which rely heavily on a method of drawing blood known as *plasmapheresis*. In plasmapheresis, after the donor has given a

Table .7.3 Number of Blood Banks and Transfusion Services
            and Units of Blood Drawn, 1961 and 1971

	1961	1971
Hospital-based blood banks	4,400	5,124
Non-hospital blood banks	123	217
Red Cross regional blood centers	55	59
Total facilities	4,578	5,400
Units of blood collected (in millions)	6.2	8.8

pint of blood, the red cells are separated from the plasma and injected back into the donor. Under ideal conditions, an individual can make several plasmapheresis donations per week. Of the known blood banks in 1971, 53 percent were nonprofit, 35 percent were government-owned, and 12 percent were proprietary. At present, the Red Cross draws and processes 45 percent of all units of blood.

The first dilemma of blood banks concerns the morality of the marketplace. The opposing views are:

1. The donation of blood is a gift, a gesture beyond price; blood is not an economic good and to associate it with a commercial market is to degrade the donor; donating blood is a moral gesture that society should encourage; shortages of blood exist because of self-seeking commercialism.

2. There is no essential difference between blood and many other commodities normally exchanged in the market place; the absence of payment to the personal supplier means that the recipient of blood does not pay the full cost of the commodity and hence is not discouraged from wasting it (20 percent of all blood units are wasted); less blood is supplied than would be if payment were made; shortages are caused by fickle philanthropy.[22]

The dilemma boils down to paid donors versus voluntary donors and the wide range in between. Table 7.4 estimates the sources of blood as a percentage of donors and as a percentage of blood units.[23]

Few individuals give blood with no strings attached. In 1967, hospitals began to experience shortages of blood; as a result, elective surgery often had to be postponed.[24] All sorts of schemes have been devised to get volunteer blood—from football tickets to the requirement that blood bills be paid with blood from friends rather than with money. Patients may even have to get predeposits of blood before surgery is performed, or a cost penalty may be incurred if blood is not replaced after surgery. Some companies have set up "assurance clubs," and communities have established "blood replacement plans."

In the United States the paid donor is a major source of blood.[25] Blood banks that pay donors are sometimes located along skid row and use

Table 7.4 Estimates of Source of Blood by Donors and Blood Units in the United States, 1965-1967

Source of Blood	Percentage of Donors[a]	Percentage of Blood Units
Paid or professional donor	47	29
Paid-induced voluntary	3	4
Responsibility fee or family credit	39	52
Captive voluntary	4	5
Fringe benefit voluntary	1	1
Voluntary community	7	9

a Includes plasmapheresis programs.

questionable recruiting practices and standards in attracting donors, who are often derelicts, winos, and individuals with contagious diseases.[26] Serum hepatitis is a major problem:

> The best available statistics (and these are none too good) show that hepatitis in the blood of paid donors occurs in about 30 cases per 1000, as opposed to 3 cases per 1000 among volunteers. It is estimated that 1 in 150 patients receiving transfusions is inoculated with the disease, and of these, 15 percent of persons over 40 years of age die from it. The Center for Disease Control in Atlanta estimates that hepatitis resulting from transfusions accounts for some 3,500 deaths a year, but many doctors believe that, because of unreliable and inconsistent reporting, the total is closer to 35,000. The Australian antigen test developed a few years ago is now almost universally used, but this test detects hepatitis in only 25% of affected blood.[27]

The risk of contracting serum hepatitis from transfusions derived from prison and skid row populations is at least ten times that from the use of voluntary donors. Paid donors are less likely to respond accurately to medical histories and are more likely to wander from blood bank to blood bank in search of $15 donating sessions. Ironically, hospital blood banks located in wealthy suburban areas pay $25 to $30 for a pint of blood. Commercial blood banks, after processing the blood, turn around and sell it to hospitals or drug companies, so that the consumer is charged a considerable amount more than the donor is paid. Neither the donor nor the recipient has much control over the process, which is a significant change from the days when blood was transfused directly from the arm of a donor to the arm of a recipient (as in World War II battle movies).

Because it is difficult to establish negligence in serum hepatitis cases, a blood recipient who contracts the disease may seek recovery by bringing suit against a hospital or blood bank. Originally, the courts refused to apply product liability principles (if someone sells a customer a faulty product, the customer may recover his original cost or even damages) to blood cases. Later, several courts applied the principle; most states then enacted laws that expressly provide that the *furnishing of blood is a medical service* and that no warranties are implied in blood transfusions. Therefore, it is necessary to prove negligence in order to establish liability (for example, if the blood was labeled with an incorrect blood type).[28]

The blood banks' second major problem is the territorial battle between the AABB and the American Red Cross (ARC).[29] The AABB is the national organization that includes most hospital blood banks, but it has never developed a simple, unified donor-recruiting program. Instead, hospitals guard donor lists, penalize nondonors who are recipients, and make individual arrangements with donors. By contrast, the ARC's unified program treats donors equally. The AABB and ARC have fought in community after community across the United States for control of blood collection. In 1973, the secretary of health, education and welfare took two steps. First, the governmental regulatory authority for blood was placed (in the Bureau of Biologics) within the Food and Drug Administration. The bureau *declared blood to be a product,* subject to regulatory authority whether shipped interstate or intrastate. In July 1973, HEW announced a National Blood Policy that would reorganize the blood service system. A major objective of the policy is to establish an all voluntary blood donation system and eliminate the commercial system. However, leeway is given on the question of credits and penalty fees. Whether the paid donor can be eliminated without creating a blood shortage remains to be seen. The AABB and the ARC have been forced to merge their policy boards into the American Blood Commission, and there are indications that the two organizations may not be able to work together.

Summary

Volunteers are being phased out of emergency medical transportation, but are actively sought in the donation of blood. The American Red Cross puts a great deal of emphasis on volunteers and donations and quietly derives income from other sources. In many communities, emergency medical transportation, the Red Cross, and blood banks are disorganized, fragmented, and misunderstood, but at the same time those who are going through personal health crises deeply appreciate them.

Questions

1. You are the president of the local unit of the American Heart Association. The president of Americans for National Tax Reform comes to your town. She wants to debate you on the topic: "Resolved: Charitable Contributions Should Not Be Tax Deductible." Her organization believes that wealthy individuals pay less taxes than they should, they take advantage of "loopholes" by picking out pet organizations and centering their social life on these organizations. Your goal in the debate is to defend the present tax system and your association. Outline your arguments.

2. You are in charge of a blood donor drive. What methods would you use to induce donors to participate? How much money or man hours should you use to induce participation?

3. What implied warranties are involved in blood transfusion?

4. Should the legal standards of care that apply to emergency rooms apply also to ambulances—that is, all patients must be transported, regardless of ability to pay?

5. To what hospital should an ambulance driver take a patient if the patient is unconscious and no one knows anything about the patient's background?

Notes

1. John J. Hanlon, *Principles of Public Health Administration* (St. Louis: C. V. Mosly, 1969), pp. 241-49.

2. Ibid., p. 246.

3. S. Levine, P. White, and B. Paul, "Community Interorganizational Problems in Providing Medical Care and Social Services," *AJPH* 53:1183-95 (August 1963).

4. Richard Carter, *The Gentle Legions* (New York, N.Y.: Doubleday & Co., 1961), p. 299.

5. Ibid., p. 299.

6. C. W. Hartman and L. Thomas, "Sweet Charity Gone Sour: San Francisco's United Fund," *Society* 12:54-58 (November/December 1974).

7. Robert H. Hamlin, *Voluntary Health and Welfare Agencies in the United States* (New York: Schoolmaster's Press, 1961).

8. *Uniform Standards of Accounting and Reporting for Voluntary Health and Welfare Organizations.* National Health Council and National Social Welfare Assembly, 1964.

9. Alan M. Nahum, "Emergency Medical Care Systems," *JAMA* 217:1530-32 (13 September 1973).

10. John Hanlon, "Emergency Medical Care as a Comprehensive System," *Health Services Reports* 88:579-87 (August/September 1973).

11. Irona W. West et al., "Emergency Medical Transportation," *California Medicine* 116:35-43 (February 1972).

12. Triage is a concept developed on the battlefield. Soldiers who will die if they do not receive immediate treatment are treated first. Soldiers who will live regardless of whether they are treated immediately get treated second. Soldiers who will die regardless of whether they are treated immediately get treated third or not at all. A trained dispatcher can make these decisions based on a description of the patient and thereby allocate ambulances.

13. "Ambulance Aid Found Deficient," *New York Times,* 19 August 1973, pp. 33 and 46. "Mobile Units to Treat Heart-Attack Victims Gain Widespread Use," *Wall Street Journal,* 27 November 1973, pp. 1 and 25.

14. R. J. Joling, "Legal Aspects of Emergency Medical Services," *Journal of Trauma* 15:392-97 (May 1975); also, West, "Emergency Medical Transportation," p. 42.

15. C. A. Aldrich et. al., "An Analysis of the Demand for Emergency Ambulance in an Urban Area," *AJPH* 61:1156-69 (June 1971).

16. American Red Cross publications 626, 1316, 1640, 893, 2507, 1157, 573, 1316, and 565; F. R. Dulles, *The American Red Cross* (New York: Harper & Row, 1950); Wesley A. Sturges, "The Legal Status of the Red Cross," *Michigan Law Review* 56:1-32 (November 1957).

17. American Red Cross, *The American National Red Cross Annual Report for the Year Ended June 30, 1973* (Washington, D.C.: ARC, 1973).

18. "Red Cross Puts Reserves at Zero," *New York Times,* 5 June 1973, p. 44.

19. Richard Carter, *The Gentle Legions* (1961), pp. 38-62.

20. August Gribbin, "Stodgy Ways Blur Its Mercy and Make the Red Cross a Bitten Hand," *National Observer,* 7 October 1972, pp. 1 and 18; David Adams, "The Red Cross: Organizational Sources of Operational Problems," *American*

Behavioral Science 13:392-403 (September 1969-70). The entire September issue focuses on organizational and group behavior in disasters. Organizations studied include the police, the general hospital, the Salvation Army, and the Department of Public Works.

21. *Health Resources Statistics* (1974), p. 423.

22. Michael H. Cooper and Anthony J. Culyer, *The Price of Blood* (London: Institute of Economic Affairs, 1968), pp. 10-11.

23. Richard Titmuss, "The Gift of Blood," *Transaction* 8:18-26 and 62 (January 1971). For an interesting review of the controversy Dr. Titmuss's publication aroused, see D. Mac N. Surgenor, "Human Blood and the Renewal of Altruism: Titmuss in Retrospect," *International Journal of Health Services* 2:443-53 (August 1972).

24. "Operations Postponed As Hospitals Encounter an Increasing Demand," *Wall Street Journal*, 1 March 1967, pp. 1 and 22.

25. A recent study of the blood-service complex could not determine the volume of paid blood. See U.S., DHEW, National Heart and Lung Institute, Summary Report: NHLI's blood resource studies (DHEW publication no. [NIH] 73-416). (Bethesda: National Institutes of Health, 30 June 1972).

26. One technique of reimbursing an alcoholic is to give him or her a slip of paper after he has donated a pint of blood; the paper is redeemable for a pint of whiskey at a nearby bar.

27. Constance Holden, "Blood Banking: Money Is At Root of System's Evil," *Science* 175:1344-48 (24 March 1972). Detection of hepatitis is difficult because of its long incubation period—sometimes up to six months. Newly developed detection tests will increase the predictability.

28. *Problems in Hospital Law*, 2nd ed. (Rockville, Md.: Aspen Systems Corp., 1974), p. 42.

29. Douglas Mac N. Surgenor, "Progress Toward a National Blood System," *New England Journal of Medicine* 291:17-22 (4 July 1974).

Further Reading

Collins, John A. "Problems Associated with a Massive Transfusion of Stored Blood." *Surgery* 75:274-95 (February 1974).

Cumming, P., et al. "Blood Services: Price and Public Policy." *Science* 180:385-89 (27 April 1973).

Freeze, Arthur S. "Trauma: The Neglected Epidemic." *Saturday Review* 55: 58-62 (13 May 1972).

Gibson, Geoffry. "EMS: A Facet of Ambulatory Care." *Hospitals* 47:59-60 (16 May 1973).

Gross, Malvern J. "A New Study of the Cost of Fund Raising in New York." *Philanthropy Monthly* 9:1-4 (April 1976).

Horn, Francis H. "The Voluntary Health Agency—Is It Still Necessary?" *Rhode Island Medical Journal* 57:367-72 (September 1974).

Kessel, Reuben A. "Transfused Blood, Serum Hepatitis, and the Coase Theorem," *Journal of Law and Economics* 17:265-89 (October 1974).

Oswatt, R. M., and Hoff, T. E. "The Motivations of Blood Donors and Nondonors: A Community Survey." *Transfusion* 15:68-72 (January-February 1975).

Prybil, Lawrence D. "Operational Characteristics of 911 Systems." *Hospital Progress* 56:64-69 (May 1975). "Size Scope of 911 Systems." *Hospital Progress* 56:51-54 (March 1975).

Swisher, John. "A National Blood Program for the U.S." *Archives of Internal Medicine* 135:1344-49 (October 1975).

"*U.S. Using Its Clout to Force Its Resolution in Blood Banking: Government* Impact on Hospital Practice." *Hospital Practice* 11:141, 146 (February 1976).

8. Medical Business in the Private Sector

There is much more hope for humanity from manufacturers who enjoy their work than from those who continue in irksome business with the object of founding hospitals.
—Alfred North Whitehead

Along with the for-profit components of the health care delivery system—such as proprietary hospitals, nursing homes, ambulances, and blood banks—there are private businesses that have an impact on the delivery of health care. With the exception of private investment analysis, which rarely gains wide public circulation, next to nothing has been written about the medical supplies and equipment industry. Slightly more is known about clinical laboratories; the pharmaceutical industry, starting in 1962, has come in for considerable criticism (some beyond reason).

Consulting Firms and Contractual Arrangements

A growing number of private companies contract with hospitals, group practices, and the government. Some of the services they can provide are:

1. fund raising and public relations
2. facility design and construction
3. medical information systems (computer technology): design and installation
4. accounting, financial, and investment management
5. manpower forecasting
6. continuing education
7. clinical, technical, and legal assistance

It is not unusual for a highly specialized consultant to charge $300 per day for his or her services. Consultants are an excellent means of supplementing and improving a wide range of specialized services, but technical advice, like personal advice, can be very good or impractical and useless.

Medical Supplies and Equipment

There is no reliable estimate of the number of different products manufactured in this field, but it probably exceeds 20,000.[1] Nor is there a reliable estimate of the number of manufacturers of these products. Medical products we might expect to find on the floor of a general hospital are: beds, bedpans, laundry supplies, chairs and dressers, thermometers, heating pads, dressings, syringes, monitoring devices, record-keeping systems, charts, wheelchairs, stretchers, cribs, intravenous hookup equipment, bottles and glasses, trays, charts, uniforms, signs, name plates, paging devices, and oxygen tents. This list does not include all the equipment required for x-ray, surgery, laboratory tests, and other specialized procedures or food preparation. Nor does it include the medical products a patient might use outside the hospital (such as hearing aids, crutches, braces, casts, whirlpool baths, and contraceptive devices). Nor does it include the equipment found in non-hospital-based institutions such as reducing spas, schools and private medical research organizations, or other independent practitioners, including dentists, optometrists, podiatrists, chiropractors, and veterinarians.

The companies that manufacture and distribute these products have quietly grown and prospered. Few restrictions are placed on them. Under the limited powers it was granted in 1938, the Food and Drug Administration could remove dangerous products from the market and control the promotion of spurious devices.[2] The Medical Device Amendments of 1976 gave the FDA new authority over the safety and effectiveness of medical devices, including many diagnostic products.[3] Medical devices are placed in three classes according to the difficulty in assuring their safety and effectiveness:

> Class I—General Controls: all devices are subject to general controls, which include the registration of manufacturers and record-keeping requirements.
> Class II—Performance Standards: devices for which general controls alone are insufficient to assure safety and effectiveness are required to meet performance standards established by the FDA. Performance standards may concern the construction, components, ingredients, and properties of the device.
> Class III—Premarket Approval: all implanted and life-supporting devices require FDA approval for safety and effectiveness before they can be marketed unless the FDA determines that premarket approval is not necessary.

Any manufacturer who develops a new device has to give the FDA ninety days notice before the product can go on the market. During this period, the FDA will determine the regulatory class to which the device belongs. The FDA continues to publish additional rules in the weekly *Federal Register*.

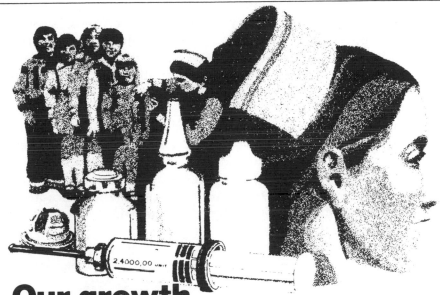

Our growth is healthy.

O-I's Kimble Division has
an impressive growth record.
One reason: our increasing
strength in the expanding health
care field. Kimble produces
precision laboratory products;
containers for injectable
and diagnostic applications;
and sophisticated systems
for blood collection,
transportation and
analysis. Kimble. It's
a name people trust.

OWENS-ILLINOIS

Toledo Ohio 43666

Clinical Laboratories

Laboratory medicine—a combination of hematology and pathology—began during World War I, when a number of clinical laboratories were established. Clinical laboratories examine human blood, urine, and tissue by microbiological, cytological, serological, immunohematological, hematological, chemical, biophysical, or pathological procedures so as to provide information for the diagnosis, treatment, and prevention of disease.

State and federal control over clinical laboratories is complicated. Twenty-four states, the District of Columbia, New York City, and Puerto Rico have requirements for clinical laboratories. Laboratories in hospitals accredited by the Joint Commission on Accreditation on Hospitals (JCAH) are automatically eligible for medicare reimbursement. Laboratories in nonaccredited hospitals and unlicensed independent laboratories are subject to medicare regulations. The Clinical Laboratories Improvement Act of 1967 provides for federal licensure of both hospital and independent laboratories—with two exceptions: (1) laboratories licensed in states whose laws are at least as stringent as federal laws and (2) laboratories that analyze no more than 100 specimens per year in each of six license categories. The laboratory accreditation programs of the American College of Pathologists and of the state of New York are the only two private programs to adjust their standards to comply with those established for interstate federal licensure.[4]

The first national census of clinical laboratories was conducted in 1971.[5] Since 80 to 85 percent of all clinical laboratories were included in the census, it may be concluded that in 1971 there were between 14,466 and 15,387 clinical laboratories in the United States. Clinical laboratories seem to be about equally divided in number between hospitals and private, non-hospital-based offices; the rest are in the state and local health departments (which have the primary responsibility for testing for contagious diseases, such as venereal diseases). Ninety-seven percent of the non-hospital-based independent clinical laboratories are privately owned.

In recent years, two innovations have changed the industry. In 1967, Technicon Corporation perfected the SMA-12, an instrument that can analyze sixty blood specimens per hour for twelve different components. Before this, tests on the twelve components had to be run separately. The savings from economies of scale are significant. Second, the SMA-12 can be put "on-line" to a computer, which means that the computer can directly analyze the values for the twelve components and print out the results on a medical report—again, the savings in man hours are immense. Other medical equipment—EKGs, EEGs, blood pressure and so on—can also be put "on-line" to a computer. In addition, samples need not be analyzed locally—instead, thousands of samples can be sent to a distant laboratory on a twenty-four hour basis. Ironically, whether a consumer realizes the savings from these devices is not up to the consumer or the laboratory. The patient's cost for these services is determined by the middleman—the hospital or the physician who ordered the tests; the markup on laboratory services can be substantial.

Drug Manufacturing and Wholesale Distribution

Before 1900, any drug, including narcotics, could be manufactured and sold by anyone. After a number of children contracted tetanus from a contaminated diphtheria antitoxin and died, the Virus-Toxin Law of 1902 (Biologics Control Act) was passed: licenses were now required for the manufacture and sale of *biologics* (any virus, therapeutic serum, toxin, antitoxin, or analogous product used for the prevention of disease). A number of other scandalous conditions prompted the Pure Food and Drug Act of 1906, which specified that certain drugs are to be sold by prescription only and that the federal government ensures that drug packages accurately state the names and quantities of the active ingredients. As a rule of thumb, a prescription drug (known as an *ethical drug*) is any drug of which two times the normal dose leads to harmful results. An over-the-counter drug (known as a *proprietary drug*) is any drug of which twenty times the normal dose is not fatal. Most new drugs start out as prescription drugs; only after a number of years of safe public usage does a drug become classified as an over-the-counter drug.

In 1938, a mistake by a chemist preparing an elixir of sulfanilamide with the S. E. Massingill Company led to deaths of 100 persons. Congress swiftly passed the Federal Food, Drug, and Cosmetic Act, which required that drugs must be proved safe before marketing and must be labeled. Drug manufacturing boomed after World War II. In 1953, the FDA became part of the Department of Health, Education, and Welfare. In 1961, large numbers of congenitally malformed babies were born to women who had taken thalidomide during their pregnancies. Fortunately, the stubborn insistence of FDA researcher Dr. Frances Kelsey had delayed the marketing of thalidomide in the United States. This near-tragedy and the Kefauver Senate hearings (the marketing practices and profits of pharmaceutical companies were scrutinized and severely criticized) prompted the passage of the 1962 Kefauver-Harris Drug Amendments. The amendments require drug manufacturers to submit proof that a new drug is safe and efficacious (effective) before it can be marketed, to give physicians information about a drug's side effects and contraindications as well as potential benefits, and to report (immediately) any unusual side effects before and after the drug is marketed.[6] The FDA also monitors ethical drug advertising for honesty. In addition, the National Academy of Sciences/National Research Council was assigned the responsibility for reviewing for efficacy the 4,349 drugs approved between 1938 and 1962.

NAS/NRC were asked to rate each drug in terms of four categories: (1) effective, (2) probably effective, (3) possibly effective, and (4) ineffective. As of February 1974, approximately 3,360 drugs had been reviewed; of these, 529 had been rated ineffective, and at least 450 had been removed from the market. The federal government will not reimburse for drugs rated "ineffective" or "possibly effective" in government-financed programs. In 1972, the U.S. district court in Washington, D.C., ordered NAS/NRC to complete the review within four years. In 1971, the FDA set up advisory committees for the purpose of evaluating over-the-counter drugs as safe and effective. The panels will provide effectiveness standards for an estimated 100,000 to 500,000 over-the-counter products. Removal of specific ingredients that cannot be clinically proven to be effective and required changes in label claims will be the most important problems facing the pharmaceutical industry.[7]

Drugs are known by three names:

1. chemical name—the terminology that defines its chemical structure, for example, 2 methyl—2 propyl—1, 3 propanediol dicarbonate
2. generic name—the established, short name for the drug, for example, meprobamate
3. brand or trade name—the registered trademark of a drug established by the owner of the trademark, for example, Miltown or Equanil

There are approximately 22,000 trade-name prescription drugs on the market for some 700 different chemical entities. New drugs can be patented. A patent is a legal right to exclusive ownership granted by the federal government for a period of seventeen years from the time the patent is issued. A patent holder may allow other companies to manufacture and sell his or her patented drug, usually in exchange for royalties. The patent system is supposed to ensure profits and protection for research and development resources invested in a new drug. Patents encourage discoveries, but they also allow a patent holder to reap monopolistic returns. A patent can cover new chemical entities and new processes of making drugs, but not dosage forms (tablets or capsules). Patents can be taken away (ruled invalid) if a company withholds critical information and knowingly presents false information to the patent office.[8]

Figure 8.1 shows the process of new drug development.[9] The FDA monitors almost each step in biological development; applications must be approved before clinical trials can begin and before final marketing begins. Five to seven years can elapse, and $2.5–$4.0 million dollars can be spent before a new product is marketed. For each successful product,

Figure 8.1   The Process of New Drug Development

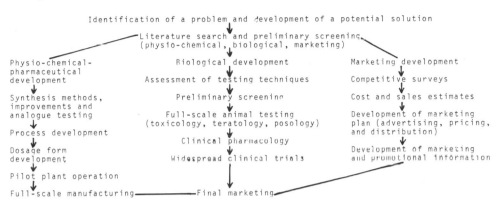

six to ten additional ones fail along the developmental process, which runs the cost of a successful new drug to an average $10–$11 million.[10] As seen in Figure 8.2,[11] the introduction of new clinical entities has decreased markedly since Congress passed the Kefauver-Harris Amendments, but introduction of new combinations and new dosage forms were decreasing before 1962. There has been much speculation about the cause-and-effect relationship between the decline in new drugs and the Kefauver-Harris Amendments.[12]

Although fewer new drugs are being introduced, the pharmaceutical industry has been highly profitable. As indicated in Table 8.1, the average net after-tax profits as a percentage of stockholders' equity, and net after-tax profits on sales for the drug industry, have consistently run higher than those for all U.S. manufacturing corporations.[13] Ordinarily, in evaluating an industry, one might hypothesize that the greater the risks, the larger the returns. After all, risk results from aggressive competition, volatile upturns and downturns in revenues (cycles of major break-through discovery followed by a long dry spell), and constant business failures. But the drug industry has experienced no major corporation failures in the past twenty-five years and little change in the percent share of the prescription market for the past ten years (when mergers are taken into consideration). Table 8.2 shows that the sixteen largest pharmaceutical companies have 68 percent of the prescription market.[14] Stock prices for drug companies have been sold at 155 to 165 percent of stock prices of industrials, and the price/earnings ratio (P/E ratio) has been running around 27 to 35X.[15] The pharmaceutical industry is second only to mining in profitability.

Manufacturers' sales of prescription drugs have grown steadily. As indicated in Figure 8.3, sales of prescription drugs more than doubled between 1962 and 1971—from $1.89 billion to $4.11 billion (in wholesale value).[16] Cardiovascular drugs and drugs that affect the central nervous

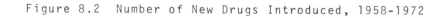

Figure 8.2 Number of New Drugs Introduced, 1958-1972

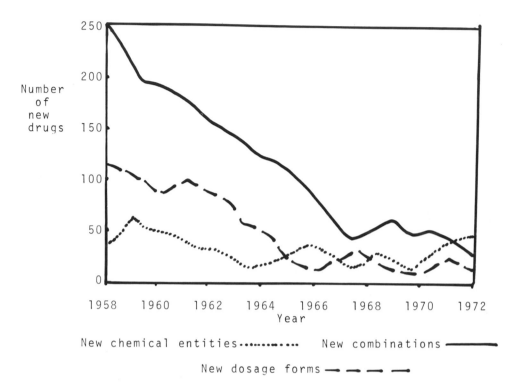

Table 8.1 Net Profit for Drug Companies and Manufacturing
Corporations (in percentages)

	On Stockholders' Equity		On Sales	
Year	Drug Manufacturers	All U.S. Manufacturing Corporations	Drug Manufacturers	All U.S. Manufacturing Corporations
1973-3Q	19.8	12.3	10.7	4.6
1973-2Q	18.6	14.0	10.1	5.1
1973-1Q	19.7	11.6	10.5	4.5
1972	18.6	10.6	10.2	4.3
1971	17.9	9.7	9.5	4.2
1970	18.2	9.4	9.4	4.0
1969	18.7	11.7	9.6	4.3
1968	18.4	12.2	9.7	5.1
1967	18.7	11.8	10.1	5.0
1966	20.8	13.6	10.8	5.6
1965	20.5	13.1	11.3	--
1964	18.4	11.7	10.7	--

Source: Calculated from information available in Quarterly Financial Report for
Manufacturing Corporations, Federal Trade Commission-Securities and Exchange
Commission.

Table 3.2   Dollar Volume of Prescription drugs and Percentage Share of Prescription Market, for the Sixteen Largest Companies

Company	Pharmaceutical Divisions	1972 Dollar Volume Sales of Prescription Drugs (in million dollars)	Percentage Share of Prescription Market
Hoffmann La Roche	Roche	271.2	9
American Home Products	Ayerst, Wyeth, Ives	221.2	8
Merck	Merck, Sharpe & Dohme	206.0	7
Eli Lilly & Co.	Lilly, Elanco	188.5	6
Warner-Lambert	Warner-Chilcott, Parke-Davis	122.5	4
CIBA-Geigy	Ciba, Geigy	131.8	4
Smith Kline & French	--	121.0	4
Squibb	--	110.3	4
Chas. Pfizer & Co.	Pfizer, Roerig	103.2	4
Bristol-Myers	Bristol, Mead-Johnson	95.0	3
Searle	--	89.5	3
Upjohn	--	84.4	3
Abbott	Abbott, Ross	81.7	3
Burroughs Wellcome	--	80.5	3
Schering	--	66.0	2
Sterling	Winthrop, Breon	39.3	1
Total			68

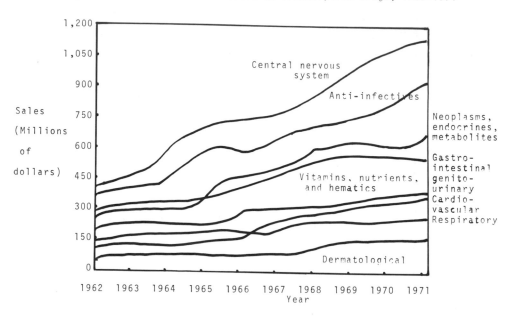

Figure 8.3 Manufacturers' Sales of Prescription Drugs, 1962-1971

system demonstrated sharp increases. About 76 percent of the pharmaceutical industry's sales are prescription drugs, and these sales are distributed as follows:

Wholesalers	46.4 percent
Retail pharmacies	30.0
Hospital pharmacies	20.8
Practitioners	1.5
Federal government	0.9

These figures do not include foreign sales, which are about half of U.S. sales but are increasing faster than U.S. sales. Approximately 1.5 billion drug prescriptions are written per year—an average of twenty per capita per year. The average cost of a prescription continues to climb despite little change in the cost per unit (pill or dose) of medicine; the reason is that more medicine is being prescribed per prescription.

The sales dollar for the leading pharmaceutical house breaks down as follows:

1. cost of goods sold	35 percent
2. general and administrative	10
3. marketing	25
4. research and development	7
5. total costs	77

6. gross income		23
a. corporate income tax	10	
b. net income	13	
7. total revenues		100

The pharmaceutical industry pays relatively less tax than the average middle-class taxpayer. Nearly four times as much money is spent on marketing as is spent on research and development. Marketing expenses include the salaries of detail men (individuals who call on physicians to explain new drugs and encourage physician acceptance of their company's products); direct mail pieces, including imprinted rulers, ashtrays, and samples; seminars; educational films; exhibits at conventions; underwriting the cost of medical conventions; advertisements in health journals; and special advertising (giveaways such as golf balls, freezers, trips to the Caribbean—sometimes based on how much is prescribed). Prescription drugs are among the few items available for sale in the United States about which the consumer exercises few decisions in his purchase; physicians decide which drug is purchased, and as a consequence, drug manufacturers spend more than $5,000/physician/year trying to influence their prescribing preferences. Drug companies are even generous enough to give medical students black bags and discounts on the other accoutrements of practice. Manufacturers allow wholesalers and retailers to return unsold merchandise for credit.

Total retail sales of all over-the-counter drugs were $2.9 billion in 1971. As indicated in Figure 8.4, cough and cold medicines and internal analgesics (such as aspirin) are big sellers.[17] Some nonprescription drugs advertised heavily. This advertising is watched over by the Federal Trade Commission, which must sort out the numerous claims and counterclaims that aspirin and buffered aspirin manufacturers make.

A drug wholesaler consolidates large quantities of different manufacturers products and distributes them in smaller quantities to retail outlets. Wholesalers may stock 100,000 items, or two to three times the number of different items the average retailer may stock. In many instances, wholesalers can provide one-day service for hard-to-find items; rapid distribution is one of their services. Since World War II, pharmaceutical manufacturers have been bypassing wholesalers and selling directly to retailers. Pharmacies increasingly have been willing to stock larger inventories in order to avoid the wholesaler's markup. However, wholesalers have responded by stocking increasing numbers of other drugstore items (from shampoo to paperback books).

The pharmacy industry has been criticized for more than just their profits. In 1973, after reviewing the number of punitive FDA actions against each company, the Council on Economic Priorities found that several companies were weak in terms of safety, efficacy, and research

Figure 8.4   Consumer Expenditures for Non-prescription
              Drugs, 1960-1971

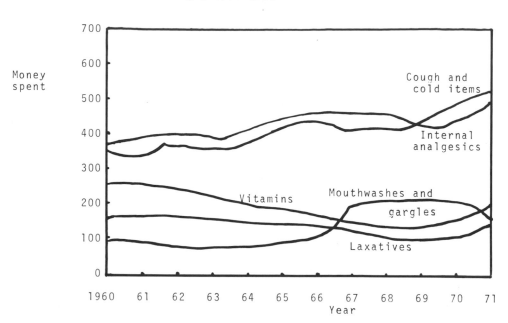

productivity.[18] Abbott Laboratories and Bristol-Meyers were singled out
as having had problems with their quality control. Smith Kline was rated
worst in a review of efficacy: only one of the sixty-two drugs it
introduced before 1962 was rated effective for all indications. Smith Kline
also had no drugs on a list of fifty-six significant drugs introduced from
1966 to 1973.

In April 1973, the Monopolies Commission in the United Kingdom
concluded that Hoffman-LaRoche had been profiteering in the sale of
Librium and Valium, the world's leading tranquilizers. The commission
based its rulings on the large disparity in selling prices for the same drug in
different countries. Next, the Common Market Commission moved
against the company in Europe. These price inquiries may stimulate price
inquiries in the United States. Late in 1973, HEW announced it was moving
to a generic price base for prescription reimbursement on medicare,
medicaid, and all other prescription drugs it paid for in programs it
administered. The drug industry then waged a long and bitter battle to
block imposition of the cost controls, which would limit federal purchases
under medicare and medicaid to the lowest-priced generally available
product. Under the plan (called MAC), maximum allowable costs would
be established for a drug, and only that amount would be paid by the
government. If a physician ordered a higher-priced product, a pharmacist
would not be able to fill the prescription under medicaid unless the
physician noted on the prescription that the higher-priced product was

necessary for the patient. Sales of Darvon, Orinase, and antibiotics such as ampicillin and penicillin should be affected.

Physicians fear that the new regulations might intefere with their freedom to prescribe, and the drug industry claims that inferior products will be purchased. The proposal was supposed to go into effect April, 1976, but the program has been delayed. The cost controls will probably lower retail prices by encouraging more competition within the industry and will give pharmacists more autonomy in the selection of drugs.[19] Currently, 10 percent of all prescriptions are written generically. When a prescription specifies a trade-name drug, the pharmacist must fill the prescription with that drug; however, when it specifies a generic drug, the pharmacist may fill it with any generic equivalent on his or her shelves. Sometimes this saves money for the consumer, but not always. Pharmacists should find the MAC generic pricing plan to their liking, since it restores some of their lost professional status.

Pharmacy

Pharmacy is one of the most interesting systems of health care: it is to some extent an independent practitioner, yet it is also dependent on physicians, drug manufacturers, the government, and the consumer. Obviously, it has come a long way from the corner apothecary store that ministered to the neighborhood ills.

Early drugstores were of three types: (1) stores owned by physicians and operated by them and their apprentices, (2) stores owned by pharmacists who had either migrated to the United States or had served as apprentices, and (3) general stores that stocked the drugs and sidelines customarily found in apothecary shops. Around the middle of the eighteenth century, pharmacy and medicine gradually became differentiated. In the early 1800s, pharmacies were often combinations of miniature importing establishments, manufacturing plants, wholesale drug houses, and community pharmacies. Four southern states led the way in pharmacy licensing (Louisiana, 1808; South Carolina, 1817; Georgia, 1825; Alabama, 1852). Drugs and medicines could no longer be purchased from a general store (unless a pharmacist was present).

The first drug "chains," or drugstores under common ownership, began to appear around 1900, primarily through the independent efforts of Charles R. Walgreen and Louis K. Liggett.[20] The chains grew fast and adopted price-cutting techniques. However, the depression of the 1930s dampened the appeal of price competition. Many states adopted *fair trade laws*, which allowed manufacturers and retailers to set a uniform minimum price for their products. The National Association of Retail Druggists (NARD), an organization composed largely of pharmacist-owners of drugstores, was a strong advocate of fair trade principles and lobbyist for fair trade legislation. From 1937 to 1951, fair trade laws proved to be legally sound and allowed drug manufacturers and retailers to fix prices under what was known as a *resale price maintenance contract.* In 1951, however, the U.S. Supreme Court held that those who do not sign these contracts are not bound to respect minimum prices established by the contractual arrangements of others.[21] The Schwegmann decision set off gigantic price wars, and eventually the fair trade edifice crumbled. Chain pharmacies began to take advantage of their economies of scale and sell drugs at lower prices.

The major legal barrier to pharmacist control over drugs has been the Durham-Humphrey Amendment (1951) to the Federal Food, Drug and Cosmetic Act. This amendment prohibited pharmacists from dispensing "legend" drugs (drugs that must bear the following legend, "Caution: federal law prohibits dispensing without a prescription") on his or her own accord without a physician's prescription. According to the amendment, however, a pharmacist is the only one, aside from a physician, who may legally dispense legend drugs. Nurses and other health care providers are not allowed to do so. A *pharmacist* is a health provider who dispenses legend drugs on the prescription of a licensed physician, dentist, or veterinarian. Any individual can sell nonlegend or over-the-counter drugs, but since the demand for many nonlegend drugs is so sporadic, drugstores may be the only retail outlets that stock them.

In 1973, the United States had 132,900 active licensed pharmacists and a pharmacist/population ratio of 62.6/100,000, a ratio that has been declining slightly.[22] Active pharmacists are distributed over the following types of practices:

1. community pharmacy   83 percent
2. hospital pharmacy   10
3. manufacturing and wholesale   4
4. teaching, government, and other   3

Of all community pharmacists, 42.3 percent own or are partners in their pharmacies, a percentage that has been slowly decreasing as more pharmacists become employees. Of the detail men employed by manufacturers and wholesalers, 10 to 15 percent are pharmacists. There are seventy-four colleges of pharmacy, which graduate approximately 16,000 pharmacists per year. Most colleges have a five-year program; upon graduation, a student receives a bachelor of science in pharmacy (B.S.) or a bachelor of pharmacy (B. Pharm.). To become a registered pharmacist, a pharmacist must spend a one-year postgraduate apprenticeship under a registered pharmacist. Pharmacy assistants aid in the storage and maintenance of an inventory of drugs, and pharmacy technicians perform the repetitive tasks in preparing and distributing medications.

In 1973, the 50,602 pharmacies in the United States were distributed as follows:

1. chain pharmacies: 10,604
2. independent pharmacies: 39,998
3. hospital pharmacies: 5,174

Approximately 2,000 hospitals had no pharmacy. Both pharmacies and pharmacists are required to have a state license. So many organizations are related to drug distribution that one needs a score card (Figure 8.5[23]) to keep track of them. Not all these organizations have the same philosophy or compatible goals.

A practicing pharmacist generally dispenses a prescription drug according to the following procedure:[24]

1. receives the prescription (3 to 5 percent of all prescriptions go unfilled because patients fail to purchase the drugs)
2. certifies the prescription order (checks physician's narcotics number, etc.)
3. prepares the prescription (well over 98 percent of prescriptions dispensed are prefabricated; less than 2 percent require compounding)
4. labels the prescription (label instructions must be clear)
5. certifies the finished prescription (label matches contents)
6. issues the prescription to the patient (gives advice and makes sure the patient understands instructions)

Pharmacists also supervise other personnel, control inventory and purchases, and, in some instances, look after the pharmacy's other activities (finances, hiring, accounting, and so on).

Pharmacists are struggling to maintain a "professional" identity.[25] In theory, at least, a professional—especially in the delivery of health care—is more concerned with helping other people, technical proficiency, and the client's welfare than with business interests and making a profit. Thus, the reasoning goes, the more business activities a health provider has, the less "professional" he or she is. Our discussion of pharmacy thus takes us into advertising, fees for service, markups, prices, ownership, and chain stores.

Pharmacists price their product in two ways: (1) fee for service and (2) percentage markup on cost. Table 8.3 shows how these two methods of pricing differ on high and low cost prescriptions: As these examples show, a fee-for-service method will make the low-cost drug more expensive than the markup method would, but the opposite occurs with the high-cost drug—even though it may take exactly the same amount of

142

Figure 8.5 Major Pharmacy Organizations and Their
            Constituents

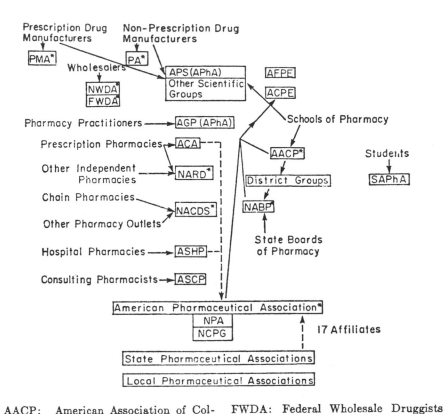

AACP: American Association of Colleges of Pharmacy

ACA: American College of Apothecaries

ACPE: American Council on Pharmaceutical Education

AFPE: American Foundation for Pharmaceutical Education

AGP: Academy of General Practice of Pharmacy

APhA: American Pharmaceutical Association

APS: Academy of Pharmaceutical Sciences

ASCP: American Society of Consultant Pharmacists

ASHP: American Society of Hospital Pharmacists

FWDA: Federal Wholesale Druggists Association

NABP: National Association of Boards of Pharmacy

NACDS: National Association of Chain Drug Stores

NARD: National Association of Retail Druggists

NCPG: National Catholic Pharmacists Guild

NPA: National Pharmaceutical Association

NWDA: National Wholesale Druggists Association

PA: Proprietary Association

PMA: Pharmaceutical Manufacturers Association

SAPhA: Student American Pharmaceutical Association

Dotted lines indicate affiliation.

_____
* Member, National Drug Trade Conference.

Table 8.3 Pricing Methods of Pharmacists

	Low-cost Prescription		High-cost Prescription	
	Fee for Service ($1.50)	Markup (50%)	Fee for Service ($1.50)	Markup (50%)
Cost of good sold	$2.00	$2.00	$10.00	$10.00
Pharmacy expense	1.50	1.00	1.50	5.00
Price to consumer	$3.50	$3.00	$11.50	$15.00

work to dispense both drugs. Fee-for-service pricing is considered more "professional," but many large stores use the markup method.

Most professions' codes of ethics and licensing laws prohibit advertising and the solicitation of customers. In pharmacy, this has taken the form of forbidding the advertising of prescription drug prices.[26] Such restrictions exist in thirty-five states. Pharmacists have maintained that advertising is unprofessional, that it depreciates the profession and makes it a business rather than a part of the health care team. Studies have revealed a wide variation of prices for prescription drugs among pharmacies in the same community,[27] a fact that has been attributed to a lack of competition due to restrictions on advertising.[28]

In May 1976, the U.S. Supreme Court held that "commercial speech" of all kinds is protected by First Amendment guarantees of free expression.[29] In so doing, it upheld a Virginia case initiated by a consumer group and the state AFL-CIO against the Virginia State Board of Pharmacy, a case in which a lower court held that a ban on such advertising violates the First Amendment right of consumers to receive essential information. This Supreme Court decision may bring an end not only to some pharmacy statutes that prohibit advertising, but also to similar statutes governing physicians, dentists, optometrists, and other health providers. For example, the Justice Department and the Federal Trade Commission have attacked advertising restrictions imposed by states and professional groups.[30]

Pharmacy boards have been more successful in controlling other aspects of their occupation. Fifteen states require that a pharmacist be on the premises during the hours a pharmacy is open for business. Four states (Michigan, North Dakota, South Dakota, and Montana) require pharmacies, or a certain percentage thereof, to be owned by pharmacists (minimum 25 percent pharmacist ownership seems to be the rule of thumb). The ownership requirement supposedly protects public health, since pharmacists might otherwise be subjected to improper pressure from nonpharmacist owners. In December 1973, the U.S. Supreme Court upheld North Dakota's right to restrict majority ownership of the state's pharmacy to registered pharmacists.[31] NARD and APA have opened a campaign to encourage state associations to seek legislation limiting pharmacy ownership.[32] On the other hand, pharmacy boards have been most unsuccessful in preventing discount pharmacies, chain pharmacies, mail order prescription purchase plans, pharmacies owned by food supermarkets, and in enforcing laws requiring pharmacist-managers and minimum drugstore operating hours.[33]

Independent community pharmacists tend to cling to the operational philosophy of high prices and low volume. However, chain pharmacies are taking a larger and larger share of the retail pharmaceutical market— because they draw a tremendous amount of traffic (customers). Soon the typical American pharmacy will be a cross between a department store, a supermarket, and a general store with a pharmacy. Gone will be the apothecary (stocks only drugs), or the "chemist," as it is known in the United Kingdom. Private enterprise and technological innovation will replace the corner pharmacy with a pharmacy strategically placed in a medical arts building or with a gigantic multipurpose store in a suburban shopping center.

Summary

Health industries in the private sector supply a vast amount of resources to the health care system. Some participants from the private sector claim altruistic goals, wish to be treated as "professionals," and have attempted to restrict competition, but others have been growing quietly at an unwavering pace with no particular regard for altrusim, unless a high rate of return on investment can be considered stockholder altruism. All participants in the private sector fear increasing government involvement unless that involvement means guaranteed reimbursement for their products or services.

Questions

1. The FDA does not have to show that a certain device is an "imminent hazard"before it can be removed from the market, as is the case with drugs. A showing that the device presents a substantial deception or a substantial and unreasonable risk is sufficient for its removal from the market. Why do you suppose there is one FDA standard for drugs and another for medical devices?

2. Is seventeen years too long or too short a time for the owner of a patent to reap monopolistic returns?

3. Should the pharmaceutical industry pay more taxes? If they do, the cost of medical care will rise. Consider other industries and personal income taxes in your answer.

4. Why might the same drug manufactured by the same company sell for different prices in different countries?

5. Can a pharmacist be a professional and a business person at the same time— are the two roles compatible? How does his role or identity compare with that of a "professional" football player? What is a professional?

6. Assume that the Supreme Court decides that any health care provider can advertise. Design a newspaper ad for a psychiatrist just starting his or her practice.

7. Assume you are a family practitioner in a state that is considering removing its prescription drug antisubstitution laws. You are opposed to this change. Why?

Notes

1. James L. Goddard, "The Medical Business," *Scientific American* 229:161-66 (September 1973).

2. In an upcoming chapter, we will discuss how the FDA moved on a curious black box promoted and used by Scientologists.

3. Linda R. Horton, "Medical Devices: Strengthening Consumer Protection," *FDA Consumer* 10:4-9 (October 1976). Horton cites a description by the FDA commissioner of a number of medical device problems that the FDA has had to deal with in recent years: "intrauterine devices that could perforate the uterus, poorly designed and manufactured artificial heart valves, faulty cardiac pacemakers, heart monitors that electrocuted patients or would not work, improperly designed respirators, electric beds that killed people, a cobalt therapy unit that crushed a woman to death, another that broke ribs . . . contaminated catheters, unsafe x-ray machines, inaccurate thermometers, unsterile disposable surgical sets, unsafe anesthesia machines, unsafe pumping oxygenators, and the list goes on."

4. *Health Resources Statistics* (National Center for Health Statistics, Washington, D.C.: Superintendent of Documents, 1974), pp. 427-28; M. M. Brooke, "Quality Clinical Laboratory Services for the American People," *Public Health Reports* 85:155-59 (February 1970).

5. *Lab World* 23:1262-64 (November 1972).

6. The FDA recently lost an interesting court case involving an in-home pregnancy kit. The judge ruled that the FDA has the authority only to regulate the sale of drugs that are designed to cure diseases; pregnancy, he said, is a normal physiological function of all mammals and cannot be considered a disease of itself. In 1969 the U.S. Supreme Court ruled that a device consisting of a piece of cardboard impregnated with chemicals prescribed for use in a litmus-type test to determine what kinds of antibiotics should be prescribed was a drug and could be regulated by the FDA. "Loss of Decision on Pregnancy Kits Concerns the FDA," *Wall Street Journal*, 21 July 1975, p. 17.

7. This brief history of legislation and regulation was pieced together from three sources: Goddard, "The Medical Business," pp. 162-65; Florence A. Wilson and Duncan Neuhauser, *Health Services in the United States* (Cambridge, Mass.: Ballinger Publishing Co., 1974), pp. 200-1; Hayden Stone Inc., "The Health Care Industry" (February 1974), pp. 13-14.

8. "Pfitzer Inc. Patent on Doxycycline Is Ruled Invalid," *Wall Street Journal*, 21 July 1975, p. 6.

9. Mickey C. Smith and David A. Knapp, *Pharmacy, Drugs and Medical Care* (Baltimore, Md.: Williams and Wilkins, 1972), p. 159.

10. Louis Lasagna, "Research Regulation and Development of New Pharmaceuticals: Past, Present and Future," parts 1 and 2, *American Journal of Medical Science* 263:8-18 and 67-78 (January and February 1972).

11. Goddard, "The Medical Business," p. 167.

12. Richard Landau, *Regulating New Drugs* (Chicago: University of Chicago Center for Policy Study, 1973).

13. Hayden Stone, Inc., "The Health Care Industry," p. 23.

14. *In Whose Hands? Safety, Efficacy and Research Productivity in the Pharmaceutical Industry* (New York: Council on Economic Priorities, August/November 1973), p. 4.

15. Hayden Stone, Inc., "The Health Care Industry," p. 29. The price/earnings ratio (price = price of a share of stock; earnings = yearly profits per share) is an indication of how favorably investors view the company's future profit performance. A higher than average P/E ratio (the P/E ratio for industrial companies) indicates that investors believe that these companies will enjoy continued high profitability.

16. Goddard, "The Medical Business," p. 163.

17. Ibid., p. 162.

18. Council on Economic Priorities (1973).

19. "Drug Industry Fails to Block U.S. Price Plan," *Wall Street Journal,* 28 July 1975, p. 3.

20. This short history is a combination of the following: Richard A. Deno et al., *The Profession of Pharmacy* (Philadelphia: J. B. Lippincott Co., 1966), pp. 44-53; and Edward Krewers and George Urdang, *History of Pharmacy* (Philadelphia: J. B. Lippincott Co., 1963).

21. F. Marion Fletcher, *Market Restraints in the Retail Drug Industry* (Philadelphia: University of Pennsylvania Press, 1967) pp. 54-67. *Schwegmann Bros.* v. *Calvert Distillers Corporation,* 341 US 384 (1951). See also *Dr. G. H. Tichenor Antiseptic Company* v. *Schwegmann Bros. Giant Super Markets,* 231 LA 51, 9050 2d 343 (1956).

22. *Health Resources Statistics,* 1974, pp. 243-45.

23. Mickey C. Smith and David A. Knapp. *Pharmacy, Drugs and Medical Care* (1972), p. 102.

24. Ibid., p. 18.

25. Norman K. Denzim, "Incomplete Professionalization: The Case of Pharmacy," *Social Forces* 46:375-82 (March 1968).

26. Richard B. Ruge, "Regulations of Prescription Drug Advertising: Medical Progress and Private Enterprise," *Law and Contemporary Problems* 32:650-73 (Autumn 1967).

27. "Daylight on Prescription Prices," *Money* 1:31-34 (October 1972). Douglas R. Mackintosh, "Drug Price Variation Among Outlets," *Louisiana Business Survey* 4:2-4 (April 1973).

28. *Consumer Federation of America,* "Prescription Drug Pricing: An Almost Total Absence of Competition" (Washington, D.C.: The Federation, September 1972).

29. "Justices Clear Competitive Ads for Drug Prices," *Wall Street Journal,* 25 May 1976, p. 3.

30. Industries and professions such as prescription eyeglasses, optometrists, physicians, and lawyers, have been scrutinized by the government on possible antitrust grounds.

31. Fletcher, *Market Restraints in the Retail Drug Industry,* pp. 174-203.

32. William V. Toffey, "Ownership Restrictions: Headed Nowhere!" *Drug Topics* (January 1957), p. 24.

33. Fletcher, *Market Restraints in the Retail Drug Industry*, pp. 204-74.

Further Reading

Arnow, L. Earle. *Health in a Bottle*. Philadelphia: J. B. Lippincott Co., 1970.

Brooke, Paul. "Why Do We Pay So Much for Prescription Drugs," *Business and Society Review* 13:25-27 (spring 1975).

Coleman, James S.; Katz, Eliker; and Menzel, Herbert. *Medical Innovation: A Diffusion Study*. Indianapolis, New York, and Kansas City: Bobbs-Merrill, 1966.

Doherty, Neville. "Excess Profits in the Drug Industry and Their Effect on Consumer Expenditures." *Inquiry* 10:19-30 (September 1973).

Dowling, Harry R. *Medicines for Man: The Development, Regulation, and Use of Prescription Drugs*. New York: Alfred A. Knopf, 1970.

Drug Bioequivalence Study Panel. *Drug Bioequivalence*. Washington, D.C.: Office of Technology Assessment, 1974.

Krieg, Margaret. *Black Market Medicine*. Englewood Cliffs, N.J.: Prentice-Hall, 1967.

Pekkanen, John. *The American Connection. Profiteering and Politicking in the "Ethical" Drug Industry*. Chicago: Follett Publishing Co., 1973.

Public Hazards from Unsatisfactory Medical Diagnostic Products. Report to Congress by the Comptroller General of the United States (30 April 1975).

Walker, Hugh D. *Market Power and Price Levels in the Ethical Drug Industry*. Bloomington, Ind.: Indiana University Press, 1971.

9. Government Health Care Activities

*The powers not delegated to the United States by the Constitution, nor prohibited by
it to the States, are reserved to the States respectively, or to the people.*
—Article 10, Constitution of the United States

Theoretically, all governmental authority resides in the states with the exception of the authority that the Constitution delegates to the federal government or that state legislation delegates to local jurisdiction. Police power is one of the residual powers retained by the states: it is the authority to protect and promote the health, safety, and welfare of the state and its people.[1] In health matters, states began exercising their police power by attempting to prevent and control infectious diseases. Social legislation increasingly expanded health department activities into such areas as maternal and child health, environmental health, and medical care for the indigent and aged. Much of the federal government's regulatory power, on the other hand, in health derives from its constitutional power to regulate interstate commerce, but with increased urbanization, travel, industrialization, and interstate problems, the federal government has assumed responsibility for certain population groups, health insurance, and a wide variety of programs.

The increased centralization of power in the federal government has led to the popular assumption that the federal government is the ultimate source of power and money and the answer to most problems affecting the delivery of health care. We are concerned here with the structure of governmental health programs and a few of those programs involved directly in the delivery of health care. These health programs have established models for socialized medicine and give us some indication of how the federal government might expand its delivery of health care in the future.

State and Local Government

State and local health departments involve themselves in the following activities:

1. collection of vital statistics of births, deaths, and reportable diseases
2. control of communicable diseases
3. environmental sanitation, including air and water quality and supervision of foods and eating places
4. clinical laboratory services
5. maternal and child health, including school health
6. health education
7. nutrition
8. dental health
9. radiological control
10. alcohol and drug abuse
11. family planning

They have increasingly been involving themselves in housing, mental health, home health care, mass screening tests, highway safety, occupational health hazards, and chronic diseases.[2]

State health departments used to delegate most direct services to local health departments and provided only general liaison, consultation, and special services as needed. But they retained certain statewide regulatory and planning functions, such as licensure, budgeting, auditing, and personnel management. City health departments, under *the home rule doctrine,* provided direct services to the population under basic guiding principles established by the state. Recently, however, a number of state and local jurisdictions have consolidated health and welfare services by combining related smaller departments and agencies into a single administrative structure, known as an "umbrella" or "super" agency. In Louisiana and North Carolina, for example, all the activities on a state and local basis have been placed under a Department of Human Resources at the state level. Theoretically, this coordination of services leads to less duplication and more efficiency.

Most municipal, county, and state health departments have a chief executive officer (health officer, director, or commissioner, who is usually a physician with a background in public health). The director of the state health department is usually appointed by the governor, the director of the county health department by the county supervisor, and the director of the city health department by the mayor. These elected officials also appoint boards of health to help set policy for health departments. Health directors are not immune from political pressure from elected officials. Health officers and boards of health advise and sometimes promulgate administrative legislation in the area of public health. Unless they grant permission, health departments, boards, and officers cannot be sued or held liable by the public. Increasingly, state and local health departments derive large parts of their budgets from federal contracts, grants, and Social Security programs.

Federal Government Efforts at the State and Local Level

Much of the federal government's efforts to affect the delivery of health care take place at the state and local level. These efforts involve federal, state, and locally administered programs for health services, manpower training, and research. Federal funding sources for health services at the state and local level are:

1. federally administered programs
   a. medicare
   b. CHAMPUS, Department of Defense
   c. Veterans Administration
   d. Public Health Service
2. state-administered programs
   a. medicaid
   b. Cuban refugees
   c. maternal and child health
   d. other public health, including drug abuse, family planning, dental care, mental health, environmental health, financial assistance by geographic area, school health, health planning, community health services, vital statistics, and special projects and studies
3. locally administered programs
   a. maternal and child health
   b. other public health including financial assistance by geographic area, school health, and environmental health

Federally administered programs usually account for over half of all federal health funds coming into a state. State-administered programs often involve a contribution of state funds. *Grants-in-aid* are authorized in various federal laws for stated purposes and are distributed to state and local organizations, agencies, and individuals. Table 9.1[3] lists two types of grants-in-aid: (1) *formula grants,* which are allotted by a formula that takes into account factors like state populations, per capita income, and the extent of health problems; and (2) *matching grants,* which must be matched up to a specified percentage by the state, agency, or institution receiving the grant. Confusion can arise over these terms because formula grants may involve matching funds and therefore are also matching grants; the terms are used interchangeably.

State, regional, or local agencies, colleges, universities, and private

Table 9.1 Health Formula and Matching Grants Received by State Agencies,
Based on Louisiana FY 1974

Grant Number, Name, and Authorization	Use	Financial Information			
		Federal		State	
		Amount (in dollars, 000)	Percentage	Amount (in dollars, 000)	Percentage
13.714 Medicaid Social Security Act Title 19	Direct services: Family planning Other services Administration: Professional health administrators Licensing Development of mechanized systems Operation of mechanized systems Other support	$82,668 1,640	90 90 72.8 75 100 90 75 50	$30,885 1,204	10 27.2 25 0 10 25 50
13.754 Social Services "Health Related" Social Security Act Title 4a	Family planning Health information and referral services Social support services delivered by state health agencies	5,361 90 1,428	90 75 75	690 30 476	10 25 25
13.210 Comprehensive Health Services Section 4140	Public health services	1,439	54	224	46
13.207 Comprehensive Health Planning Public Health Service Act Section 314a	Planning	220		39 "Maintenance of effort"	
13.220 Health Facility Construction "Hill-Burton" Public Health Service Act	Facility construction, renovation, and equipment purchasing	4,139 "Obligated"		Varies by project	
13.756 Special Projects for the Aging Social Security Act Titles 3 and 7	Transportation to health facilities Nursing services Other "health related" services	Separate figures for health-related activities were not readily available			
13.232 Maternal and Child Health Social Security Act Title 5	Health services for low income mothers and children	Fund A: 672 Fund B: 713	50 100	672 0	50 0
13.211 Crippled Chrildren Social Security Act Title 5	Services for crippled children	Fund A: 717 Fund B: 798	50 100	717 0	50 0
13.257 Alcohol Abuse Alcohol Abuse and Alcoholism Prevention, Treatment and Rehabilitation Act, 1970	Alcohol treatment programs	582	100	0	0
13.269 Drug Abuse Planning Drug Abuse Office and Treatment Act, 1972	Planning and operation of drug abuse treatment programs	171	100	0	0
13.746 Vocational Rehabilitation, Basic Support Vocational Rehabilitation Act, 1973	Medical services such as as examinations and physical restorations	2,236	80	584 Small number cf services to the blind reimbursed at 100 percent.	20

nonprofit institutions and organizations also receive *project grants* made available through grants-in-aid: (1) *research grants,* which are (competitively) awarded for specified research work; (2) *training grants,* which are granted competitively to institutions engaged in certain health manpower training activities; and (3) *capitation grants,* which involve funds allotted to educational institutions in proportion to student enrollment.[4] All three project-grant categories may fit under two types of specified grants: (1) *categorical grants,* which are made for narrowly defined problems such as venereal disease or drug therapy tests in treating heart disease; and (2) *block grants,* which are for more broadly defined purposes (such as a five-pronged attack on cancer) and which permit more discretion in the use of funds. Currently, the government seems to be emphasizing massive block grants that address themselves to large applied health research problems such as the "war on cancer."

Grants-in-aid usually require strict adherence to federal guidelines and standards, the assignment of the responsibility for administration of the grant to a single agency (although more than one agency or institution may be involved), and may require the submission of a state plan concerning the problem or purpose in question.[5] Many state and local agencies have complained of the federal red tape, bureaucratic bungling, and long delays before monies reach the area or people they were intended for. In 1972, the State and Local Fiscal Assistance Act created "revenue sharing," which cuts through the federal bureaucracy, has relatively few restrictions, and allows states and local governmments more discretion in how federal funds are spent. Under revenue sharing, funds must be spent for such "priority expenditures" as necessary capital expenditures and operating expenses in the areas of health, recreation, public safety, environmental protection, social service for the poor and aged, public transportation, libraries, and financial adminstration.

Health monies filter down to state and local agencies as a result of several acts and their amendments:

1. Social Security Act (1935), HEW
2. Public Health Service Act (1944), HEW
3. Mental Retardation Facilities and Community Mental Health Centers Construction Act (1963), HEW
4. Economic Opportunity Act (1964), ACTION
5. Demonstration Cities and Metropolitan Act ("Model Cities," 1966), Department of Housing and Urban Development
6. Occupational Safety and Health Act (1970), Department of Labor
7. National School Lunch Act (1946) and Child Nutrition Act (1966), Department of Agriculture
8. Dependents Medical Care Act ("CHAMPUS," 1956), Department of Defense
9. Clean Air Act (1963) and Water Quality Act (1965), Environmental Protection Agency

Each act has its own administrative unit, sometimes within a governmental department or independent agency, to carry out the provisions of the act. Many of the grant-in-aid programs are authorized for stipulated periods of time only, usually two to five years. Amendments are being added continuously.

Family Planning

Today, many of us take for granted the government's participation in helping families control and limit their size. Not so many years ago, however, individuals were arrested for openly discussing contraceptive methods in their lectures. This government action was prompted by the Catholic church and a "bluenose" named Anthony Comstock, who believed that the advocates of contraception were doing the devil's work and who institutionalized his prejudices through his New York Society for the Suppression of Vice. Comstock, as special inspector for the Post Office Department, personally arrested many individuals between 1873 and 1882 and seized thousands of "obscene" books and "immoral" articles.

Fortunately, the influence of Havelock Ellis and Dr. Marie Stopes, and the example of Charles Bradlaugh and Annie Besant, had an effect on Margaret Sanger, whose mother died at age forty-eight after bearing eleven children. Born in 1883, Sanger agitated for women's suffrage, became a nurse and socialist, and decided to take on Comstock by publishing material on venereal disease, condoms, and family limitation. Her work suppressed, she founded the National Birth Control League in 1915. She decided to defy the law by opening a birth control clinic in Brooklyn. On 16 October 1916, when the clinic opened, 150 women lined up outside. Nine days later Mrs. Sanger, her sister, Ethel Byrne (a nurse), and another woman helper were arrested. Each was sentenced to thirty days in the workhouse. Mrs. Sanger, released on bail, immediately reopened the clinic and was rearrested and charged with "maintaining a public nuisance." Her sister went on a hunger strike for 103 hours and was force-fed through a rubber tube. Mrs. Sanger's case received such widespread publicity that her publications *(The Birth Control Review)* were in much demand, and she began to speak before large crowds. She organized conferences, the International Federation of Birth Control Leagues, and eventually Planned Parenthood. She was the single most important contributor to the family planning movement.[6] Later, a second revolution was started by William Baird, who allowed himself to be arrested numerous times when he demonstrated birth control devices and arranged abortions during the 1950s and 1960s.

At about the same time as Margaret Sanger began her birth control clinic, clinics were opening to provide prenatal care for expectant mothers in the lower-income groups. In 1912, the Children's Bureau was established to enable, through grants-in-aid, the extension and improvement of health services for mothers and children. Eventually a network of prenatal, postnatal, and well-child clinics was constructed. Until the 1960s, there was little interaction between maternal and child health agencies and the more independent birth control movement.

Research during the 1960s found that:

1. many men and women did not understand reproductive physiology;
2. many individuals reported having conceived a significant number of unplanned pregnancies;
3. many individuals believed that couples had the right to decide for themselves when to stop having children;
4. many individuals wanted more information about family planning and believed that family planning services should be available to the medically indigent.[7]

In short, people wanted to limit the size of their families but lacked the knowledge and community resources to do so. We will turn our attention to one family planning program to see how federal-state efforts can produce success and failure.

Louisiana Family Planning Program (LFPP)

LFPP was the first statewide family planning program in the United States, servicing over 70,000 indigent Louisiana families through 170 facilities. A large part of its success was due to four factors:

1. postpartum women were contacted by LFPP personnel before they left the hospital; the postpartum period is considered the most crucial time, when a woman is most highly motivated to adopt family planning
2. outreach community workers made house calls to encourage women who missed their appointments to come into the clinic; LFPP had a low dropout rate
3. LFPP clinics were cheerful and dignified; patients were treated well
4. LFPP was well funded through a variety of sources

The ultimate objectives of the program were to reduce the incidence of unwanted pregnancies, infant deaths, stillbirths, premature births, abortions, and illegitimate births, and to augment significantly the delivery of maternal and child health care for the medically indigent. Figure 9.1 shows how LFPP fit under the umbrella of the Family Health Foundation (FHF). Money was plentiful, for the FHF received large amounts of federal money through matching funds (the state puts up 10 percent, the federal government 90 percent; see Table 9.1). At its peak (1973), FHF had an annual budget of $18 million and was internationally

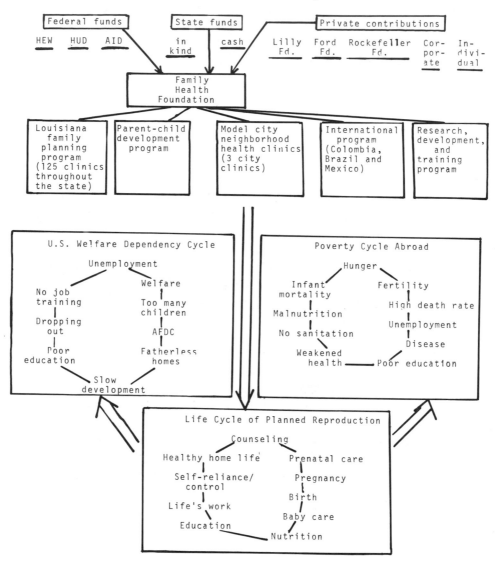

Figure 9.1 Family Health Foundation Program Thrust

known for having developed a family planning model suitable for replication.[8]

In 1974, FHF became the first major U.S. health program to be forced into receivership. Federal indictments accused FHF executives of using Title 4a funds (to be used only for providing family planning services to poor families) to make political payoffs, of "laundering" 4a funds through a consulting firm and another private foundation so that federal funds eventually would be matched by more federal money in grants to the foundation; additionally, FHF, using creative accounting techniques, shuffled 4a money into "discretionary" accounts as a way of generating funds for lavish apartments, meals, and airplanes. Thus far, several high ranking FHF officials have been convicted on several of the indictments, and each has been sentenced to two years in federal prison. In their defense, they argued that HEW spending guidelines are vague, that only the state had a right to monitor their activities (a job the state was ill equipped to perform), that officials in state and federal government wanted to make an example out of their case, and that the spending irregularities amounted to a small percentage of the total budget.[9]

Federal spending on local health programs is caught in a dilemma. Too many controls on how the money is spent create a large bureaucracy, which overshadows the actual delivery of the services; too few controls lead to abuses, which may cause the collapse of the program. FHF's misfortune raises the question of whether federal programs are doomed to failure regardless of their popularity and political support. Finally, we are reminded that health programs and federal health dollars are as susceptible to fraud and mismanagement as any other business endeavor.

Inside the Federal Government

Many different federal agencies are involved in health. As indicated in Figure 9.2, 74 percent of the 1974 federal health budget goes to the Department of Health, Education and Welfare, 10 percent to the Veterans Administration, and 9 percent to the Department of Defense.[10] Since these three agencies consume 93 percent of the total budget, they will be examined in detail. As shown in Figure 9.3, 79 percent of the budget goes to financing and providing health services, a category that is growing fast, accounting for 87 percent of real growth in the federal health budget since 1969.[11] The remaining real growth comes primarily from increases in health research expenditures and in outlays for the training of health care providers. Figure 9.4 shows that besides HEW and USDA, the Agency for International Development (AID) within the State Department is active in the prevention and control of health problems abroad.[12]

Several new programs for the prevention and control of domestic health problems have been established. These include the National Institute of Occupational Safety and Health (HEW), the Occupational Safety and Health Administration (DOL), and the Consumer Product Safety Commission. Recent legislative trends suggest that a Consumer Protection Agency will soon be spending monies on the prevention and control of health problems. The Atomic Energy Commission (AEC) is currently the fourth largest spender in this area.

Department of Defense (DOD)

The mission of the military health care system is to provide the health services necessary to support and maintain all military forces in fulfilling their own missions, to create and maintain high morale in the uniformed

Figure 9.2 Federal Health Outlays by Activity, 1969 and 1974

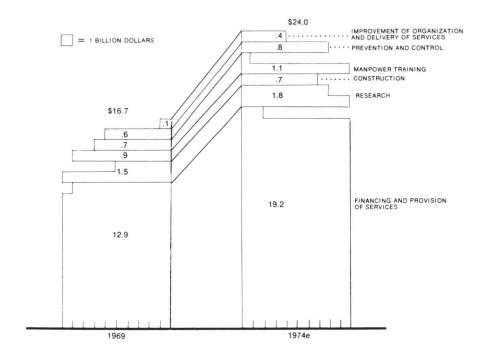

Figure 9.3 Total Federal Outlays by Agency, 1969 and 1974

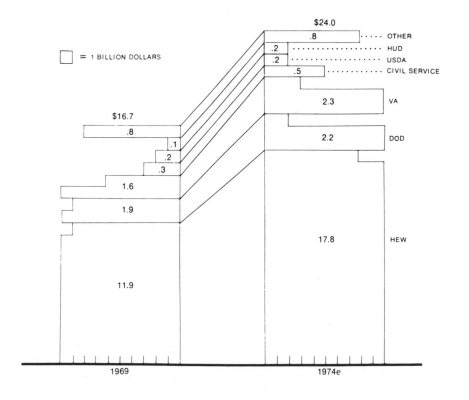

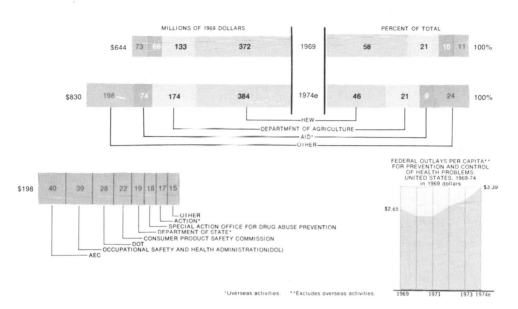

Figure 9.4 Federal Outlays for the Prevention and Control of
Health Problems and Distribution by Agency,
1969 and 1974

services by providing a comprehensive and high-quality uniform program of health services for members and other eligible beneficiaries, and to be responsive to missions directed by the executive branch of the government. The four major components of the military health care system are (1) the Army Medical Department; (2) the Navy Medical Department, which also provides health services support to the Marine Corps; (3) the Air Force Medical Service; and (4) the Office of the Assistant Secretary of Defense (Health Affairs).

DOD provides health care to (1) active-duty service members, (2) their dependents, (3) retired military members and their dependents, and (4) survivors of both active-duty and retired members. The worldwide military system has about 190 hospitals and 120 free-standing clinics providing direct care, with payment for supplementary civilian care made through the Civilian Health and Military Program of the Uniformed Services (CHAMPUS).[13] CHAMPUS amounted to 20 percent of DOD outlays for the provision of health services in 1974. As seen in Figures 9.5[14] and 9.6[15], the number of people eligible for services provided or financed by DOD has declined, but the outlays per eligible beneficiary have increased sizably.

In July 1973, the draft was eliminated. Since the introduction of an all-volunteer army, the armed forces have relied on increased benefits—including pay bonuses, training scholarships, and promises of health training at their own facilities—to help recruit their manpower. The Uniformed Services Revitalization Act of 1972, which established a

Figure 9.5   Number of People Eligible for Services Provided or
Financed by the Department of Defense, 1969-1974

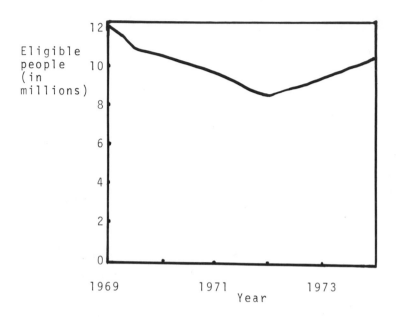

Figure 9.6   Outlays by the Department of Defense per Eligible
Beneficiary, 1969-1974 (in 1969 dollars)

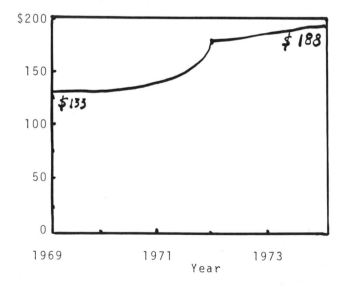

university of health sciences (including a medical school), was designed to increase the DOD's ability to attract and retain health manpower (an M.D. trained at the university would have a seven-year additional commitment). The university has had a tough time getting congressional appropriations: cost of DOD physician training is higher than the training cost at a non-DOD medical school. However, the medical school is now admitting students. The DOD's research accounted for 5 percent of the total federal research expenditure in 1974.

Veterans Administration (VA)

A veteran is one who has served no less than ninety days in the U.S. armed forces. The VA provides health services to (1) veterans age sixty-five and over, (2) veterans with service-connected disabilities, and (3) medically indigent veterans. The VA health care system was established at a time when alternative facilities were not available, when the federal government had almost no responsibility for the health care of the public, and when health insurance was almost nonexistent.

A recent controversial report on health care resources in the VA recommended that because these circumstances have changed, VA policies and programs should now be designed to permit the VA system ultimately to be phased into the general delivery of services in communities across the country.[16] In short, the VA health care system should be phased out, and other public and private mechanisms should be phased in.

The VA now serves about 29 million veterans through its 169 hospitals and ambulatory clinics and 101 long-term care facilities. About 10 percent of VA health care outlays pay for services to veterans by non-VA facilities. As seen in Figure 9.7, VA outlays per U.S. veteran have increased significantly, particularly as a response to public reaction to the Vietnam war and to veterans' criticism of the inadequacies of the VA.[17] There is currently excessive reliance on hospital care and inadequate ambulatory services. This pattern has led to substantial overuse of inpatient resources. Whether any substantial changes will occur in the VA health system is a matter of conjecture.

Health, Education and Welfare

Federal laws authorize the federal government to undertake and sponsor many health-related activities. Most health monies are administered by the spawling Department of Health, Education and Welfare. Since 1953, HEW has been reorganized many times. Figure 9.8 shows a simplified organizational chart of HEW and the location of some of its more important health programs and activities.[18] The HEW secretary is appointed by the president. The assistant secretary for Health is appointed by the secretary and usually is a physician, as are the heads of the six operating agencies of the Public Health Service (PHS). The head of the

Figure 9.7   Outlays by the Veterans Administration per
              U.S. Veteran for 1969-1974

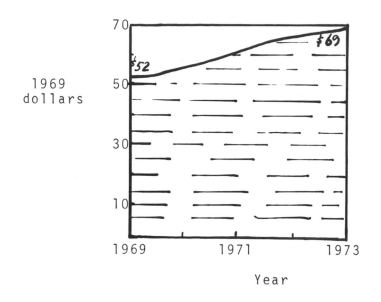

Year

PHS used to be the surgeon general, but this position has been vacant for some time. The National Institutes of Health perform basic and applied health research and administer the outflow of grant monies. A close look at Figure 9.8 reveals that several HEW agencies are concerned with maternal and child health, the aged, and drug abuse. To make matters more or less confusing—depending on your knowledge of the bureaucracy—in 1971 a Special Action Office for Drug Abuse Prevention was established within the Executive Office of the President to plan and coordinate federal drug abuse prevention programs.

HEW has five broad areas of responsibility:

1. the provision of financial assistance to individuals
2. the provision of financial assistance to state and local governments
3. federal assistance in building the capacity of human services institutions to meet human needs
4. the direct federal provision of services
5. the setting of regulations and standards

These areas sound simple enough until we find that HEW currently administers over 300 programs, 54 of which overlap each other and 36 of which overlap programs of other departments. In all, the government had more than 500 categorical programs of aid to states in 1971. The complexity (and fragmentation) of HEW programs is staggering. Rules and regulations for categorical programs are restrictive, conflicting, and overlapping. Bureaucrats suspiciously defend their programs. Legislators

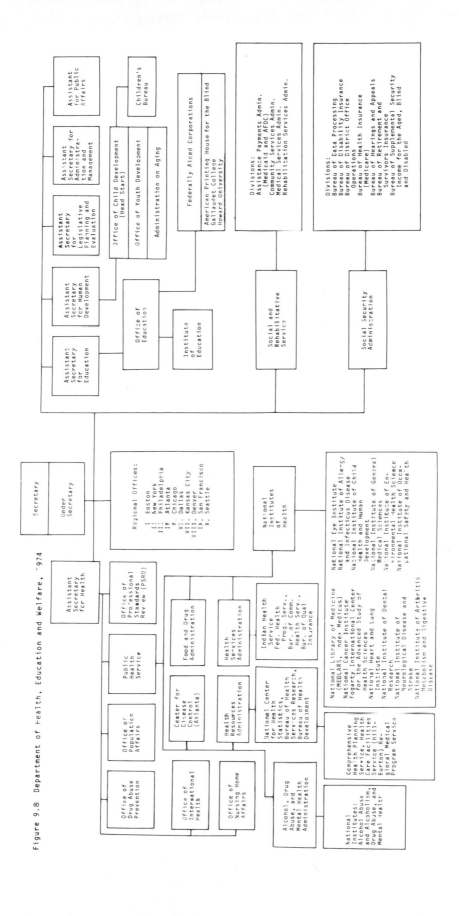

Figure 9.8 Department of Health, Education and Welfare, 1974

loudly push and protect their favorite categorical programs (Sickle Cell, Cooley's Disease, or whatever is expedient politically). HEW is forced to promise more and deliver less: in 1961, nearly all of HEW's authorizations (promises) were matched by appropriations (delivery); in 1971, only one third of HEW's authorizations were matched by appropriations. The agency finds itself caught between preserving incrementalism (business as usual) by Congress and a "hardening of categories," on one hand, and seeking the perfect at the expense of the good, on the other hand. Each year HEW is given the responsibility over dozens of new categorical programs, and each year HEW finds it more difficult to deliver on its promises.

According to policy analysts Lynn and Seidl:

> In short, HEW was expected by Congress and the American people to deliver a scope, quantity, and quality of services which it was not even within hailing distance of achieving and each year the problem was getting worse, not better. If the term "unmanageable" meant the inability to provide coherent and consistent leadership in establishing and meeting deliberate goals, HEW seemed to be truly unmanageable.[19]

Former HEW secretary Elliot Richardson explains: "HEW's problem was both simpler and far more fundamental than unmanageability. The plain fact was that the system—of which HEW itself was but a part—was out of control."[20] HEW is a product of hundreds of different legislative plans, compromises, and personal ambitions. It is subjected to much political pressure but still manages to accomplish its short-range tasks. One of its tasks is to deliver health care to American Indians and Alaskan Natives.

Indian Health Service

The story of the American Indian is one of broken promises.[21] Battle after battle followed broken treaty after broken treaty. Indians were continuously uprooted from their land and confined to reservations against their will. Their human rights were blatantly abused. The "Great Council" in Washington was for the most part unfeeling and rigid. Small armies of traders made fortunes selling bad food, shoddy merchandise, and whiskey to thousands of Indians trapped on reservations. Investigations of atrocious treatment of Indians by the military-political reservation complex were little more than whitewashes. All in all, much of the history of the American Indian is a record of disgraceful U.S. government behavior.

The federal government has provided health care to Indians since the 1800s. During the first half of the nineteenth century, the War Department, through its army physicians at military posts, was responsible for the health of nearby Indians. Military physicians were concerned that communicable diseases (smallpox and tuberculosis) would spread from the Indians to soldiers. Large-scale vaccination programs were initiated.

In 1832, the first treaty was negotiated that committed the federal government to provide health services as partial payment for rights and property ceded to the government. Whether by design or by omission, many of the treaties imposed time limits of five to twenty years for the provision of care; the federal government, however, adopted a policy of continuing service after the original benefit period expired. In 1849, the Bureau of Indian Affairs (BIA), which had been directed to take measures "for the relief of distress and the conservation of health," was transferred from the War Department to the Department of the Interior. A corps of civilian health employees was established, both in the field and in Washington. Between 1880 and 1900, many hospitals and infirmaries were built on reservations and at boarding schools. Despite these changes, the health of American Indians remained marginal at best, and the BIA retained many inadequate and understaffed facilities.[22]

In the 1930s, the BIA established eligibility requirements for health services. In general, to be eligible, Indians must (1) belong to a recognized Indian tribe, (2) be a descendent of Indians who lived on a recognized tribal reservation, (3) be one-half or more Indian blood. For an individual to receive federally funded health care, therefore, he or she must be recognized by the tribal council as a member of the tribe, and the tribe must in turn be recognized by the federal government; he or she need not live on the reservation to be eligible for health care. To be recognized by the federal government, a tribe must have a specific treaty or have land set aside in trust for it and have a tribal council or some representative form of government. Several Indian tribes have no treaties or no land held in federal trust and therefore are not eligible for federal Indian health programs. Some tribes live on state reservations and are cared for by individual states.

In 1955, as a result of hearings on the health of the American Indian, responsibility for health was shifted from the BIA to the Public Health Service (PHS). The PHS was instructed to assume all functions, responsibilities, authorities, and duties relating to the maintenance and operation of hospital and health facilities for Indians and the conservation of the health of the Indians (and Alaskan Natives—Aleuts and Eskimos). Within the PHS, the Indian Health Service (IHS) has three objectives:

1. to deliver comprehensive health care
2. to assist in the development of Indian self-sufficiency and administrative authority
3. to act as an advocate for Indians in the health field

According to these objectives, therefore, the IHS is to work toward the day when it can be staffed entirely by Indians and Alaskan Natives. This policy is an abrupt change from the previous government policy of assimilation of Indians and their culture.[23]

When the PHS took over from the BIA, the Indian population had many of the same problems typically found in an undeveloped country. Contagious diseases, particularly tuberculosis, and diseases related to unsafe water supplies and lack of basic sanitary facilities were a constant source of ill health. The IHS's immediate objective was to vaccinate all Indians and to decrease births occurring outside of hospitals. It achieved remarkable success, but as can be seen in Table 9.2,[24] the Indians had many health problems still remaining in 1967. Comparatively, Indians tend to die of violence and excessive consumption of alcohol. The Indian arrest rate for crimes related to alcohol is twelve times the national average. The Indian birthrate is twice the U.S. birthrate. Dental problems are severe among Indians. Socioeconomic problems abound: in 1970 the median family income for reservation Indians was $3,800 compared with $10,826 for U.S. whites. Housing is inadequate and unemployment is high. Students drop out of high school. Communication and transportation, particularly public transportation, is almost nonexistent in remote areas. Dysentery among IHS Indians is thirty times that of the general population. The IHS had and continues to have a formidable task.

In 1970, the total U.S. Indian and Alaskan Native population was 827,000.[25] In the same year, the IHS service population was 478,000, which included approximately 422,000 Indians belonging to more than 250 tribes and 53,000 Natives living in 300 Alaska villages. Figure 9.9 shows the structure of the IHS. The tribal councils are the local administrative units that negotiate with the IHS at all levels. More than 55 percent of the 6,000 IHS employees are Indians, but most of the Indians are in lower-level positions. Very few M.D.'s—no more than five—are Indians. Much work is contracted out; non-IHS providers are reimbursed for services rendered to eligible Indians. The IHS has put a lot of effort into educating and training new personnel, such as nurse extenders, practical nurses, dental assistants, radiological technologists, environmental health workers. Since 1955, appropriations from Congress have increased markedly. In

Table 9.2   Ratio of Indian and Alaska Native Age-Adjusted Death Rates to U.S Rates for All Races, Calendar Year 1967

Cause of Death	Ratio of Indian Rate to U.S. Rate
Accidents	3.9
Influenza and pneumonia (excluding newborn)	2.4
Cirrhosis of the liver	4.4
Homicide	3.5
Diabetes mellitus	2.1
Suicide	2.1
Tuberculosis, all forms	8.0
Gastritis	3.3
All causes	1.4

Figure 9.9   Indian Health Service

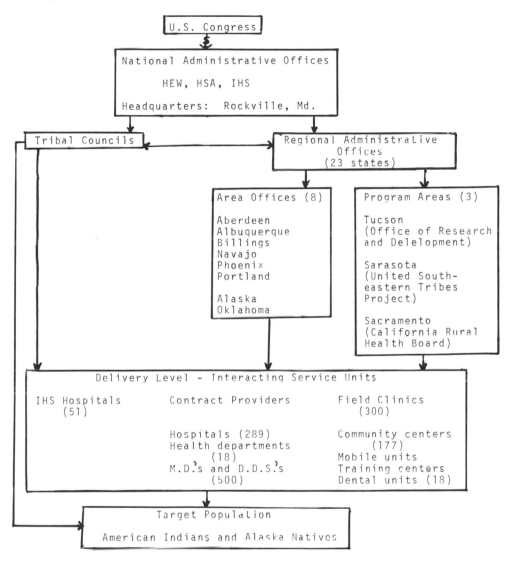

fiscal 1975, the IHS received $283.5 million, which was approximately $500 per IHS eligible Indian.

The IHS is not without its own problems. Much like any other federal program or agency, it can become bogged down with bureaucratic inefficiency and red tape. Its headquarters are a long way from the people it services. It is trying to alleviate health problems caused, in part, by the cycle of poverty. After the physician draft came to an end (June 1973), fewer physicians have volunteered for the PHS, which has created a shortage of IHS physicians.[26] However, most PHS physicians stay only two years and tend to clash with both the PHS careerist and the Indians themselves. Kane and Kane contrast the two types of PHS provider:[27]

Two-Year Individual	*Careerist*
younger	older
more educated	less educated
change-oriented	favoring status quo
short-term outlook	long-term outlook
liberal	conservative
uncontrollable	dependent on the system
involved in Indian culture	ambivalent about Indian culture

Indians see the two-year provider as an intern on temporary assignment with little definitive interest in the Indian's cyclical plight. Many Indians would prefer to be treated by private physicians because of the long waiting lines in PHS outpatient clinics and because the private physicians tend to make greater use of shots.[28] Authoritarian personalities clash.

Indians living on reservations are wards of the federal government. Tribal councils can make their own local laws and establish their own form of justice. Tribal councils may find themselves caught in between the wishes of the tribe and the federal government. Impoverished and isolated, the Indians find themselves culturally adrift, neglected, discriminated against off the reservation, and dependent on federal assistance. Sickness is viewed as a loss of harmony between the patient and the world. Disharmony is everywhere. Yet Indians survive and endure.

Summary

The federal government is quite active in the direct and indirect provision of health services. The Department of Health, Education and Welfare has been growing and expanding its activities, but some of its programs, such as the Public Health Service, appear to be in administrative limbo. The federal bureaucracy is a series of contradictions: many Americans depend on its resources, but many other Americans resent the dependency and inefficiency it has fostered. There seems to be no end in sight for the increasing tendency of the federal government to assume the authority that at one time resided with state and local governments; health care seems to be at the forefront of this centralization of power.

Questions

1. The following news brief appeared in the 13 November 1972 issue of *American Medical News:*

> U. of New Mexico has been awarded a five-year, $4.7 million grant by the U.S. Dept. of Health, Education, and Welfare to establish on the Navajo reservation at

Window Rock, Arizona, a health education center that will eventually become the nation's first medical school *specifically designated* for Indians.

Assume you are each of the following individuals; describe how you feel about this announcement by analyzing the grant and the new medical school.

    a. an Indian living on a reservation in Utah
    b. a coal miner in West Virginia
    c. a New Orleanian with an annual disposable income of $60,000
    d. a health economist

2. Assume you are a city health director. Would you like to see the federal government pour more money into revenue sharing and less money into grants-in-aid?

3. What happens to a government-funded program when the organization running the program goes into receivership?

4. In examining the organization chart of HEW, we find medicare and medicaid in different sections of the department; do you believe that the two programs ought to be housed in the same section; if so, why?

5. If the draft is ever reinstituted, would you favor a special draft for nurses and physicians based on manpower needs?

Notes

1. Police power originated in the doctrine of overruling necessity, which states that in times of stress such as fire, epidemic, and so one, the private property of an individual may be appropriated summarily or even destroyed if the ultimate relief, protection, or safety of the group indicated such action as necessary. In *Miami County v. Dayton* (92 O.S. 215) the court defined police power as "that inherent sovereignty which the government exercises whenever regulations are demanded by public policy for the benefit of the society at large in order to guard its morals, safety, health, order, and the like in accordance with the needs of civilization." By the way, what are the "needs of civilization?"

2. Ernest L. Stebbins, "The Provincial or State Health Organization" and "Local Health Services" in *Preventive Medicine and Public Health*, Philip E. Sartwell, ed. (New York: Appleton-Century-Crofts, 1965), pp. 1007-35.

3. *Flow of Federal Health Funds*, Comprehensive Planning Associates and Arthur D. Little, May 1975.

4. In the latter part of this chapter, we will discuss the problem one quasiprivate organization had with HEW guidelines.

5. Florence A. Wilson and Duncan Neuhauser, *Health Services in the United States* (Cambridge, Mass.: Ballinger Publishing Co., 1974), pp. 119-20.

6. Peter Fryer, *The Birth Controllers* (Briarcliff Manor, New York: Stein & Day, 1966), pp. 201-19.

7. Joseph D. Beasley and Carl L. Harter, "Introducing Family Planning Clinics to Louisiana," *Children* 14:188-92 (September-October 1974).

8. Joseph D. Beasley and John P. Wells, "Louisiana: Developing and Managing a Statewide Family Planning Program," *Family Planning Perspectives* 3:68-79 (October 1971).

9. For a more complete analysis of the Family Health Foundation's rise and fall, see Douglas R. Mackintosh, "How Family Health Foundation was Mau-Maued," *New Orleans Magazine,* pp. 44-58 (May 1975).

10. Center for Health Policy Studies, *Chartbook of Federal Health Spending 1969-1974* (Washington: National Planning Association, 1974), p. 5.

11. Ibid., p. 4.

12. Ibid., p. 55.

13. Ibid., p. 40.

14. Ibid.

15. Ibid., p. 41.

16. National Research Council, *Health Care for American Veterans* (Washington, D.C.: National Academy of Sciences, May 1977).

17. Center for Health Policy Studies, *Chartbook of Federal Health Spending,* p. 41.

18. Adopted from Florence Wilson and Duncan Neuhauser, *Health Services in the United States* (1974), p. 112.

19. L. E. Lynn and J. M. Seidl, "Introduction—Policy Analysis at HEW: The Story of the Mega-Proposal," *Policy Analysis* 1:232-37 (spring 1975).

20. Elliot L. Richardson, Preface to a Special Issue on the HEW Mega-Proposal, *Policy Analysis* 1:223-31 (spring 1975).

21. Dee Brown, *Bury My Heart at Wounded Knee* (New York: Bantam, 1970).

22. *The Indian Health Program of the U.S. Public Health Service,* HEW, HSMHA, PHS (Washington, D.C.: Superintendent of Documents, 1973), pp. 30-31.

23. Sar A. Levitan and Barbara Hetrich, *Big Brother's Indian Programs—with Reservations* (McGraw Hill Book Co., 1971).

24. *Indian Health Trends and Services,* HEW, HSMHA, PSH, IHS (PHS publication no. 2092, January 1971), p. 30.

25. *1970 U.S. Census,* final reports. A curious phenomenon took place in the 1970 census. An individual could declare himself or herself whatever race he or she felt was most accurate. Due to a resurgence of Indian pride, many more individuals declared themselves to be Indians than population experts expected based on the 1960 census. For example the IHS estimated the total Indian and Alaska Native population to be approximately 620,000 in 1968.

26. "Indians Health Care in U.S. May Worsen, Partly Due to Slump," *Wall Street Journal,* 19 March 1975, pp. 1 and 16.

27. Robert L. Kane and Rosalie A. Kane, *Federal Health Care (With Reservations!)* (New York: Springer-Verlag, 1972), p. 27.

28. Richard P. Bozof, "Some Navajo Attitudes Toward Available Medical Care," *AJPH* 62:1620-24 (December 1972).

Further Reading

Child Health in America. DHEW publication no. (HSA) 76-5015 (1976).

Corey, Marsha. "U.S. Organized Family Planning Programs in FY 1974," *Family Planning Perspectives* 7:98-103 (May-June 1975).

Forward Plan for Health FY 1978-82. DHEW, PHS, GPO (August 1976).

Sheppard, Harold L. *Effects of Family Planning on Poverty in the United States.* Kalamazoo, Mich.: Upjohn Institute for Employment Research, October 1967.

"Special Bibliography on American Indian Health," *Health Services Reports* 88:727-29 (October 1973).

10. Independent Practitioners

Logic only gives man what he needs. Magic gives him what he wants.
—Tom Robbins

Many independent health practitioners other than physicians deliver health care—although discussions and texts on health care delivery systems often ignore them. These practitioners make a significant contribution to the well-being of health consumers, but for the past fifty to seventy-five years, some of them have been in a constant battle with organized medicine (M.D.'s and the AMA) for recognition and survival. At times organized medicine has tried to absorb them, eliminate them, or degrade them; at other times it has ignored them and hoped they would go away. Because of the tenacity of these independent practitioners and the tremendous demand for health care, however, they have survived and prospered.

Faith Healers and Marginal Practitioners

Indian Medicine Men

According to the Indian view, particularly the Navajo view, sickness is a loss of harmony between the patient and the world. Thus, almost all Navajo religion is concerned with health and healing, and all Navajo healing is religious. A Navajo religious ceremony is a symbolic reenactment of what went wrong in the supernatural past and how the supernaturals corrected it. Physicians can set a broken leg and provide relief for painful symptoms, but a medicine man (often they are women) can determine what was the cause of the broken leg and what disharmony led to the broken leg. Only then can he restore harmony.

There are several types of medicine men:

1. singer or ceremonialist—he treats the basic causes of illness by performing complex symbolic ceremonies using music, dance, drama, oratory, chants, sculpture, and painting
2. herbalist—he provides symptomatic relief by administering prayers and ground up plants, some with known pharmacologic action; most of these plants have never been studied
3. diagnostician—(a) shaman: he diagnoses illness by inspiration, foretelling the future, and stargazing, and (b) hand trembler: he says prayers and goes into a trance in which one hand begins to shake and move; he then thinks about the possible causes and treatments of illness and judges among them by the behavior of his trembling hand; finally he refers the patient to an IHS hospital or a singer or both

In the Navajo hierarchy of values, the medicine man is far more important than the physician. In an unpredictable world where supernatural powers abound, the medicine man creates harmony and order, imparts strength and inner peace, and assures physical safety and emotional security.

The BIA and the IHS at first rejected the Indian medicine man as just so much foolishness. But the federal government has slowly begun to recognize that healing—especially treating the unconscious, a Freudian concept—involves cultural and religious factors. Indians have a great deal of respect for age, the extended family, wisdom, history, and the supernatural. Therefore, IHS psychiatrists have begun to work with some 300 singers to teach apprentices who eventually will become medicine men. Indians, following the warrior ethic, are reluctant to discuss their mental health problems with outsiders (IHS staff). The singer not only has an effect on the patient and his problems, but he also brings harmony to the family and the spectators at his ceremony. Unconscious mental processes, such as prolonged grief reactions, are treated with a ceremony, in this case to remove the influence of the dead from the living and turn the patient's attention back toward life. The pastoral response is stimulated, group therapy takes place, and the entire gathering feels a stronger social bond and the restoration of universal harmony. The effect of the medicine man is impossible to measure or test empirically—a notion the medicine man himself would find foolish, an example of the white man's blindness.[1]

Miracles, Shrines, and Exorcism

The four Gospels of the Bible attribute about fifty paranormal events to Christ. If resurrection from the dead is excluded, fewer than three dozen of these miracles can be considered healing. Many of Christ's healing sessions dealt with psychological disorders and involved exorcisms of evil spirits. Christ cured at least four cases of blindness, cured a sufferer who did not know he was being treated, and replaced an ear that had been sliced off. He also appears to have presided over ten mass healings. He used prayers, commands to be well, the laying on of hands, and instructions to the patient to pursue a certain course of action. The faith of the sufferer was sometimes important, and in one case, that of the witnesses also. Christ's disciples carried on the healing. Sickness was hardly distinguishable from sin and salvation; it had to do with the mental and spiritual as well as with the physical. In later centuries, the church continued to treat large numbers of patients.[2]

A Christian tradition developed that cures could be obtained by the intervention of certain saints, whose shrines were said to have brought miraculous cures. Although the Roman Catholic church has not shown more interest in faith healing than any other religion, it has established a strict set of standards that must be satisfied before it considers a cure miraculous. To be a miracle, a cure must be (1) noteworthy, edifying, and reasonable, (2) instantaneous, (3) in answer to a prayer, (4) supported by overwhelming evidence that the cure did in fact take place and that any natural explanation is supremely unlikely, (5) impossible or very difficult to reproduce by known medical means, (6) for illnesses not declining or likely to improve, (7) accompanied by no medical treatment or if medical treatment is rendered, it should have been proved ineffective sometime before, and (8) permanent (no relapse occurs for at least several years).[3]

Worldwide attention has focused on shrines and springs discovered as a result of revelations to otherwise unremarkable individuals. Popular healing shrines include Lourdes in France, Guadalupe in a suburb of Mexico City, Knock in Ireland, Loreto and Pompeii in Italy, Beauraing in Belgium, Saint Anne de Beaupre in Quebec, Our Lady of Loreto in Roxbury, Massachusetts, and the Shrine of the Little Flower in Nasonville, Rhode Island.[4] These shrines are the sites of miraculous cures; their altars are surrounded by discarded crutches and plaster casts as well as devotional plaques attesting to their healing powers.

Despite all the testimonials as to the healing power of Lourdes, the Catholic church has documented only forty-nine miracle cures.[5] Those who remain entirely unmoved by the ceremonies do not experience cures. On the other hand, most of the pilgrims to Lourdes derive some psychological benefit from the experience. The spiritually uplifting atmosphere creates hope, a new feeling of strength, remarkable serenity, and a desire to be of service to others. As Frank writes:

> In short, the healing ceremonials at Lourdes, like those of primitive tribes, involve a climactic union of the patient, his family, the larger group, and the supernatural world by means of a dramatic, emotionally charged, aesthetically rich ritual that expresses and reinforces a shared ideology.[6]

We should not take the psychological power of religious healing rituals for granted. Ceremonies such as exorcism have a forceful impact on those without hope and those with high expectations of release from misery, insecurity, and the detached cold objectivity of scientific medicine.

Christian Science

For most of her adolescent and adult life, Mary A. Morse Baker Grover Patterson Eddy (she had a few husbands) suffered from ill health characterized by psychotic egocentricity, chronic invalidism, and functional paralysis. Despairing of conventional practitioners, she traveled at age forty to Portland, Maine, to visit faith healer Phineas Parkhurst Quimby. Quimby restored her health and tutored her in his techniques. Eddy reworked Quimby's theories and came up with Christian Science. In 1875 she published *Science and Health,* and in 1879 she founded the Church of Christ, Scientist, in Boston. According to Christian Science literature, she healed malignant diptheria and cancer, restored both sight and hearing, and cured various other ills.[7]

According to Christian Science, man is created in God's image and therefore is forever in a state of perfect being. Only wrong thinking, fear, ignorance, and sin cause many of the physical illnesses from which man suffers. The correction of a physical condition must begin with healing of the spirit: the first step is to eliminate the false thinking that produces the disease. Mental discord and belief in the reality of sin and disease, give way to spiritual radiance and divine love. Material methods of treatment (based in some cases on the germ theory of disease) consistently regard suffering as a reality but a Christian Scientist must be alert to deny that scientific medicine is effective and thereby to affirm that man enjoys original perfection. Illness, age, and death are imagined; they are misconceptions of physical imperfection.

For Christian Scientists, healing is accomplished through prayer, either directly through reading *Science and Health* or indirectly through a Christian Science practitioner. There are approximately 5,000 Christian Science practitioners in the United States. One becomes a practitioner upon proof of one's understanding with God and of one's effectiveness in healing (usually testimonials). Practitioners receive a salary from the church and charge a nominal fee per office visit; in return, they work as full-time practitioners. They heal the whole person and, in addition to strictly physiological disease, handle family problems, moral problems, unhappiness, and questions of employment. Practitioners do not diagnose—a patient need not be present in the practitioner's office. Through prayer, healing in absentia is possible, for example, by phone or over the radio.

In only two conditions would a Christian Scientist seek the help of a physician: childbirth and the setting of broken bones (no medication is involved). Christian Scientists cooperate with health departments in reporting contagious diseases as required by law. But the law itself is unclear as to what happens to a practitioner whose actions lead to the deterioration of a patient (for example, antitoxin is not administered to a patient with diphtheria). The doctrine of separation of church and state seems to protect Christian Science practitioners; both they and Christian Science families are free to practice their religion with almost no infringements—no malpractice and no licensure. Practitioners are reimbursed by health insurance, including medicare and medicaid.[8]

Evangelism and Charismatic Healing

Charismatic healers usually have much in common: (1) they are brought up in fundamentalist families; (2) they undergo a debilitating disease; (3) they observe other faith healers at work; (4) they are cured by another faith healer or themselves; (5) they discover their own curing power; (6) they credit God with this power and begin to heal others; (7) they then lead charismatic, flashy lives, leading to bigger and better facilities, houses, cars, and broadcasts; and (8) they rarely invite scientific investigation and confirmation of their healing powers and patients.

The United States has had many evangelists and charismatic healers. As a boy, Edgar Cayce (1877–1945) had visions and total clairvoyance combined with an *eidetic* memory. When he was twenty-one, his throat muscles went into slow paralysis, and he feared he would lose his voice. A hypnotist put him in a trance, and a disembodied voice gave a detailed explanation of his throat condition and recommended certain medications (poultice prescription) and therapy. Cayce began by going into trances, diagnosing illness, specifying the diet, exercises, and medication to correct it. (In all this he used medical phraseology.) He might call for raw apples, castor or olive oil, or obscure drugs. He went into partnerships with various physicians. His fame and fortune spread. Several businessmen from Chicago and New York who had benefited from his readings underwrote a foundation—the Association for Research and Enlightenment (A.R.E.) in Virginia Beach, Virginia—to maintain and analyze records of his activities. Cayce, at his death, left 14,238 documented readings, which have been compiled, cross-indexed, printed, and made available to anyone wishing to study them. Since 1965, a physician has maintained an A.R.E. clinic in Phoenix, Arizona.[9] Castor oil packs, diet, low-voltage electricity, and massage are used in addition to conventional medicine.[10]

Oral Robert's father was a gospel circuit rider in small towns in Oklahoma. Young Roberts (1918–) stammered and had tuberculosis of both lungs. At a back country revival meeting, he was miraculously cured. The miracle worker laid hands on him and murmured a brief prayer. Roberts took on a pentecostal ministry, but not until ten years later, after he made a dramatic auditorium performance, did he begin evangelical healing. Eventually, Roberts had offices in six foreign countries, distributed more than 100 million pieces of literature annually, and had a central office in Tulsa, Oklahoma, with a staff of 600 persons and a multimillion-dollar university (accredited and now famous for its basketball team). He claims to have healed cancer, tuberculosis, paralysis, congenital deformity, spinal incapacitations, headaches, and psychological problems. He says, "I am simply God's instrument. Faith in Him does the healing." Roberts, like many evangelical healers, has several simple devices to combine faith and health with monetary contributions.[11] Roberts, after accumulating a fortune, now does little personal healing, leaving this work to other evangelists.[12]

A thousand acres in Cochise County, Arizona, has become known as Miracle Valley. A. A. Allen Revivals, Inc., developed it into a liquorless, tobaccoless bible college and large-scale enterprise. A. A. Allen (1911-1970), a nostalgic holdover from the canvas cathedrals of Billy Sunday, was converted to the pulpit and faith healing by an itinerant female revivalist. He himself became capable of whipping a crowd into a frenzy using his hypnotic oratorical skills. Don Stewart (1939–), the son of two pentecostal ministers, has succeeded Allen. Although cured of a hip injury by a healing evangelist, Stewart drank, lied to his parents, gambled away his earnings, and frequented local whorehouses. Luckily, one day God told him to go into the world and preach the gospel. He heard A. A. Allen speak on the radio and raise a crippled woman to health from her stretcher. Allen became Stewart's hero. Stewart was one of the first settlers in Miracle Valley. His association with Allen gradually turned from preaching to faith healing to leadership of Allen Revivals and Miracle Valley. Stewart and his staff attempt to heal and persuade through television and radio broadcasts, crusades, and their sixteen page glossy official journal, *Miracle*. Stewart says of his healing power:

> My power to act as God's agent in healing was a gift, a result of the accumulated faith I had inherited from my folks, from Brother Allen, from Christ coming to me as a brother during my time of fasting, prayer, and meditation.[13]

Kathryn Kuhlman (1901?–1976) was perhaps America's foremost healing minister. She found true religion at the age of fourteen, while attending a Methodist church service. She underwent considerable material deprivation, but became a teenage preacher. In an old Billy Sunday tabernacle in Franklin, Pennsylvania, a woman stood up and announced that Kuhlman had cured her malignant tumor. Said Kuhlman, "Since that time there have been thousands and thousands of healings." She claimed to be neither a miracle worker or faith healer; instead, she attributed her power to the Holy Spirit. She apparently took sources of energy, prayers, and the Holy Spirit, and used this energy (force) like a laser beam, as she pointed toward those who need help. The ill person was "recharged," and the physical body is healed. Her services were powerful, moving, electric, switched-on spectaculars that produced testimonial after testimonial.[14]

Charismatic crusades are similar to rock concerts—the listeners temporarily forget their troubles as they give themselves over to a pulsating force. Even those who attend out of curiosity get caught up in the ritual, performance, and tempo. Crowds have strange effects on some people. Although healing arts fall under the police power of the state, faith healing employs no physical means or agencies, rarely has harmful effects, and is therefore allowed to continue. If the state interfered with evangelists and charismatic healers, there would be an even more vocal outburst than when it interferes with rock concerts.[15]

Psychic Surgery

Unlike charismatic healers, psychic surgeons remain out of the public eye. Perhaps the most famous was Arigo (1922–1971) of Congonhas do Campo, Brazil. Arigo practiced in a modest one-story cement building. Although he had no medical training whatsoever, he treated hundreds of thousands of patients. He would go into a trance and begin speaking in a harsh German accent; he used an unsterilized paring knife and no anesthesia; he rarely asked a question of a patient; his diagnosis was wordless and immediate; he used no hypnosis; there was little bleeding or pain; he wrote extraordinary and baffling prescriptions. He claimed no credit for his skill. Instead, during his trance, Adolpho Fritz, a German physician who died in 1918, supposedly performed the surgery and understood the pharmacology. Arigo never accepted any remuneration for his services. He was prosecuted by the Brazilian government and ostracized by the Catholic church. Despite medical confirmation of his diagnostic and healing powers, no scientific explanation has been made of Arigo's techniques.[16]

The Union Espiritista Christiana de Filipinas is a spiritualistic congregation and cult that has about three dozen psychic surgeons for members. Many Americans have flown to the Philippines to have appendixes, kidney stones, fatty tissues lodged near the heart, stomach tumors, and cataracts removed. Anthony Agpaoa (1939–), the best known of these healers, apparently presses his fingertips into the patient's diseased area; the flesh opens and his hand enters the incision; blood pours out but congeals about six inches from the opening; his fingers search for and find the tumor or diseased fibrous matter; he removes it; and the wound closes over. There is no antiseptic or anesthetic; there is no pain or infection. Agpaoa does not cure everyone (bad Karma can hinder his healing techniques), and as a result of a partially unsuccessful tour-pilgrimage from Detroit in 1967, he was charged with fraud. He will be arrested if he again sets foot on U.S. soil. His healing is carried on in Chicago by a psychic healer named Rosita Rodriguez, who because of state laws preventing the practice of medicine, uses massage, a small amount of back manipulation, and some mesmerism. Empirical studies of Filipino techniques have been ambiguous and inconclusive.[17]

First Time In New Orleans and Here To Stay.
Come Visit Her At Her Church.

Spiritual Reader, Healer And Advisor
MOTHER MARGARET

½ HOUR OF YOUR TIME TO SEE MOTHER MARGARET WILL BRING PEACE IN HOME AND HAPPINESS AND SUCCESS AND HEALTH AND LOVE IN LIFE.

SEE MOTHER MARGARET, SHE HAS GOD GIVEN POWER TO HEAL BY PRAYER.

WELCOME AT MOTHER MARGARET'S CHURCH. WHAT YOU SEE WITH YOUR EYES YOUR HEART WILL BELIEVE. ARE YOU SUFFERING? DO YOU NEED HELP? DO YOU HAVE BAD LUCK? BRING YOUR PROBLEMS TO MOTHER MARGARET TODAY AND BE RID OF THEM TOMORROW. SHE ADVISES ON ALL AFFAIRS OF LIFE. THERE IS NO PROBLEM SO GREAT SHE CAN'T SOLVE. (HOW TO HOLD YOUR JOB WHEN YOU HAVE FAILED, AND HOW TO SUCCEED. CALLS YOUR FRIENDS AND ENEMIES BY NAME WITHOUT ASKING YOU A SINGLE WORD. AND REUNITES THE SEPARATED). UPON REACHING WOMANHOOD SHE REALIZED SHE HAD THE GODGIVEN POWER TO HELP HUMANITY. MOTHER MARGARET HAS DEVOTED A LIFETIME TO THIS WORK. FROM THE FOUR CORNERS OF THE WORLD THEY COME TO HER. MEN AND WOMEN OF ALL RACES AND WALKS OF LIFE. GUARANTEED TO REMOVE EVIL INFLUENCE AND BAD LUCK. THERE IS NO PITY FOR THOSE KNOWING THEY ARE IN HARDLUCK AND NEED HELP AND DO NOT COME FOR — ONE VISIT WILL CONVINCE YOU SHE GIVES LUCKY DAYS AND HANDS YOU OUT OF SORROW AND DARKNESS AND STARTS YOU ON THE WAY TO SUCCESS AND HAPPINESS. DON'T FAIL TO SEE THIS GIFTED WOMAN WHO INVITES YOU TO HER CHURCH.

HOURS 7:00 A.M. to 10:00 P.M. Daily and Sunday
NO APPOINTMENT NECESSARY. SEE HER TODAY

3300 SOUTH BROAD
Corner Washington and Broad on top of Broadmoor Druggists
NEW ORLEANS. LOUISIANA 70125

IF YOU CAN'T COME, WRITE

Brazilians and Filipinos are more likely to accept these healers because they accept paraphysical events as basic realities. This acceptance of the rational reality of the spiritual world is known as *Kardecism,* a philosophy that emerged from the writings of a nineteenth-century French mystic known as Allan Kardec, a professor whose real name was Denizard Rivail. Kardecists reject ritual and paganism, but believe in reincarnation and in drawing on the power and knowledge of the spiritual world through mediums. Kardec theorists believe that communication with, and effective use of, spirits is a neglected area of modern psychotherapy and a new development on the rapidly closing frontier of medicine.

A curious example of this phenomenon is Reverend William Brown (1914–) who lives in an unpretentious house in an undisclosed small town in or near North Carolina. When he diagnoses and operates (all this takes place in his house), twenty-eight dead physician-specialists take over his body. A patient dressed in a hospital gown rests on his operating table, and these departed entities inhabit Brown's body one by one. Brown's hands never touch a patient—they work quickly in the air a few inches over the body—and the surgery takes place on the etheric, not the physical, level. The etheric body of the patient is an exact copy of the actual bones, muscle, organs, and nerves of the patient's body. Bloodlessly, each disease is corrected in the etheric body, and these corrections are reflected back into the physical body. Brown works on invisible wounds with invisible needles, thread, and instruments. Patients rest and sleep in one of four of Brown's recovery rooms. In 1954 Brown was ordained a minister of the Spiritualist Episcopal Church, and he now belongs to the Church of Revelation. While still a child, Brown was visited by a deceased Presbyterian minister and a Sioux Indian medicine man.[18]

There are an unknown number of psychic surgeons practicing in the United States. Most of them get their patients through word of mouth. As long as they remain underground, organized medicine ignores them. We have no methods for measuring their impact on health care. There may be a sizable number of quacks among them, but we are at a loss as to how to approach unorthodox, paranormal healing with rational analysis.

Mesmerism and Hypnotism

Friedrich Anton Mesmer (1734-1815) held four doctorates; he was a physician, astrologer, and astronomer. He revived interest in the treatment of patients with hypnotism, which he called animal magnetism or mesmeric sleep. *Hypnotism* occurs when one individual captures the attention of another to such a degree that it is possible to lull him into a trance such that commands and suggestions could be implanted. Unfortunately, Mesmer took a potentially powerful technique and surrounded it with hokum. Sufferers were led into a large room filled with mirrors, stained glass, incense, and soft music. In the center of the room was a tub of iron filings, from which protruded rods. Patients sat around the tub and held the rod or each other's hands. Mesmer entered in a lilac silk robe and held another iron rod. He would pass around the circle, staring into patients' eyes, touching them and making passes over their heads.

Mesmer influenced several areas of the scientific and nonscientific community. Scattered medical groups in the United States adopted mesmerism to treat neuralgias, migraine, inflammatory maladies, and hysteria.[19] He also stimulated psychiatric interest in hypnosis. Last, he inspired countless quacks to develop ever more bizarre techniques— bimetallic tractors that were stroked over diseased organs, artificial lodestones, and magnetic vapors—with which to fleece the susceptible public.

Fortunately, James Braid, a Manchester physician, took the showmanship out of mesmerism. He suggested that hypnotism, when used to induce analgesia, anesthesia, and relaxation, would be an important healing agent.[20]

Voodoo

Voodoo, a ritualistic following linked with serpent worship and (in extreme cases) with human sacrifice and cannibalistic ceremonies, came to the southern United States from the West Indies, particularly from Haiti, a little over 200 years ago. During the nineteenth century, it flourished in southern Louisiana and was practiced by such colorful characters as Dr. John, Dr. Yah Yah, Dr. Jim Alexander, Marie Laveau, and her daughter Marie Glapion. Voodoo practitioners usually worked separately and in competition; they developed a mixture of snake worship, charms, Catholic rituals, fortune-telling, blackmail, and prostitution. Charms, amulets, talismans, secret potions, gris-gris, and topical ointments were prescribed for everything from chest pains to marital problems. Wild orgies—secret but racially integrated—were performed on religious holidays and special occasions. Local laws and the organized church kept voodoo underground and suppressed.[21]

Yet voodoo practices, like folk medicine, persist in twentieth-century America. According to a study of the effect of voodoo on health practices in Louisiana,[22] 44 percent of the patient-respondents believed that one could cause pain or illness to another by putting a spell on him—a voodoo practice. Numerous other voodoo superstitions were discovered as well. Patients still go to traiteurs for rheumatism, tumors, inflammations, angina, nosebleeds, warts, dislocations, and arthritis. Voodoo practitioners may prescribe a novena and apply an ointment or lotion made from ingredients such as dew gathered in May or water from the first rain of the month. Patients wear copper, gold, or silver wires, coins or rings tied around the neck, waist, or ankle. Forty percent of the patient-respondents believe that nonmedical practitioners can cure.

Scientology

Scientology was the brainchild of science fiction writer Lafayette Ronald Hubbard. His creation was called Dianetics, based on a best-selling periodical in the 1950s, *Astounding Science Fiction.* Hubbard claimed he had been blinded by a World War II explosion but cured as a result of a personal reexamination of the accident and the attitudes he had derived from the experience. He described the human mind as a machine filled with accumulated errors that needed to be removed if a person is to function happily in a state of near-genius. These errors or hang-ups, called "engrams," resulted from emotional pain or shock suffered either earlier in life or during a previous existence. Getting "cleared" (cured) resembled climbing a very tall ladder, and the ascent cost plenty of money. The process employed an E-meter: two empty cans wired to a battery and to a gauge—a simple galvanometer—supposedly designed to detect suppressed engrams and improve intelligence. Because of tax, medical, and legal difficulties, Hubbard reformulated his creation into the Founding Church of Scientology in 1955. Branches developed in major U.S. cities and foreign lands. In 1969, the U.S. Court of Claims denied the church a tax exemption as a religious organization, and the FDA impounded the E-meter because of false and misleading claims made by Scientologists.

In the resulting court battles, the government won a bittersweet victory.[23] The E-meter could be used to monitor the spirit or soul of man, for example, for religious purposes, but it must be clearly marked with a warning that it is not to be used for diagnosis, treatment, or prevention of disease. Scientology kept its tax exemption, and the E-meters were returned, and Hubbard took off for his Mediterranean floating castle with a sizable sum of money. Scientology persists.[24]

Homeopathy

Samuel Hahnemann (1755-1843), a German physician, experimented with various drugs using himself as a subject. He developed the principle of "like cures like," that is, if a drug administered to a healthy person causes certain symptoms, the same drug will cure a sick individual who presents similar symptoms. *Homeopathy* ("like-disease") is a system of treating disease by drugs that produce in healthy persons symptoms similar to those of the disease being treated. Homeopaths attempt to provide a remedy that will stimulate the body's vital forces to heal itself. The importance of diet is stressed.

Homeopaths are almost always physicians with special training in homeopathy. About 5,000 physicians call themselves homeopaths but use both homeopathic and orthodox methods. They often examine the results of laboratory studies before they prescribe a medication. Hahnemann Medical College was at one time the Homeopathic Medical College of Pennsylvania. Great Britain has relatively more homeopaths than the United States.[25]

Naprapathy and Naturopathy

Naprapathy is "a system of manually applied movements, both passive and active, designed to bring motion, with consequent release of tension, into abnormally tensed and rigid ligaments, muscles, and articulations of the human body." Naprapaths concentrate on increasing the resistance of the body through manipulation, diet, and hygiene. They are aligned closely with the natural foods movement (granola, nonprocessed foods, and the like).

There are approximately 500 naprapaths in the United States. Naprapathy was started by Oakley G. Smith, who established the first college of naprapathy in 1908. One other college, also located in Chicago, has since been established to grant the degree of Doctor of Naprapathy (D.N.). Entrants have a high school degree and must complete 144 weeks of study, including the basic sciences.

Naturopathy is the prevention and treatment of disease by use of biochemical, psychological, and physical methods that assist the body's own healing processes. When the mechanical, mental, and physiological principles of life are upset and disease occurs, the naturopath restores normal body balance by applying natural agencies in conformance with the principles or laws of life. Naturopaths use corrective nutrition, body mechanics, physiotherapy, and remedial psychology. Naturopaths, sometimes known as naturopathic physicians, diagnose and treat any and all conditions that one might find in an M.D.'s general practice.

There are about 5,000 naturopaths in the United States. The National College of Naturopathic Medicine in Seattle, Washington, is the only U.S. institution granting the degrees of Doctor of Naturopathic Medicine (D.N.M.) and Doctor of Naturopathy (D.N.). There are no naturopathic hospitals, and naturopaths have no hospital privileges. Naturopaths (specifically) are licensed in five states and the District of Columbia. In most states, naturopaths may use only natural remedies (whatever *natural* means), although a few states (Florida and Utah) grant virtually unlimited licenses.[26]

Naprapaths and naturopaths (and chiropractors) have for some time been the target of excessive abuse from the American Medical Association. No one is quite sure how these independent practitioners affect health consumers.

Chiropractic

The chiropractor is the most controversial practitioner in the United States. In 1895, David Daniel Palmer, a tradesman who operated a magnetic healing studio in Davenport, Iowa, adjusted the vertebrae of his deaf janitor and restored the man's hearing. Palmer believed that he had relieved pressure on a spinal nerve, removed interference with the nerve supply, and thereby allowed the body to cure itself. Misaligned vertebrae, or subluxations, according to Palmer, were the cause of most diseases. Theoretically, mechanical disturbances of the nervous system impair the body's defenses, including its resistance to germs. Gravitational strains, asymmetrical activities and efforts, developmental defects, or other mechanical, chemical, or psychic irritations may also trigger nerve disturbance. Some chiropractors follow Palmer's theories and use only adjustments of the spine to restore proper nerve function; however, most also use diet and vitamins, physical therapy including massage, and psychosomatic counseling.

In the same year he discovered chiropractic principles, Palmer founded the Palmer College of Chiropractic. This college, one of eleven schools in the United States that grant the degree of Doctor of Chiropractic (D.C.) and an unknown degree, Ph.C., trains one-third of all chiropractors. Most entrants to the college have college degrees or at least two years of college. The faculty is composed almost entirely of D.C.'s who have graduated from Palmer. The grandson of D. D. Palmer is now the college's president. The curriculum is patterned after the medical school curriculum—two years of basic science and two years of clinical practice—and includes courses in public health, diagnosis, ophthalmology, pediatrics, radiology, pathology, psychiatry, obstetrics and gynecology, business administration, and ethics. The curriculum and admission standards of chiropractic colleges have been improved in response to severe criticism that course offerings are inferior and inadequate.[27] In August 1974, the U.S. Commissioner of Education recognized an accrediting agency—the Council on Chiropractic Education—for chiropractic colleges. As a result of official national standing, accredited chiropractic schools are eligible for financial assistance from a variety of federal funding programs.

The greatest opposition to chiropractic has come from organized medicine, especially from the American Medical Association. The AMA has branded chiropractic an unscientific cult and a significant hazard to the public, and it has relentlessly warned that chiropractic treatment diverts patients from seeking appropriate orthodox medical attention in time to prevent serious or fatal consequences. Around 1920, organized medicine harassed chiropractors in California and had about 75 percent of them arrested for practicing medicine without a license. Many of the chiropractors, instead of paying fines when convicted, went to jail. In 1922, when the California legislature was considering a bill to license chiropractors, the jailed chiropractors created such tremendous public sympathy that the bill was approved by a wide margin. After many court battles and jail sentences, chiropractors are now licensed in all states.

In the 1960s, the AMA, through its investigatory arm and Committee on

Quackery, attempted to discredit chiropractic by the dissemination of highly slanted propaganda; this misinformation was passed on and published in subsequent research reports and the press.[28] When the attempt to discredit the chiropractors appeared doomed, the AMA began a strategy of absorption and control of chiropractors; specifically, it tried to convince state legislatures that chiropractors, like physiotherapists and other health auxiliaries, should be placed under the formal supervision of physicians. The AMA failed miserably; the chiropractors had overwhelming political clout.[29]

At present, chiropractors cannot prescribe drugs or perform surgery, but in many states they can sign birth and death certificates. The federal government reimburses them for treating Workmen's Compensation, medicare, and medicaid patients. They work at their own hospitals and clinics and at Veterans Administration and armed forces hospitals. In one survey, more than 20 percent of M.D.'s received some referrals from chiropractors, and 5 percent of the M.D.'s sometimes referred patients to chiropractors.[30] Chiropractors seem to develop excellent patient relationships and have a low incidence of malpractice claims.

Yet controversy still plagues the chiropractor. He stands accused of excessive and dangerous use of x-rays, unsupported healing claims, shallow and deceptive promotional techniques,[31] and ignorance of fundamental biochemical life processes.[32] Sociologists have labeled chiropractors as marginal practitioners.[33] Perhaps because of fierce rivalry between health providers or perhaps because of a lack of funds or motivation on the part of chiropractors, not one well-executed scientific study in the eighty-year history of chiropractic or in the entire history of medicine shows that manipulation can affect any of the basic life processes. In 1973, HEW decided it would sponsor a scientific evaluation of chiropractic.[34] Yet, whatever the outcome of these studies may be, chiropractors, now 20,000 strong and earning an average income of $31,000 per year, will doubtlessly prosper and expand their role in the health arena.[35] They have fought a strong, uphill battle against organized medicine, they have political allies, and their message reaches the public despite an unfavorable press.[36]

Podiatry

Podiatry, in contrast to chiropractic, has maintained a low public profile. Until 1958 podiatrists were known as chiropodists (Chirogen: "surgeon"; pod: "foot"). Perhaps the name change was the result of confusion with chiropractic. Podiatry deals with the examination, diagnosis, prevention, treatment, and care of the human foot. The origins of podiatric foot care go back to the European barber-surgeons of the fourteenth century. During the latter half of the eighteenth century, the itinerant corncutter disappeared from the streets and was replaced by the office-based practitioner. Chiropody was considered a craft until 1895, when New York State passed the first law to license the chiropodist. In 1912, the New York College of Chiropody opened to teach some of the fundamental principles of medicine and surgery as they related to the foot. Today, podiatrists are licensed in all fifty states and the District of Columbia. In the United States, there have been no direct confrontations between podiatry and organized medicine, and podiatrists have maintained their independence. The British Medical Association gave formal recognition to chiropody in 1938 but placed them, along with other technical health services, in an auxiliary position to the physician.[37]

The five colleges of podiatric medicine in the United States are in Chicago, Cleveland, New York, Philadelphia, and San Francisco. The states in which these cities are located account for nearly one-half of all practicing podiatrists—7,100 in 1970. Applicants to a college must have completed two years of college. The first two years of podiatric training cover the basic sciences; the last two years cover clinical experiences. Upon graduation, an individual becomes a Doctor of Podiatric Medicine (D.P.M.), Doctor of Podiatry (Pod. D. or D.P.), or Doctor of Surgical Podiatry (D.S.P.). Many graduates do an internship, either in a general hospital or in a podiatric hospital in California. An internship or practice is not required, except in three states, for licensure. Podiatric specialties include foot orthopedics, foot roentgenology, foot surgery, and podiatric dermatology.[38]

Ninety-four percent of active podiatrists fit corrective and supportive devices, prescribe proper footware, perform physical therapy, and write prescriptions for, and administer, drugs. Podiatrists perform foot surgery in their offices. Orthopedic surgeons tend to ignore this intrusion on their business because most of the surgery takes place outside of the hospital. In some states, (depending upon whether physicians sit on their licensing board), podiatrists may operate above the ankle. Podiatrists may not amputate the foot or leg; they are limited to the use of local anesthesia. One in eight podiatrists had malpractice claims filed against him or her in 1973; one in forty had claims filed in 1963.[39] Children, the elderly, pregnant women, and people with decreased vision or blindness are more frequently podiatric patients than others.[40] Podiatrists are reimbursed by public (medicare and medicaid) and private insurance programs. A podiatrist's average net income is about $35,000 per year.

Dentistry

In the eighteenth century, dentistry was practiced almost exclusively in emergency situations—by barber-surgeons and local blacksmiths. Tooth drawers were trained by apprenticeship.[41] During the early nineteenth century, schools of medicine in the United States had departments of dental medicine. In 1839, two physicians, Horace Hayden and Chapin

Harris, founded the Baltimore College of Dental Surgery, the first dental school in the world. *Dentistry* is the art and science of healing the oral cavity, its connective tissues, teeth, and organs contained in the mouth.[42]

In 1972 there were 119,700 dentists in the United States and a dentist/population ratio of 57.1/100,000, a ratio that has been holding steady for twenty years. The optimum ratio is 100/100,000. In 1972 there were 47.3 active civilian dentists per 100,000 population.[43] Fifty-six dentistry schools in the United States grant either the degree of Doctor of Dental Surgery (D.D.S.) or the degree of Doctor of Medical Dentistry (D.M.D.). These schools graduate about 4,000 per year. A small number of dentists, approximately 400, come into the United States each year. A dental education mirrors a medical education: two years of basic sciences and preclinical sciences and two years of clinical practice. Upon graduation, a dentist who wishes to practice obtains a license by passing both a written and a clinical examination. Most states accept the written examination given by the National Board of Dental Examiners. In 1972, there were two regional clinical examinations for twenty states; in the other thirty states, a dentist's clinical skill was examined by the state board of dental examiners (or its equivalent).

Dentists also specialize. A specialist is one who completes two or more academic years of advanced education and passes the American Board of Examinations (the specialist is then a diplomate) in one of the specialties shown in Table 10.1.[44] Orthodontics is by far the most popular specialty. Oral surgeons practice both in their office and in the hospital. When practicing in the hospital, they sometimes come in conflict with physician-surgeons who feel that dentists do not treat the "whole" patient and that oral surgeons are poaching on their territory. Dentists can administer general anesthesia, usually intraveneously, either in a hospital or in their offices.

About 91 percent of active dentists are in private practice. A small, but slowly increasing, number are in group practice (approximately 3 percent of active dentists).[45] Since 1960, the number of dental auxiliaries has increased markedly; they now account for 63 percent of the total dental work force. Table 10.2 shows the number and type of dental auxiliaries.[46] The dental hygienist is the only dental auxiliary required to obtain a license to practice in each state. In general, a dentist can increase his or her income by efficient use of auxiliary personnel and by increasing the number of chairs he or she has to work over. Dentists usually charge by the cavity, and a tooth may have more than one cavity. They are reimbursed by a few insurance programs. Some unions have prepaid dental programs.[47]

For some reason—either because those who have a weak self-concept become dentists or because dentistry involves little job satisfaction or is associated with pain or lacks public recognition—dentists have the highest rate of suicide and divorce of all occupational groups.[48]

Table 10.1   Number of Dental Specialists by Specialty, 1972

Specialty	Number of Dentists
1. Orthodontist: Concerned with the position of the teeth in the jaw and with the shape of the jaw. They correct malocclusions and improve appearances. Two additional years of training are required.	4,566
2. Oral surgeon: Performs simple and complicated surgery. Takes additional courses in anatomy, radiology, and anesthesiology. One year internship and two years as a resident are required.	2,714
3. Periodontist: Works on the soft and hard tissues surrounding the teeth. The soft tissues are the gums, and the hard tissues are the bony structures (sockets) that the teeth fit into.	1,114
4. Pedodontist: Children's dentist. Two years post-graduate work required.	1,225
5. Prosthodontist: Replaces missing teeth with false teeth; the architects and engineers of dentistry.	702
6. Endodontist: Works deep down in the tooth, with the nerves, blood vessels, and roots that reach into the bone. The highest paid specialty.	585
7. Oral pathologist: Makes microscopic diagnoses of oral conditions.	120
8. Public health: Promotes oral health through organized public effort.	116
Total	11,142

Table 10.2 Number of Dental Auxiliaries, By Type, 1972

Type of Auxiliary	Number
1. Dental hygienist: Performs dental prophylaxes (cleans and polishes teeth), takes and processes X-rays, applies preventive agents (fluorides), and does patient education. Two- or four-year program at the college level required.	21,000
2. Dental assistant: Prepares the patient, passes instruments and material to the dentist, prepares materials, and helps around the office. On-the-job training or one year at a community college or vocational school required.	116,000
3. Dental laboratory technician: Works with acrylics, ceramics, and metals to construct dentures, crowns, bridges, and orthodonic devices. Uses precision instruments, casting machines, furnaces, and other special equipment. On-the-job training or two years of post-secondary education required.	32,000

The public tends to neglect dental care. Dental caries is our most prevalent disease. An astonishing number of adolescents suffer from periodontal disease in its more distinctive stages. Perhaps as one way of encouraging the public to utilize dentists, organized dentistry is working toward hospital-based dentistry, which would integrate medicine and dentistry and allow for a more ideal treatment of the whole person. Postgraduate courses listed in various dental journals emphasize "hospital orientation" for general practitioners. Someday dentistry may be part of a hospital-based, primary-care group practice.[49]

Optometry

Vision care in the United States is delivered by three groups of practitioners: ophthalmologists, optometrists, and opticians. Most consumers have only a vague idea of the differences among the three groups. Table 10.3 compares these groups and their auxiliary personnel.[50] *Optometrists* are vision specialists, and *ophthalmologists* are eye specialists. *Opticians* fill their prescriptions.

There are twelve schools of optometry in the United States. Since 1950 the number of practitioners per 100,000 has been decreasing; according to the American Optometric Association, the optometric ratio is now 14/100,000. Upon graduating with an O.D. degree, an optometrist must pass an optometry board examination. Optometrists perform refraction and use various pieces of sophisticated equipment to diagnose and treat vision problems. Optometrists examine an estimated 60 percent of all patients who seek eye care. They tend to locate their practices in shopping centers, optical departments of department stores, and neighborhood health care centers.[51]

The dispute between optometry and ophthalmologists goes back to the nineteenth century, when optometry made a dramatic split from organized medicine after it appeared as though the two would be compatible.[52] Since then their organizations have gone their separate ways, but the dispute continues to center on training, diagnosis, and the fitting of contact lenses. The ophthalmologists' concern is that optometrists desire to practice medicine without the necessary medical training. Recent activities by segments of organized optometry—such as a change in the licensing laws to allow the topical application of drugs to the eye— reinforce this concern.

For their part, optometrists are concerned about the orthoptist and other assistants working under ophthalmologists; more and more of these auxiliary personnel are being trained to test visual acuities, make visual field examinations, test for binocular vision, perform tonography, and fit contact lenses. In short, personnel working under an ophthalmologist can and do perform many of the same functions that an optometrist performs—which is highly threatening to the optometrist.

Table 10.3 Comparison of Opticianry, Optometry, and Ophthalmology

	Opticianry	Optometry (O.D.)	Ophthalmology (M.D.)
Number of practitioners	8,000 in 1965 10,963 in 1969 11,715 in 1972	21,000 (18,000 active), constant since 1960	2,849 in 1950 7,660 in 1967 9,578 in 1969 10,443 in 1972
Practitioners per 100,000	5.5 in 1972	13.9 in 1951 12.0 in 1959 10.7 in 1967	2.2 in 1950 3.7 in 1967 4.9 in 1972
Educational requirements	Mostly on-the-job training.	Usually 4 years college + 4 years in accredited school of optometry.	4 years college + 4 years medical school + completion of residency program in ophthalmology.
Licensing requirements	15 states as of February 1971	All states	All states
Functions	Make, fit, supply, and adjust eyeglasses according to prescriptions written by O.D. and M.D.	Examine the eye and related structures to determine the presence of vision problems, eye diseases, or other abnormalities. They do not prescribe drugs, make definitive diagnoses of or treat diseases, or perform surgery.	Diagnose and treat all eye diseases and abnormal conditions, including refractive errors. They may prescribe drugs, lenses, or other treatment, or perform surgery to remedy these conditions.
Allied personnel:	Optical Technicians	Ophthalmic Assistants	Orthoptists
Functions	Grind and polish the lenses and assemble in a frame.	Take histories, assist in refractions, administer local medications, apply surgical dressings, fit and adjust spectacles, and neutralize lenses.	Specializes in the field of diagnosis and treatment of eye muscle and fusion anomalies. Teaches patients exercises.

Optometrists believe that the expanded utilization of modestly trained technicians for refraction and contact lens procedures is not in the best interest of maintaining a high level of patient care. Ophthalmologists usually charge one-fifth to one-half more than optometrists for the same services. Recent licensing laws hold the optometrist responsible for detecting the presence of eye disease and making a timely referral to an M.D. Thus O.D.'s have taken on additional medical responsibilities, but without the additional status or compensation.[53]

Veterinary Medicine

In the United States, more than 30 million families own dogs, over 25 million cats and 15 million birds are kept in homes, and the pet population is growing faster than the human population. Food, dog houses, cages, leashes, collars, sweaters, coats, bowls, and accessories accompany the pet boom.

The friendly veterinarian is cashing in on the pet boom. *Veterinary medicine* is the health practice concerned with the prevention, cure, and alleviation of disease and injury in animals. Veterinarians treat sick animals, advise on the care and breeding of animals, and help prevent the

Table 10.4   Type of Activity of Members of the American Veterinary
             Association, 31 December 1972

	Percentage in Specialty
Private practice	
Large animal	6.9
Small animal	32.1
Mixed	37.0
Total	76.0
Regulatory	3.9
Public Health	1.2
Military	4.0
Miscellaneous, including laboratory services	13.5
Total, non-private	22.6

outbreak and spread of animal-borne and animal-transmitted diseases.

In 1972, there were 28,337 veterinarians, or 40 per 100,000 pet dogs, cats, and birds. As seen in Table 10.4, most veterinarians are in private practice and treat primarily small animals.[54] Veterinarians are educated largely at the public's expense. Sixteen of the eighteen veterinary schools are land grant colleges (A & M colleges), where tuition is subsidized.[55] Veterinary school is the most difficult to gain admission to of any type of health school.[56] It consists of two years of basic science and two years of clinical work. Graduates receive the degree of Doctor of Veterinary Medicine (D.V.M.). Then, to obtain a license (which is required in all states), an applicant must pass a state board examination. Veterinarians can specialize and become board-certified in the following areas: public health, toxicology, theriogenology, microbiology, ophthalmology, pathology, radiology, surgery, internal medicine, and preventive medicine.

Large animal practice, which is a dying field, concentrates on preconditioning herds of animals. Preconditioning is a form of insurance, and the veterinarian trains farmers and lay helpers to perform these tasks (vaccination, dehorning, needle pushing, etc.). Because of small profit margins per animal, the veterinarian concentrates more on the herd as a whole and less on the health of an individual animal. However, thoroughbred race horses still get individual attention.

Small animal practice has been called a luxury—that is, in relation to large animal practice—yet it makes up the largest segment of veterinary practice. In a small animal practice, the clinic must often deal with the worried owner: veterinarians see 1.71 owners for every 1.00 animals in the examining room. Thus, a veterinarian faces the emotional challenges of the patient-owner-vet triangle:

1. treat the whole patient, not merely the injured area
2. act as a "parent" in vet-owner relations
3. analyze and capitalize on the owner-pet relationship by judging the owner's degree of concern—a possible index of the quality of home care

4. recognize that the conduct of seriously ill animals closely resembles that of pediatric patients
5. recognize that the emotional security of the human population is, in part, dependent on the physical and emotional security of pet animals[57]

Approximately 98 percent of the drugs prescribed by veterinarians—which are considerably more expensive than human drugs—are filled by veterinarians. Over 3,500 of the roughly 4,500 animal hospitals in the United States are for small animals. Standards for these hospitals are set by the American Animal Hospital Association.

What does the future hold for veterinarians? The following list is, of course, incomplete.

1. veterinary mobile care and emergency units
2. twenty-four-hour monitoring of hospital patients
3. franchised veterinary hospitals
4. centralized hospitals with outpatient and satellite clinics
5. expansion of group practice
6. pet insurance programs
7. hospital accreditation
8. certification for specialized practice

In short, we can expect veterinary medicine to follow many of the trends of human medicine.

Intermediate-Level Health Practitioners

During the 1960s, the Department of Defense realized that there would not be enough military physicians to staff clinics in remote areas, in combat, and on board ship. The solution it found was to give medical corpsmen special training and to allow them to handle routine illnesses using medical decision guides. Medics provided life-saving procedures in emergencies as well as preventive medicine. They gradually gained physician acceptance and are now an important part of the military health care system.

Efforts to duplicate this success in the civilian health care system have been less well defined. A handful of academic programs for inter-mediate-level health practitioners began in the 1970s. This new health practitioner has several names:

physician's assistant
physician's associate
physician-extender
health associate

nurse practitioner
nurse-midwife
nurse clinician

Most provide primary care skills, and some specialize in pediatrics or childbirth.

In only a few states do licensing laws grant physician's assistants a well defined, semiautonomous role. At issue is whether physician's assistants can and should function independently of licensed physicians.[58] A key to this issue is their method of reimbursement. Until 1978, they could be paid only through a physician. In December 1977, President Carter signed into law a bill that authorized, for the first time, medicare and medicaid payments on a cost basis for services of physician's assistants, nurse practitioners, and nurse-midwives. To be eligible, they must work in a rural health clinic in a medically underserved area. Although the clinic must be under a physician's "general" direction, the new law eliminates any requirements for "on the spot" physician supervision. In a few years, intermediate-level health practitioners may be billing patients directly on a fee-for-service basis.

Summary

Independent practitioners are a curious group. Several of them got started with a miraculous cure and proceeded to develop a following—which in some cases is so enamored with the healing process that despite evidence to the contrary, they have an absolute faith in the healing process. Occasionally, legal authorities step in and make arrests or seize equipment, but very few independent practitioners are put out of business. Instead, accreditation and licensure give these practitioners credibility and status. The tremendous demand for health care almost guarantees that any practitioner will find patients.

Questions

1. Pharmacy and chiropractic have been labeled incomplete or marginal professions. What does this description mean? How has, and/or will, professional identity shifted, and/or shift, as a result of legislation and successful law suits? Discuss.

2. Should Christian Science practitioners be allowed to practice in government hospitals? Explain.

3. Suppose your aunt wanted to go to a psychic surgeon for a gall bladder operation. What would you tell her?

4. Should podiatrists and dentists be able to write prescriptions for drugs and not optometrists?

5. Why is getting into veterinary school more difficult than getting into medical school?

Notes

1. This section on the Indian medicine man was taken from two sources:

Robert L. Bergman, "Learning from Indian Medicine," *Diversion* 3:8-9, 34-35 (February-March 1975), and "Navajo Medicine Men Are Busier Than Ever Bringing Peace of Mind," *Wall Street Journal,* 26 March 1973, p. 1.

2. Louis Rose, *Faith Healing* (Middlesex: Penguin, 1971), pp. 27 and 28.

3. Ibid., pp. 89 and 90.

4. In 1531, an Indian, Juan Diego, had a vision of the Virgin at Guadalupe; the Virgin left an imprint of herself on Diego's cape, which is on display in Our Lady of Guadalupe Church. In 1858 the Virgin appeared to an illiterate and asthmatic fourteen-year-old girl, later canonized Bernadette Soubirous; the apparition told Bernadette where to dig for a spring; Bernadette dug and struck water. Between 1 and 2 million people visit Lourdes each year, including over 30,000 sick. The following is an account of what a visitor might expect:

The pilgrims' days are filled with religious services and trips to the Grotto, where they are immersed in the ice-cold spring. Every afternoon all the pilgrims and invalids who are at Lourdes at the time—usually forty or fifty thousand—gather at the Esplanade in front of the shrine for the procession that is the climax of each day's activities. The bedridden are placed nearest the shrine, those who can sit up are behind them, the ambulatory invalids behind them, while the hordes of visitors fill the rest of the space. The enormous emotional and aesthetic impact of the procession is well conveyed by the following quotation:

At four the bells begin to peal—the Procession begins to form. The priests in their varied robes assemble at the Grotto. . . . The bishop appears with the monstrance under the sacred canopy. The loud-speakers open up. A great hymn rolls out, the huge crowd joining in unison, magnificently. The Procession begins its long, impressive way down one side and up the other of the sunny Esplanade. First the Children of Mary, young girls in blue capes, white veils . . . then forty or fifty priests in black cassocks . . . other priests in white surplices . . . then come the Bishops in purple . . . and finally the officiating Archbishop in his white and gold robes under the golden canopy. Bringing up the rear large numbers of men and women of the different pilgrimages, Sisters, Nurses, members of various religious organizations; last of all the doctors. . . . Hymns, prayers, fervent, unceasing. In the Square the sick line up in two rows. . . . Every few feet, in front of them, kneeling priests with arms outstretched praying earnestly, leading the responses. Nurses and orderlies on their knees, praying too. . . . Ardor mounts as the Blessed Sacrament approaches. Prayers gather intensity. . . . The bishop leaves the shelter of the canopy, carrying the monstrance. The Sacred Host is raised above each sick one. The great crowd falls to its knees. All arms are outstretched in one vast cry to Heaven. As far as one can see in any direction, people are on their knees, praying.

4. Jerome D. Frank, *Persuasion and Healing* (Baltimore, Md.: Johns Hopkins University Press, 1973), pp. 66-72.

5. Rose, *Faith Healing*, p. 95.

6. Frank, *Persuasion and Healing*, p. 72.

7. *The Scope of Christian Science Healing* (Boston, Mass.: The Christian Science Publishing Society, 1967), pp. 11 and 12. See also, *A Century of Christian Science Healing* (Boston, Mass.: The Christian Science Publishing Society); and *Radical Reliance in Healing* (Boston, Mass.: The Christian Science Publishing Society, 1958).

8. This section is assembled from Aubrey C. McTaggart, *The Health Care Dilemma* (Boston, Mass.: Holbrook Press, 1971), pp. 59-62. Paris Flammonde, *The Mystic Healers* (Briarcliff Manor, N.Y.: Stein & Day, 1974), pp. 34-44.

9. The clinic consists of eight examining rooms, one emergency room, six M.D.'s, seven R.N.'s, and a large auxiliary staff.

10. Flammonde, *The Mystic Healers*, pp. 61-68. David St. Clair, *Psychic Healers* (New York: Doubleday & Co., 1974), pp. 289-307.

11. An ill person who attends a crusade is not required to give money but usually finds himself making numerous contributions. He cannot receive a healing without a prayer card, and he must attend every nightly session since he never knows when his card will be called. The collection plate is passed around at each session. The ill person believes his chances of having his prayer card called increase with his contributions. Love-gift contributions also are made to ensure the giver health and prosperity (a sort of preventive medicine).

12. Flammonde, *The Mystic Healers*, pp. 69-77.

13. Ibid., pp. 117-31. St. Clair, *Psychic Healers*, describes a Kuhlman service:

The service was about to begin. For at least an hour the two-hundred-voice choir had been singing hymns. Their voices filled the vast auditorium before the people did, setting up vibrations and creating an atmosphere.

When it was time for the service to begin, amid very little fanfare, Miss Kathryn Kuhlman walked out onto the stage. No, it was more than just walking out; it was a quick, energy-laden movement almost like the arrival of a volt of electricity. She was wearing a white blouse with light, puffy, wrist-length sleeves. She wore a simple knee-length, pleated, white skirt. High-heeled white shoes were on her feet and her auburn hair was hanging freely to her shoulders.

The choir behind her began to sing and she sang right along with them in that deep throaty voice that has become familiar to so many television viewers. She wasn't asking for anything, or even that you believe in what she was about to do. She was singing because she was happy to be there and to be beginning her service.

After that she told a few stories about her childhood and showed a gift that she had received from one of her small nieces. She loves those girls and wistfully told all of us that it was a shame that she had never had any children of her own. (She was married once, years ago, but it ended in divorce.) From there a male vocalist sang two songs and she rested a bit. She must have been tired for she hadn't stopped moving, talking, praising, since she had first appeared.

Then she began to preach. It was from the book of John and told of Christ's tribulations. As she was speaking, she suddenly stopped and pointed out into the audience. "Someone out there has been cured of a fused disc in the spine. He is wearing a body truss and it is beginning to burn. Take it off! Jesus has touched you! You have been blessed by the touch of the Lord!"

There was a murmur as heads turned to look at a man who was struggling excitedly to his feet. He began to unbutton his shirt as she went back to her sermon. "Up there," she pointed to the other side of the balcony, "there is a woman who can see again! Oh, praise Jesus that this dear soul has been given her sight. Praise him!" and back she went to her message.

This happened several times during the sermon. She announced—she didn't go down there and touch, but announced from the stage—that a hip socket was well, that an ulcer had vanished, that a severe itching had ceased, that a swollen throat had returned to normal, that a broken ankle was well, that a migraine headache had stopped, etc., etc., etc. People cried out, others shouted praise to Jesus, others sobbed or sat there praying that this miraculous power would touch them, too. They had come for a miracle. They were praying to get what they came for.

Her oft-interrupted sermon over, she had them pass the collection plate as the choir sang. Some people put in checks, others threw in large-size bills. Most people dropped a few coins and those who didn't have anything to give at all let the plate go by.

Then she asked that those who had been healed, who had "been touched by Blessed Jesus," come forth onto the stage. All over the auditorium people rose and moved toward the aisles. They came down to the steps leading up to the platform. Many carried canes and crutches in their hands. One woman was pushing her own wheel chair. Ushers at the steps asked a few brief questions before they permitted the healed to come up next to Miss Kuhlman.

With a portable microphone around her neck, she began talking to those who said they had been healed. A woman began sobbing as she told her story of feeling a stomach tumor burn up and go away. "All the pain is gone," she kept saying. "It's the first time in months there hasn't been any pain."

Then Kathryn Kuhlman did something extraordinary. She reached out and prayed for the woman, but as her fingers touched the woman's forehead the woman fell backward. She seemed to be jolted by an unexpected lightning bolt that knocked her off her feet and into the waiting arms of one of Miss Kuhlman's helpers. She lay there, on the stage, for a few seconds before regaining consciousness. When they helped her to her feet, she, still in tears, thanked Miss Kuhlman again. "It is not me, my dear, that you must thank," said the evangelist. "I have no power. It is the power of Jesus that cured you. Please don't give me your praise. Give it to the Lord." And she reached out again and again the woman fell over backward onto the floor.

And that's the way it went for another two hours. A steady parade of people who claimed to have been instantly cured *before* she ever touched them, cured while she was preaching her sermon. And as she prayed for each of them, over onto the floor they went.

A young girl came up a specially constructed ramp, pushing her own wheel chair. She was with her teen-age sister. Both were in tears. Miss Kuhlman managed to get their story through the sobbing. The girl had been crippled since she was six years old and confined to that wheel chair for life. Then two years ago, when she was sixteen, the doctors had discovered cancer. Desperate for anything that would help, their brother had heard of Kathryn Kuhlman and had paid their airplane expenses from Arizona to California. Miss Kuhlman asked the brother to come on stage and a young sailor, wearing his summer whites, joined his two sisters. He was also crying. Miss Kuhlman began to pray for all three and as she did, she reached out and touched them. One at a time they fell over backward, sisters and brother alike. They lay on the stage as she continued to pray for them.

Then there was a young Mexican boy whose mother confessed she had taken him from the state hospital for incurables that morning on a pretext of a family picnic. The boy was in his late teens and he had been unable to walk. He felt something surge down through his legs as Miss Kuhlman was speaking and told his mother he had been cured. Miss Kuhlman asked that he run down the ramp and up the aisle to the rear of the auditorium and back to the stage. As his mother sobbed and cried out, *"Gracias a Dios,"* the young man—incurable just minutes before—raced up and down the aisle.

I had noticed a woman with a withered leg as I came into the auditorium. One leg was normal, the other was like a dry stick, and about three inches shorter. She walked with a heavy limp, leaning on a thick wooden cane. Now she came onto the stage. She walked evenly. There was no more limp. The difference in the leg, somehow, was gone. One leg was still withered, but it gave her support. She held out her cane and Miss Kuhlman took it, touched her on the forehead, and she fell over backward. There wasn't a dry eye in the house.

15. Of the big-time healers, only Rex Humbard and his "Cathedral of Tomorrow" (Cuyahoga Falls, Ohio) and the Moral Rearmament movement have run afoul of the law. Humbard and his church representatives agreed in 1973 to a consent order of the Securities and Exchange Commission that they illegally sold unregistered securities (church bonds).

16. John G. Fuller, *Arrigo: Surgeon of the Rusty Knife* (New York: Thomas Y. Crowell, 1974).

17. Condensed from Flammonde, *The Mystic Healers,* pp. 203-07; and St. Clair, *Psychic Healers,* pp. 58-88.

18. St. Clair, *Psychic Healers,* pp. 254-85.

19. New Orleans, Philadelphia, and Cincinnati had physicians who practiced mesmerism. Wallace K. Tomlinson and John J. Perret, "Mesmerism in New Orleans, 1845-1861," *American Journal of Psychiatry* 131:1402-04 (December 1974).

20. Rose, *Faith Healing,* pp. 52-56 and 128-29.

21. Robert Tallant, *Voodoo in New Orleans* (New York: Macmillan, 1966). The wild orgies involved huge bonfires, trance-inducing naked dancing, and uninhibited debauchery. Officials believed these gatherings would lead to a black slave uprising and moved to suppress any signs of slave unrest.

22. Julie Y. Webb, *Superstition's Influence—Voodoo In Particular—Affecting Health Practices in a Selected Population in Southern Louisiana* (New Orleans, La.: Tulane University School of Public Health and Tropical Medicine, special thesis, 1971).

23. *The Founding Church of Scientology* v. *United States,* 133 U.S. App. D. C. 229, 409 F. 2d 1146 (1969) and *United States* v. *An Article of Device. . . . "Hubbard Electrometer" or "Hubbard E-Meter," Etc., Founding Church of Scientology, et al.,* U.S. Dist. D. C. (30 July 1971).

24. Condensed from James H. Young, "The Persistence of Medical Quackery in America," *American Science* 60:318-26 (May-June) 1972, and Flammonde, *The Mystic Healers,* pp. 210-20.

25. McTaggart, *The Health Care Dilemma,* pp. 62-63.

26. Ibid., pp. 63-66.

27. Stanford Research Institute, *Chiropractic in California* (Los Angeles: Haynes Foundation, 1960). Wilber Cohen, *Independent Practitioners Under Medicine: A Report to Congress from HEW on Chiropractic* 28 December 1968.

28. Samuel Homola, *Bonesetting, Chiropractic and Cultism* (Panama City, Fla.: Critique Books, 1963); Joseph Sabatier and H. Fineberg, "Chiropractic Education," *Science* 152:1329-30 (3 June 1966); Ralph Lee Smith, *At Your Own Risk: The Case Against Chiropractic* (New York: Pocket Books, 1969). Smith, the AMA, and Sabatier colluded to produce this one-sided book. In the 1970s other equally distorted material was published: H. J. Ballantine, "Will the Delivery of

Health Care Be Improved by the Use of Chiropractic Services?" *New England Journal of Medicine* 286:237-42 (3 February 1972); Robert B. Hunter, "Health Quackery: Chiropractic" *Journal of Louisiana State Medical Society* 124:114 (April 1973); Joseph Simanaites, "Law and Medicine: The Right and Duty of Hospitals to Exclude Chiropractors," *JAMA* 226:829-30 (November 1973); Barbara B. Erickson, "The Controversial Chiropractic Schools," *Change* :15-17 (September 1974); Alfred A. Angrist "Inevitable Decline of Chiropractic," *New York State Journal of Medicine* 73:324 (15 January 1973). Many of these studies predict the decline of chiropractic; these predictions reflect the personal biases of the authors.

29. William Trever, *In the Public Interest* (Los Angeles: Scriptures Unlimited, 1972). This book documents the AMA's subversive methods and makes the organization appear guilty of using CIA tactics.

30. *Medical Economics* (April 1975).

31. Chiropractors publish newspapers and promotional flyers for their patients (testimonials from movie stars are a favorite in this material) and sometimes give patients their x-rays to take home to show their family and friends.

32. For an excellent summary of the problems with chiropractic: "Chiropractors: Healers or Quacks? Part I: The 80-Year War with Science." "Part II: How Chiropractors Can Help—or Harm," *Consumer Reports* 40:542-47 and 606-10 (September and October 1975); David Lisher, "Manipulation of the Patient. A Comparison of the Effectiveness of Physician and Chiropractic Care," *Lancet* 1:1333-36 (29 June 1974).

33. W. I. Wardell, "A Marginal Professional Role," *Medical Care*, Scott and Volkart, eds. (New York: John Wiley & Sons, 1966), pp. 51-67.

34. Edward S. Crelin, "A Scientific Test of Chiropractic Theory," *American Scientist* 61:574-80 (September-October 1973); C. Holden, "Chiropractic: Healing or Hokum? HEW is Looking for the Answers," *Science* 185:922-23 (13 September 1974).

35. According to the American Chiropractic Association.

36. Julius Dintenlass, *Chiropractic: A Modern Way to Health* (New York: Pyramid Books, 1973); Chester Wild, *Chiropractic Speaks Out: A Reply to Medical Propaganda, Bigotry and Ignorance* (Park Ridge, Ill.: Wild Publishing Co., 1973).

37. Jules Shangold and Frank Greenberg, *Opportunities in a Podiatric Career* (New York: Universal Publishing and Distributing Corporation, 1971), p. 13; Frank Weinstein, *Principles and Practice of Podiatry* (Philadelphia: Lea and Febiger, 1968), pp. 1-2. The American Medical Association gave formal recognition to podiatry in 1939.

38. *Health Resources Statistics* (National Center for Health Statistics, 1974), p. 265.

39. Leonard Zimmerman, "Podiatry and the Law," *Journal of the American Podiatric Association* 63:543-44 and 691-93 (October and December 1973).

40. Frazier Todd, "Podiatric Care," *Urban Health* 3:63 (October 1974); see also, Donald C. Helms, "Podiatry: A Needed Dimension of Medical Care," *New England Journal of Medicine* 284:613 (18 March 1971).

41. Perhaps one of the great moments in American dentistry occurred in 1639,

when William Dinly of Roxbury, Massachusetts, became the first dentist to die in the line of duty: during a violent snowstorm while trying to make a house call. No house calls have been made since that time.

42. M. D. K. Bremmer, *The Story of Dentistry* (New York: Dental Items of Interest Publishing Co., 1964).

43. *Health Resources Statistics*, pp. 67-72.

44. Ibid., p. 73.

45. In 1970, 3,148 dentists worked in 715 group practices; ibid., p. 446.

46. Ibid., pp. 69-70.

47. In an effort to encourage preventive dentistry, some of these contracts allow for a greater percent of reimbursement for dental work if a union member has had an annual dental checkup. If there has been no checkup, the member has higher out-of-pocket expenses when he has dental work performed. Just slightly more than 40 percent of the U.S. population visits a dentist at least once a year.

48. Psychiatrists have the second highest rate of suicide. Dentists definitely lack public recognition; can we name one famous U.S. dentist besides Dr. West (and his toothbrushes)?

49. See William McIntosh, "Future Shock in Dentistry," *Oral Surgery, Oral Medicine, Oral Pathology* 34:251-56 (September 1972); Victor Kessel, "Relationship Between Medicine and Dentistry," *JAMA* 226:199-200 (8 October 1973).

50. David E. Shaver, "Opticianry, Optometry and Ophthalmology: An Overview," *Medical Care* 12:754-65 (September 1974); *Health Resources Statistics* (National Center for Health Statistics, 1974), pp. 235-36.

51. Shaver, "Opticianry," *Health Resources Statistics*, pp. 235-36.

52. Rosemary Stevens, "Delineation of a Specialty: Ophthalmology, Optometry and the First Specialty Board," in *American Medicine and the Public Interest* (New Haven, Conn.: Yale University Press, 1971), pp. 98-114.

53. This feud was compiled from R. Ball and J. Henderson, "Interprofessional Relations: A Solvable Dilemma?" *Sightsaving Review* 41:5 (1971); R. Stevenson, "Optometry: Ophthalmology's Obligation," *Military Medicine* 137:243 (1972); David Shaver, "Opticianry, Optometry and Ophthalmology: An Overview," *Medical Care* 12:760-62 (September 1974).

54. *Health Resources Statistics*, p. 310.

55. What this means is that taxpayers subsidize veterinarians to take care of dogs and cats.

56. There are more applications per opening than any other type of health school or any school for that matter.

57. Michael Fox, "Neurosis in Dogs," *Saturday Review of Science*, November 1972, pp. 58-63; Calvin Schwabe, *Veterinary Medicine and Human Health* (Baltimore, Md.: Williams and Wilkins Co., 1969).

58. Sidney Shindell, Jeffrey C. Salloway, and Colette M. Oberembt, *A Coursebook in Health Care Delivery* (New York: Appleton-Century-Crofts, 1976).

Further Reading

Adair, John, et al. *The People'sHealth: Medicine and Anthropology in a Navajo Community.* New York: Appleton-Century-Crofts, 1976.

Ballantine, H. Thomas. "Federal Recognition of Chiropractic: A Double Standard," *Annals of Internal Medicine* 82:712-13 (May 1975).

Finman, Gregory J., and Goldstein, Michael S. "The Future of Chiropractic: A Psychosocial View," *New England Journal of Medicine* 293:639-41 (25 September 1975).

Schafer, R. C. "Chiropractic: A Challenge for Health Education," *Journal of School Health* 45:52-3 (January 1975).

11. Economics and Finance of Health Care

You never gain something but that you lose something.
—Henry David Thoreau

Economics is the study of the distribution of scarce resources. For many people, health care—like adequate housing and transportation, recreation, higher education, and proper foods—is a scarce commodity. Those with limited or moderate incomes may have difficulty deciding how to allocate their money among these competing needs. Purchasing one item means that one can purchase less of the other items. Few people in the world have enough money to buy almost anything. Health care, with several exceptions, is bought and sold like any other commodity and is subject to the same laws of supply and demand. The health care delivery system is subject to the same economic trends, pressures, and constraints as other commodity systems.

We are concerned here with some simple indicators and principles of the economics of health care as well as with some of the more complex economic factors that determine the price and quantity of health care.

Gross National Indicators

One of the best ways to study health economics is to examine the national indicators of health expenditures. Figure 11.1 shows the distribution of health expenditures by type from 1929 to 1975.[1] As we can see, relatively more money is spent on hospital and nursing-home care, and relatively less on physicians' and dentists' services. Figure 11.2 shows where the money comes from.[2] There has been a dramatic rise in the government's share in funding health care, particularly since the introduction of medicare and medicaid in 1965. Private health insurance has also grown tremendously. In contrast, less and less money is coming directly out of the pockets of consumers. As seen in Figure 11.3, per capita

Figure 11.1   Distribution of Aggregate National Health
              Expenditures by Type of Expenditure, Selected
              Fiscal Years, 1929-1975

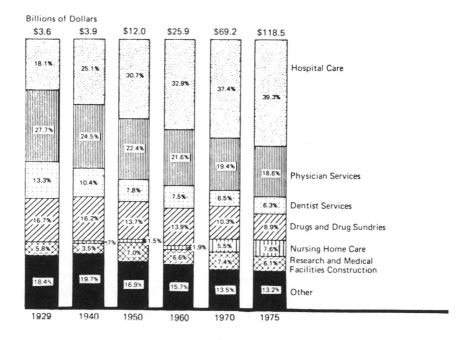

Figure 11.2   Sources of Funds for Personal Health Care
              Expenditures, Selected Years, 1929-1975

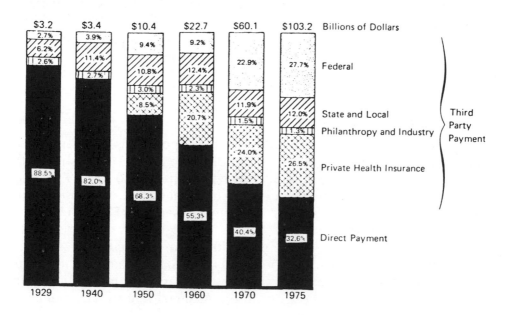

Figure 11.3   Estimated Per Capita Personal Health Care
Expenditures, Fiscal Years 1967-1972

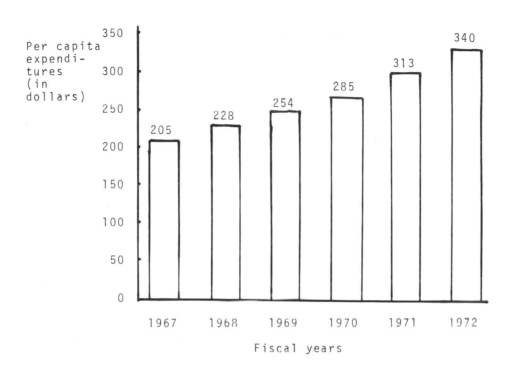

health care expenditures rose 65 percent from 1967 to 1972.[3] Does this mean that consumers are purchasing larger quantities of health care?

Part of this dramatic increase in per capita health expenditures is accounted for by an equally dramatic rise in the cost of health care. Figure 11.4 shows the increase in the price index for health care.[4] The price of health care, especially hospital and physician care, has risen faster than the price of all consumer goods. On the other hand, the price of drugs has not changed much in twenty years. Thus, much of the rise in health expenditures is due to a rise in prices rather than a rise in the quantity of care demanded.

However, the quantity of health care demanded has increased relative to the quantity of other goods and services in the U.S. economy. As seen in Figure 11.5, national health expenditures as a percentage of the gross national product increased from 4.6 percent in 1950 to 7.7 percent in 1973.[5] Since 1955, the relative growth of health care expenditures has accelerated, but it may have leveled off in the early 1970s.

Figure 11.4 Medical Care Price Index and Consumer Price Index, Base Year 1967 = 100, Selected Years 1950-1977

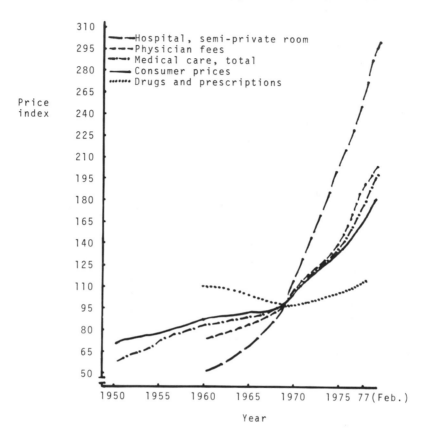

Figure 11.5 National Health Expenditures as a Percent of Gross National Product for Selected Fiscal Years, 1950-1975

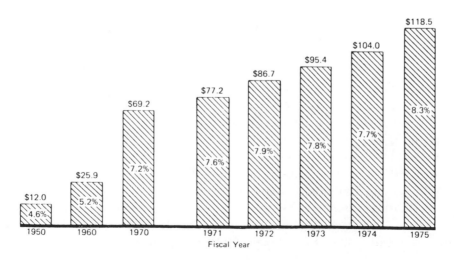

Macro Model of the Health System

The health system, like the education system, is part of a circular flow of economic activity. Figure 11.6 diagrams this flow. Money flows counterclockwise, and goods and services flow clockwise. Health care providers and drug manufacturers supply their products for a price to consumers. The *product market* is where provider supply meets consumer demand. Prices coordinate the independent decisions of physicians, hospitals, manufacturers, and consumers.

The *factor market* is where the prices for the factors of production—

Figure 11.6   Circular Flow of Economic Activity in the Health
Care Delivery System

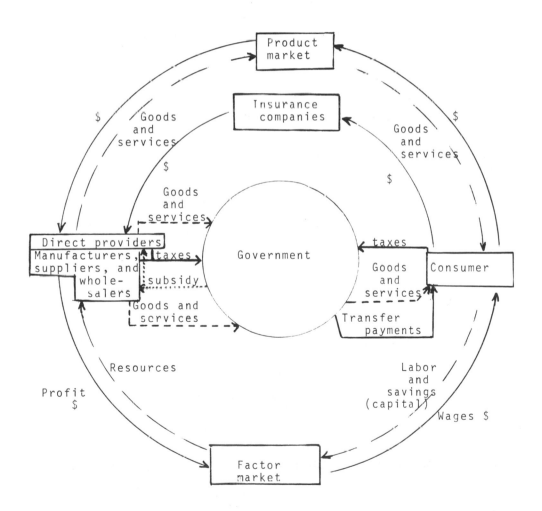

land, labor, and capital—are determined. (Capital includes buildings, equipment, and investment money.) The consumer, in his role as employee, landowner, and investor, supplies his working talents, land, and savings to health providers. Health providers, in turn, pay wages, interest, and dividends to consumers. Production creates income, and income is used to purchase output. The flow of money around the outside of the diagram in Figure 11.6 is called the *money supply*. In our dual role, we receive income as productive agents, and we spend our income on health services (as well as other items) as consumers. The circular flow of economic activity of the health system would be, if government were not present, an uninterrupted four-way flow. A laissez-faire economic system is one in which perfect competition prevails with minimum government intervention. The purpose of governmental intervention is to make sure that consumers and providers are well informed, to prevent collusion and fraud, and to facilitate the easy and orderly entrance (incorporation) and exit (bankruptcy) of firms. Ideally, the supply of health care goods and services is responsive to changes in the demand for health care.

The government of the United States increasingly affects the circular flow of health care goods and services. First, it collects taxes from both providers and consumers. Second, it purchases goods and services from providers and manufacturers. Third, it provides health care directly to consumers through such agencies as the Department of Defense and the Veterans Administration. Fourth, it provides transfer payments and Social Security benefits (medicare and medicaid) to health consumers. Fifth, it provides subsidies to health providers and manufacturers in the form of grants, special tax write-offs, and loans (Hill-Burton monies, for example). Sixth, it controls the money supply through the Federal Reserve System. The Federal Reserve System expands and contracts the money supply by:

1. buying and selling government bonds
2. establishing an interest rate at which it lends money to its member banks
3. establishing a reserve requirement (a percent of total cash) for member banks

The interest rate at which health care providers borrow, especially hospitals and nursing homes, directly affects the growth of new health facilities. High interest rates tend to discourage borrowing, which, in turn, discourages building new facilities or purchases of equipment. In short, the Federal Reserve System directly influences the cost of the factors of production. From time to time, the federal government also intervenes in the product market by controlling prices of goods and services; most economists, however, believe price controls have little long-run effect on prices. Increasingly, the government is monitoring the quality of health

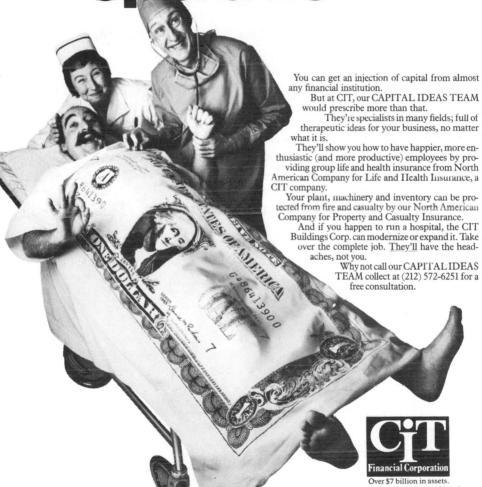

products through such agencies as the FDA and such programs as utilization review (PSRO). It also attempts to control the supply of health providers by subsidizing medical schools and students and by instituting mandatory regional health planning for providers who receive federal reimbursement.

The cost of health care is related to the price of land, labor, and capital in the factor market, which in turn is related to the supply of money. The price of health care is set through the relationship between supply and demand.

Supply and Demand for Services

Demand has to do with the amount of a particular good or service that a consumer is willing and able to purchase at each possible price during a specified time period. That is, willingness or need alone does not create demand. Effective demand also measures the consumers' financial resources, including credit. Demand may be represented by a demand curve, which relates price and quantity of a good or service. *Supply* is the amount of a particular good or service that providers are willing and able to sell at each possible price during a specified time period. Supply is represented by a supply curve.

Figure 11.7 shows that a fundamental characteristic of demand is the inverse relationship between price and quantity; in contrast, a

Figure 11.7   Supply and Demand Curves

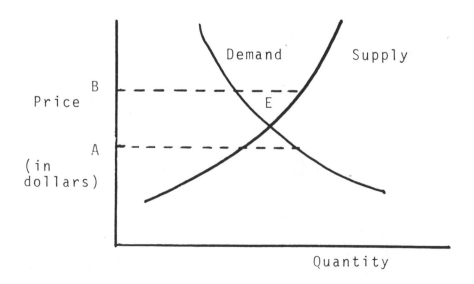

fundamental characteristic of the supply curve is the direct relationship
between price and quantity. The demand curve slopes downward from
left to right because as price increases, the quantity demanded by consumers decreases. The supply curve slopes upward from left to right because
at a higher price, more goods and services will be supplied by providers. If
the price of a drug increases, for example, consumers will be less willing to
buy it, but providers will be more willing to provide it. A change in
quantity demanded or supplied refers to a movement along a given
demand or supply curve, and it results from a change in the price of the
good under discussion with all other factors held constant. In situation A,
known as a *sellers' market*, demand exceeds supply. If the price is allowed
to rise, eventually the quantity demanded will decrease, and the amount
supplied will increase to the point where supply equals demand, at an
equilibrium point *E*. In situation *B*, known as a *buyers market*, supply
exceeds demand. If the price is allowed to drop, eventually the quantity
demanded will increase, and the amount supplied will decrease. The
equilibrium price will again be reached. The *equilibrium price* is known as
the going market rate or prevailing market rate, for example, $15 for a
physician's office visit.

Other factors, known as *exogenous changes*—such as tastes and
preferences, money income, and prices of substitute or complementary
goods or services—also can influence demand. Three exogenous factors
influence supply: technology, prices of the factors of production, and
prices of related goods. Changes in these factors cause shifts in either the
demand or supply curve.

Figure 11.8 shows the shifts in supply and demand. Suppose, as a result
of changes in consumer preferences, the demand curve for drug *X* shifts
from *DD* to *D'D'*. The price increases from P_1 to P_2. There is a temporary
move along the supply curve SS to satisfy this increased demand. Next,
suppose a technological advancement allows for increased production at
lower unit cost. The supply curve shifts down and to the right from SS to
S'S'. Price decreases from P_2 back to the original equilibrium price of P_1. In a
perfectly functioning market, shifts in demand will be met by increases or
decreases in supply. If supply does not shift, however, then a shift from
DD to *D'D'* will be accompanied by a long-term price increase. As we shall
see, there is some evidence that parts of the health care delivery system
are not responsive to shifts in demand.[6]

Deviance from the Competitive Model

Health care markets, like many other industries, depart substantially
from competitive conditions. First, many areas have limited numbers of
sellers. If there is only one hospital in town, it has a monopoly on hospital
beds (as well as on hospital-based jobs). Some think this is healthy: after
all, there is no duplication of services. Second, there may be some

Figure 11.8   Shifts in Supply and Demand

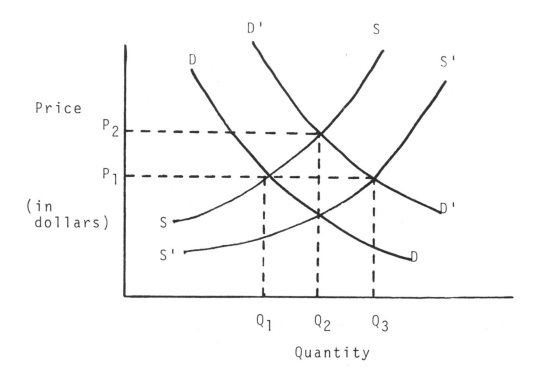

collusion among sellers in setting prices. For example, pathologists have been found guilty of price-fixing and price discrimination. Third, there are restrictions placed on the entry of additional providers. Licensure and limited hospital privileges, are two such restrictions. Fourth, significant disequilibriums in supply and demand continue to exist. For example, there seems to be excess demand for house calls. If insurance companies allowed the going rate for house calls to go up to $150 per fifteen-minute visit, physicians would be willing to make more house calls. There also seems to be an excess supply of general surgery—the quantity of surgery that surgeons are willing and able to do at the going rate is much greater than the quantity demanded. Excess supply probably is also present in radiology.

Fifth, consumers seem to lack a great deal of information for decisions involving choice of providers and choice of procedures. Most consumers are dependent on health providers for information about the quality of the good or service. The concept of demand implies consumer sovereignty, or autonomy of the individual to decide his or her own preferences: "the consumer knows best." However, in its ex- treme form, the concept of need implies that a health provider knows what is best for a consumer, regardless of what the consumer wants or even is willing and able to pay. Once a consumer puts himself under the control of the health provider, demand disappears, and the health provider attempts to satisfy most, if not all, of the consumer's needs. One result may be the overconsumption of goods and services. Thus, the way in which health care goods and services are purchased differs markedly from the way food is purchased in a store, but it may be quite similar to the way cars are fixed by automobile mechanics.[7]

Sixth, consumers are not well informed about the prices of health care goods and services. Pharmacies or surgeons may charge markedly different prices for the same product. Price discrimination—charging two different consumers two different prices for the same procedure—has long existed in medicine. Under the principle of helping the medically indigent, the well-to-do are charged a higher price than the poor. Wealthy and middle-class patients often have no idea how much of their fee represents a subsidy to poorer patients. Most health care providers do not provide price lists, post prices, or advertise, so consumers cannot make price comparisons.

Seventh, an individual's consumption of health care tends to be uneven and unpredictable, and therefore financial planning is more difficult for health care. Health insurance helps to alleviate some of the uncertainty involving adequate financial resources, but not everyone is willing or able to take even the most minimal steps to plan for medical emergencies.

Eighth, many health providers have nonprofit motives or function in nonprofit institutions. Profit and competition are frowned on: no one should make profits from other people's sicknesses or compete for patients. Without the profit motive, however, performance and efficiency are hard to measure and perhaps are difficult to instill as sources of motivation. The philanthropic motive tends to clash, and sometimes obscure, standards for optimum operation of personnel and facilities.

Ninth, many independent health care practitioners face a curious phenomenon not found in other industries: a backward bending supply curve (as seen in Figure 11.9). As the price of health care rises, say from P_1 to P_2, providers reach a point where working longer hours and employing more personnel is so unwieldly and distasteful that they instead choose to spend more time with their families and less time making money. After a certain income is achieved, money is no longer an incentive for these individuals to increase output. The supply curve then begins to bend backward: at price P_2, for example, the quantity produced decreases to Q_2.

Tenth, supply tends to create demand. Hospital admissions and surgical procedures per 1,000 population appear to be directly related to the number of available beds and practicing physicians in a community.

Finally, health care has some curious economic spillover effects. An individual consumer, in the case of a communicable disease, may

Figure 11.9   Supply Curve for Independent Health Care Practitioners

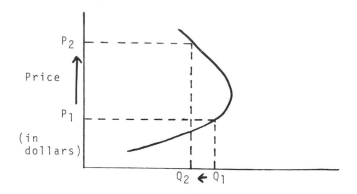

underestimate the marginal benefits of certain medical services. For example, it is extremely important to society for someone with the plague or venereal disease to get treatment, but he or she may not care or tends to undervalue the benefit of receiving fast, thorough treatment. As a result, the government may intervene and attempt to force him or her into treatment. Public health represents society's attempts to make up for deficiencies in a freely competitive economic system.[8]

Price and Income Effects

Health care can be looked on as a special industry: sometimes it saves lives. However, not all health services are quite so urgent. In fact, the demand for health services can be divided into three classifications:

1. demand arising from an emergency or serious situation, where life or death are the alternatives
2. demand for treatment of non-life-threatening situations, such as chronic illnesses, elective surgery, outpatient care, and minor problems
3. demand for health services to detect developing medical problems early such as annual physical checkups and other preventive health services[9]

Each type of demand is affected differently by changes in price and consumer income.

The *price elasticity* of a good or service measures the responsiveness of quantity demanded to changes in its price (*P*). The *income elasticity* of a good or service measures the responsiveness of quantity demanded to changes in consumer income (*Y*). If an equation for the demand curve is unknown and if one has information only on two price-quantity combinations, an arc price elasticity of demand coefficient can be calculated:

$$\text{elasticity coefficient } (e_p) = \frac{Q_2 - Q_1}{Q_2 + Q_1} \div \frac{P_2 - P_1}{P_2 + P_1}$$

Elasticity of demand is summarized as follows:

Elasticity	e_p
inelastic	less than one
elastic	greater than one
unitary elastic	one

Figure 11.10 shows the effect of price and income demand for the three different types of health services. Emergency care is price-inelastic, and chronic care is price-elastic. That is people are willing to pay the price of emergency care no matter how high it is, but they are not willing to do so for chronic care. For some forms of preventive care, such as polio vaccine, most people will pay any price (*DD*); for other forms of preventive care, such as physical checkups, people would buy much less if the price went up even slightly (*DD*$_1$). Emergency and preventive care are income-inelastic. A large increase in income will lead to only a small increase in the purchase of these types of care. However, a small increase in income may lead to large increases in the purchase of chronic and nonemergency care. Federal subsidies to low-income consumers have blurred these relationships.

Insurance

Insurance is a financial method used to handle risks. Not all risks are insurable, but insurance reduces risk by combining a sufficient number of exposure units (individuals, companies, providers, etc.) to make the loss predictable. A basic principle of insurance buying is that the most economical use of insurance premiums (payments to the insurer by the consumer) is first against the serious loss and then against the less serious losses, and not vice versa. Another principle is that the insured should not protect himself with insurance against a highly probable loss. At a certain point, the loss becomes so certain that it makes better financial sense for the insured to pay his premium to himself rather than to someone else.

Health Insurance

Health insurance may be defined broadly as that type of insurance that provides indemnification for expenditures and loss of income resulting from loss of health.[10] In general, five types of health insurance benefits may be offered on separate contracts or in combinations in a single contract, as shown in Table 11.1. Normally, regular medical and major medical insurance are written in conjunction with other types of health

Figure 11.10   Effect of Price and Income on the Demand for Three
Types of Health Services

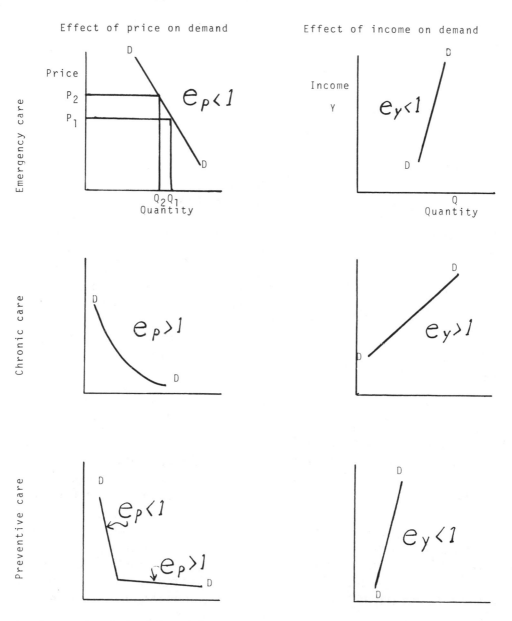

Let's examine price elasticity for emergency care.   Assume P_1, the price
per minute for treatment =$1.00, P_2 =$2.00, Q_1 = 1.1 million visits and
Q_2 = 1.0 million visits.

$e_P = \dfrac{1.0 - 1.1}{1.0 + 1.1} \div \dfrac{2 - 1}{2 + 1} = \dfrac{.1}{2.1} \times \dfrac{3}{1} = \dfrac{1}{7}$ ignoring the minus sign e = 0.14

Therefore emergency care is price inelastic; a large change in price
(doubled) causes a small change in quantity demanded.

Table 11.1 Types of Health Insurance

Type	Coverage
Hospital	Hospital expenses, including room and board, laboratory fees, nursing care, use of operating room, and certain medicine and supplies
Surgical	Different surgical procedures set forth in a schedule of operations, with maximum allowances for each type of operation
Regular medical	Physician's services, including visits other than surgical procedures
Major medical	Large medical bills such as intensive care, special procedures, etc.
Disability income	Periodic payments when the insured is unable to work as a result of illness, disease, or injury

insurance and are not written as separate contracts. Single-plan insurance, known as comprehensive major or medical, integrates regular and major medical coverages and features maximum benefits ranging from $10,000 to $50,000 or more.

There is almost no uniformity in policies among companies. Benefits vary extensively, and policies have many different provisions. Most policies have deductibles, coinsurance, and elimination periods. A *deductible* refers to that portion of covered hospital and medical charges that an insured person must pay before his policy's benefits begin. Coinsurance is a provision whereby both the insured person and the insurer share in a specified ratio the hospital and medical expenses resulting from an illness or injury. An *elimination period,* or waiting period, specifies that no benefits may be paid until a certain number of months have elapsed since the policy went into effect. A second type of waiting-period clause, found in loss-of-income policies, specifies that no benefits will be paid until the disability, once it has occurred, has lasted a certain length of time. Health insurance policies are sometimes cancelable by the consumer or the company during the policy term. The safest type of health insurance contract is one that is both noncancelable and guaranteed renewable at a constant premium. This type of policy costs more than one that is cancelable or that does not guarantee the premium rate at which it is renewable. Most policies also have numerous clauses covering special hazardous activities, misstatements in the application, and coordination of benefits if the insurer has more than one policy. Interestingly, if the insured has two or more private hospitalization policies, some companies allow him to collect in full from each of these policies.

In 1972, group health insurance accounted for 72 percent of the total health insurance premiums paid to insurance companies.[11] Blue Cross /

Blue Shield associations and the other private health insurance companies cover about equal numbers of individuals. In the public sphere, various social insurance programs, such as medicare and medicaid, represent group health insurance programs. Group health insurance offers several advantages over individual policies:

1. lower costs: freedom from adverse selection, lower administrative costs, lower acquisition costs, exemption from taxes (nonprofit), and economies of scale[12]
2. more generous benefits
3. higher payback on premium dollar

A group policy is a contract between the employer and the insurer; individual employees are third-party beneficiaries. An insurer is more likely to settle a claim in favor of a group policy holder than an individual policy holder, because the insurer may jeopardize the entire plan if employees become upset over miserly claim settlements.

Private health insurance poses difficult problems for health consumers. A consumer has little information on which to base a purchasing decision but obviously prefers those companies that pay back a sizable portion of their premium dollar. A health insurance company can do one of five things with its incoming premiums: (1) pay claims, (2) cover operating expenses and taxes, (3) hold the money in reserve, (4) invest, and (5) retain or distribute profits. The larger the proportion of the premium dollar devoted to items 2-5, the lower the proportion will be of paid claims. Table 11.2 shows the percentage of claims incurred to net premiums written for twenty-two large national companies.[13]

Obviously, some companies return a much lower portion of the premium dollar than others. Some companies write a larger proportion of group policies than others. Some companies operate inefficiently or take higher profits.[14] Despite the introduction of sophisticated data-processing equipment, there are indications that the operating expenses per enrollee for Blue Cross and Blue Shield have risen faster than the consumer price index and an index of physician' fees.[15]

Insurance companies are regulated by the states. States establish rate-making organizations, which are usually financed by member companies and are supposed to see that rates are not excessive or discriminatory. State insurance departments may also enforce minimum standards of financial solvency and control business practices (acquisition practices and certain contractual provisions). State insurance commissions generally are understaffed and are not overly aggressive.[16] State regulations have pushed companies toward uniform policy provisions, but exact standardization of policies has yet to occur. Cooperative rate making does not violate federal antitrust laws as a result of the 1945 McCarran-Ferguson Act, which exempts insurance companies from the

Table 11.2 The Ratio of Claims Incurred to Net Premiums Written for Twenty-two Large
Insurance Companies, 1970-1972[a]

Company	Three-Year Average	1970	1971	1972
Aetna	92.7	111.2	97.1	79.9
Occidental	92.6	90.7	95.8	91.3
Union Labor	91.7	93.6	93.2	88.3
Connecticut General Life	90.5	97.6	89.2	84.7
Republic National	89.9	88.9	90.5	90.3
Lincoln National	89.5	92.0	91.2	85.3
Equitable Life	88.5	91.8	90.3	83.3
Pacific Mutual	88.3	91.9	88.4	84.6
Travelers Insurance	88.1	94.5	86.7	83.0
Provident Life and Accident	86.3	88.0	83.4	82.5
Banker's Life	84.1	83.9	86.5	81.8
Metropolitan	83.8	88.4	85.9	77.1
John Hancock	83.6	88.9	88.2	73.6
Prudential	82.6	83.7	84.3	79.9
Union Mutual	81.0	85.7	85.0	72.2
New York Life	80.7	79.1	85.0	78.1
Continental Assurance	78.2	81.9	76.5	76.3
Washington National	75.1	77.6	74.6	73.2
Life of North America	72.1	62.4	79.2	74.3
Mutual of Omaha	71.9	72.0	71.0	72,8
Bankers Life & Casualty	55.4	55.4	54.6	56.3
Combined of America	40.7	41.0	40.6	40.5
Weighted average: claims/premiums written	81.2	83.6	82.4	77.7

a Companies included in the analysis have written annual health and accident premiums
exceeding $100 million.

Sherman Act, the Clayton Act, the Robinson-Patman Act, and the Federal
Trade Commission Act.

A third problem with health insurance is overutilization. Many
individuals tend to feel that they have not received any value from their
health insurance policy unless they have been ill and collected a claim
from their insurer. Hospitalization costs may also tend to rise because
insurance enables consumers to pay more for hospital services. Insurance
thus distorts care toward hospital care and specialists and away from
goods and services not covered by health insurance policies. Often the
excluded services represent less costly alternatives to hospitalization and
specialized care. As seen in Figure 11.1, the net cost of hospital care (out-
of-pocket expense) in constant dollars has scarcely risen since 1950, but
the average cost per patient-day in community hospitals has risen from
$16 to $103 in 1972.[17] In current dollars, the out-of-pocket cost per patient-
day has risen from $10 to $19. Whereas private insurance paid $6 (37
percent) of a day's hospital cost in 1950, it paid $84 (82 percent) in 1972. The
growth of insurance has played a dominant role in increasing the demand
for health care by distorting consumer choices toward increased
utilization of a more expensive product than the consumer actually
wishes to purchase. Because the net (out-of-pocket) cost appears so

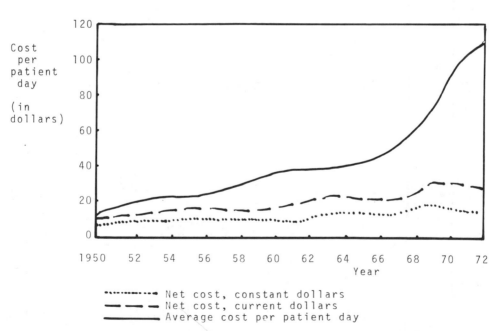

Figure 11.11   Hospital Cost per Patient Day, 1950-1972

Note: Net cost = average cost - insurance coverage

modest, the patient is willing to buy more expensive care than he would if he were not insured.

Overinsurance is a fourth problem. There is a tendency to insure the "first dollar" of claims instead of the "last dollar." Funds that could be used to insure severe and catastrophic losses are being used instead to insure small and somewhat predictable losses, which could be more economically paid by the individual directly. Health insurance is increasingly being used to finance expenses not meant to be covered by insurance per se.

Social Insurance

Social insurance plans tend to be introduced when a social problem exists that cannot be solved by the private sector. Governmental agencies either administer or finance the insurance plan. The economic problems involved are such that governmental action is necessary to solve legal difficulties, to supplement financing, to introduce forceful incentives, to provide organization, or to supply other ingredients in a successful insurance plan.

Workmen's compensation was the first type of social insurance legislation adopted in the United States.[18] Because of the industrial revolution and the rise of job-related injuries in the 1800s, injured employees increasingly had to sue their employer for damages at common law for presumed employer negligence. These suits, rarely successful, resulted in meager awards and long delays. Workmen's compensation insurance represents a merging of private and government insurance and combines two types of insurance: employer's common-law liability and workmen's disability benefits for victims of industrial accidents or occupational disease.

There are three methods by which an employer can provide workmen's compensation and employer's liability coverage:

1. purchase from private insurers (63 percent)
2. purchase through a state fund set up for this purpose (23 percent)
3. self-insure (14 percent)

All states require selection of one of these methods. Half the states have enacted laws that allow employers to select from all three options; other states limit the various options. Self-insurers must generally be large companies with adequate diversification of risks in order to qualify under state laws. In most states, if an employer decides not to use an insurer, the employer loses his three common-law defenses to negligence,[19] which makes it easier for a successful law suit. Most policies have two insuring agreements:

1. coverage pays all claims for job-related injuries

2. coverage pays to defend all employee suits against an employer and pays any judgments resulting from these suits

Although the intention of this coverage is to facilitate payment of claims and discourage employee litigation, a surprising number of suits are still brought against employers.[20] Benefits vary from state to state, but usually cover income, survivor, and medical provisions.

Medicare and medicaid were passed in 1965 to provide financial assistance for the medical needs of the elderly and of the poor. Medicaid is not social insurance, because its recipients make no direct payments into the fund; instead most of the care is paid for by nonrecipients. Nevertheless, it sometimes is thought of as medical insurance for the poor.

Title 18 of the Social Security Act, known as medicare or Health Insurance for the Aged, began paying benefits in July 1966. The passage of this amendment ended a protracted, bitter fight by organized medicine to defeat the bill.[21] This probably is the most important piece of health legislation passed in the United States in this century. With the enactment of this legislation and medicaid, third-party payments by the government have exceeded third-party payments by insurance companies.

Medicare consists of two parts: Part A provides for obligatory hospitalization insurance, and Part B provides for voluntary medical insurance.

1. *Part A*
   a. coverage: (1) inpatient and outpatient hospital care; (2) extended-care services; (3) home health services.
   b. financed: (1) compulsory payroll tax of 0.6 percent on employers and employees alike; (2) in industries covered by the SSA; (3) patient pays the national average cost for his first day of hospital care, then receives fifty-nine days of free hospitalization.
2. *Part B*
   a. coverage: (1) home health services; (2) physician's services and supplies that are part of a physician's practice; (3) diagnostic x-ray and radiotherapy; (4) surgical dressings; (5) rental of durable medical equipment used in the home; (6) prosthetic devices and braces; (7) independent laboratory services; (8) ambulance services.
   b. financed: (1) monthly premium ($6.70 in 1974) paid by the elderly and matched out of general revenues by the federal government.

Although medicare meets well over 50 percent of an aged person's hospital care and physicians' bills, it pays only a small percentage of bills for drugs, nursing care, dentistry, eyeglasses, and so on, which in total make up 44 percent of an aged person's total personal health care expenditure. Despite medicare's lack of comprehensive coverage, the program annually lowers financial barriers to health care for approximately 22 million people. The heart of medicare's problem is rising costs and how to contain them. When Congress adopted medicare in 1965, it was more intent on increasing the aged person's access to health care than on holding down costs. As hospital costs skyrocketed over the first ten years, the actuarial soundness of the insurance trust fund became questionable, and it became necessary to increase the hospital insurance tax. As physicians' fees increased, it became necessary to raise the monthly premium for Part B coverage (the premium was $3.00 in 1966). In the past few years, the government has suggested numerous ways of making medicare patients' payments closer to the actual cost of care. These proposals would lead, so the proponents claim, to elimination of wasteful use of health services and would make physicians more cost-conscious.[22] The direction of the medicare program is bound to be an indicator of what type of national health insurance program will emerge in the future.

Title 19 of the Social Security Act, known as Grants to the States for Medical Assistance Program, or medicaid, was passed in 1965 as a companion measure to medicare. Medicaid establishes a program of medical assistance for persons receiving federally aided public assistance and extends eligibility to similar individuals, that is, needy families with dependent children, and blind, disabled, or elderly persons who do not receive welfare. Coverage and financing are as follows:

1. coverage
    a. inpatient and outpatient hospital services
    b. laboratory and x-ray
    c. skilled nursing-home services
    d. physician's services plus these optional services: (1) medical care furnished by licensed practitioners (dentists, psychologists, speech pathologists, chiropractors, Christian Science practitioners, etc.); (2) home health care; (3) drugs; (4) dentures; (5) prosthetic devices; (6) eyeglasses; (7) private duty nursing services; (8) medical transportation.
2. financing
    a. federal general revenues matched to state funds (the federal contributions vary from 50 to 83 percent, inversely in relation to a state's per capita income)

Two states, Arizona and Alaska, do not participate in the medicaid program. The program has gone through a number of eligibility and financial changes and thus has left itself open to charges that it is plagued with bureaucratic paper shuffling and lack of planning. In addition, the

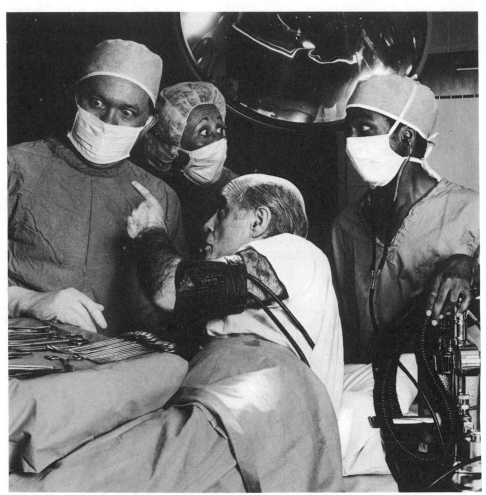

"$1500 for everything... and that's my final offer!"

How absurd it sounds—a consumer of medical care who's actually concerned about the price!

But while he may be greeted with amazement by the hospital staff, it isn't really *he* who's amazing—it's the rest of us, who've been buying health care as if money grew on trees.

The result has been a staggering inflation of the cost of health care and health insurance.[1]

(In 1950, for example, our intrepid bargainer's hospital bill would have run about $15 a day. Today, it'll be close to $175 a day!)

Ætna is working to slow that inflation.

We're going back, claim in hand, to doctors whose charges seem out of line. Ætna did that half a million times last year—and reduced those claims by an average of $50 each.[2]

We're advocating more "same-day surgery,"[3] we're pushing "co-payment," where the actual users of health care pay for a piece of it.[4]

These positions do not always make Ætna popular, but they *do* help make health insurance affordable. Insurance costs *can* be controlled. Don't underestimate your own influence. Use it, as we are trying to use ours.

Ætna
wants insurance to be affordable.

[1] "Staggering" is probably too weak a word. The share of the gross national product which goes for health services has virtually doubled in the past 15 years. The Government's share of the national health bill is now $70 billion—a sum second only to national defense.

[2] This requires Ætna knowing what the prevailing charges are for every type of medical service in every area of the country. and examining each claim against that standard. Costs vary wildly from city to city. In Philadelphia. $413 is the average surgeon's charge for the removal of a gall bladder; in Manhattan. the same operation averages $813!

[3] Many minor operations—as many as 20% of all hospital operations –can properly be performed without the patient staying at the hospital overnight. At the now-prevailing rate of $175 a day. this could mean enormous savings. Ætna also advocates peer-group review by doctors of cases of improper hospitalization

—again. to prevent misuse of hospital facilities.

[4] "Co-payment" reduces premiums: it also gives the consumer a reason to *care* about health costs. and to demand reasonable ones. Today. frankly, too many consumers of health care have too little stake in controlling costs.

LIFE & CASUALTY

program has had its share of graft, double-billing, and charges for services not rendered. However, the effect of medicaid has been to expand the quantity of care delivered to the poor, and what used to be "charity" patients are now freer to choose a provider.

Both medicare and medicaid are handled at the local level by nongovernmental organizations that act as intermediaries between the providers and the government. In the medicare program, these organizations are called "intermediaries" under Part A and "carriers" under Part B. In the medicaid program, they are called "fiscal agents" or "fiscal intermediaries." Theoretically, these intermediaries make a small profit by being reimbursed by the government for processing claims made by the providers. In many states, Blue Cross handles medicaid institutional claims, and Blue Shield handles independent practitioner claims. Intermediaries often receive the brunt of providers' wrath over the problems of the programs when, in fact, this wrath should be directed at the federal government for not properly containing bureaucratic inefficiencies.

Alternative Methods of Financing Health Care

Given the availability of scarce health resources as well as the rules of liability for negligence under which providers must function, what is the best method of allocating resources? In general, there are five ways in which health care could be distributed among consumers:

1. patient may determine his own health needs; system has price barriers
2. patient may determine his own health needs with no price or financial barriers; willingness to sacrifice time in order to obtain medical care
3. each individual M.D. or health provider, rationing his or her time, imposes judgement as to how much care, for example, how many office visits, the patient needs
4. allocated administratively using rules to establish priorities
5. automated multiphasic health screening and testing

All five methods are currently in use in the United States.[23] The price system is the most efficient method of allocating care, but it certainly does not lead to equality. On the other hand, governmental determination could lead to a highly equitable system but might in turn prove highly inefficient. Few people would argue in favor of long waiting periods before treatment. We thus must choose among inequities, waiting times, and inefficiencies.

There is also a fourth dimension that affects our choice of financial mechanisms. Health care utilization—the extent to which supply keeps

Table 11.3 Alternative Financial Arrangements for Health Care

Providers Face:	Consumers Face: Direct out-of-pocket expense at time of delivery	Consumers Face: Third party payment; no direct out-of-pocket expense at time of delivery
Fee-for-service (profit possible)	A	B
Hospital and clinic average cost; salaries for providers	C	D
Fixed prepaid annual capitation fees	E[a]	F[b]

a Utilization fee per visit
b No utilization fee

pace with demand—is affected by how providers are reimbursed. Reinhardt has delineated six types of financial arrangements that could be superimposed upon any particular technology, as seen in Table 11.3.[24]

Third party payments might include insurance companies or government transfer payments or both. A fixed prepaid annual capitation fee is much like an insurance premium except that it goes directly to the provider, who, in turn, must bear the risk of the consumer's ill health. In cell A or B, providers will tend to maximize the number of services they sell per unit of time and will be less likely to discourage any overutilization of health services. Within any row, one would expect the utilization of health services to increase as one moves to the right; within any column, one would expect utilization of health services to decrease as one moves from top to bottom. Under arrangement E, the utilization of services is likely to be lowest, and under arrangement B it is likely to be highest.

Whatever financial arrangement prevails, some individuals are bound to be dissatisfied. Harm in the form of inequities and inefficiencies will accrue to either poor or nonpoor consumers, providers, taxpayers, insurance companies, or individuals working for the government.

Summary

Consumer prices for medical care have risen rapidly for the past ten years. Demand has surpassed supply as a result of the change in government financing of health care. Despite the general rise in consumer prices, the net cost to the patient for hospital care has changed little in twenty years. There are few incentives, given third-party payments, for consumers to ration their consumption of scarce health services. Insurance may have contributed to the increased utilization of services. No matter what system of financing is used to pay for health care, some individuals are bound to suffer either inequities or inefficiencies.

Questions

1. *Socioeconomic Issues of Health* (Chicago: American Medical Association, 1974), p. 147.

2. Martin S. Feldstein, "The Medical Economy," *Scientific American* 229:151-59 (September 1973).

3. *Socioeconomic Issues of Health* (Chicago: American Medical Association, 1974), p. 156.

4. *Monthly Labor Review* (April 1977). The consumer price index is an accumulation of prices for various goods and services collected periodically in fifty-six American cities. The 1977 index is a ratio of 1977 prices to 1968 prices.

5. Assume you are going to buy an individual health insurance policy. How would you decide on a health insurance company and a specific policy?

Notes

1. *Socioeconomic Issues of Health* (Chicago: American Medical Association, 1974), p. 147.

2. Martin S. Feldstein, "The Medical Economy" *Scientific American* 229: 151-59 (September 1973).

3. *Socioeconomic Issues of Health* (Chicago: American Medical Association, 1974), p. 156.

4. *Monthly Labor Review* (April 1977). The consumer price index is an accumulation of prices for various goods and services collected
periodically in fifty-six American cities. The 1977 index is a ratio of 1977 prices to 1968 prices.

5. *Socioeconomic Issues of Health*, p. 149. See updated version, 1976.

6. For a discussion of supply and demand, see Hirsch S. Ruchlin and Daniel C. Rogers, *Economics and Health Care* (Springfield, Ill.: Charles C. Thomas, 1973), pp. 54-70.

7. Kenneth E. Boulding, "The Concept of Need for Health Services," in *Economic Aspects of Health Care*, John B. McKinlay, ed. (New York: Prodist, 1973), pp. 3-22. Mark E. Schaefer, "Demand versus Need for Medical Services in a General Cost-Benefit Setting," *AJPH* 65:293-95 (March 1975).

8. Victor R. Fuchs, "Health Care and the United States Economic System. An Essay in Abnormal Physiology," in McKinlay, *Economic Aspects of Health Care;* Herbert E. Klarman, "The Distinctive Economic Characteristics of Health Services," *Health and Human Behavior* 4:44-49 (spring 1963).

9. Richard M. Bailey, "An Economist's View of the Health Services Industry," *Inquiry* 6:3-18 (March 1969).

10. Mark R. Greene, *Risk and Insurance* (Cincinnati: South-Western Publishing Company, 1973), pp. 555-77.

11. *Source Book of Health Insurance Data* (New York: Health Insurance Institute, 1973-74).

12. Adverse selection occurs when large numbers of unhealthy individuals sign up for policies or programs. Group policies tend to be sold to groups with a

smaller percentage of unhealthy individuals than exists in the population at large.

13. Table 11.2 also shows a decrease of 6¢ return on the premium dollar from 1970 to 1972. The rise in health care costs would tend to push up rather than down the percentage of claims incurred—a possible explanation is that the price of insurance premiums is rising faster than health care costs.

14. Douglas R. Mackintosh and Dennis A. Duclaux, "Monitoring the Performance of Health Insurance Companies in Louisiana," 5:9-12 (July 1974). See also *1973 Argus Chart of Health Insurance* (Cincinnati: The National Underwriting Company, 1973). Douglas R. Mackintosh, "A Consumer's Guide for Quality Commercial Health Insurance" (Lake Charles, La.: The Research Institute for Quality Health Plans, 1973). Although a claim may be incurred, the company may not pay the claim; therefore, the percentage of premium actually returned to the consumer may be less than the percentages listed in Table 11.2.

15. Robert J. Weiss, William H. Wiese, and Josel C. Klein, "Trends in Health Insurance Operating Expenses," *New England Journal of Medicine* 287:638-42 (28 September 1972).

16. "The State's Regulation of Insurance Companies Often Viewed as Farce," *Wall Street Journal,* (2 August 1973), p. 1.

17. Feldstein, "The Medical Economy," p. 155.

18. In 1884 Germany passed the first modern workmen's compensation statute under the leadership of Bismarck.

19. See the following section on negligence and malpractice.

20. Greene, *Risk and Insurance,* pp. 595-601.

21. American Medical Association, *The Case Against the King-Anderson Bill* (Chicago: The Association, 1963). Russell B. Roth, "Medicare: Its Problems for Practicing Physicians," *JAMA* 197:125-37 (1 August 1966). For a more detailed account of medicare's coverage, see *Your Medicare Handbook,* DHEW publication 74-10050 (January 1975), and Florence Wilson and Duncan Neuhauser, *Health Services in the United States* (Cambridge, Mass.: Ballinger Publishing Co. 1974), pp. 126-34.

22. "Should Old Folks Pay More for Medicare? Would That Curb the Misuse of Services?" *Wall Street Journal,* (23 March 1973), p. 26. See also Paul M. Densen, "Public Accountability and Reporting Systems in Medicare and other Health Programs," *New England Journal of Medicine* 289:401-06 (23 August 1973).

23. Automated multiphasic health testing (AMHT) is in limited use and is discussed in Chapter 14.

AMHT and the price system probably are the most coldly objective of the five methods of allocating care. See Rita R. Campbell, *Economics of Health And Public Policy* (Washington, D.C.: American Enterprise Institute, 1971), pp. 65-75.

24. Uwe E. Reinhardt, "Proposed Changes in the Organization of Health-Care Delivery: An Overview and Critique," *Milbank Memorial Fund Quarterly* 51:169-222 (spring 1973).

Further Reading

Bailey, Richard M. "Philosophy, Faith, Facts and Fiction in the Production of Medical Services." *Inquiry* 7:37-66 (March 1970).
Cooper, Michael H. *Rationing Health Care.* London: Croom Helm, 1975.

Cooper, Michael H., and Culyer, Anthony J., eds. *Health Economics.* Harmondsworth: Penguin Books, 1973.

Feldstein, Martin S. *The Rising Cost of Hospital Care.* Washington, D.C.: Information Resources Press, 1971.

Fuchs, V. R. *Who Shall Live? Health Economics and Social Choice.* New York: Basic Books, 1974.

Fuchs, Victor, ed. *Essays in the Economics of Health and Medical Care.* New York: National Bureau of Economic Research, 1972.

Glaser, William. *Paying the Doctor: Systems of Remuneration and Their Effects.* Baltimore, Md.: Johns Hopkins University Press, 1970.

Harris, Seymour E. *The Economics of Health Care.* Berkeley, Calif.: McCrutchan Publishing Co., 1974.

"Hospital Costs, Biggest Piece of the Health Care Bill." *Medical World News,* 2 May 1977, pp. 49-60.

Kramer, M. S., and Kramer, C. "Fragmented Financing of Health Care." *Medical Care Review* 29:878-943 (August 1972).

Krizay, Johna, and Wilson, Andrew. *The Patient as Consumer: Health Care Financing in the United States:* Lexington, Mass.: D. C. Heath & Co., 1974.

Law, Sylvia. *Blue Cross: What Went Wrong.* New Haven, Conn.: Yale University Press, 1974.

Medicare and Medicaid: Problems, Issues and Alternatives, Report of the U.S. Senate Committee on Finance. Washington, D.C.: U.S. Government Printing Office, 1970.

Mique, Jean-Luc, and Belanger, Gerard. *The Price of Health.* Toronto: Macmillan of Canada, 1974.

Myers, Harold B. "The Medical-Industrial Complex." *Fortune* 81:90-95 (January 1970).

Newman, Howard N. "Medicare and Medicaid." *Annals of the American Academy* 399:114-24 (January 1972).

Perlman, Mark, ed. *The Economics of Health and Medical Care.* New York: Halsted Press, 1974.

Rafferty, J., ed. *Health Manpower and Productivity.* Lexington, Mass.: D. C. Heath & Co., 1974.

Stevens, Rosemary, and Stevens, Robert. "Medicaid: Anatomy of a Dilemma." *Law and Contemporary Problems* 35:348-425 (spring 1970).

Taylor, Vincent. "How Much is Good Health Worth?" *Policy Science* 1:49-72 (1970).

U.S. Council on Wage and Price Stability. *The Rapid Rise of Hospital Costs.* Washington, D.C.: Executive Office of the President, 1977.

Weisbrod, Burton A. *Disease and Economic Development.* Madison: University of Wisconsin Press, 1973.

Yett, Donald E. *An Economic Analysis of the Nursing Shortage.* Lexington, Mass.: D. C. Heath & Co., 1975.

12. Negligence and Medical Malpractice

Whoever pays the piper, calls the tune.
—Anonymous

Medical malpractice is an injury to a patient caused by a health care provider's negligence. Some, but not all, physical and mental medical injuries are caused by negligence. *Negligence* is failure to exercise the degree of care required by law. The law requires conduct expected of a reasonably prudent individual in the same circumstances. Acts of negligence that cause injury are considered torts. A *tort* is a legal injury or wrong to another that arises out of actions other than breach of contract in which courts will provide a remedy by allowing recovery in an action for damages. Patients who believe thay have iatrogenic injuries are increasingly making claims to insurers and bringing suits against health care providers. Physicians, hospitals, and other health providers cover the risk of malpractice claims and suits by purchasing malpractice Insurance. In spring 1975, several insurance companies that write malpractice insurance announced large increases in premiums or cancellations of policies.[1] Organized medicine loudly protested and turned to the state legislatures for governmental relief. This situation had been building up for a number of years and is one of the causes of the increased prices of medical care.

Frequency and Distribution of Claims

In 1970, there was less than one chance in 100,000 of an incident occurring that would give rise to a medical malpractice suit when a physician or dentist treated a patient.[2] However, with a total of 382,000 physicians, dentists and hospitals at risk, one out of every twenty-one health care providers was the object of a malpractice claim in 1970. Claims occur more frequently in some states than others, more frequently against physicians in some specialties than others, and more frequently against some hospitals than others. Figure 12.1 shows that physicians practicing in

231

Figure 12.1   State to State Differences in Number of Claims Closed
               in 1970 per 100 Physicians Providing Patient Care

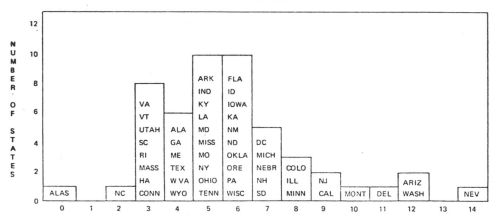

AVERAGE U.S. = 6.54

CLAIMS CLOSED PER 100 PRACTICING PHYSICIANS

Nevada have a high number of malpractice claims brought against them.[3]
    Physicians pay malpractice premiums based on rating experience for
their specialty. Table 12.1 indicates which physician specialties fall into the
five classes upon which premium rates are calculated.[4] Anesthesiologists
and orthopedic surgeons have the most claims and suits brought against
them. Seventy-four percent of all alleged malpractice incidents occur in
hospitals, but approximately 15 percent of the nation's 7,000 hospitals
accounted for more than half the claims against hospitals. This statistic is
biased, in part by the immunity of state government hospitals

Table 12.1   The Ratio of the Base Rate For Classes Two Through
              Five Physicians and Surgeons to the Base Rate For
              Class One Physicians, 1966-1972

	Class[a]				
Year	1	2	3	4	5
1966	1.00	1.25	2.40	3.60	NA
1967-1972	1.00	1.75	3.00	4.00	5.00

a There are exceptions to these ratios, most notably, New York
City (1969-1972). However, they are correct for most rating
territories in most years.
    The class definitions are:
Class 1: Physicians who do not perform or ordinarily assist
in surgery; Class 2: Physicians who perform minor surgery or
assist with major surgery on their own patients; Class 3:
Physicians who perform major surgery on patients other than
their own, plus opthalmologists and proctologists; Class 4:
Cardiac surgeons, otolaryngologists-no plastic surgery,
surgeons-general, thoracic surgeons, urologists, and vascular
surgeons; and Class 5: Anesthesiologists, neurosurgeons,
obstetricians-gynecologist, orthopedists, otolaryngologists-
plastic surgery, and plastic surgeons.

Table 12.2 Location Within Hospital Where Incidents
Which Give Rise to Malpractice Claims Occur

Location	Percentage of Incidents
Operating room	39
Patient's room	34
Emergency room	12
X-ray room	3
Labor and delivery room	3
Other	9
Total	100

(approximately one-half the states have this protection), under the concept of sovereign immunity ("the king can do no wrong"), from suits by citizens.[5] Table 12.2 shows that most of the malpractice incidents in the hospital occur in the operating room and the patient's room.[6] Hospitals, according to the American Hospital Association, are dangerous places:

> Simple logic would suggest that hospitals have a special affinity for the practice of safety. The evidence, however does not bear out this idea. The safety record of health care facilities is inferior to that of many industries that send them accident victims, studies by the National Safety Council indicate.[7]

Many providers feel that numerous claims and suits are entirely without foundation and that these actions ask for astronomical amounts of money. Furthermore, they claim that greedy lawyers, spurred on by the contingency fee system, push patients into suits. Table 12.3 shows that approximately 45 percent of all claims result in some payment to the patient.[8] Only 6.5 percent of all claims ever reach a trial verdict. Interestingly, three times as many trials end up in favor of the health provider (the defendant) as for the patient (the plaintiff). Clearly, malpractice claims and suits, based on settlements alone, have some merit. Table 12.4 indicates the amounts paid on medical malpractice claims in 1970.[9] Most paid claims, over 78 percent, were under $10,000. Very few paid claims (3 percent) were over $100,000. However, there is a prevailing practice of naming extremely high dollar amounts, the *ad damnum* clause, in the pleading of malpractice actions. An analysis of 2,784 liability claims brought against members of the California Hospital Association in 1969-72 showed that damages asked were fifty-three times greater than damages eventually recovered.[10]

Table 12.3   Percentage of Medical Malpractice Claims Files
Closed at Each Stage in the Process, With
and Without Payment

Stage Claim Closed	Total	With Payment	Without Payment
Incident report/pre-claim	28.6	7.4	21.2
Claim/pre-suit	21.7	7.4	14.3
Suit/pre-trial	38.2	24.9	13.3
Trial/pre-verdict	5.0	3.5	1.5
Verdict	6.5	1.6	4.9
Totals	100.0	44.8	55.2

Table 12.4   Distribution of Amounts Paid on Medical
Malpractice Claims Closed in 1970

Total Settlement Costs of Incidents (in dollars)	Percentage of Incidents	Cumulative Percentage of Incidents
1-499	21.1	21.1
500-999	16.0	37.1
1,000-1,999	12.3	49.4
2,000-2,999	10.1	59.5
3,000-3,999	3.0	62.5
4,000-4,999	2.7	65.2
5,000-9,999	13.4	78.6
10,000-19,999	10.0	88.6
20,000-39,999	5.3	93.9
40,000-59,999	1.3	95.2
60,000-79,999	1.0	96.2
80,000-99,999	0.8	97.0
100,000 and up	3.0	100.0
Total percentages	100.0	

Attorneys generally take malpractice cases on a contingent fee system. If the plaintiff wins the case, the lawyer will receive anywhere from one-third to one-half of the amount settled on or won. A large amount won could mean a large fee for a lawyer. However, an attorney takes home no income from lost cases and instead has to absorb the expenses of witnesses, his own overhead for maintaining his practice, and court costs. The average hourly fee for plaintiff lawyers is $63 as compared to an average of $50 for malpractice defense lawyers. Thus, the contingency fee, based on total hours devoted to malpractice cases, does not lead to any greater riches than other types of fee systems.[11]

Malpractice claims take a long time to settle. Figure 12.2 shows that in comparison to personal injury cases involving automobile accidents, mal-

Figure 12.2   Duration of Closing Files for Auto Claims versus
              Medical Malpractice Claims, 1970

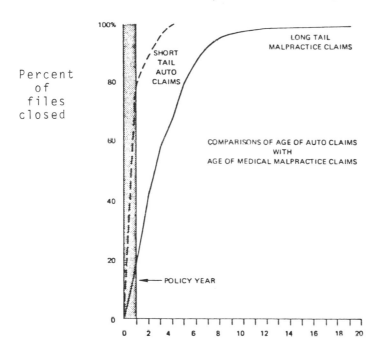

practice claims take a long time to close after the policy year.[12] The most
important reason for the long tail on malpractice claims is the discovery
rule, which holds that the two-year statute of limitations, or the time
period in which a plaintiff must file suit after the incident giving rise to the
suit has occurred, does not begin to run until the patient discovers the
injury or negligence.[13] Since rate making for insurance companies is
based on past experience, the long tail of malpractice claims makes
premium determination a vexing problem.

Principles of Negligence

Hospitals are sued for the wrongful acts of their employees under the
doctrine of *respondeat superior,* which necessitates that a "master/
servant" relationship exist between employer and employee. The
employer's conduct may be without fault. The doctrine does not absolve
the employee of liability for his wrongful act; the hospital may turn
around and sue the employee. A hospital generally is not liable for the
wrongful act of a physician-member of the medical staff in the treatment
of his patients in the hospital. Most physicians on the medical staff, with
the exception of the employed physicians, are not working in a
"master/servant" relationship, and the hospital theoretically is powerless
to command or forbid them as to how to practice. Matters become more

complex in the operating room, where the surgeon is the "captain of the ship" and the nurse is the "borrowed servant." Under the "borrowed servant" doctrine, the general employer is not liable for injury negligently caused by the servant if the latter is at the time in the special service of another. The problem, as yet unresolved, is to determine which party, the hospital or the surgeon—who supposedly is in total command of the operating room—is liable for the wrongful acts of nurses, interns, residents, or other hospital personnel.[14] The effect of this uncertainty leads to physician doubts over the delegation of responsibility to other health care providers.

In order to prove negligence, four conditions must be met:

1. duty owing to someone else (contractual and/or implied based on reasonable standards for care)
2. breach of duty (a mistake)
3. injury (harm and damage)
4. proximate cause (cause and effect relationship between the mistake and the injury)

In some situations, negligence, under the doctrine of *res ipsa loquitur* ("the thing speaks for itself"), can be inferred from the circumstances surrounding the injury. The plaintiff can collect without actually proving negligence on the part of the defendant. This doctrine is an evidentiary rule that is permitted to be invoked when:

1. an injury occurs that is of a type that ordinarily does not occur except from someone's negligence
2. the conduct or mechanism that caused the injury was within the exclusive control of the person from whom damages are sought
3. the complaining party was free of any contributory negligence

Health care providers believe this rule is a form of judicial discrimination, which shifts the burden of proof over to the provider to prove that he was not negligent. Whether health care providers are losing cases solely on the basis of circumstantial evidence is difficult to tell. However, the common law defenses to negligence (contributory negligence on the part of the patient, assumed risk, and the fellow-servant rule) have slowly been removed from judicial consideration. Nonprofit hospitals also used to invoke the doctrine of charitable immunity to avoid litigation, but this doctrine slowly is losing favor in malpractice cases.

A test of negligence often requires expert witnesses. Some states, under the *locality rule*, require that only local physicians be allowed to testify as to what the prevailing standard of care is in the community. But this rule is slowly being abolished in favor of expert testimony from outside the locality. This rule tended to protect rural physicians.

Effects of Malpractice Suits

All these changes have brought more and more claims as more and more attorneys learn the complexities of taking on these cases. Increasingly, physicians are practicing defensive medicine by ordering additional x-rays and tests to make certain of diagnoses; and by not performing certain procedures or tests out of fear of a later malpractice suit.[15] Over-utilization and under-utilization occur. Informed consent and its ramifications are being taken more seriously. Finally, various states have passed legislation that changes the litigation and insurance process to affect the health provider more favoraby. These changes include trials without juries, limitations on the contingency fee system, strict enforcement of the locality rule, the pooling of premium risks for awards over $100,000, and the placement of a $500,000 ceiling on recovery. In some states, physicians are forming their own insurance companies.

There are a few conclusions we can make about the so-called malpractice crisis. First, malpractice insurance costs do appear to be passed on to patients.[16] One estimate indicates that a 1 percent increase in malpractice costs lead to an increase of about 0.5 percent in physicians' fees. Second, defensive medical practices resulting from the threat of malpractice appear to contribute to medical costs, but the effect is not large. Finally, the fear that physicians will retire early or move out of suit-prone areas of the country seems to be seriously exaggerated.

Summary

In recent years, medical malpractice has become an emotional subject that has physicians, lawyers, and insurance companies accusing one another of increasing health care costs. Negligence and liability litigation is rooted firmly in the U.S. judicial system, but with increased discontent over the malfunctioning of malpractice insurance, legislators may attempt to remove medical malpractice cases from the traditional judicial arena.

Questions

1. Dr. X, who is not a member of your hospital staff, visits a friend in your hospital and writes notes and procedural directions on his friend's chart. You as the administrator of the hospital, find out about this situation and further learn that Dr. X's orders have been followed by the nurses caring for the friend. What should you do? How would your answer differ if X were unlicensed and/or not a physician?

2. Assume you are an attorney and a client comes to you with a malpractice case. You ascertain that there is a fifty-fifty chance of winning the case, that it will take two years to complete, and that your client may win between $25,000 and $100,000. What other factors would you consider in deciding whether to take the case? Would you prefer to take it on a contingency or fee-for-service basis?

"Think you have problems? Next case
I'm operating on a malpractice
attorney."

3. What do you suppose was the basis for establishing the doctrine of charitable immunity for non-profit hospitals?

4. Assume you are the president of an insurance company that does not write malpractice insurance. Argue against a state provision that forces all insurance companies doing business in the state to contribute money to a state malpractice insurance pool.

5. Some physicians, rather than pay high malpractice insurance premiums, are "going bare" and carrrying no insurance while putting all their personal assets in their spouse's name. What dangers are there in following this strategy?

Notes

1. "Doctors' Protest Spreads in California: Bay Area Hospitals Feel Financial Pinch," *Wall Street Journal*, 21 May 1976, p. 15. "Job Actions by Doctors Spread as More Join Protest Against Insurance Costs," *Wall Street Journal*, 3 June 1975.

2. *Medical Malpractice Report of the Secretary's Commission on Medical Malpractice*, DHEW publication no. 73-88 (16 January 1973), pp. 6 and 8.

3. Ibid., p. 8. Commission study of Claims Closed in 1970; Distribution of Physicians in the United States, 1970, American Medical Association.

4. Ibid., p. 43.

5. Ibid., p. 9. A patient cannot sue a government hospital, but he can sue a provider working in a government hospital.

6. Ibid., p. 10. Commission Survey of Claim Files Closed in 1970.

7. *Safety Guide for Health Care Institutions* (Chicago: American Hospital Association and the National Safety Council, 1972), p. 3.

8. *Medical Malpractice Report of the Secretary's Commission on Medical Malpractice*, p. 10. Commission Study of Claim Files Closed in 1970.

9. Ibid., p. 11.

10. Ibid., p. 38.

11. Ibid., p. 33.

12. Ibid., p. 42. Estimate of Auto Claims Based on Testimony.

13. An extreme example of the discovery rule occurs with children; the statute of limitations does not begin to run with children until a child reaches legal adulthood, age eighteen. Thus a suit for injuries occurring at childbirth can be brought twenty years after it happened.

14. Health Law Center, *Problems in Hospital Law* (Rockville, Md.: Aspen Systems Corp., 1974), pp. 32-39.

15. *Medical Malpractice Report of the Secretary's Commission on Medical Malpractice*, pp. 14-15.

16. B. Greenwald, M. Mueller, and A. Marcus, "Medical Malpractice and the Cost of Doctor's Services" (Presented at the American Economic Association Meeting, 18 September 1976).

Further Reading

"Medical Malpractice Insurance, 1975." Hearings before the Subcommittee on Health of the Committee on Labor and Public Welfare, U.S. Senate 94th Congress. Washington, DC: U.S. Government Printing Office, 1975 and 1976.

13. Sociopolitical Aspects of Health Care

If a free society cannot help the many who are poor,
it cannot save the few who are rich.
—John F. Kennedy

Control of health resources is important to both providers and consumers. In addition, the government, that is, legislators and bureaucrats, would also like to increase its power over the allocation of resources. Our concern here is with various mechanisms used by those attempting to control the health system and to determine who will reap the benefits of mainstream U.S. medicine. Perhaps the most invisible group recently made visible as a result of dramatic confrontations is the impoverished black consumer. Much state and federal activity has been directed toward improving the health care of minority Americans.

Poverty and Minority Participation in the Health System

The Extent of Injustices

Being poor and black or belonging to some other minority ethnic group is to be invisible. Many of these individuals carry a heavy baggage of profound suspicion, subliminal rage, and covert hatred.[1] The great majority, (70 percent) of Negroes live in the decaying central cities. Housing units, schooling, and hospitals are substandard. Life for the low-income black youth consists of either ripping and running, watching ripping and running, or avoiding ripping and running. Young people of the ghetto are increasingly conscious of a system that seems to reward those who exploit others (narcotics sellers, and so forth) and punish those who struggle under traditional responsibilities. The ghetto resident has far less political representation, employment, housing, public services, and protection from dangerous situations than his suburban counterpart. Urban and rural poverty, in combination with racism, has led to the initiation of countless federal programs.

Yet medicare and medicaid programs have helped relieve the burdensome medical costs for the nation's poor. As seen in Figure 13.1,

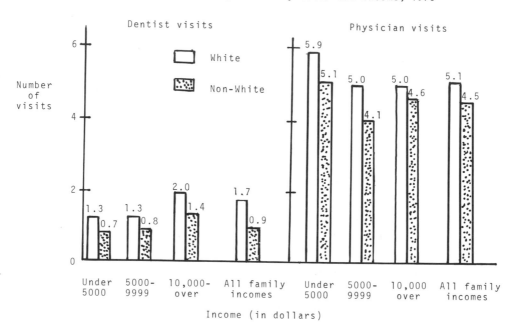

Figure 13.1   Visits to Dentists and Physicians in the U.S.
per Person per Year by Color and Income, 1973

nonwhites in all income groups have slightly fewer physician visits per person per year than whites in equivalent income groups.[2] Lower-income individuals also have more physician visits per year than those in middle or upper income groups. Contrary to popular belief, low-income families do not receive less medical care than the rest of the population. But they do receive less dental care. Evidence indicates that the poor get as much hospital care as people with higher incomes; differences among income groups in the use of health care are relatively unimportant.[3] However, low-income families suffer greater financial hardship when they incur medical expenses that are large with respect to their income; upper class and middle class families spend relatively less of their income on health care. Second, ghetto residents are prevented by their form of employment (or lack of employment) from buying adequate insurance at a fair premium; they are therefore much more likely to confront large out-of-pocket expenses or to be deterred from seeking needed medical care. Neither do the above statistics show the quality of these physician visits. The visits may well be contacts with medical students in teaching institutions. Peer review, involving medicare and medicaid, is one governmental attempt to see that low-income patients get equal, adequate, and timely treatment.

Neighborhood Health Centers

In the 1960s, the idea of a decentralized health center placed in the heart of an underserved area was revitalized from fifty years of dormancy.

Antipoverty programs were looking for a way to structure health care in impoverished areas.[4] The Office of Economic Opportunity (OEO) began funding health care centers sponsored by hospitals, medical schools, citizen groups, medical societies, and health departments. OEO's directives for its funded centers were as follows:

1. The center must serve everyone living below a given income level who resides in a designated "target area." In a city, the target area may be a compact neighborhood; in a rural area, the area may be a group of communities.

2. The center must be equipped for comprehensive health services, including physical checkups, pre-symptom screening, immunization, health education and family planning, in addition to general outpatient treatment.

3. Center staffs are organized into "family care teams." Patients are seen not merely as individuals, but as members of families as well.

Each family was to be assigned to a family care team, centers were to have community boards to make policy decisions, and employees were to be hired from the local neighborhood. In short, the centers were to be responsive to community needs. At the peak of the neighborhood health center movement, nearly 500 centers were operational. Many of the centers were supposed to become self-sufficient and eventually self-supporting.

Unfortunately, the antipoverty program, for all its rhetoric, did not function well in practice.[5] Many of the projects ran into protracted community fights over control of the facility. Others simply had their funding cut when the federal government moved to scuttle the antipoverty program.[6] Once again, poverty and minority groups were let down, "sold out," by the federal government. OEO was the first program to be reduced; Vista and Model Cities had a more lingering, more politically controversial death. The neighborhood health center program may be revitalized by a change in federal administration. The movement toward reallocating medical resources into poverty areas generated a lot of excitement and a good deal of disappointment.

Free Clinics and Radical Politics

The free clinic movement emerged at about the same time as the neighborhood health center movement. "The movement for social change" was a distillation of the experience and beliefs of the New Left, the underground counterculture, the black power movement, and OEO. The consensus of the founders of this movement was that the U.S. health care system did not meet the people's needs and had to be restructured radically. These feelings can be summarized by the following principles:[7]

1. health care is a right and should be free at the point of delivery
2. health services should be comprehensive, unfragmented, and decentralized

3. medicine should be demystified
4. health care should be deprofessionalized; health care skills should be transferred to worker and patient alike
5. community-worker control of health institutions should be instituted

Starting by providing medical presence at civil rights demonstrations in the South in the early 1960s, the New Medical Left began the free clinic movement in 1967, when the Haight-Ashbury Free Medical Clinic opened its door to the hundreds of young people pouring into San Francisco for a summer of hallucinogens, love, and rock music. Soon, free clinics sprang up in store fronts, second-story offices, and church basements in major U.S. cities. The resistance from organized medicine and local health departments was sometimes fierce. Drug problems, venereal disease, unmarried pregnancy, and runaways were treated in a patient, supportive manner. Patients were encouraged to volunteer their help in all clinics. Two-thirds to three-quarters of the patients were women, and a high proportion were young white dropouts. Gradually the clinics began to treat a less hip, older, more working-class group of patients.

Funds and a supply of licensed physicians were a constant problem. Voluntary contributions rarely were enough to pay for supplies. Gradually, friendly drug detail men and, ironically, the local health departments began to furnish supplies. Physicians, like the rest of the staff, maintained a flexible schedule whereby they might or might not show up for a night clinic. Underutilization was never a problem; most of the clinics decided that it was better to turn people away or limit the scope of their services than to sacrifice the quality of their services. Built into that quality was a sense of purpose that these clinics were not just a place to see patients, but a political force in the community.

> The fact that the care came free not only fulfilled the need to provide medical services to people who had no money, it was also groovy! It supported and gave testament to the idea that alternative institutions can survive in the belly of the beast, that they can be developed on principles of sharing, not exploiting, and that they can subsist on the surplus of a materialistic economy.[8]

As of 1974, there were an estimated 175-200 such clinics around the country.[9] Participants in free clinics and neighborhood health centers have raised the important issue of who should control local resources devoted to health care.

Community and Consumer Control

The patient does not exercise the same degree of consumer sovereignty as he does in purchasing goods and services in other industries. In the

Figure 13.2   Spectrum of Consumer-Provider Control of Various
Health Resources

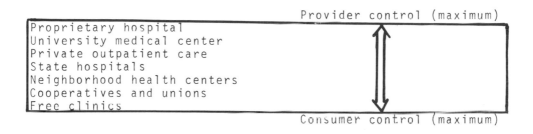

United States, as Sheps points out, a pluralistic society leads to varying degrees of consumer and community control.[10] Figure 13.2 schematically shows the spectrum of consumer-provider control for various health resources. Voluntary hospitals theoretically are controlled by a board of trustees that makes policy decisions. However, as in many corporations, a group of absentee individuals often must defer to the wishes of a powerful group of insiders—in the case of the community voluntary hospital, the medical staff may run the hospital and the board of trustees often run the errands. Throughout the late 1960s and early 1970s, voluntary hospitals found themselves confronted with the demand for a new type of accountability—to people of their neighborhood, often an underprivileged group of residents frustrated by the lack of services available to them. Tactics included militant sit-ins and confrontations. Many hosptials reluctantly began providing satellite clinics, additional treatment centers for emergency room care of lead poisoning and narcotic addiction, and improved prenatal care. They even went so far as to provide patient advocates and put minority consumers on the board of trustees.[11]

In general the politicalization of health care seems to involve two distinct consumer strategies:

1. the consumer is primed for problem analysis—a consumer group may accept as its objectives helping consumers understand why the health system operates as it does, promoting the appropriate use of services, identifying consumer needs, and interpreting the limited role of consumer committees to consumers
2. the consumer is primed for bargaining—a consumer group may accept as its objectives the determination of rules of eligibility, vigorous pursuit of representation on personnel committees, achieving the authority to participate in financial decisions, and achieving the authority to set the priorities of health programs[12]

Most providers prefer that consumer groups follow the first strategy. When community groups move toward adoption of the second strategy, which represents a loss of power for providers, intense conflict may prevail.[13] "Maximum feasible participation" has emotional appeal, but, in practice, this concept is difficult to structure into a meaningful decision-making process. At the heart of the conflict are the issues of loss of power and maintenance of quality of care. Providers understandably are upset when such participation requires the delegation of agency and private decision-making autonomy to groups of neighborhood citizens. Current health-planning legislation represents just such a transition of power and control.

State and Areawide Control

Health Planning

In 1965, the Comprehensive Health Planning and Public Health Services Amendment became law. Few major interest groups advocated the legislation, and almost none opposed it because the legislation sounded so innocuous.[14] The objective of the act was to promote and assist in the extension and improvement of comprehensive health planning (CHP) and public health services and to provide for a more effective use of available federal funds for such planning and services. Although the wording of the law was unclear, the spirit of the law was to prevent needless duplication of costly health services and to promote the construction of badly needed facilities through the development of voluntary planning agencies. These agencies were to be funded by federal project grants. Planning was to be statewide and areawide. CHP has been amended four times.

In 1967, the Partnership for Health Amendments required representation of the interests of local government in areawide planning agencies. The Public Health Service Amendments of 1970 included additional provisions concerning the broad composition of the governing board and advisory councils of areawide health planning agencies. A majority of the members of such councils were to be representatives of consumers.

In 1972 Congress passed Section 1122 of the Social Security Act to assure that federal funds are not used to support unnecessary capital expenditures for health care facilities such as hospitals, nursing homes, and health centers. A capital expenditure is a financial outlay that buys a fairly permanent asset, such as a new building, a new wing to an existing building, a renovation of a facility or a portion of one, or a major piece of equipment. Section 1122 applies to capital expenditures that:

1. amount to over $100,000, including the cost of studies, surveys, planning and other preliminary expenses; or
2. increase or decrease the bed capacity of a facility; or
3. add or terminate a clinically related service (diagnostic, curative, or rehabilitative)

Section 1122 probably is the federal government's most aggressive attempt to date to change the supply of health care. Providers who fall under the above categories request a *certificate of need* from their designated health planning councils. The councils delegate the task of analyzing the request to a project review committee. The certification of need is evaluated on the following criteria:

1. community need
2. adequate staffing and operation of the facility
3. economic feasibility
4. cost containment and improved productivity

If the request for a certificate of need is denied by the health planning council, the law authorizes HEW to withhold from the provider that submitted the proposal payments for services provided patients under the maternal and child health, medicare and medicaid programs in an amount related to the capital expenditure. Most health care institutions are dependent on medicare and medicaid as a source of cash flow.

The National Health Planning and Resources Development Act of 1974 replaces Comprehensive Health Planning, Regional Medical Program, Hill-Burton, and the Experimental Health Service Delivery System authorities. The act creates a network of health systems agencies serving geographically defined health services areas. In addition to performing capital expenditure reviews, the agencies approve or disapprove applications for federal funds for health programs within the area. Certificate-of-need laws, which incorporate an important element of public utility regulation, place regulatory controls on entry into the health services industry and on new investments in health care facilities.

The 1974 act provides the health systems agencies with two additional forms of leverage:

1. agencies will be allowed to direct state hospital licensing agencies to refuse to grant licenses to hospitals that have not obtained certificates of need.

2. health systems agencies, beginning in 1978, will review *existing* hospital facilities; hospitals with a low census will be asked to close down beds or be faced with loss of Title 5, 18, and 19 funds or loss of state license or both. Many of the decisions of the project review committee will be based on policy guidelines established in master plans for each local area. Figure 13.3 shows the structure of the health planning system for the United States.[15]

Recently, the CAT scanner (computerized axial tomography, or whole body scanner) has become symbolic of the difficult decisions facing health systems agencies. In 1977, a CAT scanner cost about $500,000. Should every hospital have one? When considering the needs of their own individual hospitals (particularly in attracting and retaining

Figure 13.3   Health Planning Structure in the United States,
              1977[a]

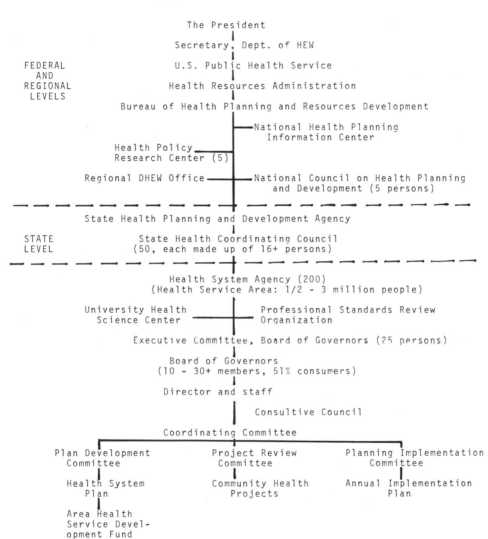

FEDERAL
AND
REGIONAL
LEVELS

The President

Secretary, Dept. of HEW

U.S. Public Health Service

Health Resources Administration

Bureau of Health Planning and Resources Development

National Health Planning
Information Center

Health Policy
Research Center (5)

Regional DHEW Office ─── National Council on Health Planning
                         and Development (5 persons)

State Health Planning and Development Agency

STATE
LEVEL

State Health Coordinating Council
(50, each made up of 16+ persons)

Health System Agency (200)
(Health Service Area: 1/2 - 3 million people)

University Health   Professional Standards Review
Science Center   Organization

Executive Committee, Board of Governors (25 persons)

Board of Governors
(10 - 30+ members, 51% consumers)

Director and staff

Consultive Council

Coordinating Committee

Plan Development   Project Review   Planning Implementation
Committee   Committee   Committee

Health System   Community Health   Annual Implementation
Plan   Projects   Plan

Area Health
Service Devel-
opment Fund

[a]PL 93-641, 1974:   National Health Planning and Resources Development Act

radiologists), most hospital administrators would say "yes." When considering the community as a whole, however, most health planners would say "no." But it is very difficult to say "no" to "progressive patient care" and to "maintaining high-quality services." A few years from now, some other new piece of equipment will replace the CAT scanner as the leading controversy in health planning.

Licensure

All states have extensive licensing powers for health manpower and institutions. They may require that individuals meet stated educational and, frequently, examination criteria to engage in certain health activities. Licensure can take two forms: (1) mandatory licensure regulates practice, and (2) voluntary licensure protects a person's title (some states protect the R.N. title, but allow non-R.N.'s to practice skilled nursing). State legislation usually establishes boards of licensure to implement provisions, make rules and regulations, and make decisions in the issuance and revocation of licenses. These boards are largely made up of members of the provider group being licensed. In addition to manpower, the states license health care institutions. Practicing or providing health care without a license is normally a misdemeanor.

Licensure establishes a monopoly and has allowed occupational groups to gain cartel powers in exchange for high standards of performance (in theory) and protection from inadequate providers. We will examine how licensure and accreditation have affected the supply of health care providers.

Provider Control

Education and Manpower

The history of the American Medical Association (AMA) and medical education in the United States could be characterized as one of restrictionism and self-interest thinly disguised as actions for the public interest. When the AMA was founded in 1847, there were a large number of medical schools, mostly proprietary institutions, which supposedly had low levels of educational quality. In fact, more than 400 medical schools were founded in the nineteenth century.[16] All kinds of practitioners— from natural healers to graduates of Edinburgh—claimed the title of doctor of medicine. The AMA initiated a reform campaign to secure state licensing laws with AMA-approved examiners.[17] By the turn of the century, the AMA had control of almost all state licensing boards: each state law provided that only graduates of AMA-accredited schools could sit for the licensing exams.

In 1904, the AMA's Council on Medical Education accelerated its drive to raise the standards of medical education. In 1907, an AMA report found many of the nation's 161 schools "doubtful" or "unsatisfactory." In 1908, Abraham Flexner, under the auspices of the Carnegie Foundation, began a comprehensive inspection of medical schools. His report (issued in 1910) was highly critical of schools that did not follow his ideal model, the medical school of Johns Hopkins University, which had a graduate program consisting of two years of basic science and two years of clinical medicine. The AMA called for implementation of Flexner's report, and soon standards rose markedly, and the number of medical schools and medical students fell sharply. Between 1904 and 1920, the number of medical schools decreased from 161 to 88, the number of students from 28,142 to 14,088, and the number of graduates from 5,747 to 3,047. By 1922, the number of graduates had fallen to 2,629, and all-time low for this century and only 46 percent of the number graduated in 1904.[18] The restriction on opportunities to study medicine in this country was particularly oppressive for Jews, Negroes, and women.

Flexner made no attempts to evaluate the outputs of medical schools; there was no investigation of what medical graduates could or could not do. The entire scope of improving standards was to be borne by changes in how physicians should be trained. (Medical education was made artificially expensive owing to the overspecification of how it was to be produced, especially, but now exclusively, during the first two years of school.) Kessel believes that Flexner and the Carnegie Foundation "unwittingly served the highly parochial interests of organized medicine."[19] Shryock, writing on the AMA's council on Medical Education, observes:

> Competing within a free economy they [organized medicine] observed that the scientific motive for educational reform coincided with their own professional ambitions. They became increasingly aware that too many schools were turning out too many graduates to make practice profitable.[20]

One of the effects of this AMA reform was an artificial scarcity of physicians in the United States. During a shortage or artificial restriction of supply, the income of physicians relative to the income of others will tend to rise.

Restrictionism increased during the Great Depression (1932 to 1940), when the AMA openly advocated and successfully carried out a policy of restrictionism. In 1932, the Association of American Medical College's Commission on Medical Education issued its final report, financed in large part by the AMA; the report states "it is clear that in the immediate past there has been a larger production [of M.D.'s] than necessary and that at the present time we have an oversupply . . . of at least 25,000 physicians in this country. If the present rate of supply is continued the number of physicians in excess of indicated needs will increase."[21] The report agreed that "an over-supply is likely to introduce excessive economic competition, the performance of unnecessary services, and elevated total cost of medical care, and conditions in this profession which will not encourage students of superior ability and character to enter the profession."

Sharply falling medical incomes were thought to be the result of excessive economic competition and an oversupply of physicians. The AMA's Council on Medical Education and Hospitals was delegated the responsibility of readjusting the ratio of physicians to population. An income-producing livelihood rather than patient welfare was the criterion used to make this assessment. The AMA's pressure on medical schools to cut back enrollment, or at least not to expand enrollment, had a substantial impact.[22] The success of organized medicine's restrictionist activities during the 1930s contributed to the shortage of physicians, which has persisted since the end of World War II. By 1962, the AMA had retreated from its position that there was no current or prospective danger of a physician shortage, and it eventually supported federal aid-to-medical-education bills.

The key to the medical model of controlling supply is the process of accreditation of medical schools combined with state licensing laws that require practitioners to graduate from accredited schools.

Qualifications for licensure of physicians educated in foreign medical facilities is controlled by the Educational Council for Foreign Medical Graduates. The test administered by this council can be made more or less difficult depending on the desired supply. In 1966, the ratio of Americans studying medicine abroad to foreigners studying medicine in the United States exceeded three to one; in all other fields—business administration, agriculture, education, engineering, and physical and natural sciences— the opposite was the case. Kessel concludes that the restriction of opportunities in this country continues to affect the number of Americans studying medicine abroad.[23]

Licensure has resulted in an extraordinary discontinuity in the skill distribution of personnel in the health industry. If we assume that the annual earnings of full-time workers are an index of the demand and supply of an individual's skills, we can compare mean earnings of health care providers with other large industries. Figure 13.4[24] shows there is an unusually large percentage of health workers at the low end of the distribution, a small percentage with earnings between the mean and

Figure 13.4   Percentage Distribution of Annual Earnings of
Providers of Health Services versus Workers in
a Composite of 19 Non-Health Industries

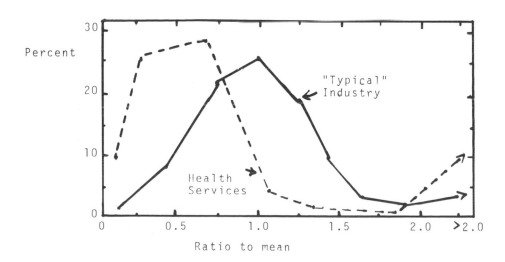

twice the mean, and an unusually high percentage earning more than twice the mean. The manpower gap in the health industry is most severe in earnings from the mean to 50 percent above the mean. These are individuals whose education and experience justify $15,000 to $30,000 in annual earnings. In other industries, these persons take on middle-level management or technical functions, thus freeing the most skilled and experienced to concentrate on the most important and demanding tasks.

Licensure is the key to the expanded use of allied health personnel, including physician assistants (or extenders) and nurse practitioners.[25] Provider control—physician dominance over other practitioners in this instance—is an important determinant in the supply of health manpower. Restrictionism is not limited to physicians; nurses demonstrate the same characteristic.[26]

Professional Organizations and Lobbying Efforts

Organized medicine has a clear record of anticompetitive behavior. Pathologists and radiologists often refuse to participate in any enterprise that they themselves do not own or run and in which all profits do not go solely to them. Prices for the services are fixed through sub-rosa agreements made through organized contacts. The AMA was prosecuted and convicted of a criminal conspiracy to destroy the Group Health Association of Washington, D.C., one of the earliest HMOs in the nation.[27] Organized medicine's control over licensure was used in an attempt to kill the Kaiser-Permanente Plan as well as the Farmers Union Hospital in Elk City, Oklahoma.[28] Medical-practice acts that forbid the corporate practice of medicine when the corporation is owned by nonphysicians have been used in San Antonio to deter a Mexican-American clinic (*Garcia* v. *the State Board of Medical Examiners;* Texas is one of twenty-two states with such a prohibition) and in New Orleans to hinder the growth of Louisiana's first abortion clinic (*Delta Women's Clinic* v. *State of Louisiana*). Antipoverty clinics have been attacked vigorously in Marianna, Arkansas, and Elps, Alabama, by entrenched county medical societies. Interference with private practice as a result of not belonging to the county medical society or to the AMA has arisen in Spokane, Washington, and in New York state.[29]

Physicians, partly as a result of further efforts to foster anticompetitive behavior, practice price discrimination. Theoretically, rates are higher for affluent patients and lower for less affluent patients; this practice is known as charging what the traffic will bear. The medical profession maintains that price discrimination exists because physicians represent a collection agency for medical charities; that is, if physicians themselves are not to finance the cost of operating medical charities, they must price their services to wealthier patients disproportionately high. Economists, on the other hand, believe this behavior represents the profit-maximizing behavior of a discriminating monopolist. Why should medical charity function differently from other charities? Evidence indicates that if income and wealth differences are held constant, people who have medical insurance pay *more* for the same service than people who do not have such insurance. In addition, physicians practice inconsistent price discrimination: typically, they do not charge one another for medical services. As real per capita income rises, price discrimination ought to fade away. Affluent patients are not informed of, nor do they give their consent to, the loading charges imposed.[30] Schuck concluded that "the medical profession has simply been the most successful of all the occupational monopolists."[31]

Occupational monopolists remain politically successful because they have sizable campaign funds to influence legislators. The AMA is the leading proponent of using campaign funds to affect legislation on Capitol Hill. The American Medical Political Action Committee (AMPAC) spent $636,500 in campaign contributions before the 1970 elections.[32] The AMA claims that the AMPAC is a separate organization, but AMPAC and the AMA share board members and resources. In addition to the AMA, the Federation of American Hospitals and the Pharmaceutical Manufacturers Association also maintain active lobbies. Washington lawyers are retained, and suites of offices are maintained, to keep track of health legislation and influence key legislators. Timely campaign contributions and continuous application of pressure require on-the-spot analysis and action.

Politicians also are susceptible to funding projects that have little impact but that satisfy certain constituents and ethnic groups. Congressional declarations of war on Cooley's anemia, sickle-cell anemia, G6PD, and Tay-Sachs disease duplicate existing efforts and tend to be unscientific, but legislators can not resist the political appeal of combating rare, dread diseases.[33]

Utilization and Peer Review

The debate over utilization review perhaps is one of the greatest furors ever to develop in health politics. *Utilization review* is a system for reviewing patient records to determine whether the care rendered is adequate and necessary. Hospitals are now required to exercise one of three options in order to be reimbursed for services to medicare and medicaid patients:

1. have staff physicians perform the review
2. have a combination of staff physicians and a separate group of members from the local medical society perform the review
3. hire an outside group of physicians to perform the review

A hospital can exercise the third option only if it is too small or otherwise unable to make an objective review itself. Another requirement of utilization review is that records of hospitalized medicare and medicaid patients must be reviewed within twenty-four hours of their admission. The objective of this program is, in part, to reduce unnecessary tests and procedures while improving the quality of care rendered to public patients. If the review committee finds treatment to be unsatisfactory, the hospital or physician or both will not be reimbursed by the government for services.

HR 1 of amendments to the Social Security Act (1974) established provisions for professional standards review organizations (PSRO). A PSRO will be a locally based entity that will oversee the quality, necessity, and appropriateness of medical services paid for, wholly or partially, under provisions of the Social Security Act. Qualified organizations, consisting primarily of physicians, will review medical records for institutions and organizations that cannot demonstrate effective quality and utilization controls. Each PSRO will start by making use of professionally developed "norms" and standards of treatment, diagnosis, care, and utilization. Inappropriate treatment will not be reimbursed, and practitioners who demonstrate gross or repeated impropriety may be barred from further reimbursement under federal health programs, either permanently or temporarily. PSROs will be reimbursed by HEW for expenses.

Under the 1974 law, each hospital—or PSRO, if a hospital does not have an effective review process—must establish standards for care. PSRO coordinators in each institution will use these norms to approve admissions, assign appropriate length of stay, approve extensions of the initial length of stay, and ensure that all patients are cared for in an appropriate manner. Extensive profile reports will be developed for every hospital physician and facility. Reports will summarize surgical rates, frequency of complications, length of stay, etc. Aberrant trends will be identified and corrective actions taken.[34]

Providers claim that PSROs will disrupt the physician-patient relationship and lead to government abuse of patient records. The AMA has temporarily blocked the implementation of federal PSRO regulations. The fight over this legislation is far from over.[35]

A 1977 HEW study evaluating the performance of PSROs found no evidence that they had saved money in most cities or achieved reductions in hospital use nationally, although improvement was found in some areas. The Office of Management and Budget recommended the elimination of federal funds for PRSOs from the fiscal 1979 budget.[36]

Summary

The public knows little about how health legislation is influenced by groups of providers. Recently, two important pieces of legislation involving health planning and utilization review have been enacted to increase the government's control over the quality and quantity of health care delivered to low-income consumers. The government, as a powerful third party, will supposedly protect the relatively powerless consumer from abuse by, and the excesses of, providers. The history of provider professional groups, such as the AMA, has been restrictionism based on self-interest and on maintaining control over the health system. Recent health legislation may signal a shift in this power away from the providers.

Questions

1. The 1976 federal poverty level for a nonfarm family of four was $5,500. Let's assume that you are a congressman and several poor families in your area each consume more than this amount in medicaid payments each year. Your opponent in the upcoming congressional race accuses you and your colleagues in the House of runaway spending and wasteful use of taxpayers' money; he cites the above situation. How would you answer him?

2. If the federal government again began funding neighborhood health centers, what suggestions could you make to improve their effectiveness and longevity?

3. Assume you are the director of your state's medicaid program. Would you support reimbursement by medicaid of services provided to the indigent in a free clinic? How about reimbursement for abortion services?

4. What advantages would consumers gain if hospitals, both private and public, were regulated as if they were a public utility such as the phone company?

5. How have new campaign financing laws affected AMPAC's political spending?

Notes

1. John C. Norman, "Medicine in the Ghetto," *New England Journal of Medicine* 281:1271-75 (4 December 1969). See also John C. Norman, *Medicine in the Ghetto* (New York: Appleton-Century-Crofts, 1969); J. Kosa, A. Antonovsky, and I. Zola, *Poverty and Health* (Cambridge, Mass.: Harvard University Press, 1969); Pierre Devise, *Slum Medicine: Chicago's Apartheid Health System* (Chicago: University of Chicago Press, January 1969).

2. *Minority Health Chart Book* (Washington, D.C.: American Public Health Association, 1974), p. 63.

3. Martin S. Feldstein, "The Medical Economy," *Scientific American* 229:151-61 (September 1973).

4. John D. Stoeckle and Lucy M. Candib, "The Neighborhood Health Center—Reform Ideas of Yesterday and Today." *New England Journal of Medicine* 280:1385-91 (19 June 1969).

5. Dr. Andrew Dott, author of the foreword in this book, has provided the following government-funded health center terms:

   a. *duplication of service*—a term used by someone who wishes to eliminate competition and maintain a monopoly (a captive patient population)

b. *freedom of choice*—a term used by someone who wishes to break up a monopoly and introduce competition
c. *a demonstration*—offering services to a limited number of people since the government is too cheap to offer what it should to everyone (also called a *pilot project*)
d. *consumer board*—a group of people inexperienced in health programs who will be blamed when an underfinanced project fails
e. *maximal feasible community participation*—creating a management structure of inexperienced people under the control of community people knowing nothing of health who must hire and train inexperienced personnel to operate an underfinanced project in a neighborhood of high social discontent and high expectations (another definition—*political patronage*)
f. *management information system*—gathering information about everything since you don't know what someone will want in five years and writing lengthy reports no one reads
g. *a budget*—a document that will be revised next week when someone in Washington changes his mind
h. *guidelines*—vague rules issued by Democratic bureaucrats that will be reinterpreted by a Republican politician next year
i. *audit*—learning about the reinterpretation
j. *a federally financed health project*—something which will be terminated about the time people figure out how to make it work
k. *fraud, waste, mismanagement*—the mistakes made figuring out how to make it work.

6. For an interesting discussion of the death of one of the most famous health centers, see Joseph Huttie's, "New Federalism and the Death of a Dream in Mound Bayou, Mississippi," *New South* 28:20-29 (fall 1973). What makes the demise of the health center movement so ironic is the tremendous enthusiasm the movement generated. See "Medicine on the Firing Line." *Hospital Practice* 7:154 (March 1972); S. Bellin et al., "Impact of Ambulatory Health Care Services on the Demand of Hospital Beds." *New England Journal of Medicine* 280:808-12 (10 April 1969); J. Elinson and C. Herr, "A Sociomedical View of Neighborhood Health Centers." *Medical Care* 8:87-103 (March-April 1970); R. Fein, "An Economist's View of the Neighborhood Health Centers." *Medical Care* 8:104-7 (March-April 1970); H. J. Geiger, "Health Center in Mississippi." *Hospital Practice* 4:68-81 (February 1969); G. A. Goldberg, F. L. Trowbridge, and R. C. Buxbaum, "Issues in the Development of Neighborhood Health Centers." *Inquiry* 6:37-48 (March 1969); J. Hatch, "Community Shares in Policy Decisions for Rural Health Center." *Hospitals* 43:109-12 (1 July 1969); E. Langer, "Medicine for the Poor: A New Deal in Denver." *Science* 153:508-11 (29 July 1966); Mark H. Lepper et al., "An Approach to Reconciling the Poor and the System." *Inquiry* 5:37-42 (March 1968); J. D. Synder, and M. J. Enright, "Free Neighborhood Health Centers Promise Big Impact for Hospitals." *Hospital Management* 103:38-44 (March 1967); G. Sparer, G. B. Dines, and D. Smith, "Consumer Participation in OEO-Assisted Neighborhood Health Centers." *AJPH* 60:1091-102 (June 1970); G. Sparer and Anne Anderson, "Cost of Services in Neighborhood Health Centers." *New England Journal of Medicine* 286:1241-45 (8 June 1972); Peter E. Dans and

Samuel Johnson, "Politics in the Development of a Migrant Health Center. *New England Journal of Medicine* 292:890-95 (24 April 1975); Robert Hollister et al., *Neighborhood Health Centers.* Lexington, Mass.: Lexington Books, 1974.

7. "Free Clinics." Health/Pac Bulletin 34:1-17 (October 1971). See also, R. Corner, "Appraisal and Health Care Delivery in a Free Clinic." *Health Services Reports* 87:727-33 (October 1972); A. J. Carniello, "Setting Up a Dental Free Clinic Component." *Journal of Social Issues* 30:115-22 (1974); David Smith et al., eds. *The Free Clinic: A Commentary Approach to Health Care and Drug Abuse* (Beloit, Wisc.: Stash Press, 1971).

8. Ibid., p. 6.

9. Florence A. Wilson and Duncan Neuhauser, *Health Services in the United States* (Cambridge, Mass.: Ballinger Publishing Co., 1975), p. 186.

10. Cecil G. Sheps, "The Influence of Consumer Sponsorship on Medical Services," in Irving K. Zola and John B. Mckinlay, eds., *Organizational Issues in the Delivery of Health Services* (New York: Prodist, 1974), pp. 365-93.

11. For an examination of the movement toward the consumer-community control of health facilities, see M. Frankel, "In the Watts Health Center, the Customer is Nearly Always Right." *National Tuberculosis and Respiratory Diseases Association Bulletin* 55:14-16 (February 1969); C. B. Galiher, "Consumer Participation." *HSMHA Reports* 86:99-106 (February 1971); T. Goldberg, "A Consumer Looks at Medical Care." *Medical Care* 5:9-18 (January-February 1967); J. Graves, "Involvement of Consumers." *Hospitals* 44:46-49 (October 1970); S. Krevitz and F. K. Kolodner, "Community Action: Where Has It Been? Where Will It Go?" *Annals of the American Academy of Political and Social Science* 385:30-40 (September 1969); Mary L. Moore, "The Role of Hostility and Militancy in Indigenous Community Health Advisory Groups." *AJPH* 61:922-30 (May 1971).

12. George L. Maddox and Eugene A. Stead, "The Professional and Citizen Participation," in *The Citizenry and the Hospital* (Durham, N.C.: Duke University, 1974), pp. 71-84.

13. Jeoffry B. Gordon, "The Politics of Community Medicine Projects: A Conflict Analysis." *Medical Care* 7:419-28 (November-December 1969).

14. Symond R. Gottlieb, " A Brief History of Health Planning in the United States," in Clark C. Havighurst, ed., *Regulating Health Facilities Construction* (Washington, D.C.: American Enterprise Institute, 1974), pp. 7-25.

15. David A. Dittman and Jeffrey A. Peters, "A Foundation for Health Care Regulation: PL 92-603 and PL 93-641." *Inquiry* 14:32-42 (March 1977). For a dissenting view, see Clark C. Havighurst, "Regulation of Health Facilities and Services by Certificate of Need." *Virginia Law Review* 59:1143-1233 (October 1973). See also, Richard A. Posner, "Certificates of Need for Health Care Facilities: A Dissenting View," in Clark C. Havighurst, ed., *Regulating Health Facilities Construction* (Washington, D.C.: American Enterprise Institute, 1974), pp. 113-17 and 123-124.

16. Bonnie Bullough and Vern Bullough, "A Brief History of Medical Practice," in Eliot Freidson and Judith Lorber, eds., *Medical Men and Their Work*, (Chicago: Aldine Publishing Co., 1972), pp. 86-102.

17. Texas was the first state to establish such a licensing board in 1875.

18. Elton Rayack, *Professional Power & American Medicine* (Cleveland: World Publishing Co., 1967) pp. 66-72.

19. Reuben Kessel, "The AMA and the Supply of Physicians." *Journal of Law*

and *Contemporary Problems* 35:267-83 (spring 1970).

20. Richard Shyrock, "Women in American Medicine." *Journal of the American Medical Women's Association* 5:371-79 (September 1950).

21. *Final Report of the Commission on Medical Education* (New York: Association of American Medical Colleges, 1932), pp. 93, 100.

22. E. Rayack, *Professional Power & American Medicine,* p. 78.

23. "The AMA and the Supply of Physicians," p. 272.

24. Victor Fuchs, Elizabeth Rand, and Bonnie Garrett, "The Health Manpower Gap Re-Examined," *New England Journal of Medicine* 282:338-39 (5 February 1970).

25. See F. N. Lohrenz, "The Marshfield Clinic Physician-Assistant Concept." *New England Journal of Medicine* 284:301-04, (11 February 1971); A. Robbins, "Allied Health Manpower—Solution or Problem." *New England Journal of Medicine* 286:918-23 (27 April 1972). Since 1971 there has been an incredible number of articles written about physician extenders and assistants.

26. In order to expand the supply of nurses, suggestions have been made that institutions such as hospitals educate their providers on the job and issue their own license to practice in their respective institutions. These limited licenses then could be cross-recognized by other institutions in the community and perhaps also be recognized by the state. Institutional licensure was first proposed to relieve the nursing "shortage," which, according to hospital administrators, has resulted from moratoriums imposed by nursing associations on the development of new nursing schools. See Lawrence R. Tancredi and John Woods, "The Social Control of Medical Practice: Licensure Versus Output Monitoring." *Milbank Memorial Fund Quarterly* 50:99-125 (January 1972), and R. J. Carlson, "Health Manpower Licensing and Emerging Institutional Responsibility for the Quality of Care," *Law and Contemporary Problems* 35:849-78 (autumn 1970), and L. Y. Kelly, "Institutional Licensure," *Nursing Outlook* 21:566-72 (September 1973).

27. Peter H. Shuck, "A Consumer's View of the Health Care Sytem," *Ethics of Health Care,* edited by Laurence Tancredi (Washington: National Academy of Science, 1974), pp. 95-118.

28. R. Kessel, "Price Discrimination in Medicine." *Journal of Law and Economics* 1120-53 (October 1958).

29. *Competition in the Health Services Market,* Hearings before the Subcommittee on Anti-Trust and Monopoly of the Committee on the Judiciary U.S. Senate, 93rd Congress, (1974), 3 vols.

30. R. Kessel, "Price Discrimination in Medicine," p. 1120-53.

31. Schuck, "A Consumer's View", p. 107. For an extended discussion of organized medicine's restraint of trade, see Douglas R. Mackintosh and G. Kent Stearns, "Occupational Licensure, Professionalism, and Restraint of Trade: The Medical Model," Working Paper #103, Division of Business and Economic Research, University of New Orleans, 1975.

32. John Iglehart, "Washington Pressures/Skyrocketing Health Care Costs Aggravate Mission of Hospital Lobby." *National Journal* 4:680-89 (22 April 1972). For a brief glimpse of the difference between lobbying efforts of two associations, see the following capsule from the above article:

Because the American Hospital Association considers its cause always to be in the public interest, it sees no need to build political power by making contributions to the campaigns of Members of Congress, and this has been a source of frustration at times to the AHA's lobbyists.

The "public interest" argument wore thin at times, recalls Lacey C. Sharp, who served as a legislative representative for the AHA from 1961 to 1969.

Sharp, who supports the idea of a campaign fund for hospitals, remembered that he once asked a Member of the House to support an AHA-backed bill in committee, and was greeted with this response "What's the AMA's (American Medical Association's) position on the bill?"

"I asked him, 'What's the AMA got to do with it?' He said: 'The AMA contributed $9,000 to my campaign last time.'"

Sharp said he would find out what the AMA's position was. He telephoned James W. Foristel, an AMA lobbyist, and Foristel said the medical association had no problem with the bill.

"I asked Jim to call the Member and tell him that," Sharp said. "He did call and the Member ended up voting to support the bill."

If there is any question about the AMA stand on current health policy issues, glance over the following letter from the AMA to a past member who has not paid his 1976 dues:

Dear AMA Member:

I was very sorry to learn that you have apparently chosen not to join the American Medical Association this year. It may be possible that you have paid your AMA dues for 1976 and either your county or state medical society has not as yet sent your dues to us. Your AMA wants to respond quickly to your membership, but in some instances medical societies hold AMA dues dollars in local banks for interest and do not report membership to us for as long as six months after they receive your dues check.

If you have not paid your 1976 dues I can only speculate that you have concluded that AMA membership is not of importance or value to you, and that it is something you can do without.

But can you really? Did you ever think about what the AMA is worth to you?

What is it worth to you to have your American Medical Association take the Department of Health, Education and Welfare to court over the Utilization Review Regulations? These regulations would have required that a physician justify admittance for all his Medicare or Medicaid patients within 24 hours before a hospital review committee. AMA contended that these regulations constituted unlawful interference with the rights of physicians and patients. AMA won the suit and HEW withdrew the regulations for re-writing.

What is it worth to you not to have the government interfere with the drugs you prescribe to patients under federal health care programs? Under the Maximum Allowable Cost (MAC) Regulations, you would, in effect, be expected to prescribe drugs primarily on the basis of price considerations rather than your clinical experience and patient's acceptance. The AMA has taken HEW to court on this one, too, seeking a permanent injunction.

What is it worth to you that the AMA lobbied effectively and had the most substantial impact with respect to Congressional modification of the self employed retirement plan tax shelter (Keogh Law) which increases the annual limits of contributions you can make to a qualified retirement plan to 15% of earned income or up to $7,500 a year? If you are in the 40% tax bracket, you could potentially save $1,500 a year, which is *six times the $250 annual AMA dues.*

What is it worth to you to prevent the federal bureaucracy from telling us and our patients what type of health facilities we will have, what services will be provided, how these services will be organized, and when and where these services will be rendered? Well, that's exactly what the National Health Planning and Resources Development Act calls for. By this law, Congress has created a health planning empire for HEW in the avowed interests of cost containment and efficiency. In short, the basic decisions about quality of care no longer will be made by those of us closest to the patient, whose emphasis is on the quality of care; instead, the decisions will be circumscribed by governmental rules and regulations, and be made by those whose emphasis will be on cost. The AMA believes this is one of the most potentially destructive pieces of health legislation ever enacted by Congress and to prevent its implementation, the AMA plans to file suit challenging the constitutionality of the law on behalf of the entire profession and our patients.

There's still another example of how the American Medical Association is working to protect the interests and integrity of the profession. As you know, the Federal Trade Commission has filed a formal complaint challenging the AMA's code of ethics, charging that the ethical ban on solicitation is in restraint of trade. The AMA defends its code of ethics as a protection of the public against unscrupulous or mercenary practitioners. We will fight the F.T.C. action because we believe that solicitation is the very antithesis of professionalism.

I could go on at considerable length about why AMA membership is of value to you. But I hope these few examples demonstrate that the AMA is indeed worthy of your support.

I ask that you give serious consideration to joining your AMA. Particularly in these difficult and challenging times, we need a strong and vigilant American Medical Association. Your support, through your membership, will help keep it that way.

For your convenience you may forward your dues check along with the top portion of the membership form in the enclosed business reply envelope.

I sincerely hope you will join us. We can do even *more* together.

Sincerely,
Max H. Parrott, M.D.
President

For a lengthy discussion of the fierce lobbying over medicaid, see Robert Stevens and Rosemary Stevens, *Welfare Medicine in America* (New Haven, Conn.: Yale University Press, 1975).

33. "Congress Pushes Fight on Ailments That Afflict Ethnic Groups; Some Doubt Wisdom of Such Acts." *Wall Street Journal* (29 September 1972), p. 24. See also, "The Battle Against Sickle-Cell Anemia Progresses, But It Brings Some Problems Along With Results." *Wall Street Journal* (4 January 1973), p. 20.

34. David A. Dittman and Jeffry A. Peters, "A Foundation for Health Care Regulation: PL 92-60 and PL 93-641," *Inquiry* 14:32-42 (March 1977). Earl Brian, "Foundation for Medical Care Control of Hospital Utilization: CHAPA PSRO Prototype," *New England Journal of Medicine* 288:878-82 (26 April 1973). J. Fine and M. Morehead, "Study of Peer Review of Inhospital Patient Care," *New York*

State Journal of Medicine 71:1963-73 (15 August 1971). F. M. Richardson, "Peer Review of Medical Care," *Medical Care* 10:29-39 (January-February 1972). D. A. Soricelli, "Practical Experience in Peer Review Controlling Quality in the Delivery of Dental Care," *AJPH* 61:2046-56 (October 1971).

35. "AMA Wins First Round in Fight as Judge Blocks the Start of HEW Review Boards." *Wall Street Journal,* 28 May 1975, p. 6. See also, "Medical Care Review Stirs Fiery Debate Among U.S. Physicians." *Wall Street Journal,* 24 June 1974, pp. 1 and 15. "Is Your Doctor Good? PSROs Can Tell—and Maybe Bring Better, Less Costly Care." *National Observer,* 4 May 1974, pp. 1 and 18.

36. "OMB Seeks to End Program Reviewing Physicians' Practices," *Washington Post,* 13 December 1977, p. 12.

Further Reading

Alford, Robert R. *Health Care Politics: Ideological and Interest Group Barriers to Reform.* Chicago: University of Chicago Press, 1974.

Blackman, Allen. *A Bibliography of Bibliographies on Comprehensive Planning for Health and Related Topics.* Washington, D.C.: Association of University Programs in Hospital Administration, July 1970.

Bullough, Bonnie and Bullough, Vern L. *Poverty, Ethnic Identity and Health Care.* New York: Appleton-Century-Crofts, 1972.

Burger, Edward J. *Protecting the Nation's Health: The Problems of Regulation.* Lexington, Mass.: D.C. Heath & Co., 1976.

Cornacchia, Harold J. *Consumer Health.* St. Louis: C. V. Mosby, 1976.

Cunningham, Robert M. *The Wholistic Health Centers: A New Direction in Health Care.* Battle Creek, Mich.: W. K. Kellogg Foundation, 1977.

Derbyshire, Robert C. *Medical Licensure and Discipline in the United States.* Baltimore, Md.: Johns Hopkins University Press, 1969.

Mechanic, David. *Politics, Medicine and Social Science.* New York: John Wiley & Sons, 1974.

Navarro, Vicente. *Medicine Under Capitalism.* New York: Prodist, 1976.

Rosenberg, Ken, and Schiff, Gordon, eds. *The Politics of Health Care: A Bibliography.* Boston: New England Free Press, 1970.

Utilization Review: A Selected Bibliography 1933-1969. HEW, PHS, HSMHA, Community Health Services, 1969.

14. Future Delivery of Health Care: Emerging Concepts

He who falls in this fight falls in the radiance of the future.
—Huey P. Long

No one is quite sure in what direction health care is going. Some of the emerging concepts in the delivery of health care may never have much impact on most health consumers. On the other hand, most such concepts have theoretical merit or have proven to be effective in limited application. Several are intuitively appealing—they also make sense in the context of systems analysis and the rational allocation of scarce resources.

Automated Multiphasic Health Testing (AMHT)

AMHT is the utilization of automated equipment, computers, and allied health personnel to perform a battery of psychological and biochemical tests and measurements that, in combination with a self-administered medical history, lead to an integrated analysis of the data and a synthesized health report to a physician. The primary objective of this procedure is to help alter the natural course of an asymptomatic person's disease in a favorable direction by providing a physician with information that will lead to an early detection of the disease. The sooner a disease is detected and treated, the less likely it is that harmful consequences will occur.

AMHT originated from periodic medical examinations and industrial health programs. In the early 1950s, in order to detect employee health problems efficiently during the annual physical checkup, employers began using automated equipment.[1] Slowly, as computer hardware and software became more sophisticated, the state of the art progressed. The design of the flow of employees through the testing facility also was streamlined. The following tests are usually performed at an AMHT facility: medical history, electrocardiography, blood pressure, tonometry, visual acuity, spirometry, anthropometry, audiometry, clinical laboratory, and chest x-ray. The tests may also include cervical cytology, sigmoidoscopy, thyroid activity, and serology. Some of the testing equipment may be directly "on line" with a central computer so that test information is fed in while the patient is being tested. Other test information must be fed into the computer using data punch cards or through the use of optical scanning devices. Some data, such as the chest x-ray, must be read by specialists before the information can be stored in the computer. Finally, the computer prints out the examination results, as seen in Figure 14.1.[2] One of the strong points of AMHT is that it allows for a comparison of patient results with previous test results and with standardized results for healthy males or females within his or her age range. These comparisons are seen in Figure 14.2.[3]

Figure 14.1   Computer Printout of AMHT Questionnaire

```
                I B M MULTIPHASIC SCREENING SUMMARY 07/13/72
EXAM DATE 09/25/71                                        PAGE 1

DOE          , JOHN                    IBM NO: #88888
62 YEAR OLD MALE                       PERM LOC: 001 ARMONK
MARRIED    3 CHILDREN
TYPE OF EXAM: PROGRAM          4 EXAMS    EXAM LOC: 001 ARMONK

          ON THE IBM HEALTH QUESTIONNAIRE (M04-8060-0)
          THIS INDIVIDUAL INDICATED HEALTH TO BE GOOD.

HISTORICAL REVIEW OF SYSTEMS:     A=09/01/69  B=09/20/70  C=09/25/71

EYES:                             NO POSITIVE RESPONSES

ENT:                              NO POSITIVE RESPONSES

RESPIRATORY:
A B C     77: WHEEZING IN CHEST

CARDIOVASCULAR:
A B C     23: SHORTNESS OF BREATH
A B C     73: HIGH BLOOD PRESSURE

GASTROINTESTINAL
A B C     28: RUPTURE OR HERNIA
A B C     66: ON A SPECIAL DIET

GENITOURINARY:
    C     90: GETS UP EVERY NIGHT TO URINATE

MUSCULOSKELETAL:
A B C     10: BACKACHE
A B C     45: BACK TROUBLE
A B C     51: BACK INJURY

NEUROLOGICAL:                     NO POSITIVE RESPONSES

ENDOCRINE:
  B C     15: DIABETES
A B C     64: SUGAR WAS FOUND IN URINE

ALLERGIES:                        NO POSITIVE RESPONSES

*    *    *    *    *    *    *  PAST HISTORY  *    *    *    *    *    *

GENERAL:
A B C     34: WAS HOSPITALIZED
A B C     36: HAD A JOB WHERE FREQUENT HEALTH EXAMS WERE PAID FOR BY EMPLOYER
A B C     61: LOST 5 POUNDS OR MORE DURING THE PAST YEAR
A B C     92: EXCESSIVE THIRST
A B C     94: TAKES MEDICINE, DRUGS, OR VITAMINS REGULARLY
A B C    157: SAW MD FOR OTHER THAN ROUTINE CHECK OR MINOR ILLNESS IN PAST 5 YR
```

Figure 14.2   Computer Printout of Comparative Results for Several
Examinations and Standardized Ranges

```
            I B M MULTIPHASIC SCREENING SUMMARY 07/13/72

EXAM DATE 09/25/71                                    PAGE   4

DOE          , JOHN                      IBM NO: #88888
62 YEAR OLD MALE                         PERM LOC: 001 ARMONK


URINALYSIS:               09/69      09/70      09/71
   *GLUCOSE              *POSITIVE  *POSITIVE   NEGATIVE
    ALBUMIN              NEGATIVE   NEGATIVE    NEGATIVE
    PH                    6          5          6
    SPECIFIC GRAVITY      1.013      1.012      1.014

BLOOD:                    09/69      09/70      09/71    EXPECTED RANGE-MALES
    HEMATOCRIT            41%        43%        39%         38% - 53%
    HEMOGLOBIN           15.0       14.3       15.1     12.5-17.1 GM/100 ML

BLOOD SERUM:                                             5%-95% RANGE FOR
                  09/68    09/69    09/70    09/71    HEALTHY MALES(61-65)
*GLUCOSE, FASTING  130+    150+++   180+++    125+     87-124 MG/100 ML
 UREA NITROGEN      15       17      18        16      11- 24 MG/100 ML
 TOTAL BILIBUBIN    0.6      0.9     0.8       0.2      0.0-0.9 MG/100 ML
 URIC ACID          5.0      6.2     5.6       7.0      4.5-8.2 MG/100 ML
 LDH                85       85     NOT INC   NOT INC   74-138 WACKER U.
 SGOT               21       25      17        20       12- 30 KARMEN U.
*TOTAL CHOLESTEROL 326++a  365++a   300++a    275a     164-278 MG/100 ML
 TRIGLYCERIDES     NOT INC NOT INC  NOT INC   140       55-285 MG/100 ML

    CODES:   +  = VALUE GREATER THAN THE 95TH PERCENTILE OF MALES
            ++  = VALUE GREATER THAN THE 97.5TH PERCENTILE OF MALES
           +++  = VALUE GREATER THAN THE 99.5TH PERCENTILE OF MALES
             a  = CHOLESTEROL VALUE GREATER THAN 232, (THE 75TH PERCENTILE).
```

Another important feature of AMHT is its low cost.[4] The entire procedure can cost as low as $25 per individual when large numbers of people are being tested—which is obviously a considerable savings over the cost of a comprehensive medical examination performed by a separate group of testing facilities. Although AMHT does not take the place of a thorough work-up by a physician, the employees are usually enthusiastic about it. Because most Americans may be reluctant to purchase additional units of preventive care, however, AMHT may never receive widespread acceptance outside of an industrial setting.

Computer Diagnosis

We have seen how computers can be used to test, standardize, and integrate patient information. The next logical sequence in this chain of events is medical diagnosis by the computer. An essential part of diagnosis consists of culling out relevant from irrelevant information and developing hypotheses from the available, incomplete data presented by the patient. A computer has the ability to store vast amounts of data, to perform complex sequences of operations, and to enumerate possible causes of disease symptoms. However, the diagnostic process is not yet routine science. A physician may use varying sets of criteria in determining the diagnosis depending on the total clinical situation;

different decisions can and are made on the basis of the same information. Until the methodology of medical diagnosis can be made more exact, computer technology will be able to achieve only scattered success.[5]

Nevertheless, recent advances at integrating automation and medicine have led to the following applications: cerebral blood flow, assignments of genotypes, classification of human chromosomes, monitoring of childhood growth disorders, optometric scans, perspective drawings of molecular structure, implant dosimetry, attitude structures in psychiatric patients, phonocardiograms, management of gastrointestinal hemorrhage, transfusion analysis, control of ventilation and anaesthesia, and analysis of electrocardiograms. Computers are used to monitor the physiologic functions of the major organ systems (cardiovascular, respiratory, renal, cerebral, electrolytic control, etc.) so that complications can be detected immediately.

Moreover, medical record systems can be automated and integrated into a hospital information system, which might use its computer to schedule nurses and house staff, review drug usage, control inventories, and maintain security by monitoring passes and locks on doors.

Finally, computers can be used in the health planning process: in determining where to locate new facilities and expand existing facilities, in designing health care facilities, and in analyzing information for utilization and peer review.

As yet, most of these computer applications are several years away from widespread use.

New Facility Arrangements

Currently, the overwhelming emphasis in the delivery of health care is with curing sickness. There is increasing interest, however, in designing facilities that can accommodate the well and the "early sick" without drawing away large amounts of medical resources from treatment of the sick. An unstructured, heterogeneous mix of well and sick now enter into health care facilities designed for sick care.

Sidney Garfield of the Kaiser Foundation Health Plan and Hospitals has proposed a new delivery system to separate the sick from the well.[6] In the system proposed, a central medical center would provide sick care, and four or five "outreach" neighborhood centers would provide health testing, health care, and preventive care. The outreach clinics would be coordinated with the sick-care center, and all units would be tied into a centralized computer. Figure 14.3 shows the components of this system.[7] The computer center would regulate the flow of patients and information among the units and would coordinate the entire system. Three of the four divisions are primarily staffed by paramedical personnel. The entry point into the system is the health-testing and referral service, which utilizes automated multiphasic health testing. Consumers would be

Figure 14.3 The Garfield Delivery System

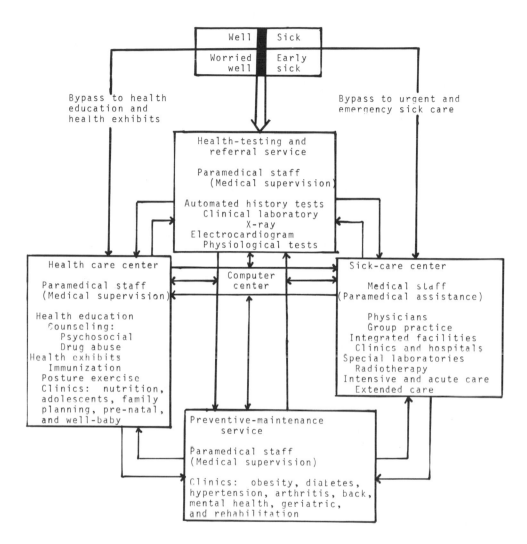

referred, depending on their test results, to the appropriate inpatient or outpatient facility. Garfield believes his system would foster the efficient use of scarce medical personnel and deliver better health care. As yet, few facilities are linked together in this fashion.

New Financial Arrangements

The three concepts we are concerned with here are controversial and may not materialize.

Health Maintenance Organization

Prepaid group practice has had a sizable impact on plans to alter the

methods for delivering ambulatory and primary care. Another form of the
delivery of medical care is the medical care foundation. Both the prepaid
group practice and the medical care foundation are health plans known as
health maintenance organizations (HMOs). An HMO is a system for
organizing and delivering health services to a voluntarily enrolled
population on a prepayment basis through groups or individual
practitioners.[8] Characteristics of an HMO include the following:

1. it provides health care directly or through arrangement with other
   health services, to enrollees on a per capita prepayment basis;
   each enrollee pays a fixed amount, regardless of the volume of
   services he or she uses
2. physician services are provided through a partnership or as
   employees or through a contractual arrangement with a group of
   physicians
3. services provided are comprehensive, including both inpatient and
   outpatient care
4. there are internal, self-regulatory mechanisms to assure quality of
   care and cost control[9]

One reason HMOs may save money and resources is that HMO physicians
will be responsible for the hospital bill incurred when they admit a patient
to the hospital and, therefore, will be careful not to admit HMO patients
unnecessarily.

In 1973, the Health Maintenance Organization Act was signed into law.
It establishes minimum requirements that HMOs must meet in order to
receive government grants to cover start-up costs. HMOs must provide
no less than the minimum benefits package to all of their enrollees for a
fixed, periodic payment calculated under a community rating system.

The minimum benefits package, as defined by the HMO act, is fairly
broad and includes physicians' services; inpatient and outpatient hospital
services; medically necessary emergency services; short-term, ambulatory, evaluative, and crisis-intervention mental health services; medical
treatment and referral services for alcohol and drug abuse and addiction;
laboratory and diagnostic and therapeutic radiological services; home
health services; and preventive services (including voluntary family
planning services, infertility services, preventive dental care for children,
and children's eye examinations).

The types of assistance provided by the legislation to qualified HMOs
are (1) grants, contracts, loans, and loan guarantees to help offset the costs
of planning; development and initial operations of HMOs; (2)
mandatory dual choice, in which most employers with more than twenty-
five employees must offer qualified HMOs in addition to the health
benefits plans they might now have; and (3) federal override of state laws
that restrict the development of HMOs. The legislation has no premium
subsidies or other incentives to motivate individuals to join HMOs. The

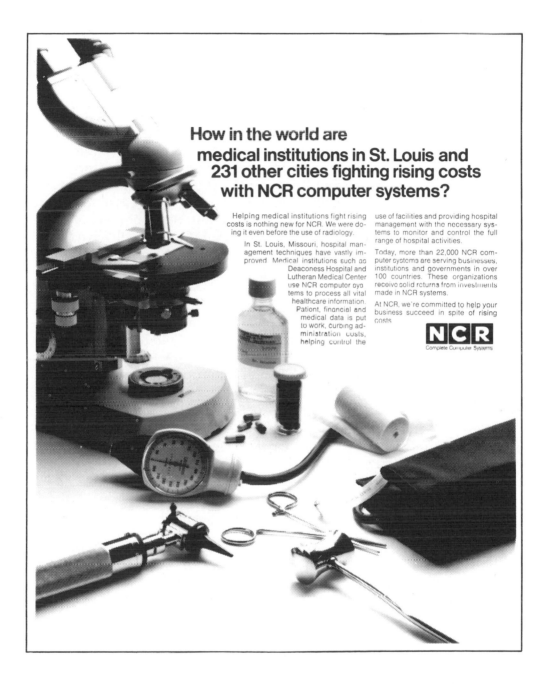

law also requires that there must be at least one thirty-day open enrollment period each year during which the HMO accepts, up to its capacity, individuals in the order in which they apply for enrollment. At least one-half of its members must be younger than sixty-five years and therefore not eligible for medicare. Not more than 75 percent of its membership can be enrolled from medically underserved populations.[10]

Since the passage of HMO legislation, HMO growth has been slow. Adverse selection—the initial enrollment of large proportions of high quantity users—has frightened away many potential providers. Adverse selection is an acute problem, particularly for the wide range of services in the minimum benefits package.[11] HMOs find it difficult to market their product to an uninformed public. The mandatory dual choice for employers has not been implemented. Several mismanaged HMOs have been reorganized under court order.[12] There is much effort in Congress to remove the open enrollment requirement and the community rating system—so that higher-risk individuals will have to pay higher capitation fees.[13] Less than 5 percent of the U.S. population is now enrolled in HMOs, but this percentage should rise.

Health Alliances

An interesting approach to lowering insurance premiums involves the formation of health alliances between consumers and providers. Under this concept, health insurance companies would "experience-rate" health providers in terms of their likelihood to order expensive procedures or lengthy hospitalizations. A large group practice might demonstrate lower utilization rates than a cross section of individual physicians in the same community.

Insurance rates would be higher for consumers allying with providers who tend more frequently to order expensive tests or hospitalizations, and rates would be lower for consumers who ally with providers less likely to incur high costs.

National Health Insurance

National health insurance (NHI) has been a subject of heated debate. There are many precedents for this form of socialized medicine, and all of the economically developed countries of the world now have national health insurance programs or national health services for large segments of their populations.

There appear to be three categories of national health insurance:[14]

1. a federal program, with compulsory coverage of all or most of the population, with broad and explicitly defined benefits, financed by a combination of payroll taxes and general federal tax revenues, and administered by the federal government without use of private insurance carriers

2. a federal program of voluntary income tax credits to taxpayers and vouchers to nontaxpayers, to help them purchase private health insurance, with minimal benefit standards, and financed entirely out of general revenues
3. various in-between proposals embodying some characteristics of the above categories

Since 1970, major proposals in all three categories have been introduced in Congress. Table 14.1 shows the seven most likely alternative national health insurance plans.[15] Each plan varies in the extent of persons not covered, of the direct patient payments, of private health insurance business, and of reimbursement of providers. Obviously, the survival of a major U.S. industry, the private health insurance business, is at stake. Also at stake are the amount of government spending and the restrictions placed on provider reimbursement.

Two plans—that of the past Nixon administration and that of Representative Wilbur Mills and Senator Edward Kennedy—are now the most likely to be adopted. Table 14.2 compares these two plans. Each will require a sizable infusion of new federal funds, but the Mills-Kennedy plan will be compulsory and will set up a separate agency to administer the plan. The Mills-Kennedy plan has the support of organized labor and the poor and is vigorously opposed by the private health insurance companies. Figure 14.4 shows the typical cost of both plans as a percentage of family income.[16] CHIP will take a larger bite out of lower-income families than will the Mills-Kennedy plan.

Starting in 1978 and progressing for five years, social security taxes will be raised in order to keep the social security system solvent. Because of these increases to payroll taxes, it will be more difficult politically to pass a national health insurance scheme that will further increase payroll taxes.

Whatever plan is adopted—and indications are that national health insurance may be a few years away—there are quite a few goals by which any proposal might be measured. Somers lists ten goals for national health insurance:

1. universal coverage of the resident civilian population without distinction as to income or contributions
2. comprehensive benefits
3. pluralistic and competitive underwriting
4. consumer free choice as far as is practical
5. adequate and stable income for providers
6. incentives for efficiency and economy
7. equitable financing
8. administrative feasibility
9. general acceptability to consumers and providers
10. flexibility in the face of changing supply and demand factors[17]

Table 14.1 Coverage, Financing, and Type of Provider Reimbursement under Alternative National Health Insurance Plans, Based on Prices and Population Projected for 1975

			Supporter or Sponsor of Plan				
	No National Health Insurance Plan	American Medical Association	Long-Ribicoff	Nixon Administration	American Hospital Association	Health Insurance Association of America	Mills-Kennedy
Persons not covered by the plan (millions)	--	4.0	0	6.5	3.3	25.0	3.0
Direct patient payments (billions of dollars)	30.1	21.1	28.1	22.7	16.1	21.9	20.3
Sources of financing (as percent of total cost of plan)							
premiums	6.0	57.8	4.5	51.8	53.5	50.1	4.6
Federal funds	71.5	37.1	76.4	38.3	44.1	41.8	38.8
State funds	22.4	5.1	19.0	9.9	2.4	8.1	6.6
Private health insurance business (billions of dollars)							
Income from sales	32.5	62.3	30.9	37.3	47.4	62.5	11.7
Administered claims and expenses	22.0	13.7	37.8	41.8	43.4	13.7	71.5
Extent of reimbursement of providers (in relation to total cost)	--	Unrestricted	Medicare type	Moderate	Generous	Medicare type	Moderate

Table 14.2 A Comparison of Two National Health Insurance Plans

	Nixon Administration Comprehensive Health Insurance Plan (CHIP)	Mills-Kennedy
New federal funds required yearly (billions)	6.5	9.3
Contribution of yearly premium		
a. employer	65% of $415	3% payroll tax
b. employee	35% of $415	1% payroll tax
Deductible		
a. individual	$150	$150
b. family	$450	$300
Co-insurance	25% up to $1500	25% up to $1000
Participation	voluntary	compulsory
Administration	private insurance companies	Social Security Administration would become a new independent agency

Figure 14.4 Typical Cost of National Health Insurance as a Percentage of Family Income under the Administration and Kennedy-Mills Plans, 1975

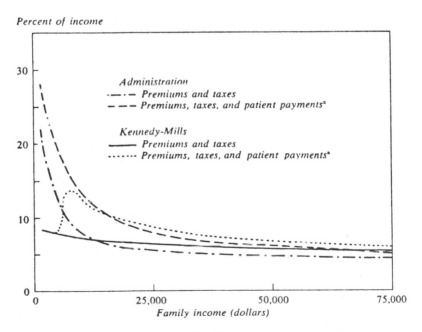

a. Assumes annual medical expenditures $1,000, which represents an average experience.

Some of these criteria may be mutually exclusive. Idealistic plans may not be pragmatic, and pragmatic plans may not offend anyone but may not change the delivery of health care measurably. Is controlled competition and supervised free choice the best possible compromise among alternatives? The decision about national health insurance revolves around the political atmosphere surrounding future administrations and Congresses. As yet, there is no perfect plan.

Summary

Advances in medical technology, particularly in computer applications, have generated widespread interest in automated multiphasic health testing. With the exception of hospital-based primary care group practices, only the Garfield plan, which separates the sick from the well, represents a significant change in health facility rearrangement. Health financial plans are methods for substantially changing how medical bills are paid. Little is known about the long-range effect of any of these emerging concepts.

Questions

1. You sit on the State Board of Medical Examiners. The Board has received a number of complaints from individuals who have had multiphasic health-screening tests performed in mobile trailers parked in the parking lots of shopping centers. The tests cost $39.95 and are performed by out-of-state companies. What additional facts would you like to know about these companies and tests before you made a decision? What actions can you take regarding the complaints?

2. Should higher-risk individuals have to pay higher capitation fees to join an HMO?

3. Supposing you were designing a national health insurance program. Draft a curve for the graph below and justify the curve's shape.

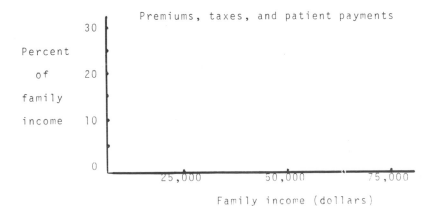

4. In the Garfield Delivery System, what mechanisms can you design to keep an excessive number of individuals from bypassing the health testing and referral service and going directly to the sick-care center?

Notes

1. E. R. Weinerman et al. "Multiphasic Screening of Longshoremen with Organized Medical Follow-Up," *American Journal of Public Health* 42:1552-67 (December 1952). See also J. M. Wilson and G. Jungner, *Principles and Practice of Screening for Disease* (New York: Columbia University Press, 1968).

2. F. W. Holcomb, "IBM's Health Screening Program and Medical Data System," *Journal of Occupational Medicine* 15:863-68 (November 1973).

3. Ibid., p. 865.

4. Douglas R. Mackintosh and Gary P. Kraus, "Cost Analysis of the Developmental Phase of an Automated Multiphasic Health Testing Facility." *Public Health Reports* 85:685-90 (August 1970). See also M. F. Collen et al. "Cost Analysis of a Multiphasic Screening Program," *New England Journal of Medicine* 280:1043-1945, (8 May 1969); M. F. Collen et al., "Dollar Cost Per Positive Test for Automated Multiphasic Screening," *New England Journal of Medicine* 283:459-63 (27 August 1970).

5. G. Octo Barnett, "Computers in Patient Care," *New England Journal of Medicine* 279:1321-27 (12 December 1968).

6. Sidney R. Garfield, "The Delivery of Medical Care." *Scientific American* 222:15-23 (April 1970). Sidney R. Garfield, "Multiphasic Health Testing and Medical Care as a Right," *New England Journal of Medicine* 283:1087-89 (12 April 1970).

7. Ibid., p. 22 and p. 1089, respectively.

8. Jeffrey Prussin, "HMOs: Organizational and Financial Models Part I and II," *Hospital Programs* 55:33-35 and 56-59, 84 (April and May 1974).

9. Florence A. Wilson and Duncan Neuhauser, *Health Services in the United States* (Cambridge, Mass.: Ballinger Publishing Co., 1974), pp. 87-88.

10. James A. Vohs, Richard V. Vohs, and Ruth Straus, "Critical Issues in HMO Strategy," *New England Journal of Medicine* 286:1082-86, (18 May 1972).

11. "Prepaid Medical Plans Run Into Difficulties as Enrollment Falters," *Wall Street Journal* (11 February 1975), pp. 1 and 25.

12. "Southern Pacific's HMO is Derailed." *Medical World News* (11 August 1975), pp. 25-26.

13. John K. Iglehart, "Health Report: HMO Act Changes Advanced to Bolster Troubled Programs," *National Journal Reports* (16 August 1975), pp. 1161-66. One of the interesting features of an HMO is its marketing strategy, which includes advertising. The ad for an HMO on page 277 ran in *Newsday*, a Long Island newspaper.

14. Anne R. Somers, *Health Care in Transition: Directions for the Future* (Chicago: Hospital Research and Education Trust, 1971), p. 129.

15. Karen Davis, *National Health Insurance: Benefits, Costs, and Consequences* (Washington, D.C.: Brookings Institution, 1975), p. 112. An excellent book for explaining the particulars of most national health insurance plans.

16. Ibid., p. 149.

17. Somers, *Health Care in Transition: Directions for the Future*, pp. 136-141.

Further Reading

Analysis of Health Insurance Proposals Introduced in the 92nd Congress. Washington, D.C.: U.S. Government Printing Office, August 1971.

Bilers, Robert. "National Health Insurance: What Kind and How Much." *New England Journal of Medicine* 284:881-86 and 945-54 (22 and 29 April 1971).

Cavalier, Kay S. *National Health Insurance: A Selective Bibliography.* RA 413, Washington, D.C.: Congressional Research Service, Library of Congress, August 1972.

Ellwood, P. M. "Health Maintenance Organizations: Concept and Strategy." *Hospitals, JAHA* 45:53-56 (16 March 1971).

Feldstein, Martin, and Friedman, Bernard. "The Effect of National Health Insurance on the Price and Quality of Medical Care," in Richard N. Roselt, ed., *The Role of Health Insurance in the Health Services Sector.* A Conference of the Universities—National Bureau Committee for Economic Research (National Bureau of Economic Research, 1975).

Giebink, Gerals A., and Hurst, Leonard L. *Computer Projects in Health Care.* Ann Arbor: University of Michigan Health Administration Press, 1975.

Gorman, Mike. "The Impact of National Health Insurance on Delivery of Health Care." *AJPH* 61:962-71 (May 1971).

Gumbiner, Robert. *HMO: Putting It All Together.* St. Louis: C. V. Mosby, 1975.

Hinman, Edward J., ed. *Advanced Medical Systems.* Chevy Chase, Md.: Society for Advanced Medical Systems, 1977.

Hirshfield, Daniel S. *The Lost Reform. The Campaign for Compulsory Health Insurance in the United States from 1932 to 1943.* Cambridge, Mass.: Harvard University Press, 1970.

Keintz, Rita M. *National Health Insurance and Income Distribution.* Lexington, Mass.: D. C. Heath & Co., 1976

McLaughlin, C. P., and Sheldon, A. *The Future and Medical Care.* Cambridge, Mass.: Ballinger Publishing Co., 1974.

Multiphasic Health Testing Services: Reviews and Annotations. HEW, PHS, HSMHA, HSM 110-69-210. Rockville, Md., March 1971.

Roemer, Milton I., and Shonick, William. "HMO Performance. The Recent Evidence." *Milbank Memorial Fund Quarterly* 51:271-317 (summer 1973).

Saward, Ernest W., and Greelick, Merwyn R. "Health Policy and the HMO." *Milbank Memorial Fund Quarterly* 50:147-76 (April 1972).

Selby, Phillip M. *Health in 1980-1990: A Predictive Study Based on International Inquiry.* White Plains, N.Y.: A. J. Phiebig, 1976.

Seubold, Frank H. "HMO's—The View from the Program." *Public Health Reports* 90:99-103 (March-April 1975).

Smits, Helen L. "Planning Health: The HMO's Opportunity." *Inquiry* 12:3-9 (March 1975).

Waldman, Saul. *National Health Insurance Proposals: Provision of Bills Introduced in the 93rd Congress as of July 1974.* DHEW publication 75-11920, February 1975.

15. National Systems of Health Care

Perspectives presented by visitors to China remind me of the perspectives of three baseball umpires I know. There is the objectivist umpire who says, "There are balls and strikes and I call them as they are." There is the subjectivist umpire who says, "There are balls and strikes and I call them as I see them." And finally there is the existentialist umpire who says, "There are neither balls nor strikes until I call them."
—Victor Sidel

With the exception of the United States, most national systems of health care are government-controlled and government-financed, either on a centralized or decentralized basis. The delivery of health care in other countries appears to reflect political philosophy and individual rights (as specified in the country's constitution or common and civil laws) as well as attitudes toward human values such as freedom, equity, upward mobility, self-protection and self-reliance, and enlightened self-interest. What follows here is a brief description of the principles, structure, administration, funding, and resources of several distinctly different national health systems.

Health Care in the United Kingdom

Before 1948, most British residents were covered for out-of-hospital medical expenses by the National Health Insurance Scheme. This scheme was administered by local insurance committees and some 1,000 "approved societies" (such as trade unions) and financed by employers, employees, and the state. However, it suffered from a severe maldistribution of medical manpower, a two-class (rich and poor) tier of care, and selective gaps in coverage.[1] A 1946 white paper proposed a system of health care "available to everyone regardless of financial means, age, sex employment or vocation, area of residence, or insurance qualification." Access of the needy to health care was to become a human right. Health resources were to be nationalized and price removed as a barrier to the acquisition of care. The system was to be financed by a progressive tax that would redistribute funds from the fit to the sick as well as from the rich to the poor.

The National Health Service (NHS), which was inaugurated in 1948, was a mammoth undertaking, representing, at that time, the tenth largest financial investment in the world. It was divided into a tripartite administrative structure, as seen in Figure 15.1.[2] Medical services were delivered on the basis of generalists first-contact services and on specialist hospital services. General practitioners kept a register of their patients. In 1970, approximately 97 percent of the population registered with a general practitioner, and each GP had about 2,500 persons on his or her register. GPs were reimbursed according to the number of individuals on their register plus additional payments for some specialty work, night and house calls, for grouping in clusters of three or more, for seniority, or for special vocational training.

In the past, GPs in contract with the NHS could engage in private fee-for-service work for persons who were not registered with them but could not treat their patients in an NHS hospital. Instead, the hospital staff were all specialists who assumed responsibility for the GP's patients while they were in the hospital. Sociomedical services such as home health care, ambulance services, and services for the handicapped and mentally ill were provided through the health departments of local governing authorities.

Figure 15.1   Administrative Structure of the
              National Health Service

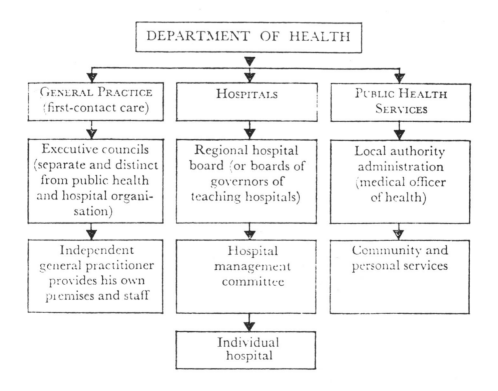

Except for patient out-of-pocket payments for dental care, eyeglasses, and a token contribution for prescriptions, all services were provided free of charge and thus regardless of an individual's ability to pay. Not much thought was given as to what allocational device would be used in the absence of prices.[3]

The NHS has had its problems. The tripartite structure has made centralized overall planning difficult. A gulf developed between hospital and nonhospital practitioners. Large regional variations in the provision of health care continued to exist. During the latter half of the 1950s, nearly a quarter of the British-born medical school graduates emigrated. The cost of the NHS has risen rapidly over the past twenty years and has been absorbing increasingly large amounts of the gross national product. Hospital and pharmaceutical services, which consume sizable resources (as seen in Figure 15.2[4]), have been consuming larger proportions of the total cost of the NHS. In 1971, only 3 percent of a total of £ 2,369 million represented out-of-pocket payment—the NHS paid the remaining 97 percent. Despite its pledge to cover all medical costs, the NHS has had difficulty deciding on such cases as whether to resuscitate elderly persons.

In 1974, the NHS was reorganized. It was broken into four health services: England, Wales, Scotland, and Northern Ireland, all of which have slightly different characteristics.[5] In addition, the previously separate hospital, general practitioner, and public health services were unified into

Figure 15.2   Specified Health Services as a Proportion of the Total Cost of the National Health Service, 1971

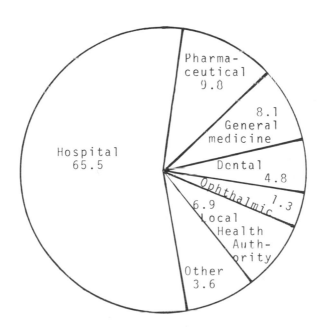

an integrated system. Clinicians were allowed to participate in management of the system through the introduction of multidisciplinary consensus teams. The reorganization recognized that excluding the GP from the hospital was a mistake, but instead pushed the GP in a new direction, that of the large health center. Grants and financial incentives are being used to expand the number of health centers and induce GPs to practice within them. The current planning is to bring together within the health center the general medical practitioner, other health practitioners (dentist, pharmacist, etc), and ancillary services. Although practitioners remain autonomous within the health centers, they share an integrated record system and nonmedical staff. More emphasis has been placed on preventive medicine, such as developmental screening of preschool children and patient education.[6]

Health Care in Sweden

Sweden is the largest (8 million inhabitants) of the Scandinavian countries, which have long been considered models of socialized health care. Sweden's system of government has long relied on extensive local autonomy, and local authorities have had to carry out most of the provisions of health legislation. The country is divided into twenty-five provincial or county councils with a population varying from 60,000 to 600,000.[7] The representative bodies of the local provinces are the elected county councils, which levy their own taxes. One of the major legal obligations of a Swedish county council is to provide hospital care for their residents. Hospitals are owned and operated by the council through health boards, as seen in Figure 15.3[8]. Each county has at least one general central hospital.

For medical care outside the hospital, there are medical officers employed by the county councils. The medical officers are GPs who provide services at fixed rates. Until 1970, fee-charging private practitioners were established mainly in the larger towns and suburbs. Since 1963, Sweden has had a compulsory comprehensive health insurance system financed out of employer, employee, and government contributions.[9] In 1970, 8.3 percent of Sweden's GNP was spent on health care.

In 1970, five factors caused the Swedish parliament to overhaul the health system—in what has come to be called the Seven Crowns Reform:

1. high medical care costs
2. high physician incomes
3. elitist physician attitudes
4. inequality of access to outpatient care and inequality in bearing these costs
5. inefficient insurance system with three-quarter-scale reimbursement

Figure 15.3 Administration of Swedish Hospital, Health and Social Services

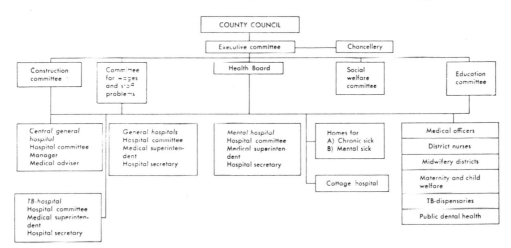

The Seven Crowns Reform instituted the following changes:

1. abolished fee-for-service outpatient care
2. instituted a uniform low outpatient fee for patients
3. put government-employed physicians (90 percent of all M.D.'s) on full salary with no additional fee collection
4. salaries were equalized among different specialities
5. fixed working hours were established
6. the insurance system was simplified and streamlined; work requirements were eased[10]

Obviously, Sweden introduced a much more socialized system of care than it previously had. The goals of the reform were equality, cost control, and de-emphasis of hospital-based care.

Health Care in the Soviet Union

The health system of the Union of Soviet Socialist Republics (the USSR is made up of fifteen Union Republics) was established after the October Revolution in 1917. Four key concepts have evolved for the Soviet health system:

1. health care services are available to all and free to all; the only exception is a nominal charge for most drugs administered outside the hospital or polyclinic, and for appliances such as eyeglasses and dental prostheses
2. health care, like other goods and services, is allocated through centralized planning and direction

3. the primary goal of the health care system is prevention of illness and promotion of health
4. the state provides for the education of all health personnel and employs all personnel in the health care system[11]

Under the principles of legislation of the Supreme Soviet of the USSR, it is not only the duty of the state to provide free medical care to the entire population, but also the duty of each citizen to take care of his own health and be considerate of the health of other members of society. In essence, the health of each citizen is the joint responsibility of an individual and the state. If the state owns and controls the means of production, and if an individual's health contributes significantly to production, then logically an individual's health is his and the state's joint responsibility.[12]

The structure of medical services in the USSR, as seen in Figure 15.4[13], is based on a hierarchical system of size, area, and diminishing responsibilities. Primary care is delivered at the neighborhod level by small teams or groups of medical or paramedical workers. Budgets are prepared at the district level and passed on up the government chain to the Ministry of Health. Since budgetary estimates are based on norms and standards

Figure 15.4   Governmental Structure of Health
             Care in the USSR

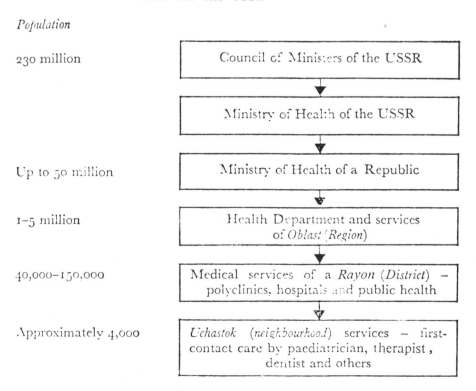

Population	
230 million	Council of Ministers of the USSR
	Ministry of Health of the USSR
Up to 50 million	Ministry of Health of a Republic
1–5 million	Health Department and services of *Oblast* (*Region*)
40,000–150,000	Medical services of a *Rayon* (*District*) — polyclinics, hospitals and public health
Approximately 4,000	*Uchastok* (*neighbourhood*) services — first-contact care by paediatrician, therapist, dentist and others

Figure 15.5   Flow of Urban and Rural Families through
the Health System of the USSR

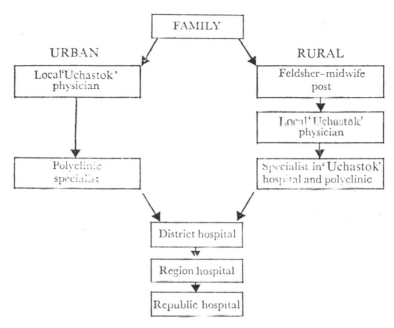

produced by the ministry, there rarely are budgetary cuts. Every five years a health inventory is carried out at the district level. Deficiencies are estimated, and plans are drawn up for the next five years. Figure 15.5 shows the flow of both an urban and rural family through the health system of the Soviet Union.[14]

Because of the difficulties of providing care for a widely dispersed population in rural areas, primary care is delivered by midwives and feldshers, the equivalent of nurse practitioners and physician's assistants in the United States. There is no free choice of physician at the neighborhood level, nor is there any effort to provide total family care. All those living in a particular neighborhood are assigned, so that planned services can be made available to all, to the care of the physician appointed to that area. Outpatient ambulatory care is provided at polyclinics. Specialists, who work in urban polyclinics, have no regular hospital duties or access to hospital beds. The staffs of the polyclinics and the hospitals are separate organizations, even though a local polyclinic is often built on the grounds of a district hospital. First-level general hospitals occur at the district level and more specialized hospitals (for example, neurology, cardiology, etc.) occur at the regional level. Patients normally are referred to these regional specialists' hospitals only through district hospitals. Republic hospitals serve as teaching hospitals and medical schools.

Mental illness is not prevalent in the USSR because the disease reflects politically a less-than-happy society. The Soviet attitude toward mental illness is that the disease is much more prevalent in "capitalist" societies.[15]

From 70 to 75 percent of the physicians in the Soviet Union are women. The path toward greater financial rewards and prestige in Soviet medicine is, after graduation, to seek advanced degrees, specialize, do research, and obtain an academic appointment. The beginning Soviet physician is paid about 105 to 140 rubles ($140 to $187) a month, some 30 percent less than an industrial worker. The physician/population ratio is 1 per 670.

Health Care in the People's Republic of China

During the period 1917-49, the People's Liberation Army (PLA) of China, led by Mao Tse-tung, fought internal wars against several governments, including the Kuomintang government of Chiang Kai-shek. From 1935 to 1945, it fought the Japanese, and from 1945 until 1949, when Mao Tse-tung prevailed, it fought against Chiang Kai-shek and his forces.[16]

Before 1949, China suffered all of the usual afflictions of an underdeveloped country heavily influenced and torn apart by outside forces. Starvation, malnutrition, communicable disease, and addiction were rampant. Environmental resources (water, housing, food, transportation, clothes) were inadequate. The health care system was a two-class system: wealthy, urban-housed individuals received care from Western-trained physicians; poor, rurally based individuals—the vast majority of the country—received care from traditional Chinese practitioners—if at all. Most health care expenditures, both private and public, were devoted to episodic, curative care.

In 1950, China's first national health congress established three basic guidelines, and the 1952 congress added a fourth: (1) health work should serve primarily the laboring people—workers, peasants, and soldiers; (2) the main emphasis should be placed on preventive medicine; (3) close unity should be fostered between Chinese and Western physicians; (4) whenever possible, health work should be conducted by mass campaigns with active participation of medical workers and the people.[17]

Mass campaigns were undertaken to eradicate contagious diseases—smallpox, cholera, and malaria—in the course of which venereal disease and schistosomiasis were wiped out. Opiate addiction, too, was attacked.

China's first Five-Year Plan (1952-1957) emphasized health activities in the urban industrialized areas. Hospitals and clinics expanded outward from the large metropolitan cities to the provincial capitals and county seats. Rural health care continued to be neglected, and there was a drift toward elitism based on the elevated status accorded to Western-trained physicians.

The Great Leap Forward (1958-1960) was a social movement that emphasized rural economic development and national and local self-sufficiency. The first communes began to appear about that time; agricultural labor became a burning passion with students and intellectuals. Chinese subservience to Soviet medicine ceased. The Cultural Revolution (1966-1969), the turning point in the delivery of health care, emphasized the accountability of leaders to the the people they served and prescribed that the delivery of health care to the rural areas should vastly improve. To this end, medical workers were sent into the countryside, and "barefoot doctors" were trained in massive numbers. Barefoot doctors are those whom their fellow workers choose to receive three to six months of training, to return to their commune or factory, and to continue to work while providing first-contact, primary care. Perhaps 1 million to 1.3 million barefoot doctors have been trained and returned to their communities of origin. Barefoot doctors serve a dual purpose: as a source of political education and as a point of entry into the medical system. Most continue to receive supervision and continuing education from teams of physicians and nurses who visit on a scheduled basis.

Health care in China is decentralized. It is based on the smallest political unit of production and progresses, as seen in Figures 15.6[18] and 15.7[19], as political subdivisions merge into larger divisions. Health facilities follow the same pattern.

In most countries, health care providers and facilities tend to be maldistributed and are clustered in urban areas near teaching facilities. China has minimized this problem for rural areas by developing large numbers of auxiliaries and health cadres who work in communes at the brigade and team level. Manpower needs are ascertained at the local level and, after some negotiation with higher levels, the local level's manpower needs are met. Although revolutionary ethics specify that health care is a right, free medical care has been available only to party cadres, government employees, members of the People's Liberation Army, certain heavy industrial workers, and some students. None of the rural population and no more than 10 to 15 percent of the urban population receive free medical care.

Health care is financed independently by local production brigades and teams, primarily through a health insurance fund known as the cooperative medical service—CMS. The CMS fund is made up of a yearly fee from each participant, which is supplemented by a per capita contribution from the production unit's welfare fund. The annual cost per individual may be as low as 50¢ or as high as $2.50 (U.S.). Copayments (out-of-pocket payments at the time of delivery of the service) have been instituted at many communes to eliminate overutilization. The cost of these copayments is about 5¢ per visit. The details of individual and collective financial responsibility vary from brigade to brigade and team to team, once again reflecting local autonomy.

Figure 15.6   Urban Health Care in the People's Republic of China

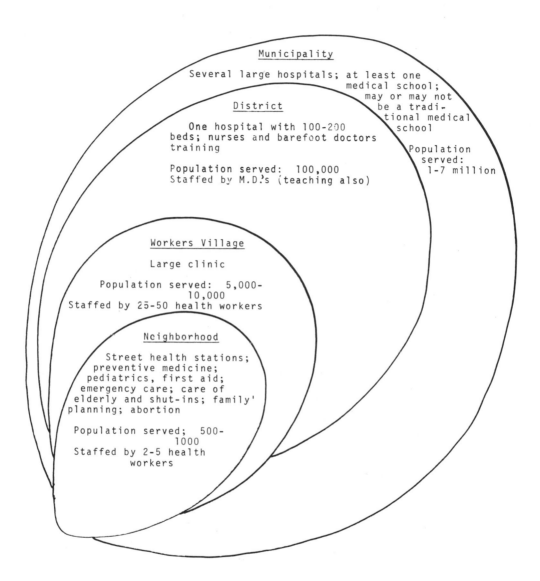

Chinese and Western medicine have been integrated. This integration gives the revolutionary movement and its participants psychological and political values with a historical foundation.

Mothers and children, though not treated at special clinics as in other countries, receive special tracking at local clinics and at school. For example, a women's menstrual periods, birth control information, and prenatal visits are posted on a large board within each nearby treating clinic. Natural childbirth, breast feeding, and spacing of children are encouraged. Abortion is available for unwanted pregnancies and for

Figure 15.7 Rural Health Care in the People's Republic of China

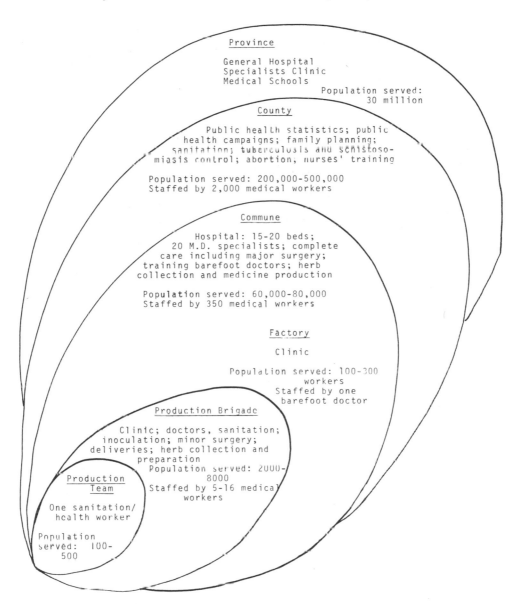

Province

General Hospital
Specialists Clinic
Medical Schools

Population served:
30 million

County

Public health statistics; public
health campaigns; family planning;
sanitation; tuberculosis and schistosomiasis control; abortion, nurses' training

Population served: 200,000-500,000
Staffed by 2,000 medical workers

Commune

Hospital: 15-20 beds;
20 M.D. specialists; complete
care including major surgery;
training barefoot doctors; herb
collection and medicine production

Population served: 60,000-80,000
Staffed by 350 medical workers

Factory

Clinic

Population served: 100-300
workers
Staffed by one
barefoot doctor

Production Brigade

Clinic; doctors, sanitation;
inoculation; minor surgery;
deliveries; herb collection and
preparation
Population served: 2000-
8000
Staffed by 5-16 medical
workers

Production
Team

One sanitation/
health worker

Population
served: 100-
500

medical purposes. Zero population growth is a political goal (for birthrates in various countries, see Table 15.1). Peer pressure and criticism reinforce use of these services.

When a student finishes our equivalent of high school in China, which may be at the ages of fourteen to sixteen, he leaves school to work for two to three years. He may join a commune, factory, or the People's Liberation Army. The work experience reminds the student that productive manual

Table 15.1

BIRTH RATES OF COUNTRIES, BY CONTINENT AND LEVEL: 1974 OR MOST RECENT DATE

BIRTHS PER 1,000 POPULATON

CONTINENT	LESS THAN 15	15-19	20-24	25-29	30-34	35-39	40-44	45-49	50 or MORE
AFRICA			St. Helena *	Cape Verde Is. 29.2 Mauritius 27.5 Reunion 28.1	Gabon * Seychelles * Tunisia 33.9	Algeria 39.3 Egypt 35.4 Equatorial Guinea * Lesotho *	Afars & Issas * Cameroon * Central African Republic * Chad * Comoro Is. * Gambia * Guinea-Bissau * Mozambique * South Africa *	Angola * Botswana * Burundi * Congo, People's Republic of * Ethiopia * Ghana * Guinea * Ivory Coast * Kenya * Libya * Malawi * Mauritania * Morocco * Namibia * Nigeria * Sao Tome and Principe 45.0 Senegal * Sierra Leone * Somalia * Southern Rhodesia * Spanish Sahara * Sudan * Swaziland * Uganda * Upper Volta * Zaire *	Benin * Liberia * Malagasy Republic * Mali * Niger * Rwanda * Tanzania * Togo * Zambia *
ASIA		China, People's Republic of * Cyprus * Hong Kong 19.3 Japan 18.6	Taiwan 23.4 Singapore 20.0	Israel 28.2 Korea, Republic of * Macao * Sri Lanka 29.5	Brunei * Viet Nam, North * India 33.4	Indonesia * Korea, North * Malaysia * Philippines * Thailand * Turkey *	Afghanistan * Bahrain * Bhutan * Burma * Lebanon * Mongolia * Nepal * Pakistan * Portuguese Timor * Viet Nam, South *	Bangladesh * Iran * Iraq * Jordan 47.8 Khmer Republic * Kuwait * Laos * Saudi Arabia * Syrian Arab Republic *	Gaza Strip * Maldive Is. * Oman * Qatar * United Arab Emirates * Yemen (Aden) * Yemen (San'a) *

	New Hebrides	Papua New Guinea	American Samoa 37.2	Cook Is. 32.8	Fiji 29.6	(20–24)	Australia 18.4 / New Zealand 19.5	Canal Zone 13.6
OCEANIA	New Hebrides *	Papua New Guinea *	American Samoa 37.2 British Solomon Is. * Gilbert and Ellice Is. * New Caledonia * Pacific Is. (Trust Territory) * Tonga * Western Samoa *	Cook Is. 32.8 French Polynesia * Guam 34.8	Fiji 29.6		Australia 18.4 New Zealand 19.5	
LATIN AMERICA	Dominican Republic * Honduras * Mexico * Nicaragua *	Bolivia * Ecuador 42.4 Guatemala * Haiti * Paraguay * Peru 40.3 Surinam 40.9	Belize * Brazil * Dominica 36.4 El Salvador 39.7 French Guiana * Guyana 36.3 U.S. Virgin Is. 39.8 Venezuela *	Cayman Is. * Colombia * Jamaica 30.8 Panama 31.3 St. Vincent 34.4 Turks & Caicos Is. *	Chile 27.6 Costa Rica 28.5 Grenada 26.2 Guadeloupe 28.0 Netherlands Antilles * St. Kitts, Nevis & Anguilla 25.8 Trinidad and Tobago 23.5	Argentina 22.9 Bahamas 22.3 Barbados 20.8 British Virgin Is. 24.5 Cuba 22.3 Falkland Is. * Martinique 22.4 Montserrat 24.3 Puerto Rico 23.3 Uruguay 20.9	Antigua 18.3	
NORTH AMERICA							Bermuda 19.1 Canada 15.4 Greenland 19.2 St. Pierre and Miquelon 16.6 United States 15.0	
EUROPE				Albania 30.4		Iceland 20.4 Ireland 22.3 Romania 20.3	Andorra * Bulgaria 17.2 Czechoslovakia 19.8 Faeroe Is. 19.9 France 15.2 Gibraltar 19.8 Greece 16.1 Italy 17.8 Liechtenstein 15.7 Malta 16.8 Poland 18.4 Portugal 19.3 San Marino 17.4 Spain 19.3 United Kingdom 17.9 Yugoslavia 17.9	Austria 12.8 Belgium 12.7 Channel Is. 11.9 Denmark 14.1 Finland 13.3 Germany, East 10.4 Germany, Federal Republic of 10.1 Hungary 13.4 Isle of Man 11.1 Luxembourg * Monaco 12.8 Netherlands 14.9 Norway 13.5 Sweden 13.1 U.S.S.R. 13.2

*Indicates incomplete registration. Placement of countries in categories is based on either data sources such as survey data and census data

Office of Population
Agency for International Development   June 1976

labor is as important a contribution to the revolution as intellectual work and further reminds him or her that elitism arising out of intellectual pursuits is to be avoided. A person who is interested in attending medical school must make application, which must be accompanied by recommendations of the individual's peer group—for example, the revolutionary committee at one's factory or commune. High political consciousness and hard work are key ingredients in such a recommendation, and applications without such are not considered. Thus, one who has not received some approval from his peers at the local level will not apply.

Medical technicians, nurses, barefoot doctors, or others with practical experience form a likely applicant pool. The medical school curriculum is three years and, as in all Chinese activities, the medical student is expected to do productive labor as an ongoing part of his learning experience. Interestingly, nurses who have had considerable experience may be elevated to the position of M.D. over a period of years. Even though a nurse may not have the "proper credentials," the fact that he or she is competent to do work of this sort is sufficient rationale to qualify her as a physician. This also may be true for a barefoot doctor who, over a period of years, learns more and more and becomes qualified as a nurse and later as a physician.

University-based research that has no relatively immediate application is discouraged, but research that can be applied practically at the local level is actively supported. Foreign medical journals and texts are available to the student. Chinese medicine, herbal medicine, acupuncture, and the like are an integral part of all curricula. Medical schools have internal Party and revolutionary committees, which establish educational, research, and training policies within their institution.

At least half of all physicians are women, and most obstetricians and pediatricians are women. Salary levels are flattened throughout China, and although there are still some small differentials, a graduating physician may make less than a nurse at the hospital to which he is assigned. Credentials are considered less important than a person's competence to do productive work. Physicians perform nonmedical labor within the hospital along with the rest of the hospital staff and patients: for example, everyone helps clean up the facility once a week.

Medical training and practice have developed along a model of patient-provider interaction that differs from Western models. In the West, the patient is generally the passive recipient of advice given by the provider, who has made a diagnosis and has prescribed a treatment program. In China, the patient is an active participant, a coequal in his own diagnosis and treatment.[20]

Health Care in Emerging and Developing Countries

Health care in developing countries is characterized by many complex problems. The most widespread diseases in these countries are probably those transmitted by human feces, such as intestinal parasitic infections and diarrheal diseases.[21] Poliomyelitis, typhoid, and cholera are common. These diseases spread in areas without community water supply systems. Vector-borne diseases—such as malaria, trypanosomiasis (sleeping sickness), chagas disease, schistosomiasis (bilharzia), and onchocerciasis (river blindness)—are also common. Malnutrition is often widespread in poor nations and by impairing normal body responses to disease and thereby reducing acquired immunity, contributes to the incidence and severity of health problems. Nutritional deficiency and immaturity (that is, premature and underweight babies) are important factors in deaths occurring before the age of five.

Developing countries have high fertility rates, which contribute to overcrowding, the easy spread of communicable diseases, and high mortality rates. High mortality rates, in turn, induce families to have many children so they can be assured of having surviving progeny. Children's diseases predominate in developing countries because children have less immunity to disease than adults. High fertility rates and insufficient maternal care lead to high maternal mortality rates, especially after the third birth. Emerging countries also have high induced-abortion rates; although abortion is illegal in most of these countries, it is a significant factor in hospital admissions and blood transfusions and is a major health risk.

Developing countries have yet other problems:

1. females may not be allowed to become primary health care providers
2. folk medicine curers and patent medicine may be the only source of health care for many rural inhabitants
3. the M.D./population ratio may approach 1/70,000 in rural areas
4. the population growth rate may hover around 3 percent per year
5. cultural and religious determinants may cause individuals to passively accept illness as a way of life, borne with resignation
6. there may be a sizable difference between government reports (epidemiological and extent of services) and field reports based on objective reporting

The governments of most of these countries have made token efforts to improve health, but these efforts are often fragmented and cover only a small proportion of the population. Moreover, they come in the form of high-cost, individual, curative medicine instead of environmental and preventive measures. Most of these limited governmental outlays, which seldom exceed 2 percent of GNP in low-income countries, go toward maintaining expensive well-equipped hospitals staffed by highly trained medical personnel. Most health expenditures, both private and public, are devoted to episodic curative care. Too much money is spent on inpatient services and too little on outpatient services.[22]

Most economists agree that health should not be isolated from other elements in the developmental process.[23] Thus, to improve health in emerging countries, agricultural production must be increased, education improved, sewerage systems built, and attitudes toward fertility and personal hygiene changed. Eventually, investment capital must be diverted away from agriculture to industry.[24]

The tremendous health gap between industrialized countries and the emerging countries appears to be widening as a result of the continuing disparity of the distribution of world resources. Corporations shy away from investment in underdeveloped countries. Many of these countries are dependent on expensive outside energy sources. They suffer from a growing brain drain. Since World War II, the developing countries' competitive position in world trade has deteriorated. They have come to demand and expect proportionately more in loans and grants, a form of indebtedness they may never be able to repay.[25]

Summary

The distribution of health care resources varies markedly among the countries of the world. Most national systems of health care provide some form of socialized medicine. Mainland China provides a dramatic example of how total reorganization of the health care delivery system has significantly improved the health of Chinese individuals. Whether or not the other underdeveloped countries attempt a similar economic and political revolution, all nations will always be faced with the problems of how to allocate scarce resources. Even well-established health systems undergo reforms to accommodate changes in resource priorities.

Questions

1. Discuss the similarities between the structure of health care delivery in the Soviet Union or China and the structure of zone mental health care in the United States.

2. England's National Health Service is a system largely governed by nonprice rationing. Instead of prices, what forces allocate health care in the NHS?

3. Assume you have been appointed minister of health for a small agricultural country that has just won independence from a powerful country. The per capita income of your country is low, the birth rate is high, and trained health personnel are few. What kind of health care delivery system would you advocate; how would you structure staff and finance your system? Would you be willing to accept aid from other countries if political strings were attached?

4. Many socialized systems experience the following dilemma: the government needs to maintain control over its expenditures while satisfying the medical providers that they are being treated fairly. How would you resolve this dilemma?

5. Assume you were a member of the 1970 Swedish parliament—given the problems facing the Swedish health system, what reforms might you have suggested?

Notes

1. M. H. Cooper and A. J. Culyer, "An Economic Survey of the Nature and Intent of the British National Health Service," *Social Science and Medicine* 5:1-13 (August 1971). See also A. J. Willcocks, *The Creation of the National Health Service* (London: Routledge and Kegan Paul, 1967); Paul F. Gemmill, *Britain's Search of Health: The First Twelve Years of the National Health Service* (Philadelphia: University of Pennsylvania Press, 1962); James Farndale, *Trends in the National Health Service* (New York: Macmillan, 1964).

2. John Fry, *Medicine in Three Societies. A Comparison of Medical Care in the USSR, USA, and UK* (New York: American Elsevier, 1970), p. 45.

3. Cooper and Culyer, "An Economic Survey of the Nature and Intent of the British National Health Service," pp. 5-9.

4. "The Cost of the NHS," *Office of Health Information Sheet* (March 1973).

5. Roger M. Battistella and Theodore E. Chester, "The 1974 Reorganization of the British National Health Service—Aims and Issues," *New England Journal of Medicine* 289:610-15 (20 September 1973).

6. "The Woodside Story," *Health Bulletin* 31:3-71 (May 1973).

7. *The Swedish Health Services System* (Chicago: American College of Hospital Administration, 1971), pp. 27-43. The three main cities—Stockholm, Gothenburg, and Malmo—are outside the jurisdiction of the county councils and have administrative units of their own.

8. Ibid., p. 33. For a discussion of the evolution of the Swedish hospital system, see John Z. Bowers and Elizabeth Purcess, *National Health Services* (New York: Josiah Macy Foundation, 1973), pp. 24-33.

9. Students and housewives were, until 1970, covered under voluntary plans.

10. Budd N. Shenkin, "Politics and Medical Care in Sweden: The Seven Crowns Reform," *New England Journal of Medicine* 288:555-59 (15 March 1973).

11. *Hospital Services in the U.S.S.R.* (HEW, PHS publication no. 930-F-10, November 1966), pp. 6-7.

12. Y. Lisitsin, *Health Protection in the U.S.S.R.* (Moscow: Progress Publishers, 1972), pp. 6-7.

Soviet physicians also must, theoretically, relinquish their skills to the state. The following oath was adopted in 1961 for the graduating class of Moscow University School of Medicine:

Solemn Oath of the Physician of the Soviet Union:

To fulfill the physician's duties, I solemnly swear in the presence of my teachers, confreres and our entire people:

to work honestly and conscientiously to promote the protection of public health and the development of the human personality in all directions;

to pursue with all my powers the study of medicine so that I contribute towards its flourishing and to seek when necessary the advice and help of my teachers and colleagues;

to love the sick, to be attentive and concerned about them;

not to apply the medical knowledge to the detriment of human health;

not to impart to others any information that was entrusted to me by patients when it does not endanger society. I shall always be mindful of any medical duty, of my high responsibility to the people, to the Communist Party and the socialist state. By selfless work I will make the effort to earn the love and the respect of the entire people. I swear to behave in an exemplary manner in my work and in my daily life and to be an active fighter for the upbuilding of communist society as well as for the formation of the communist consciousness in our people. This oath I promise to keep all my life.

This oath is unusual in that for the first time in the history of medical ethics the physician is asked to swear allegiance not only to the interests of the patient but also to the party and state.

13. John Fry, *Medicine in Three Societies. A Comparison of Medical Care in the USSR, USA and UK* (New York: American Elsevier, 1970), p. 29. See also "Soviet Health System Combines the Modern with the 'Medieval'," *Wall Street Journal,* 23 May 1977, pp. 1, 20.

14. Ibid., p. 24.

15. Pavlov is far more popular than Freud.

16. Chiang Kai-shek fled to Formosa (Taiwan) and set up a government in exile. For an analysis of events prior to 1949, see Edgar Snow, *Red Star Over China* (New York: Random House, 1937); Edgar Snow, *The Other Side of the River: Red China Today* (New York: Random House, 1961); Robert Payne, *Mao Tse-Tung* (New York: Pyramid Books, 1967). For a Canadian physician's assessment of China's health system, see Joshua S. Horn, *Away with all Pests: An English Surgeon in People's China 1954-1969* (New York: Monthly Review Press, 1971).

17. "China: Revolution and Health," *Health/Pac Bulletin* 47:2-18 (December 1972).

18. Alfred E. Kelly, "Observation of Health Services in People's Republic of China," (Mimeographed, New Orleans: January 1973), p. 19.

19. Ibid., p. 18.

20. Much of this section is a collection of material from the following: Victor W. Sidel, "Medical Education in the People's Republic of China," *New Physician* 21:284-91 (May 1972); Ruth and Victor Sidel, "The Human Services of China," *Social Policy* vol. 1:25-34 (March/April 1972); Jeoffrey B. Gordon, "The Organizing and Financing of Health Services in the People's Republic of China," (Mimeographed, San Diego, Cal.: n.d.); see also, Victor W. Sidel and Ruth Sidel, *Serve the People: Observations on Medicine in the People's Republic of China* (Boston: Beacon Press, 1974).

21. *Health* (Washington: International Bank for Reconstruction and Development, 1975), pp. 6-23. Table 15.1 reflects the tremendous difference in population growth between developed and underdeveloped countries.

22. Ibid., pp. 32-47. See also, N. R. E. Fendall, "Primary Medical Care in Developing Countries," *International Journal of Health Services* 2:297-315 (May 1972).

23. Gunnar Myrdal is a leading proponent of an integrated developmental approach toward health care. For a summary of his ideas, see John Bryand, *Health and the Developing Countries* (Ithaca, New York: Cornell University Press, 1969), pp. 96-125.

24. Robert L. Heilbroner, *The Great Assent* (New York: Harper & Row, 1963).
25. Nancy Millio, *The Care of Health in Communities: Access for Outcasts* (New York: Macmillan, 1975), pp. 5-22.

Further Reading

Adizes, Ichak. *A Management Approach to Health Planning in Developing Countries*. Rockville, Md.: Aspen Publications, 1977.

Alternative Approaches to Meeting Basic Health Needs in Developing Countries. Geneva, WHO, 1975.

Bennett, Amanda. "Canada's National Health Plan." *Wall Street Journal* 13:14 (December 1976).

Chen, Lincoln C., ed. *Disaster in Bangladesh: Health Crises in a Developing Nation*. New York: The Population Council, 1973.

"Delivery of Health Care to Children in Developing Countries." *Clinical Pediatrics* 13:777-82 (September 1974).

Douglas-Wilson, Ian, and MacLachlan, Gordon, eds. *Health Services Prospects: An International Survey*. Boston: Little, Brown & Co., 1973.

Economic Models Limited. *The British Health Care System*. Chicago: American Medical Association, 1976.

_____ . *The French Health Care System*. Chicago: American Medical Association, 1976.

"Fifth Report on the World Health Situation (1969-1972)." Geneva: World Health Organization, 1975.

Fry, John, and Frandale, W. A. J. ed. *International Medical Care*. Wallingford, Pa.: Washington Square East, 1972.

"Health: A Major Issue." *Scandinavian Review* 63: entire issue (September 1975).

Kegan, Paul. *The Changing National Health Service*. London: RGS Brown, 1973.

Maynard, Alan. *Health Care in the European Community*. Pittsburgh, Pa.: University of Pittsburgh Press, 1975.

Navarro, V. "The Underdevelopment of Health or the Health of Underdevelopment: An Analysis of the Distribution of Human Health Resources in Latin America." *International Journal of Health Services* 4:5-27 (winter 1974).

New, P. K., and New, M. L. "The Links Between Health and the Political Structure in New China." *Human Organization* 34:237-51 (fall 1975).

Newall, Kenneth W. *Health by the People*. Geneva: WHO, 1975.

Nuttall, Peggy D. "The British National Health Service," *Nursing Outlook* 25:98-102 (February 1977).

Roemer, Milton. *Health Care Systems in World Perspective*. Ann Arbor: Health Administration Press, 1976.

Rogers, E. M., and Solomon, D. S. "Traditional Midwives and Family Planning in Asia." *Studies in Family Planning* 6:126-33 (1975).

Sidel, Victor, and Sidel, Ruth. "The Delivery of Medical Care in China." *Scientific American* 230:19-27 (April 1974).

Simanis, Joseph G. "National Health Systems in Eight Countries." DHEW publication no. 75-11924 (January 1975).

Smith, K. A. *Health Priorities in the Poorer Countries*. London: Pergamon Press, 1975.

Social Security Programs Throughout the World. 1975 DHEW publication no. (SSA) 76-11805, 1976.

The Swedish Health Service System. Chicago: American College of Hospital Administration, 1971.

White, Kerr L. "International Comparisons of Medical Care." *Scientific American* 233:17-25 (August 1975).

Williams, C. D. "The Need for Family Health Services in Africa." *International Journal of Health* 3:749-52 (fall 1973).

World Health Statistics Annual, 1973-1976. "Health Personnel and Hospital Establishments." Geneva: World Health Organization, 1976.

16. Two Directions for a Health System

I must invent my own systems or else be enslaved by other men's.
—William Blake

The delivery of health care can go in only two directions: (1) toward less government involvement or (2) toward more government involvement. In examining the two alternatives, we might ask the following:

1. will the quantity and quality of care increase?
2. will consumer and provider preferences be honored?
3. will the cost of care decrease?
4. will the details of the plan be constitutional?
5. would the spillover effects be beneficial to other societal problems such as crime, delinquency, etc.?

One would have to do a tremendous amount of analysis, more than we can do here, to examine the following proposals in light of these criteria. The material we have so far digested, however, has yielded a certain amount of critical insight as to what the effects of certain changes in the health care delivery system might be.

Toward Less Government Involvement

The following is an eleven-step program for minimizing government involvement in health care:

1. Start with a *guaranteed annual income*, which would be coordinated with and administered through our tax system. A simple cash grant, based on need and measured by income, would be available. There would be no federal health services or health insurance or transfer payments except in the case of catastrophic personal disaster or to honor Indian treaties. Catastrophic personal disaster services, ambulance and emergency room

services, would be federally financed out of general revenues and administered by regional health authorities. There would be no charge for these services, but strict usage requirements and highly skilled triage would prevail. All tax write-offs for dependents' medical care and health insurance would cease except for those who have obtained annual physical checkups, have low serum cholesterol and blood pressure levels, are not overweight, and who do not consume excessive amounts of drugs (alcohol, nicotine, and so on). This proposal would not be popular with government workers, since many government jobs would be eliminated. Medicaid, medicare, Social Security, housing subsidies, food stamps, clothing allowances, and other welfare programs would be eliminated. The mechanics of the simple cash grant would be handled completely by automated data processing. If someone needed medical care after exhausting his cash grant, his needs could either go unanswered, or volunteer charitable organizations could minister to his problems.

2. Local, state, and federal government would treat medical care as if it were any other business. There would be *no licensure, no medical practice acts,* and *no government-administered peer review.* Instead, providers would undergo step-wise certification from nurse's aide all the way up to a specialized physician. Retraining—perhaps one academic year and one year of practice—would qualify a registered nurse to be certified as a nurse practitioner, a nurse practitioner to become a physician's assistant, a physician's assistant to become a physician, and a physician to be a specialist. Career mobility would increase. Stringent rules and penalties would be enforced against misleading or deceptive claims by providers. Stiff jail sentences would be given to those convicted of claiming skills beyond their certification. *Restrictions on dispensing, advertising, or usage of drugs* (including narcotics, alcohol, nicotine, and other stimulants and depressants, but excluding radioactive isotopes) *would be removed.* Self-prescribing would be encouraged through adult education courses. Possession and sale of marijuana, narcotics, hallucinogens, and so on would no longer be illegal. All prisoners being held for drug convictions or awaiting trial on drug charges would be released.

3. *No involuntary commitment of mental patients.* Individuals would be arrested and sentenced to jail for acts harmful to others or their property. There would be no prejudgment of potential criminal activities; instead, a criminal activity would have to be carried out before an arrest would be made. No criminal sentences or plea bargaining would carry a mandate for psychiatric care; instead, psychiatric care would be made available to criminals within penal institutions, and criminals would be free to reject such care at no penalty to them.

4. *No government subsidies to medical schools or other health provider schools for teaching purposes.* Research subsidies could not be

used for teaching purposes. Subsidies instead would be given to a small number of students on the basis of achievement; all other students would be eligible for guaranteed loans at prevailing interest rates; stiff penalties would be given for default of loans. Poor and middle-class taxpayers would no longer pay for the education of individuals who are likely to become wealthy.

5. *No comprehensive health planning councils or certificates of need.* No governmental subsidies would be given to health maintenance organizations, hospitals, nursing homes, or other health care facilities. There would be no special accounting tax write-offs for rapid depreciation of these facilities vis-à-vis other nonhealth types of facilities.

6. *Military medicine would be contracted out,* except where geographically impossible. The dependents program (CHAMPUS) would be eliminated.

7. *All regulated rates and premiums for health insurance companies would be removed.* Instead, state insurance commissioners would require companies doing business in their states to offer both a uniform basic and a uniform catastrophic medical policy. All companies would compete on the basis of these two policies and any other policies they wished to sell. A consumer could buy the basic policy or the catastrophic policy or both or additional policies. Insurance commissioners would continuously monitor the fiscal soundness and premium/benefit ratios of the companies and publish their findings for wide public distribution.

8. *In cases involving more than $2,000, the government would not involve itself in judicial medical malpractice proceedings.* No ceilings on recovery or pools or automatic waiver of jury trials would take place. In cases involving less than $2,000, no-fault malpractice insurance would be established, based on defined compensable events.

9. *Individual "X" would be allowed to sue for monetary recovery from individual "Y" for knowingly, and in some cases unknowingly, transmitting a communicable disease to individual "X."* This provision would provide a strong incentive for individual "Y" to take care of his or her infectious disease without government prodding. A similar principle would apply to victims of crimes, who would be compensated by the state, which would in turn monetarily penalize the criminal. This provision would eliminate much local health department activity.

10. A two-semester health course at the ninth-grade level (public and private schools) would be required, covering (1) how to take care of yourself, (2) how to choose someone to take care of you, and (3) drug education. More adult education courses in health care, especially nutrition, self-diagnosis and self-treatment, and mental health, would be developed. Patients would keep their own health records and be responsible for them. Duplicate sets, upon a patient's request, might be retained by health providers; upon a patient's request, all identifying

aspects of his records could be removed from government and insurance company computer files.

11. *Vigorous enforcement of antitrust laws.* Health providers would not be allowed to restrain trade; fix prices; or inhibit entry, exit, or ownership of the supply of health care. Insurance companies would no longer be exempt from antitrust laws.

These proposals represent a libertarian, "government that governs least governs best," philosophy. The entire package is a return to the nineteenth century, when government leaders were interested in the orderly facilitation of private transactions and in providing only those services that individuals could not provide for themselves, such as emergency health care.

Toward More Government Involvement

Many individuals feel that the United States lacks a single system of medical care. As David Rutstein writes,

> It is inconceivable that high quality efficient care for all can be provided without welding all of them (e.g., the separate components of health care) and all other existing resources into a single system.[1]

Rutstein has devised a blueprint for integrating the individual units of a national health program into a complete system; his plan, presented below in detail, involves an almost total government takeover of health care.

1. *All commonly required medical care personnel and facilities should be located within the community hospital* and should include all general physicians, frequently used specialists, allied medical personnel, and modern technology in the form of a true group-practice unit. Emphasis will be on concentrated ambulatory services as well as inpatient, convalescent, and psychiatric care. Isolated medical care units dispersed throughout the community will be reorganized into a single site.

2. Hospitals will share their resources and not attempt to provide complete medical care. *All hospitals in each medical service area must have their services so interrelated that the entire regional system should function as a single institution,* with appropriate division of labor among constituent hospitals. A highly efficient communication and transportation system is required to assure early and effective treatment of all patients. The precise distribution and balance of all medical resources between central and community hospitals will depend initially upon (1) prior knowledge, (2) computer simulation studies, (3) accumulated experience, and (4) results of definitive medical care experiments. A principle of not wasting professional time should be followed.

Two Directions for a Health System   303

3. *An integrated, reliable, and valid medical record stored in a single central computerized file* should be developed for each individual resident in each medical care region using two-way coaxial cable closed-circuit color TV with adequate resolution and true color values.

4. *Licensure laws should define more precisely the various roles of the M.D. and should expand the authority of the allied health providers* to perform tasks for which they have been qualified and that do not demand the total competence of the M.D.

5. *An areawide emergency medical care system* with a communications network, a transportation system, trained manpower, emergency treatment centers, and a central emergency authority should be developed.

6. *A district reception, triage, and minor treatment, first aid, and rehabilitation center* convenient to the patient and manned by allied medical personnel should be developed.

7. *The general physician will assume the role, responsibility, and duties of the "captain of the team."* He or she will provide personal primary care.

8. *The educational needs of the future medical student will be served by a multichannel medical curriculum* designed to educate him for a specific career. Transfer from a neutral channel to a specific pathway would occur as early as possible. Completion of the specialty pathway would result in the granting of a new special degree (in addition to the M.D.), which would become a requirement for specialty licensure in all states. The mere holding of an M.D. degree and passing of the state medical examination would no longer be sufficient to practice a specialty.

9. *Development of a regional data system* to (1) provide guidance in defining high-risk populations, doing epidemiological research, and in allowing precise case finding; and (2) provide an early warning system to identify sudden, unwarranted episodes of ill health that demand immediate action for their control.

10. *Creation of a quasi-independent Federal Board of Health* to document the potential for health improvement and provide a solid basis for specific programs. The board would set administration policy, propose legislation, recommend priority in federal health spending, and establish a national health code of board regulations concerning medicine and medical care. Regional health boards also would be created.

11. *Each physician or specialist would be paid a salary supplemented by incentive awards from the regional health board.* Salaries would be paid by the regional health authority.

12. *A single uniform national medical care program* financed by national health insurance and administered by HEW would be developed. The premiums would come from federal income, social security, and payroll taxes based on an individual's or family's ability to pay; there would also be a small direct payment by the patient at the time he or she receives care.

Rutstein's plan is a strong dose of socialized medicine characterized by government involvement in financing and delivering health care. There is quite a contrast between this plan and the one presented earlier in the chapter. One's agreement with one plan or the other depends, in part, on one's philosophy about the collective rights of society and individual rights and freedom.

Note

1. David D. Rutstein, *Blueprint for Medical Care* (Cambridge, Mass.: M.I.T. Press, 1974), p. xxi.

17. Spaceship Earth, Evolution, and Health Care

Technology is very hard to freeze.
—John Dunlap

Whether a particular country is headed toward more or less government involvement in health care is an interesting question. We should likewise be concerned with the direction in which mankind as a collective body is headed. Human beings are controlled by, and at the same time are attempting to control, their ecosystem. In the future, the flow of goods and services in the health care system may be profoundly affected by our supply and use of energy. As technology and medical research rush forward toward producing a more perfect species, other forces are at work that may short-circuit the entire evolutionary process.

We begin by examining the simplest elements of planet earth and then explaining the relationships among these elements. Finally, we discuss the survival potential of mankind's living on finite resources.

Begin at the Beginning

From previous discussions of the properties of systems (Chapter 1), we know that systems have three important features:

- Elements or components
- Attributes of the elements
- Relationships between and among elements

One of the most important elements in the universe is energy; energy can take the form of information, physical material, heat, etc. A system is considered *closed* if no energy enters or leaves it; a system is *open* if there is import and export of energies and therefore a change of elements.

Throughput is the process by which the system acts upon the energy imported, i.e., the transformation of energy from one level to another or the change of components. Cells, organisms, individuals, groups, organizations, countries, and societies—all are confronted with internal and external changes in energy.[1]

Energy originates in the ecologic system. To understand the direction of mankind, we will conceptually build a "box" around the ecologic system and examine it as a closed system.

Ecologic Systems

An ecosystem is an abstraction used to study production, distribution, exchange, and consumption in the natural world. The plants, animals, and microorganisms that live in an area and make up a *biological* community are interconnected by an intricate web of relationships. The *physical-inanimate* surroundings within an ecosystem form a second set of subsystems. An ecosystem is made up of these interdependent biological and physical subsystems. The study of these interrelationships is called *ecology.*[2]

An ecosystem can be described as a cyclical sequence of processes:

Materials and energy (source) ⟶ organic synthesis and respiration (production) ⟶ food chain (distribution and exchange) ⟶ circulation and utilization (consumption)

Ecosystems are open systems in which solar energy is incorporated into organic compounds through the photosynthetic process in green plants, and subsequently passed through a sequence of diminishing energy levels during consumption.[3] Thus, within the ecosystem one can conceptualize two subsystems interacting with each other: (1) the organic-biological-animate system; and (2) the inorganic-physical-inanimate system.

There is a tendency in nature for inanimate physical complexes to become increasingly disordered, random, and chaotic as the physical universe is forever expanding and multiplying. This tendency is called *entropy* or *positive entropy.* The second law of thermodynamics states that potential energy disappears; the available supply of energy tends to decrease as energy gradients disappear and is irrevocably converted into heat of lower and lower temperatures. Inanimate nature, a closed system, must eventually attain a time-independent equilibrium state, with maximum entropy and minimum free energy, where the ratio between its phases remains constant. In the open system of animate nature, there is a tendency, known as *negative entropy,* toward states of higher order and differentiation in organic development and evolution. Biological life sorts, selects, compacts, adapts, and regenerates with increasing orderliness of species and substances. An open system can achieve negative entropy by importing more energy than it spends. Biological life, primarily through photosynthesis and evolution, rises to states of even higher organization and increasing complexity.[4]

The macroecological system, an open system, is made up of microecosystems. The key to maintaining a properly functioning ecological system is a stable relationship between three components: (1) constant incoming energy (sunlight), (2) biological energy, and (3) physical energy. The flow of energy through the ecological system is similar to the flow of matter through a conduit. By increasing either the size of the conduit or the flow through it, the quantity of energy available to the sytem as a whole will increase. But this growth will occur only if stable conversion rates and complex self-regulating mechanisms continue; fluctuations interrupt the flow of energy and produce undesirable increases in entropy. The *teleology* of the ecological system is to maintain a stable entropy equilibrium.[5]

The Economic System

From our previous discussion of the economics of health care (Chapter 11), we conceptualize the economic system as being made up of flows of goods and services from production to consumption. When considered as a closed system, the economic system consists of producers and consumers (physicians and patients in the simplest economic system) connected by markets in which they exchange goods and services at prices that reflect both the desires (the demand) of consumers and the capabilities (the supply) of producers. When considered as an open system, the economic system utilizes resources from the ecologic system and returns waste through the three deposition media: land, air, and water. Waste is unwanted material discarded into the ecologic system.

We are ready to combine our two subsystems, the economic and ecologic sytems, into a larger system we will call "Spaceship Earth."

Spaceship Earth

Boulding and Ward developed the analogy of the human race as a ship's crew on a single spaceship; this spaceship represents the totality of the ecologic-economic interrelationship.[6] Figure 17.1 outlines the dynamics of the ecologic-economic system known as "Spaceship Earth" and helps us understand the following principles:

1. Individuals (people, mankind) are but a small part of the crew on board spaceship earth.

2. A change in one system can cause and influence profoundly a change in another system—thus we say that a "delicate" balance exists among subsystems.

3. Instead of saying a component is created or destroyed, we say that it changes into a different energy level.

4. "There is no such thing as a free lunch." In other words, changes in a subsystem always require an exchange of resources (energy).

Figure 17.1   Spaceship Earth

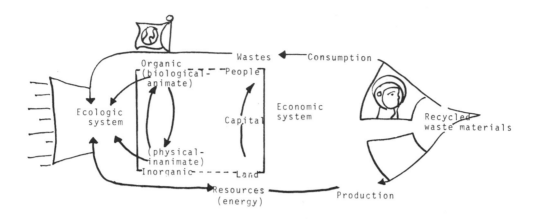

5. A health care subsystem is a delicate set of relationships operating in both the economic and ecologic systems.

6. "We're all in this together." Although we would like to maintain our individual and national sovereignty (see Chapter 2 for the balance between individual and societal rights), changes in medical research policies and health care delivery in any part of the world may affect our future collective destiny.

7. Unchecked economic growth could torpedo spaceship earth. "Slow growth" may be less dangerous.

Survival and Growth

There is, at present, a dichotomy between models of evolution: the naturalistic model versus the humanistic or anthropocentric models.[7] The humanistic approach depicts man as the central element in the universe by defining natural processes in terms of man's perceptions and interests. Natural processes, and natural selection in particular, are elevating man toward his goal of perfection. *Homo sapiens,* as we currently understand him, will be a fixture on this earth for many centuries and eons to come.

The naturalistic approach depicts man as merely another player in the game of life, not as the purpose of the game. Man is governed by natural selection, and his ultimate disappearance, like that of the dinosaur, is seen as inevitable. With either model of evolution, biological systems will evolve into higher-ordered and more complex states, and *Homo sapiens* will continue to be a central element in the economic system.

There is some speculative evidence that activities in the health care system are embarking on a course that may jeopardize the delicate systems balance that supports the humanistic approach toward evolution. These developments are listed below in no particular order:

- mind and behavior control
- DNA genetic engineering (recoupling and recombining of molecules)
- through overuse, resistance to antibiotics
- through overuse, mutations caused by x-rays
- introduction of toxic substances that are not broken down by the ecologic system
- organ transplantation
- *in vitro* conception and birth
- computer diagnosis and therapy
- changes in the quantity and quality of nutritional intake

In order for man to survive and evolve, he must continually reorganize both his thinking and the elements of the system of which he is a part or with which he interacts. *Learning* is said to occur when as a result of a given input, some element in a system is changed in such a way that when the same input is received again, either the output or the equilibrium position or both is different from its value the first time that input was received. In simpler terms, learning is said to occur when as the result of experience, a given input (stimulus) elicits a different output (response). If the process is to take place in any man-made, man-dependent system— be it a communication system, or the circulatory system (toward the conquest of arteriosclerosis)—man must assimilate, integrate, and synthesize his past experience.

History tells us that biological systems that can learn and adapt have much higher average survival potential in an changing world than those that cannot. What, ultimately, is the teleology of any health care system? In a narrow sense, it might be to maximize each individual's potential for growth. In an even more general sense, it might encompass the systematic evolution of biological system (man, the patient, and whatever else might emerge in the future) into higher-ordered and more complex states, which have a higher survival potential than the current state we now find ourselves in.

The health care system could make a positive or negative contribution to long-range negative entropy.

Summary

Spaceship Earth allows for the evolution of the human species into higher-ordered, more complex individuals. A health care delivery system can assist in this process. Redesigning present health care systems with developments such as genetic recombination and high-technology diagnostic equipment poses a difficult dilemma: because satisfying short-range needs may ultimately lead to larger problems such as untreatable genetic disease, biological warfare, energy depletion, and ecological destruction.

Question

1. Has medicine kept pace with the evolution of man, e.g., as man gets more complex, has medicine developed treatments for the more complex medical problems man has developed? Consider schizophrenia and toxicity resulting from synthetic chemicals.

Notes

1. Arnold M. Schultz, "The Ecosystem as a Conceptual Tool in the Management of Natural Resources," in *Natural Resources: Quality and Quantity,* ed. S. V. Ciriacy-Wantrup and James J. Parsons (Berkeley: University of California Press, 1967), pp. 139-161. See also Paul A. Ehrlich and Anne H. Ehrlich, *Population, Resources, Environment* (San Francisco: W. H. Freeman, 1970), p. 157; and the National Conference on Air Pollution, *Proceedings of the Third Meeting* (Washington, D.C.: U.S. Government Printing Office, 1966), p. 81.

2. Howard T. Odum, "Ecological Potential and Analogue Circuits for the Ecosystem," *American Scientist* 48 (March 1960), p. 1-8. S. Dillon Ripley and Helmut K. Buechner, "Ecosystem Science as a Point of Syntheses," in *America's Changing Environment,* ed. Roger Revelle and Hans H. Landsberg (Boston: Beacon Press, 1970), p. 1192; and Paul B. Sears, "Ethics, Aesthetics and the Balance of Nature," in *Perspectives on Conservation,* ed. Henry Jarrett (Baltimore: Johns Hopkins Press, 1958), p. 110.

3. Ludwig von Bertalanffy, "The Theory of Open Systems in Physics and Biology," *Science* 3 (January 1950): 23-29. Edwin G. Dolan, *Tanstaafl: The Economic Strategy for Environmental Crisis* (New York: Holt, Rinehart and Winston, 1971), pp. 103-105; O.R. Young, "A Survey of General Systems Theory," *General Systems* 9 (1964): 61-80; and Erich W. Zimmerman, *Introduction to World Resources* (New York: Harper and Row, 1964), pp. 65, 175. A popular interpretation of the second law of thermodynamics states "you cannot warm yourself on something that is colder than you," meaning heat cannot of itself pass from a colder to a hotter body.

4. David Pimental, "Complexity of Ecological Systems and Problems in Their Study and Management," in *Systems Analysis in Ecology,* ed. Kenneth E. F. Watt (New York: Academic Press, 1966), p. 15-35; and Jaro Mayda, *Environment and Resources: From Conservation to Ecomanagement* (San Juan, Puerto Rico: University of Puerto Rico, 1968), p. 92. The meaning of the words *entropy* and *teleology* as used in this book are based on their general systems definitions.

5. Kenneth E. Boulding, "The Economics of the Coming Spaceship Earth," in *Environmental Quality in a Growing Economy,* ed. Henry Jarrett (Baltimore: Johns Hopkins Press, 1966), pp. 3-14; and Barbara Ward, *Spaceship Earth* (New York: Columbia University Press, 1966).

6. Boulding, "The Economics of the Coming Spaceship Earth"; Ward, *Spaceship Earth.*

7. John M. Culbertson, *Economic Development: An Ecological Approach* (New York: Alfred A. Knopf, 1971), pp. 17-28.

Further Reading

Dubos, Rene. *Man Adapting.* New Haven: Yale University Press, 1965.

Fuller, R. Buckminster. *Utopia or Oblivion: The Prospects for Humanity.* New York: Bantam Books, Inc., 1969.

Schumacher, E. F. *Small Is Beautiful: A Study of Economics as if People Mattered.* London: Sphere Books Ltd., 1975.

Appendix: Gourmand and Food—A Fable

The people of Gourmand loved good food. They ate in good restaurants, donated money for cooking research, and instructed their government to safeguard all matters having to do with food. Long ago, the food industry had been in total chaos. There were many restaurants, some very small. Anyone could call himself a chef or open a restaurant. In choosing a restaurant, one could never be sure that the meal would be good. A commission of distinguished chefs studied the situation and recommended that no one be allowed to touch food except for qualified chefs. "Food is too important to be left to amateurs," they said. Qualified chefs were licensed by the state with severe penalties for anyone else who engaged in cooking. Certain exceptions were made for food preparation in the home, but a person could serve only his own family. Furthermore, to become a qualified chef, a man had to complete at least twenty-one years of training (including four years of college, four years of cooking school and one year of apprenticeship). All cooking schools had to be first class.

These reforms did succeed in raising the quality of cooking. But a restaurant meal became substantially more expensive. A second commission observed that not everyone could afford to eat out. "No one," they said, "should be denied a good meal because of his income." Furthermore, they argued that chefs should work toward the goal of giving everyone "complete physical and psychological satisfaction." For

Reprinted by permission from Judith R. Lave and Lester B. Lave, "Medical Care and Its Delivery," from a symposium on health care appearing in *Law and Contemporary Problems*, vol. 35, no. 2 (1970), published by the Duke University School of Law, Durham, North Carolina. Copyright 1970, 1971 by Duke University.

See also Reuben A. Kessel, "Higher Education and the Nation's Health: A Review of the Carnegie Commission Report on Medical Education," *Journal of Law and Economics*, 15:115-28 (April 1972).

those people who could not afford to eat out, the government declared that they should be allowed to do so as often as they liked and the government would pay. For others, it was recommended that they organize themselves in groups and pay part of their income into a pool that would undertake to pay the costs incurred by members in dining out. To insure the greatest satisfaction, the groups were set up so that a member could eat out anywhere and as often as he liked, could have as elaborate a meal as he desired, and would have to pay nothing or only a small percentage of the cost. The cost of joining such prepaid dining clubs rose sharply.

Long ago, most restaurants would have one chef to prepare the food; a few restaurants were more elaborate, with chefs specializing in roasting, fish, salads, sauces, and many other things. People rarely went to these elaborate restaurants since they were so expensive. With the establishment of prepaid dining clubs, everyone wanted to eat at these fancy restaurants. At the same time, young chefs in school disdained going to cook in a small restaurant where they would have to cook everything. The pay was higher and it was much more prestigious to specialize and cook at a really fancy restaurant. Soon there were not enough chefs to keep the small restaurants open.

With prepaid clubs and free meals for the poor, many people started eating their three-course meals at the elaborate restaurants. Then they began to increase the number of courses, directing the chef to "serve the best with no thought for the bill." (Recently a 317-course meal was served.)

The costs of eating out rose faster and faster. A new government commission reported as follows: (1) Noting that licensed chefs were being used to peel potatoes and wash lettuce, the commission recommended that these tasks be handed over to licensed dishwashers (whose three years of dishwashing training included cooking courses) or to some new category of personnel. (2) Concluding that many licensed chefs were overworked, the commission recommended that cooking schools be expanded, that the length of training be shortened, and that applicants with lesser qualifications be admitted. (3) The commission also observed that chefs were unhappy because people seemed to be more concerned about the decor and service than about the food. (In a recent taste test, not only could one patron not tell the difference between a 1930 and a 1970 vintage but he also could not distinguish between white and red wines. He explained that he always ordered the 1930 vintage because he knew that only a really good restaurant could stock such an expensive wine.)

The commission agreed that weighty problems faced the nation. They recommended that a national prepayment group be established which everyone must join. They recommended that chefs continue to be paid on the basis of the number of dishes they prepared. They recommended that every Gourmandese be given the right to eat anywhere he chose and as elaborately as he chose and pay nothing.

These recommendations were adopted. Large numbers of people spent all of their time ordering incredibly elaborate meals. Kitchens became marvels of new, expensive equipment. All those who were not consuming restaurant food were in the kitchen preparing it. Since no one in Gourmand did anything except prepare or eat meals, the country collapsed.

Selected Secondary Sources

For the most part, these books are slanted, narrow writings on what is right or wrong with the U.S. health care delivery system. They occasionally contain interesting information or provocative viewpoints, but they ought not to be taken as serious analyses of health systems. A discerning, sophisticated reader should be able to recognize their shortcomings, particularly their biases.

American Public Health Association. *Heal Yourself.* Washington, D.C.: The Association, 1972.

Burns, Eveline M. *Health Services for Tomorrow.* New York: Dunellen Publishing Co., 1973.

Carlson, Rick. *The End of Medicine.* New York: John Wiley & Sons, 1975.

Editors of Fortune. *Our Ailing Medical System.* New York: Harper & Row, 1970.

Fisher, Peter. *Prescription for National Health Insurance.* Croton-on-Hudson, N.Y.: North River Press, 1972.

Gerber, Alex. *The Gerber Report.* New York: David McKay Co., 1971.

Greenberg, Selig. *The Quality of Mercy.* New York: Atheneum Publishers, 1971.

Gray, Ed. *In Failing Health: The Medical Crisis and the A.M.A.* Indianapolis, Ind.: Bobbs-Merrill Co., 1970.

Harmer, Ruth M. *American Medical Avarice.* New York: Abelard-Schuman, 1975.

Health Policy Advisory Center. *The American Health Empire: Power, Profit and Politics.* New York: Random House, 1970.

Hepner, Donna M., and Harper, James O. *The Health Game: A Challenge for Reorganization and Management.* St. Louis: C. V. Mosby, 1973.

Jones, B. *The Health of Americans.* Englewood Cliffs, N.J.: Prentice-Hall, 1970.

Kennedy, Edward. *In Critical Condition: The Crisis in America's Health Care.* New York: Simon & Schuster, 1972.

Kime, Robert. *Health: A Consumer's Dilemma.* Belmont, Calif.: Wadsworth Publishing Co., 1970.

Klass, Alan. *There's Gold in Them Thar Pills.* London: Penguin Books, 1975.

Klaw, Spencer. *The Great American Medicine Show*. New York: Viking Press, 1975.

Kunnes, Richard. *Your Money or Your Life: Rx for the Medical Market Place*. New York: Dodd, Mead & Co., 1972.

Leininger, Madeline. *Barriers and Facilitators to Quality Health Care*. Philadelphia: F. A. Davis Company, 1975.

Levin, Tom. *American Health: Professional Privilege vs. Public Need*. New York: Praeger Publishers, 1974.

Lewis, Stephan. *The Nation's Health*. New York: H. W. Wilson, 1971.

Magnuson, Warren G. and Segal, Elliot A. *How Much for Health*. Washington, D.C.: Robert B. Luce, 1974.

Malleson, Andrew. *The Medical Runaround*. New York: Hart Publishing Co., 1973.

Murray, D. Stark. *Blueprint for Health*. New York: Schocken Books, 1974.

Ribicoff, Abraham. *The American Medical Machine*. New York: Saturday Review Press, 1972.

Rushmer, Robert F. *Humanizing Health Care*. Cambridge, Mass.: MIT Press, 1975.

Schorr, Daniel. *Don't Get Sick in America*. Nashville: Aurora, 1970.

Schwartz, Harry. *The Case for American Medicine: A Realistic Look at Our Health Care System*. New York: David McKay Co., 1972.

Tunley, Raul. *The American Health Scandal*. New York: Dell Publishing Co., 1966.

Wood, Madelyn. *Medicine and Health Care in Tomorrow's World*. New York: Julian Messner, 1974.

Index

Aged and aging, 5, 31, 95-104, 152
Agpaoa, Anthony, 179
Alabama, 84, 139
 Elps, 252
Alaska, 116, 223
Allen, A. A., 178
Ambulatory care, 49, 54, 66-68, 161, 168
 geriatric day care, 101
 mental health, 84-89
 outpatient surgery, 68
 types of clinics, 68
American College of Pathologists, 130
American College of Surgeons, 113
American Hospital Association, 233
American Medical Association (AMA), 13,
 35, 36, 50, 173, 184-186, 249-253, 254-
 255, 259-260
 American Medical Political Action
 Committee (AMPAC), 253
 Committee on Quackery, 186
 Council on Medical Education, 249
American Nurses Association, 41
American Pharmaceutical Association
 (APA), 143
American Public Health Association, 102
Arkansas
 Marianna, 252
Arigo, 179
Arizona, 223
 Chochise County, 178
 Phoenix, 177
Association of American Medical Col-
 leges, Committee on Medical Educa-
 tion, 250

Automated multiphasic health testing,
 226, 263-265

Baird, William, 154
Barton, Clara, 115
Belgium, 175
Besant, Annie, 154
Blood Services, 117, 120, 127, 293
 American Association of Blood Banks,
 120, 122
 American Blood Commission, 123
 definition, 120
 plasmapheresis, 120-121
 standards, 120
 statistics, 120-122
Blue Cross-Blue Shield, 63, 217-218, 226,
 277
Bok, Sissela, 96
Boulding, Kenneth, 307
Bradlaugh, Charles, 154
Brazil, 156, 179
Brown, William, 181
Bureaucracy, 7-8, 153, 161-164, 168, 226
Burton, Harold, 57
Byrne, Ethel, 154

California, 32, 112, 167, 185, 187
 San Francisco, 187
California Hospital Association, 233
Canada, 36
 Quebec, 175
Caribbean, 137
 West Indies, 182
Carter, Jimmy, 194

319

Cayce, Edgar, 177
Chiang Kai-shek, 286
Chiarugi, Vincenzo, 78
China, People's Republic of
  national health system, 286-292, 294
Chiropractic, 54, 128, 184-186, 223
  Council on Chiropractic Education, 185
Clinical laboratories, 130-131, 150, 263
  Technicon Corporation, 130
Columbia, 156
Columbia University Center for Com-
  munity Health Systems, 67
Computer, 63
  applications to health care, 117, 302-303
  CAT scanner, 247-248
  diagnosis, 266, 309
  electronic data processing, 54, 218, 300
  optical scanning, 264
  See also Automated multiphasic health
    testing
Comstock, Anthony, 154
Connecticut, 63, 65
Consulting firms, 127
Council on Economic Priorities, 137

Dentistry, 54, 128, 140, 143, 150-151, 166-
    167, 187-190, 203-204, 223, 231, 241,
    268, 281, 283-284
  American Board of Examiners, 188
  Baltimore College of Dental Surgery,
    188
  definition, 188
  National Board of Dental Examiners,
    188
  specialization, 188-189
  statistics, 188
Disease
  cultural perception, 168, 173-182, 286
  Cooley's, 164, 253
  definition, 13
  G6PD, 253
  iatrogenic, 14, 231
  incidence and prevalence, 15
  sickle cell, 164, 253
  Tay-Sachs, 253
  See also Prevention and control of com-
    municable, infectious, and conta-
    gious disease
District of Columbia (Washington), 36, 37,
    61, 130, 164, 184, 187
Drugs
  Abbott Laboratories, 138
  abuse, 150, 152, 162, 165, 241, 244-245,
    286

Bristol-Meyers, 138
discovery and development, 2, 133-135
Hoffman-LaRoche, 138
manufacturing and wholesale distribu-
    tion, 1, 5, 127, 131-139, 207
S. E. Massingill Co., 131
medicare, 223
patents, 132
podiatry, 187
prescription, 6, 137, 281, 283
prices, 138-139
restrictive laws, 143, 300
Smith Kline, 138
Durant, Henri, 115

Economics
  affluence, 34, 42
  capital investment, 294
  competition, 55, 133, 139, 143, 211, 294
  demand, 2, 4, 31, 34, 40, 114, 208, 210-
    215, 227
  division of labor, 7
  economies of scale, 49
  factor market, 207-210
  financial arrangements, 55, 85, 88, 119,
    132-133, 156, 158-159, 164, 167, 226-
    227
  income, 34, 52, 186-187, 214-215, 251,
    299
  inflation, 34, 96
  laissez-faire, 302
  Lorenz curve, 22-23
  maldistribution of wealth (income in-
    equality), 22, 36
  monopoly, 5, 252
  national indicators, 203-206
  poverty, 34, 241-242
  prices and changes, 23, 64-66, 81, 102,
    113-114, 121-122, 127, 138-139, 141-
    143, 176, 206, 208, 210-215, 220, 246-
    247, 268
  product market, 207-210
  supply, 2, 4, 5, 31, 40, 210-214, 246
  unemployment, 34
Eddy, Mary Baker, 176
Ellis, Havelock, 154
Emergency services, 268
  communication, 112, 113, 114
  department (room), 66-67, 71, 114, 245
  mental health services, 85
  price and income effects, 215-216
  See also Red Cross
Emerging and developing countries,
    health care, 292-294

Europe, 186
    Common Market Commission, 138
Evolution
    humanistic model, 308
    naturalistic model, 308

Faith healers, 173-182
    mesmerism and hypnotism, 181-182
    voodoo, 182
    See also Religion
Family planning, 1, 4, 150-152, 154-157,
    243, 268, 288-289
    Family Health Foundation, 155-157
    International Federation of Birth Con-
        trol Leagues, 154
    Louisiana Family Planning Program,
        155-157
    National Birth Control League, 154
    New York Society for the Suppression
        of Vice, 154
    Planned Parenthood, 154
Federal Register, 128
Federation of American Hospitals, 253
Fein, Rashi, 38
Field, Mark, 5
Flexner, Abraham, 249
Florida, 32, 184
Foundations
    Carnegie, 249
    Commonwealth Fund, 110
    Ford, 156
    Johnson, 110
    W. K. Kellogg, 110
    Lilly, 156
    Medical Foundation of San Joaquin, 52
    Rockefeller, 156
    See also Voluntary agencies

Garfield, Sidney, 266-267, 274
Geneva Convention, 115
Georgia, 139
Germany, 179, 183
Glazer, W., 24
Government
    federal, 149, 151-168, 204
    local, 1, 117, 149-157, 168, 204, 244, 246
    state, 1, 149-157, 168, 204
Government agencies, federal
    Action, 153
    Agency for International Development
        (AID), 156-157
    Atomic Energy Commission (AEC), 157,
        159
    Bureau of Indian Affairs, 165-166, 174

Center for Disease Control (CDC), 122
Children's Bureau, 154
Civil Service, 158
Consumer Product Safety Commission,
    157, 159
Department of Agriculture (USDA) 153,
    157, 158, 159
Department of Defense, 119, 151, 157-
    161, 193, 308
Department of Health, Education, and
    Welfare (HEW), 123, 131, 138, 153,
    156-158, 161-168, 186, 303
Department of Housing and Urban
    Development (HUD), 153, 156
Department of the Interior, 165
Department of Labor (DOL), 153, 157
Department of Transportation, 159
Environmental Protection Agency, 153
Executive Office of the President, 162
Federal Reserve System, 208
Federal Trade Commission (FTC), 137,
    143
Food and Drug Administration (FDA),
    123, 128, 131-132, 137, 210
Indian Health Service (IHS), 18, 164-168,
    174
Internal Revenue Service, 58
Justice Department, 143
National Institutes of Health, 163
National Institute of Mental Health, 84
National Institute of Occupational Safe-
    ty and Health, 157
Occupational Safety and Health Ad-
    ministration, 157
Office of Economic Opportunity (OEO),
    243
Office of Management and Budget, 254
Post Office Department, 154
Public Health Service (PHS), 18, 151, 162,
    164, 168
Special Action Office for Drug Abuse
    Prevention, 162
State Department, 157
U.S. Commissioner of Education, 185
Veterans Administration, 19, 157-158
War Department, 164-165
Government programs
    Aid to Families of Dependent Children,
        34
    Aid to Totally and Permanently Dis-
        abled, 84
    Civilian Health and Military Program of
        the Uniformed Services (CHAMPUS),
        151, 159, 301

Model Cities, 156, 243
VISTA, 243
See also Hill-Burton
Group practice, 49-55, 71, 190
    advantages, 53
    definition, 50
    disadvantages, 53
    Glisinger, 54
    Group Health Association of Washington, D.C., 252
    Group Health Cooperative of Puget Sound, 54
    Health Insurance Plan of New York, 54
    Marshfield, 54
    Mayo Clinic, 53
    Medical Foundation of San Joaquin, 52
    Ochsner, 54
    Palo Alto Clinic, 53
    prepaid, 54, 267
    Ross-Loos Medical Group, 53
    types, 51

Hahnemann, Samuel, 183
Haiti, 36
Hamlin, Robert H., 111
Harris, Dhapin, 188
Hayden, Horace, 187
Health
    as a right or privilege, 17-20, 22
    contrasted with medical care, 13
    definition, 13
    status indicator(s), 15, 16
Health alliances, 270
Health insurance, 52, 87-88, 213, 215-227, 253, 280-283, 287, 301-302
    private, 2, 28, 86, 187, 204, 215-221
    public (social), 2, 38, 149, 204, 221-226
    workman's compensation, 18, 221-222
    See also Blue Cross; Malpractice; Medicaid; Medicare; National health insurance
Health maintenance organization, 54, 267-270, 301
Health planning, 7, 62, 151-152, 210, 246-248, 283
    certificate of need, 247
    Section 1122, 246-247
    structure in U.S., 248
Health practitioners, intermediate level, 193-194
    barefoot doctor, 287, 292
    feldsher, 285
    health associate, 193

nurse clinician, 193
nurse extenders, 167
nurse midwife, 193, 285
nurse practitioner, 193, 300
physician-extender, 193, 252
physician's assistant, 193, 252, 300
physician's associate, 193
Health practitioners, marginal
    Homeopathy, 183
    Naprapathy and naturopathy, 184, 249
    Scientology, 183
Hill, Lister, 57
Holistic approach to medicine, 14
Home health services, 101-104, 280
    Boston Dispensary, 101
    definition, 101-102
    medicare and medicaid, 222-223
    Montefiore Hospital, 101
    standards, 102
    statistics, 102-103
Hospice, 101
Hospital
    Bellevue, 19
    Charity, 19, 23
    Community, 62, 66-67, 71, 302
    Cook County, 19, 23, 120
    costs, 63-64
    definition, 55, 57
    general medical and surgical, 57-58, 103
    history, 55-57
    Joint Commission on Accreditation of Hospitals, 61, 100, 130
    long-term, 58, 68, 71
    Los Angeles County, 23
    medical staff, 58, 61
    mental (psychiatric), 78-81, 86, 96
    organization, 60, 245
    ownership, 58-59
    short-term, 57-62
    specialty, 57-58, 71
    standards, 61
    statistics, 57
    utilization, 4, 63, 253-254
    Washington General, 19
Hubbard, L. Ronald, 183

Illinois
    Chicago, 184, 187
Indians and Alaska natives
    health services, 18, 164-168
    history, 164
    medicine men, 173-174, 181
    statistics, 166

treaty, 164, 299
Infant mortality, 15, 155
Iowa
    Davenport, 184
Ireland, 175
Italy, 78, 175

Johns Hopkins University, 249

Kaiser-Permanente, 54, 252, 266-267
Kane, Robert L., 168
Kane, Rosalie A., 168
Kansas, 81
Kardec, Allen (Denizard Rwail), 181
Kelsey, Frances, 131
Kennedy, Edward, 271
Kennedy, John F., 84
Kessel, Reuben, 251
Kuhlman, Kathryn, 178

Legal cases affecting health care
    Delta Women's Clinic v. *State of Louisi-
        ana*, 252
    Garcia v. *State Board of Medical Ex-
        aminers*, 252
    Miami County v. *Dayton*, 169
    O'Connor v. *Donaldson*, 89
    Ragsdale v. *Overholser*, 83
    Rouse v. *Carmeron*, 19, 83
    Schwegmann Bros. v. *Calvert Distillers
        Corporation*, 140
    Wilmington General Hospital v. *Man-
        love*, 19
    Wyatt v. *Stickney*, 19, 84, 91
Legislation, federal
    Biologics Control Act, 131
    Child Nutrition Act, 153
    Clayton Act, 220
    Clean Air Act, 153
    Clinical Laboratories Improvement Act,
        130
    Comprehensive Health Planning and
        Public Health Services Amendment,
        246
    Demonstration Cities and Metropolitan
        Act, 153
    Dependents Medical Care Act, 153
    Durham-Humphrey Amendments, 140
    Economic Opportunities Act, 153
    Emergency Medical Services Systems
        Act, 114
    Experimental Health Services Delivery
        System, 247

Federal Trade Commission Act, 220
Federal Food, Drug and Cosmetic Act,
    131
First Amendment, 143
Health Insurance for the Aged, 222
Health Maintenance Organization Act,
    268
Highway Safety Act, 114
Hill-Burton, 57, 63, 66, 100, 152, 208, 247
Kefauver-Harris Drug Amendments,
    131-132
McCarran-Ferguson Act, 218
Medical Device Amendments, 128
Mental Health Study Act, 84
National Health Planning and Resource
    Development Act, 62
National Labor Relations Act, 63
National Mental Health Act, 84
National School Lunch Act, 153
Occupational Safety and Health Act,
    153
Old Age Assistance, 97
Partnership for Health Admendments,
    246
Professional Standards Review Organi-
    zation (PSRO), 38, 62, 210, 253-254
Public Health Service Act, 153
Regional Medical Program, 247
Retardation Facilities and Community
    Mental Health Centers Construction
    Act, 84, 153
Robinson-Patman Act, 220
Section 1122 of the Social Security Act,
    246
Sherman Act, 220
Social Security Act, 62, 86, 96, 151-152,
    208, 222, 254
State and Local Fiscal Assistance Act, 153
Uniform Services Revitalization Act,
    161
Water Quality Act, 153
Legislation, state
    delegation of power, 149
    emergency transportation, 114
    fair trade laws, 139-140
    good Samaritan laws, 113, 114
    home rule doctrine, 150
    pharmacy licensing, 139, 143
    restricting the development of HMOs,
        268
    See also Physician (licensure)
Lewis, Sinclair, 40
Liggett, Louis K., 139

Long-term care, 85-86
Louisiana, 69, 139, 150, 152, 155, 182
  New Orleans, 252
Lynn, L. E., 164

Magic, 6
Maine
  Portland, 176
Malpractice, 4, 38, 113, 187, 231-237
  ad damnum, 233
  borrowed servant doctrine, 236
  contributory negligence, 236
  defensive medicine, 237
  informed consent, 237
  locality rule, 236
  negligence, definition of, 231
  res ipsa loquitor, 236
  respondeat superior, 235
  sovereign immunity, 233
  tort, definition of, 231
Manpower, 36-37, 40, 287. See also Dentistry; Nursing; Physician
Mao Tse-tung, 286
Maryland, 63, 167
Massachusetts, 175
  Boston, 176
Maternal and child (prenatal) health and
  care, 15, 32, 149, 151-152, 154, 245, 247,
  288-289, 293
Medicaid, 19, 62, 86, 97, 103-104, 138, 151-
  152, 177, 187, 194, 208, 218, 222-226,
  241-242, 247, 253-254, 300
Medical supplies and equipment, 5, 127-
  129
Medicare, 19, 62, 86, 97, 102-104, 138, 151,
  177, 187, 194, 208, 218, 222-226, 241-
  242, 247, 253-254, 300
Mediterranean, 183
Mental health, 5, 17, 77-88, 150-151, 268,
  280, 301
  asylums, 80
  centers and clinics, 84-89
  commitment, 82-83
  Menninger Clinic, 81
  psychiatric hospitals, 78-81
  psychiatric therapies, 77, 79, 83, 88-89
  rights of patients, 80-84
  Topeka State Hospital, 81
  USSR, illness in, 286
  zone (network of services), 84, 86
Mesmer, Friedrich Anton, 181-182
Mexico, 36, 156
  Mexico City, 175
Michigan, 143

Mills, Wilbur, 271
Mississippi, 37
Montana, 143

National Academy of Sciences (NAS), 131-
  132
National Association of Retail Druggists
  (NARD), 139, 143
National health insurance, 19, 270-274
National League of Nursing, 102
National Research Council (NRC), 103,
  131-132
Neighborhood health care center, 190,
  242-243, 282, 284
Nevada, 232
New York, 37, 130, 187
  New York City, 95, 101, 130
Nightingale, Florence, 55
Nixon, Richard, 271
North Carolina, 150, 181
North Dakota, 143
Nursing
  care, 13, 42
  conflicts in hospitals, 61
  doctor-nurse game, 24-26
  education and schools, 61, 63
  group practice, 54
  manpower, 40-42
Nursing homes, 96-101, 103-104, 127, 203-
  204, 208
  boarding, 97-100
  extended, 97-99, 103
  intermediate, 97-99, 103
  ownership, 99-101
  skilled, 97-99, 103
  standards, 97-101
  statistics, 97-100
  utilization, 100

Ohio, 61
  Cleveland, 187
Oklahoma, 167
  Elk City, 252
  Tulsa, 177
Optometry
  eyeglasses, 223, 281, 283
  medicare, 223
  ophthamologists, 190-191
  opticians, 190-191
  optometric care, 13, 190-191
  optometrists, 54, 128, 143, 190-191
  orthopist, 190-191
Organized medicine, 55, 173, 231
  definition, 13,

effect on chiropractic, 185-186
effect on the supply of physicians, 249-252
lobbying efforts, 252-253

Palmer, David Daniel, 184
Patient
  alienation and frustration, 7, 40
  control and hospitals and clinics, 244-246
  expenditures, 205
  noncompliance, 26
  participation in therapy, 88, 292
  patient-owner-veterinarian triangle, 192
  poverty and minority, 241-242
  rights, 82-84, 89
Pennsylvania, 184
  Franklin, 178
  Philadelphia, 187
Pharmaceutical Manufacturers Association (PMA), 253
Pharmacy, 137, 139-144, 213
  apothecary, 55, 139, 144
  definition, 140
  pharmacist, 138, 282
  statistics, 140
  Virginia State Board of Pharmacy, 143
  See also Drugs
Philippines, 179, 181
Physician (health providers)
  board eligible and certified, 36
  distribution and migration, 34, 50
  doctor-nurse game, 24-26
  education, 35, 38, 40, 160, 249-252, 303
  expenditures for services, 203-204
  foreign medical graduates, 36, 251
  house calls, 38
  income, 35, 52
  incorporation, 52
  licensure, 248-252, 300, 303
  manpower, 36, 51, 249-252
  patient relationship, 7, 19, 38, 42, 139
  poverty and minority visits, 242
  privileged communiation, 7
  relationship with other providers, 42
  specialization, 7, 36, 232
  strikes, 38-39
Pinel, Philippe, 78
Podiatry, 128, 186-187
  definition, 186
  statistics, 186
Population growth, 4, 289-291, 293-294
  Indian birthrate, 166

life cycle of planned reproduction, 156
net reproduction rate, 31
President's Cost-of-Living Council, 63
Prevention and control of communicable, infectious and contagious disease, 19, 150, 165-166, 213-214, 243, 286, 293, 301
  measles and polio, 1
Preventive medicine, 14, 192, 265-268, 282, 284, 286
  annual physical checkup, 14, 50, 150, 215, 243, 263, 300
  federal spending, 158-158
  price and income effects, 215-216
Primary care, 5, 49-50, 54, 67, 71, 190, 194, 280, 284, 287
  definition, 49
  physician, 7, 35
Professional
  associations, 139, 142
  image of pharmacists, 139, 141, 143
  organizations, 13, 23
Puerto Rico, 130

Quimby, Phineas Parkhurst, 176

Red Cross, 111, 113, 115-120, 122-123
  American National, 116-120
  Rare Donor Registry, 117
Religion, 6
  Association for Research and Enlightenment, 177
  Roman Catholic Church, 154, 175, 179, 182
  Christian Science, 176-177, 223
  Church of Revelation, 181
  evangelism and charismatic healing, 177-179
  Founding Church of Scientology, 183
  Kardecism, 181
  miracles, shrines and exorcism, 174-176
  psychic surgery, 179-181
  Spiritualism Episcopal Church, 181
  Union Espiritista Christiana de Filipinas, 179
  See also Faith healers
Rhode Island, 175
Richardson, Elliot, 164
Roberts, Oral, 177
Rodriguez, Rosita, 179
Rutstein, David, 302

Sanger, Margaret, 154
Saxon, M. R., 19

Scandinavia, 15, 282
Schuck, Peter, 253
Seidl, J. M., 164
Short-term care, 86
Shryock, Richard, 250
Socialized medicine and health systems,
    11, 18, 22-24, 26, 279-292, 294, 303
Somers, Anne, 35, 40, 271
South Carolina, 139
Soviet Union
    influence on medicine in China, 287
    national health system, 283-286
Stein, Leonard I., 24
Stewart, Don, 178
Stopes, Marie, 154
Sunday, Billy, 178
Sweden
    national health system, 282-283
Switzerland, 115
System
    cybernetic model, 1
    definition, 1
    ecologic, 306-308
    entropy, 306
    health care, 1, 3-4, 16, 18, 22, 24, 26, 49,
        97, 207, 241, 245, 279-292, 294, 299-304,
        305-309
    macroeconomic model, 207, 307-308
    properties of, 1-2, 305-306
    Spaceship Earth, 307-308
    teleology, 2, 307
    thermodynamics, second law of, 306
    See also Evolution

Technology, 63
    growth, 8
    technologic response, 7
    See also Computer
Texas, 32
    San Antonio, 252
Transference
    definition, 14

Unions, 18, 63, 245
    AFL-CIO, 142
United Kingdom (Great Britain), 11, 78,
    144, 184

British Medical Association, 187
Ediburgh, 249
Manchester, 182
Monopolies Commission, 138
National Health Service, 11, 279-282
Northern Ireland, 281
Scotland, 281
Wales, 281
United States, 15, 18, 31-32, 34, 36, 41, 49,
    57-58, 62, 78, 95, 102, 109, 111, 130, 133,
    136, 138-139, 161, 176, 184-185, 187-
    188, 193, 208, 221-222, 226, 241, 245,
    247, 250, 279
Utah, 184
Utilization and peer review, definition,
    253. See also Hospital; Physician

Veterinary medicine, 54, 128, 140, 191-193
    American Animal Hospital Association,
        193
    American Veterinary Association, 192
    definition, 191
    specialization, 191
    statistics, 191
Vietnam, 161
Virginia, 143
    Virginia Beach, 177
Voluntary agencies, 5, 109-111, 300
    American Cancer Society, 109
    American Geriatric Association, 109
    American Heart Association, 109
    fund raising, 110
    National Safety Council, 109
    United Fund, 110, 117, 119
    See also Blood services; Emergency
        services; Foundations; Red Cross

Walgreen, Charles R., 139
Ward, Barbara, 307
Washington
    Seattle, 184
    Spokane, 252
Welby, Marcus, 35, 40
West Germany, 15
White, Robert L., 18
World Health Organization, 13